# Foundation Macromedia Dreamweaver MX 2004

Craig Grannell
David Powers
George McLachlan

friendsof

DESIGNER TO DESIGNER™

*an Apress® company*

# Foundation Macromedia Dreamweaver MX 2004

ISBN (pbk): 1-59059-308-1

Printed and bound in the United States of America 10987654321

Distributed to the book trade in the United States by Springer-Verlag New York, Inc., 175 Fifth Avenue, New York, NY 10010 and outside the United States by Springer-Verlag GmbH & Co. KG, Tiergartenstr. 17, 69112 Heidelberg, Germany.

In the United States: phone 1-800-SPRINGER, email orders@springer-ny.com, or visit http://www.springer-ny.com. Outside the United States: fax +49 6221 345229, email orders@springer.de, or visit http://www.springer.de.

For information on translations, please contact Apress directly at 2560 Ninth Street, Suite 219, Berkeley, CA 94710. Phone 510-549-5930, fax 510-549-5939, e-mail info@apress.com, or visit http://www.apress.com.

The source code for this book is freely available to readers at http://www.friendsofed.com in the Downloads section.

## Credits

| | |
|---|---|
| **Technical Reviewers**<br>David Powers, Vibha Roy | **Production Manager**<br>Kari Brooks |
| **Editorial Board**<br>Dan Appleman, Craig Berry, Gary Cornell,<br>Tony Davis, Steven Rycroft, Julian Skinner,<br>Martin Streicher, Jim Sumser, Karen Watterson,<br>Gavin Wray, John Zukowski | **Proofreader**<br>Liz Welch<br><br>**Compositor**<br>Dina Quan |
| **Assistant Publisher**<br>Grace Wong | **Indexer**<br>John Collin |
| **Project Manager**<br>Kylie Johnston | **Cover Designer**<br>Kurt Krames |
| **Copy Editor**<br>Nancy Depper | **Manufacturing Manager**<br>Tom Debolski |

# CONTENTS AT A GLANCE

# CONTENTS

## Chapter 14: Secure Login and Registration . . . . . . . . . . . . 251

## Chapter 15: Case Study: A Content Management System . . . . . 273

# ABOUT THE AUTHORS

**Craig Grannell** was trained in the fine arts, but soon became immersed in the world of digital media and showed his work at several leading European media arts festivals. His art ranged from short video pieces to odd performances, sometimes with the aid of a computer, televisions, and a P.A. system, and other times with a small bag of water above his head.

Craig soon realized that he'd have to make a proper living. Luckily, in the mid 1990s, the Web caught his attention, and he's been working with it ever since. Along with writing for several prominent design-related magazines, he finds time to create websites for the likes of 2000 AD, work on his eclectic Veer Musikal Unit project, and occasionally delve back into the world of video. Much of his work (and dancing trees) can be found at his website, Snub Communications (www.snubcommunications.com).

**David Powers** is a writer and broadcaster on international affairs, with a particular interest in Japan. He got the Internet bug in the days when Netscape ruled the world and websites were entirely hand-coded. Then came WYSIWYDDG (what you see is what you definitely don't get) HTML editors. He tried a whole bunch, including several Japanese ones, before discovering Dreamweaver 3, and he's stayed with Dreamweaver ever since. He believes MX 2004 is the best yet, and might be persuaded to say it's finally WYSIWYG if he didn't spend so much time buried in Code view.

David started creating dynamic websites with ASP and is thankful that, unlike Cleopatra, he managed to survive before discovering PHP. When not developing websites, he spends his time writing about Japan, translating Japanese (he's translated several plays), and savoring the delights of raw fish and sake.

**George McLachlan** lives in Glasgow, Scotland, and is a freelance PHP developer. He is currently studying Software Engineering at the University of Strathclyde. As well as his studying George has contributed to previous versions of *Foundation Dreamweaver MX* and *Dreamweaver MX: Advanced PHP Web Development*. He has also written PHP tutorials for both *Create Online* and *Computer Arts* magazines, He is a strong supporter of open source and is involved in several projects, like CSSRepublic. Find his work at http://blog.untitledproject.co.uk.

# INTRODUCTION

Welcome! Macromedia Dreamweaver stands at the apex of web design software; since its original release in 1997, it has evolved from a fairly simple HTML editor into a sophisticated design tool that no serious web designer can do without. Whether you're a relative newcomer or a long-time design professional, Dreamweaver is an ideal solution: along with offering advanced visual design tools, it enables you to create dynamic websites. Graphic designers feel at home with its Design view, whereas coders can work in Code view to create documents that implement all manner of web technologies.

Dreamweaver MX introduced this flexibility in recognition of a shift in web design trends. Whereas in the past designers mostly created static web pages, **dynamic** web applications—those that inter-act with users and return information from a database—have become increasingly popular over the past few years, even for solo designers and developers. People are continuing to become aware of what the web is capable of—and in many cases, static content simply can't cut it.

Macromedia Dreamweaver MX 2004 improved the application further, centering it around **Cascading Style Sheets (CSS)**, a technology that enables designers to create low-bandwidth, accessible, flexible, cutting-edge layouts.

If you're a little worried by all this, don't be. Dynamic sites provide even more potential for creative design, and Dreamweaver MX 2004 makes integrating database elements with sites fairly easy. Likewise, Cascading Style Sheets make it much easier for designers to create and tweak page lay-outs, and again Dreamweaver MX 2004 makes this technology accessible to designers, no matter what their level of expertise.

All in all, Dreamweaver MX 2004 is the perfect choice for web designers no matter what type of site they want to create. Because it's a fantastic visual design tool with support for powerful server-side technologies, it enables you to create cutting-edge, great-looking dynamic websites efficiently and effectively. Now you *can* have it all: and this book will show you how.

## The aim of this book

This book provides you with a thorough foundation in the use of all the essential features of Dreamweaver—and even some of the lesser-known elements—starting with basic layout tasks, working through the creation of a static website based on templates, and ending with a fully dynamic, database-driven site.

We start by introducing the case study that is used throughout the book, and the planning process that you need to think through before you even open Dreamweaver. We'll then work through the various options that Dreamweaver provides for designers and developers. By the end of the first half of the book, you'll have created a CSS-based website based on Dreamweaver templates, and you will have explored Dreamweaver's Code view in depth. You'll also have learned how to validate your code against web standards, thereby ensuring that your site works well in all current browsers. (You'll also learn useful "hacks" to accommodate users running obsolete browsers.)

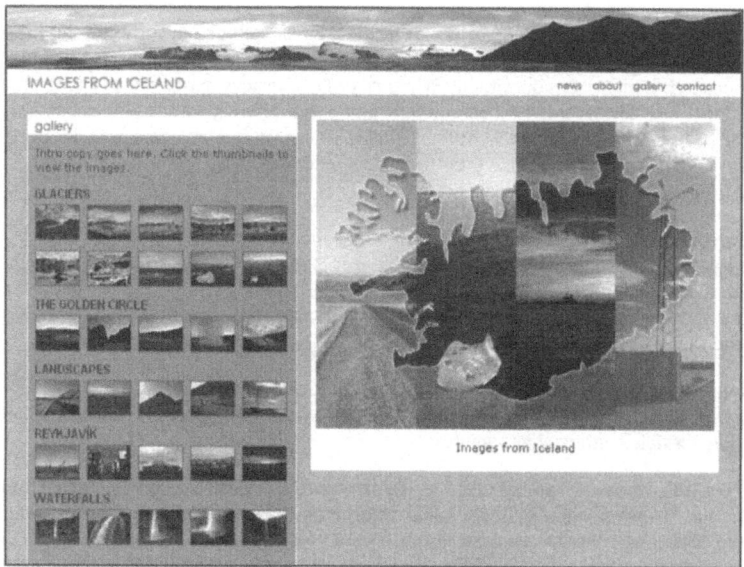

Images from Iceland

The second half of the book (Chapter 10 onward) looks at the dynamic side of Dreamweaver, and introduces databases and server-side scripting with PHP. You'll learn how PHP integrates with XHTML to change pages according to user input. After explaining how PHP, the Apache web server, and MySQL interact with each other, we'll take you through the installation process step-by-step to enable you to build and test database-driven websites on your own computer before deploying them live on the Internet. You'll then learn all the basics of PHP by building an online order form that performs calculations and makes its own decisions about which parts of the output to display. With that knowledge under your belt, you'll be ready to install MySQL and a very user-friendly interface, phpMyAdmin. This begins the next part of your journey into dynamic website construction: using Dreamweaver MX 2004's server behaviors. These take most of the hard work out of building pages to interact with databases. By the time you reach the end of the book, you will have converted the CSS-based website you built in the first half of the book into a fully operational content management system. You will be ready to deploy your skills developing modern, standards-compliant sites to meet a variety of needs.

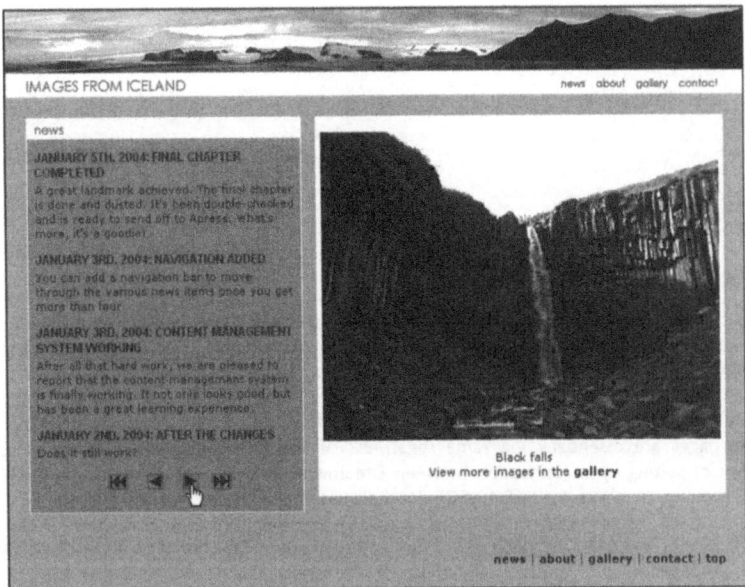

We don't believe in books that demonstrate principles by using theoretical examples that would never hack it in the real world, so our case study is based on a real-world project that demonstrates professional techniques, and is created by professional designers.

## What you'll need

You'll obviously need a copy of Dreamweaver MX 2004, and you'll need to know your way around your preferred operating system—either Windows (98SE, 2000, XP, or Server 2003) or Mac OS X 10.2.6 or higher—and be comfortable with creating folders, naming files, and so on. You also need an Internet connection if you want to download the source files.

To work with the dynamic website features of the second half of the book, you'll need to install PHP, the Apache web server, and the MySQL database management system. We also recommend that you use phpMyAdmin, a powerful but easy-to-use graphical interface for MySQL. All are available free of charge, and full download and installation instructions are given for both Mac and Windows in Chapter 10 (PHP and Apache) and Chapter 13 (MySQL and phpMyAdmin).

Apart from that, you don't need a great deal. This book makes few assumptions—we'll start at the beginning and provide instruction every step of the way. If you need additional help while working your way through the book, remember that the friends of ED forums (www.friendsofed.com/forums) are there for free technical support. Help is close at hand!

You'll notice that we don't make any recommendations regarding what platform to use, and this is for good reason. Both PCs and Macs are equally capable of creating a dynamic website, hence we will be platform-neutral throughout. Macromedia has made our job easier by unifying the Dreamweaver interface across both platforms, so our instructions will be equally useful to you whether you use a Mac or PC. Of course, we will highlight those rare cases where differences exist, and keyboard shortcuts are provided in both PC and Mac formats.

## Server technologies

We use the PHP scripting language and MySQL database solution when working on the dynamic portions of the site. For those of you who've not yet explored either technology, don't fret—this book contains exhaustive guides to installating and setting them up on your machines.

If you're a fan of ColdFusion or ASP, don't abandon ship just yet. The *concepts* behind creating dynamic pages are essentially the same regardless of the technology you're using, as are the processes of setting up a connection between Dreamweaver and a database, so you'll still learn plenty. However, we chose the PHP/MySQL duo because

- PHP, MySQL, and the third-party applications we use are 100 percent *free* for both commercial and personal use.
- PHP, MySQL, and the third-party applications we use are 100 percent *cross-platform*.
- PHP and MySQL are widely used technologies that perform well when compared to competing products, and both have a thriving community of users.

## Conventions

We've tried to keep this book as clear and easy to follow as possible, so we've used only a few layout styles.

- Important words or phrases appear in **bold type**.
- Different fonts emphasize phrases that appear on-screen, code, `filenames`, and hyperlinks, such as www.friendsofed.com. Where we're indicating that you need to input text, you'll see these styles: "type monkeyBoy into the Var field."
- Keyboard stroke sequences will be displayed in this style: *F4* and *CTRL+C*. Also, wherever possible and relevant, we'll suggest both Windows and Mac equivalents of all paths and keyboard shortcuts. For example, "Now press *CTRL/CMD+S* to save your PHP file."
- Menu commands are written in the form Menu ➤ Submenu ➤ Submenu.

> *When we want to draw your attention to something really important, we'll put it in a bubble like this.*

- Worked exercises are laid out like this:

  1. Open up Dreamweaver MX 2004.

  2. Save your file as `form.php`.

  3. And so on...

```
Blocks of code
Will appear in this style;
And we'll also use
This style to highlight new code,
Or code that deserves your attention
```

- When code is too long to fit on one line, we use a code continuation character (➡) to show that code is on the same line in Dreamweaver. If you come across such a symbol, don't go hitting the *ENTER* key just yet!

## Download files

All source files and finished versions for the exercises within this book are available for download at www.friendsofed.com. Feel free to experiment with them, and if things go wrong with your version, take advantage of the ability to compare your file with the completed one—it often helps. Also try going to File ➤ Print Code in Dreamweaver—print out your version and the downloaded one and mark any differences with a big red pen.

> *Please note that photographic images contained within the websites shown in this book remain the copyright of Craig Grannell and should not be reused without written permission.*

## friends of ED

For news, books, sample chapters, downloads, author interviews, and more, point your browser at www.friendsofed.com. Be sure to sign up for our monthly newsletter to get the latest gossip about upcoming books!

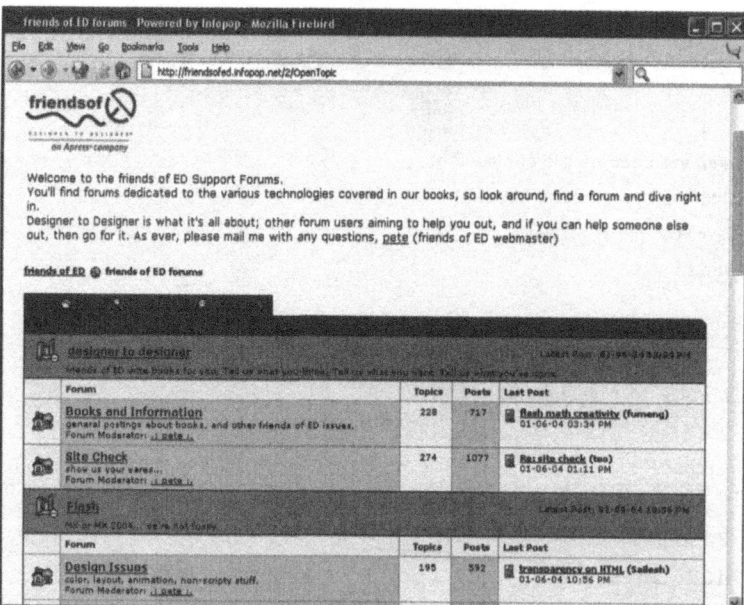

You can also visit our support forums at www.friendsofed.com/forums for help with any of the tutorials in this book, or just to chat with like-minded designers and developers. You'll find a variety of designers talking about all manner of tricks, tips, and techniques, and they might even provide you with ideas, insights, and inspiration.

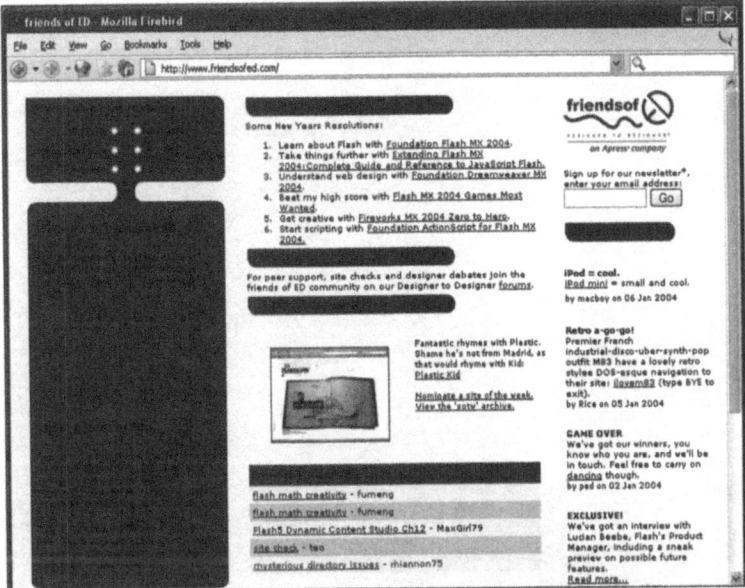

Even if you don't have problems, e-mail feedback@friendsofed.com to let us know what you think of this book—we'd love to hear from you! Whether it's to request future books, ask about friends of ED, or tell us about sites you've created after reading this book, drop us a line!

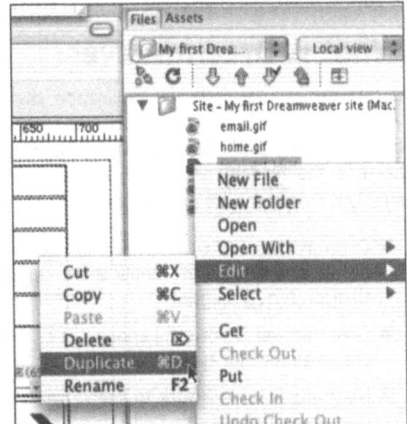

**Chapter 1**

# INTRODUCING DREAMWEAVER MX 2004

**What we'll cover in this chapter**

- Introducing Macromedia Dreamweaver
- Setting up a website
- Creating an example site with multiple pages, links, and images

# What is Dreamweaver?

Dreamweaver is a software application that enables you to create web pages. Version 1 was released way back in 1997, and since then the application has become the leading application in the field. This is largely due to three essential factors.

- Dreamweaver's interface enables people at all levels to understand the application, regardless of their preferred methods.

- Dreamweaver is powerful enough to enable you to create almost any type of website.

- Macromedia's hard work to keep Dreamweaver at the technological cutting edge.

Dreamweaver MX 2004 includes many new features; for instance, workflow elements have been improved, enabling you to work better and faster; and the application is now centered on cascading style sheets (CSS), a technology that enables you to produce low-bandwidth, flexible, cutting-edge web page layouts.

Of course, Dreamweaver MX 2004 still excels at integration with other members of the Studio MX family—Fireworks, Flash, and Freehand—and it enables you to customize your workspace, and work with Code view, Design view, or a combination of both.

Don't worry if you've never worked with Dreamweaver before—we'll start from the beginning. If you're already familiar with the application, you'll still learn plenty because the application has evolved from the previous version; of course, all changes will be highlighted.

## The start page

Like the other members of Studio MX 2004, Dreamweaver now has a **start page**, as shown in Figure 1-1.

Your first instinct might be to check the Don't show again option, especially if you're a seasoned pro, but it's worth leaving it alone for a while. Not only does it provide single-click access to various file types via the Create New column, but it also provides easy access to built-in sample sets, and the **Dreamweaver Exchange**.

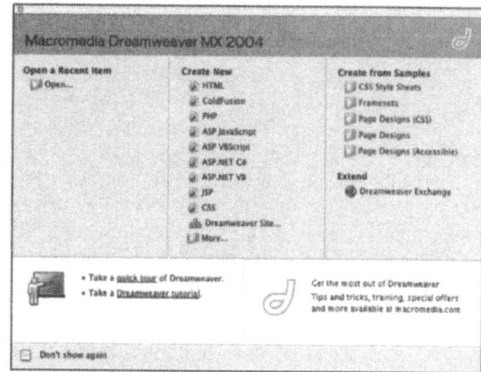

**Figure 1-1.** The start page

*Dreamweaver Exchange, which you can find at* `http://www.macromedia.com/cfusion/exchange/index.cfm`, *is a useful repository for free or affordable components that can make it easier for you to add functionality to your web pages. These components are usually built by members of the design community, and there's no doubting that this is an essential resource for any Dreamweaver user. However, be aware that some downloads function accurately only in specific browsers or on specific platforms, and any such components should generally be avoided. After all, good websites work in all browsers—imagine a scenario where a potential client cannot use all or part of your site because it won't work in his or her browser. You will almost certainly lose that business because a client may find it easier to find a competitor rather than go to the hassle of switching web browsers. Using web standards, as we will throughout this book, means such a scenario shouldn't happen.*

The folks at Macromedia are also paying attention to the working methods of web designers, and Open a Recent Item on the start page enables you to (surprise, surprise) open a file you've worked on recently. Although many applications (including Dreamweaver) contain similar functionality via File ➤ Open Recent, the start page makes this process just that little bit faster, and those few saved seconds for each opened file soon add up.

Should you decide to use the Don't show again option and later change your mind, the start page can be reactivated by going to Edit ➤ Preferences (Dreamweaver ➤ Preferences on Mac) and selecting General. Then check Show start page in the Document options area, as shown in Figure 1-2.

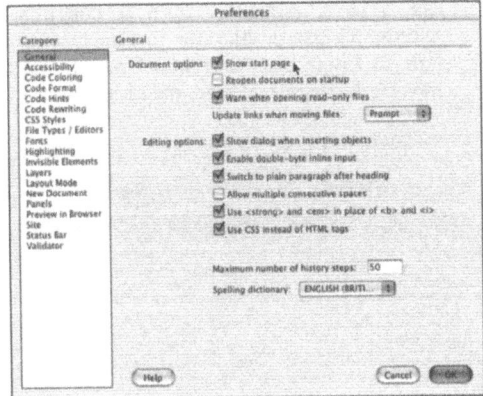

**Figure 1-2.** The Preferences panel

# Your first website

Because this is the book's first chapter, we're going to give you a taste of the power that Dreamweaver offers. The following exercise is meant to just give you an idea of what's possible, so we won't be going into much detail about the features used—that will come later on in the book. The site we're going to create is a simple, navigable journal, complete with links and images.

## Setting up browsers

Prior to creating the site, you need to take a quick trip to Dreamweaver's Preferences panel in order to define your favored web browser for web page previews.

Go to Edit ➤ Preferences (or Dreamweaver ➤ Preferences on Mac) and choose Preview in Browser. You'll see something like Figure 1-3.

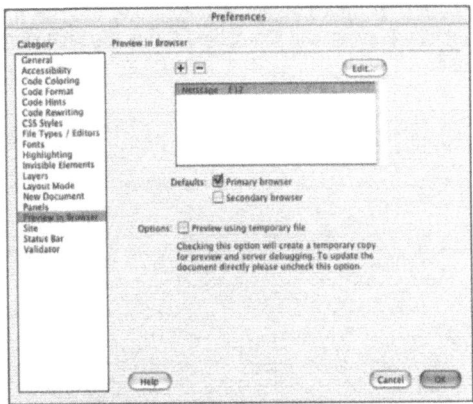

**Figure 1-3.** Specify a browser

Dreamweaver automatically detects one of your browsers (most likely Internet Explorer or Netscape) and sets it as the default, but you should add any others you have on your system. In each case this is done via clicking the plus icon, finding the application on your hard drive, and then naming it, as shown in Figure 1-4. Take note that this must be the executable file, not a shortcut or alias.

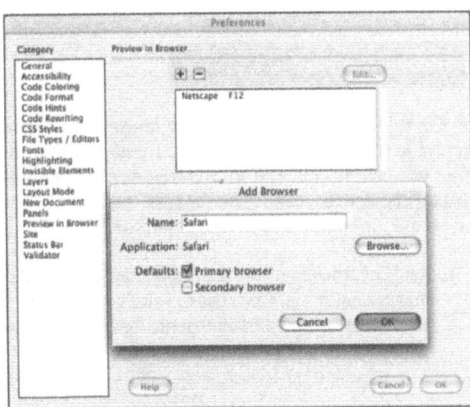

**Figure 1-4.** Adding browsers

All browsers can then be accessed via File ➤ Preview in Browser in order to test web pages in them. Browsers can be designated as Primary and Secondary via the checkboxes, which assigns a shortcut key (*F12* for the primary browser and *CTRL/CMD+F12* for the secondary one).

> Although Dreamweaver MX 2004's Design view is much improved over previous versions, you should still check your site in a range of actual web browsers in order to be sure that the site works consistently well in them. Along with perennial favorite Internet Explorer, you should install a Gecko-based browser (such as Mozilla from www.mozilla.org), or Opera (from www.opera.com). Mac users should get a copy of Virtual PC (http://www.microsoft .com/mac) because PC-based web browsers sometimes have different quirks than Mac ones. Because the Mac audience is far smaller than the PC-based one, it's perhaps less important for PC users to test on Macs (especially when using web standards, as we'll be doing throughout) but if you have the opportunity, do so.

We will go through some of Dreamweaver's other preferences options later, but for now these are the only things that need to be changed.

### Creating the page

In this tutorial, you'll use four small images that can be found in the `Images for exercises` folder within the files you can download from the friends of ED website (**www.friendsofed.com**). The images are `email.gif`, `home.gif`, `left_arrow.gif`, and `right_arrow.gif`.

**1.** Start Dreamweaver and from the start page, select Dreamweaver Site from the Create New choices. If Dreamweaver is already open, go to Site ➤ Manage Sites and select New ➤ New Site.

You should now see a dialog box like the one shown in Figure 1-5. Keep to the Basic tab for now. You're going to set up a folder where Dreamweaver can store and organize your website's files. At this stage, most of the options can be ignored because this will be a very basic site.

**2.** Give the website a suitable name (such as My first Dreamweaver site) and click Next.

**3.** You're then asked whether you're going to work with a server technology (such as ColdFusion, ASP.NET, ASP, JSP, or PHP). This isn't the case right now, so ensure that No, I do not want to use a server technology is selected, and click Next.

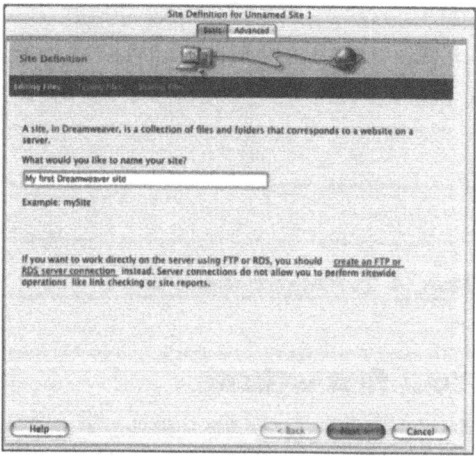

**Figure 1-5.** Defining your website

**4.** Next, select the first option, Edit local copies on my machine, then upload to server when ready (as shown in Figure 1-6), and enter a directory on your hard drive to store the files in (if this directory doesn't already exist, Dreamweaver will create it for you). Click Next to continue.

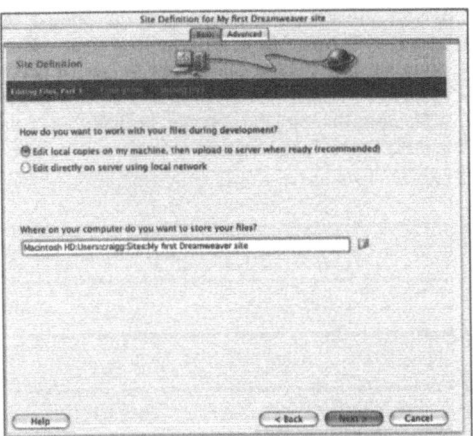

**Figure 1-6.** Specifying where your files are stored

5. You're next asked how you connect to your remote server. Select None from the drop-down menu and then Next to continue to the final set-up screen, which provides a summary of your choices, as shown in Figure 1-7. Click Done twice to finish.

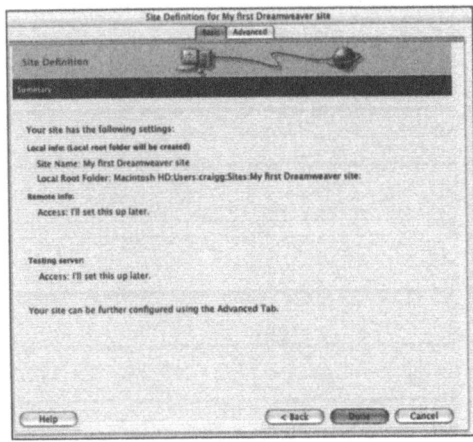

**Figure 1-7.** Summarizing your settings

6. When the main Dreamweaver interface is redisplayed, you should be able to see your root folder set up in the Files panel. Go to File ➤ New and select Page Designs (Accessible) from the General tab, and then Text: Journal Entry from the Page Designs (Accessible) menu that appears on the right. Click Create to continue, as Figure 1-8 shows.

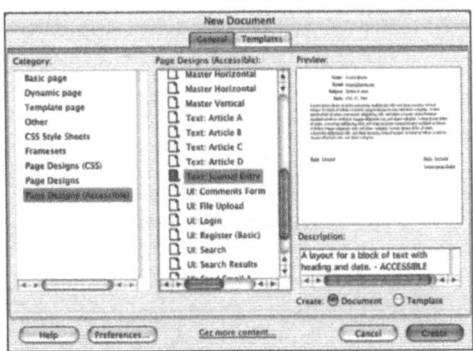

**Figure 1-8.** Creating a new document

A new document will open, filled with "Lipsum" placeholder text. This page is one of the many standard layouts that Macromedia provides with Dreamweaver.

> Lipsum placeholder text is something of a standard when you need text for a design, but don't yet have the final site content. Check out www.lipsum.com for some history, and also an online application that generates this kind of text for you to use.

**7.** You may be able to skip this step, depending on how Dreamweaver is set up on your machine. As we've mentioned already, Dreamweaver enables you to look at documents in three views: Code, Split, and Design. We'll return to the first two in later chapters, but for now choose Design (as shown in Figure 1-9), which enables you to work via a WYSIWYG (What You See Is What You Get) interface.

**8.** Now the designing can begin. You should see something like Figure 1-10 on your screen. If it's not already selected, go to View ➤ Table Mode ➤ Standard Mode, and with your mouse, highlight Name at the top left (as shown in Figure 1-10) and press *DELETE*. Type Location in its place.

**Figure 1-9.** Dreamweaver's views

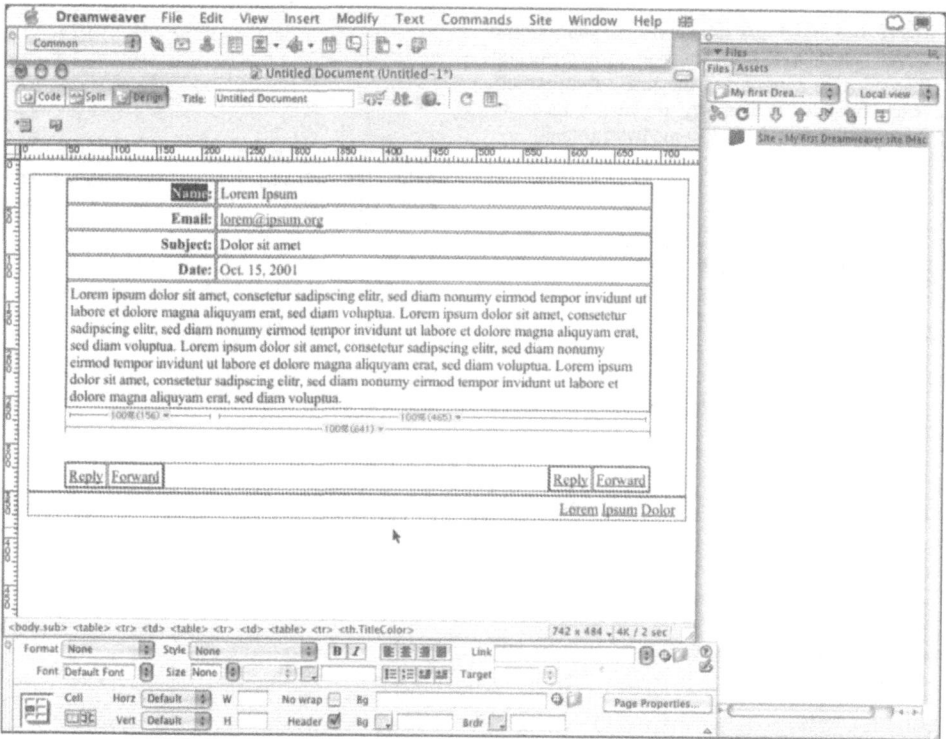

**Figure 1-10.** Designing the new document

6

9. Continue updating the text, either following our example of a simple journal (as shown in Figure 1-11), or by using your own subjects and content.

> In most cases, you can select and edit text to change it, but the lorum@lipsum.org e-mail address must be entirely deleted before you add your own copy (replaced with the time in our example). If you don't do this, Dreamweaver will continue to think that it's an e-mail address and style it accordingly.

10. Use the same technique to add appropriate text to the big text area at the bottom of the page—Dreamweaver automatically resizes the table to fit. Once you're done, go to File ➤ Save and save the file as journal_1.html.

11. Carefully select and delete all the other links on the web page (both instances of Reply and Forward).

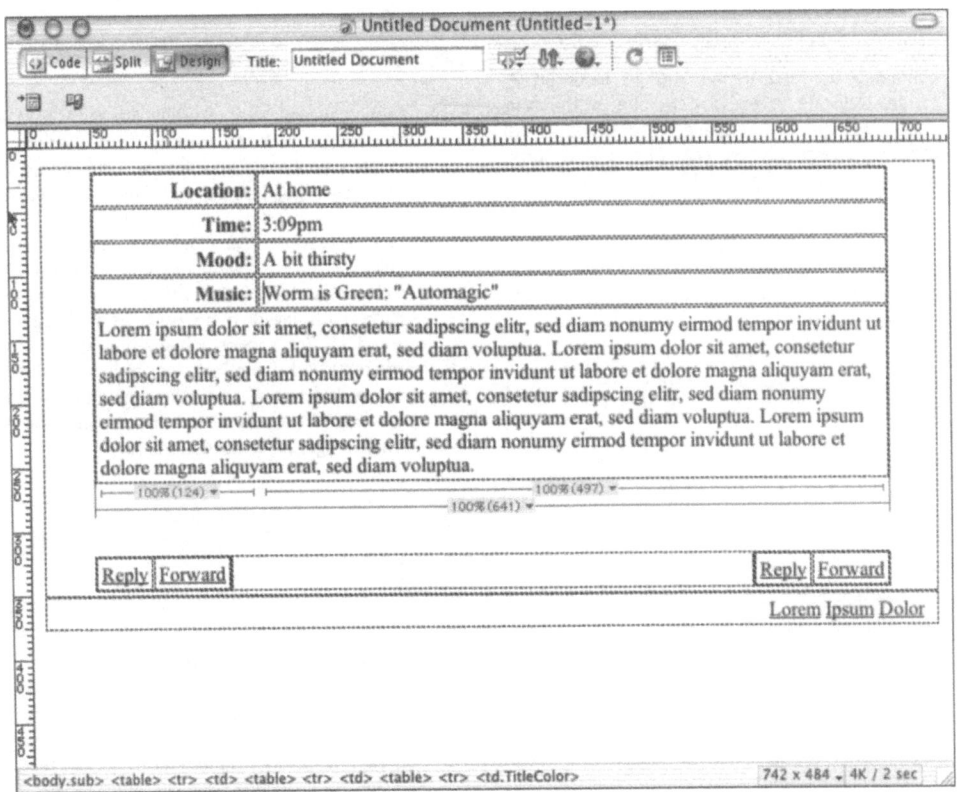

**Figure 1-11.** Continuing our example

Note the format used for file names: everything is in lower case and spaces are replaced by underscores. Some web servers—the machines that store your web pages—are case sensitive (so they see Filename, filename, and FileName differently), and spaces are always an illegal character for website file names. Get into the habit of using lower case and underscores, and naming your files in plain English for ease of recognition. Later on you may be able to create your own shorthand, but for now stick with full-length words. Also note that Dreamweaver defaults to .htm for the file type extension. Although this is fine, we prefer using the full .html, and will be sticking with that throughout the book.

**12.** Click the box furthest to the left (which originally contained the first Reply) and go to Insert ➤ Image. Navigate to email.gif—one of the four image files that are available for download from http://www.friendsofed.com. Click OK (Choose on Mac, as seen in Figure 1-12).

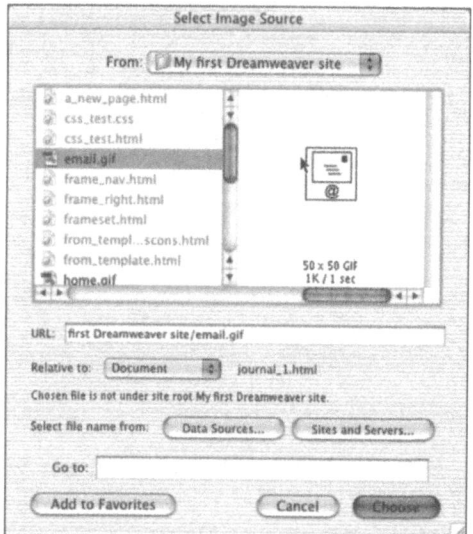

**Figure 1-12.** Downloading on a Mac

**13.** Dreamweaver prompts you to copy the file to your website folder, as shown in Figure 1-13. Select Yes. In the subsequent Copy File As dialog box, select Save. (Dreamweaver automatically chooses the root folder of the website—you're not going to start organizing website files into folders until later in this book.)

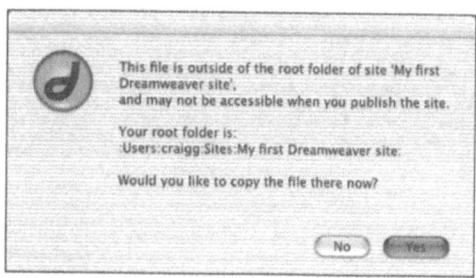

**Figure 1-13.** Copying the file to your website folder

**14.** If you've turned on accessibility attributes (by clicking Preferences ➤ Accessibility and checking the Images checkbox), the Image Tag Accessibility Attributes dialog box appears. This is one way that Dreamweaver attempts to assist you in making sites accessible for people using alternate browsers. The main element you're concerned with is **alternate text** (often referred to as *alt* text), which is displayed in browsers when images are turned off (or spoken when using speech-based browsers). Put something logical in the Alternate text field, referring to the image's purpose more than what it actually shows. (For instance, for our e-mail image, we've used Email me.)

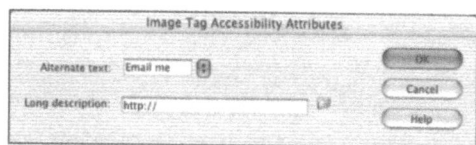

**Figure 1-14.** Specifying alternate text

**15.** Use similar techniques to place home.gif into the adjacent box and right_arrow.gif into the box on the right-hand side. Remember to add alt text.

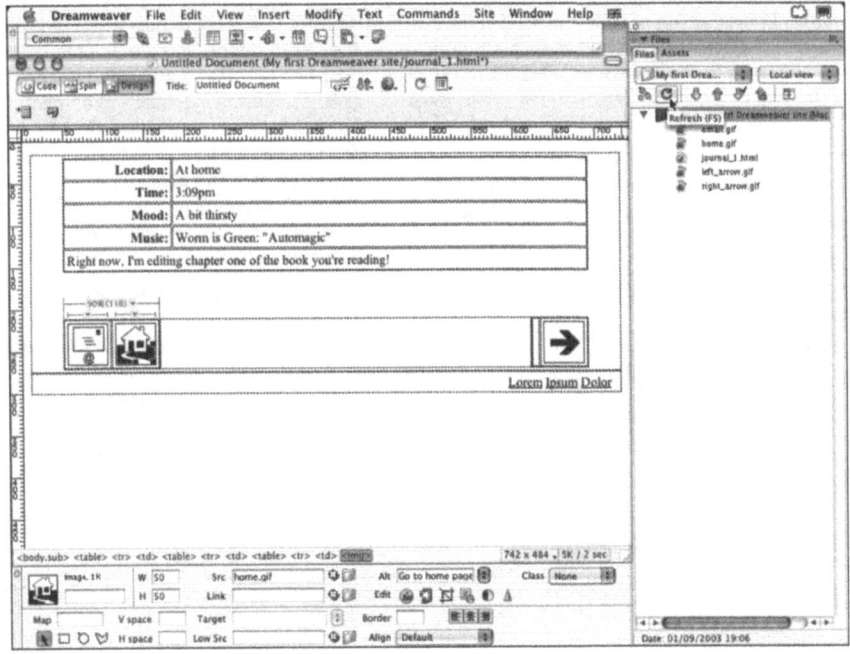

**Figure 1-15.** Placing image files

Note how the Files *panel keeps you updated about your website's files. At this point you should see* journal_1.html *and the images you've used. Clicking the* Assets *tab reveals the three images you've imported. If at any point this panel is lagging, click the Refresh button to update it.*

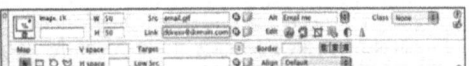

**Figure 1-16.** Adding a link to the image

*You've probably heard about and experienced spam. This method makes it easy for your address to be spidered—that is, identified and illicitly stored in the databases of some search engines and spam applications—but we'll show you some methods later in this book for dealing with this.*

16. Now add links to your images. Click the e-mail image and you'll see it appear in the Properties panel. If you don't see the Properties panel, go to Window ➤ Properties. In Windows, ensure that the Properties panel isn't collapsed. In the Link field, type mailto:youremailaddress@ wherever.com (swapping the e-mail address here with your own of course!) When the image is clicked, a new blank e-mail message is created with your e-mail address in the To field.

17. Now link the other two images in the same way. For the home page image, link to index.html and for the right arrow image, link to journal_2.html. Finally, in the Title field at the top of your

**9**

document window, give your page a title such as My journal: December 10, of course putting in the current date in place of the one we used. Save the file again by going to File ➤ Save, or using the keyboard shortcut *Ctrl/Cmd+S*.

18. In the Files panel, right-click/*Ctrl*-click journal_1.html and go to Edit ➤ Duplicate (as shown in Figure 1-17). Rename the duplicate file journal_2.html by clicking it and typing the new name. Then open this new file. If Dreamweaver displays the Update Files dialog box, click Update to get rid of it (even though there are no links to update).

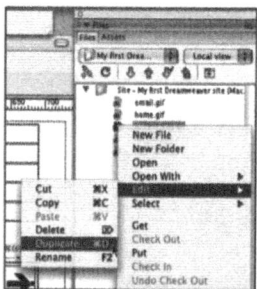

**Figure 1-17.** Creating a duplicate file

19. Switch between open files by clicking them, or by going to Window ➤ [filename]. On Windows you can also use the small tabs at the top of the document window area or *Ctrl+Tab*, whereas on Macintosh you can use *Cmd+~*. In journal_2.html, add the final image, left_arrow.gif (as shown in Figure 1-18). This should go in the space to the left of the right-facing arrow and be linked to journal_1.html.

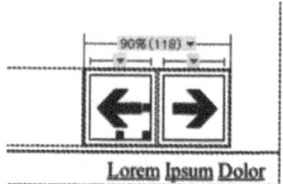

**Figure 1-18.** Adding the last image file

20. Remember, you originally linked the right arrow to journal_2.html. This now needs to be changed to the next entry in the journal (most likely journal_3.html). In that file, the left arrow would link to journal_2.html, the right arrow to journal_4.html, and so on. (In the files available for download from our website, we've only completed the first two pages outlined here, so clicking the right arrow on journal_2.html will prompt an error message in your web browser.) Save the document (*Ctrl/Cmd+S*).

21. Open a new, blank HTML document by selecting HTML from the start page's Create New selection, or by going to File ➤ New and selecting Basic Page ➤ HTML under the General tab, as shown in Figure 1-19. Then click Create.

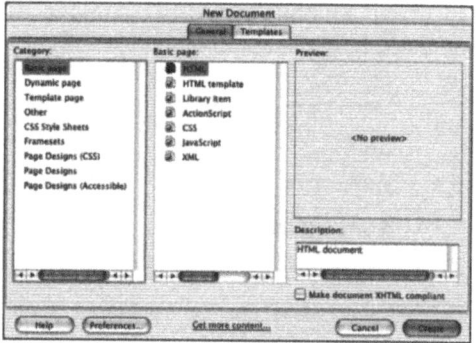

**Figure 1-19.** Opening a new document

22. Click the blank page and type My journal. Select this text and use the Properties panel to turn it into a link to journal_1.html. Give the document a title by using the Title field (as shown in Figure 1-20), and then save it as index.html.

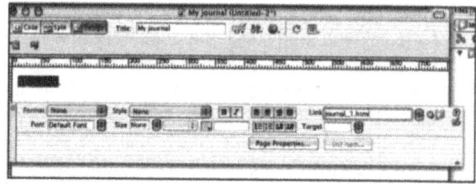

**Figure 1-20.** Titling the document

**23.** Press *F12* to preview your pages in the web browser(s) defined earlier, as shown in Figure 1-21. You should be able to navigate through the pages with ease. If not, download the example files from our website and check them against yours for possible errors. For instance, if links aren't working, you may have linked to the wrong filenames—remember that they must be *exact*.

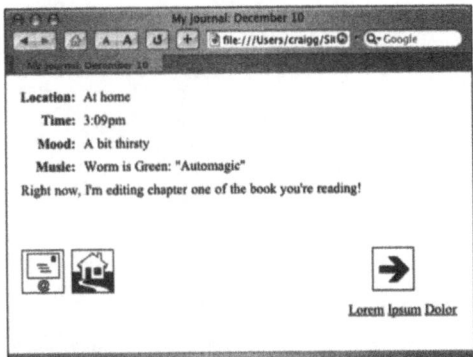

**Figure 1-21.** Previewing the page

*If you don't see anything when you press F12, you need to define your browsers, as explained earlier in this chapter. Note that you can also drop the HTML files directly onto a browser window (or use File ➤ Open in each browser) to preview them.*

And that's it—a fully usable set of web pages designed in Dreamweaver! This may not be the prettiest or best website in the world, but considering that it only took a few minutes to create, it's not too bad. And of course, over the coming chapters in this book you'll take your designs much, much further than this simple demonstration, and learn how to create exciting, innovative pages along the way.

# Summary

We're hoping by now that you have at least some idea of what Dreamweaver MX 2004 is capable of and are starting to become comfortable using it. Although this is only a small chapter, and you've only been working with Dreamweaver for a short time, here's what you've learned already:

- A little about the history of Macromedia Dreamweaver
- How to use the start page
- How to set up browsers for previews
- How to set up a basic website
- How to create web pages
- How to add images and links to your pages

In the next chapter, you're going to start working on the case study that will be used throughout the remainder of this book. And, yes, it'll look a *lot* nicer than the plain vanilla journal pages!

## Chapter 2

# INTRODUCING
# YOUR CASE STUDY

**What we'll cover in this chapter**

- Brainstorming and planning your website
- Deciding on aesthetics, content, and structure
- Creating a site map

## Introduction

In the previous chapter, you used Dreamweaver to create a very basic website. As you're probably aware, we barely scratched the surface of what the application can do. To further explore Dreamweaver, we're not going to bombard you with jargon, overlook the practical nature of web design, or throw dozens of unrelated exercises at you. Foundation books are about working with everyday practices that will prove essential in the real world of web design.

Therefore, you'll create a website from start to finish, based on a real-world project. Each step in the design process will be explored separately, and this modular approach means you'll be able to take processes, ideas, exercises, and even code, and adapt each to your own projects and needs. The project itself will highlight the power that Dreamweaver provides to web designers, and cover all aspects of site creation: layouts, content, files, templates, file management, testing, debugging, and more. At each step of the way, we'll show you the most effective and efficient means of achieving your goals.

The authors of the book are both professional, real-world designers, so you'll get plenty of insight from the field. By the time you've read the last page, you'll be well on your way to joining the world's web gurus!

## The case study

The project you'll be working on is a promotional site for unique photography. The site, called **Images from Iceland**, is based around photographic images from this distinctive and beautiful country. The first half of the book concentrates on the site's structure and content, along with aesthetics, thereby creating a photographic site with relevant supplementary information, such as an artist's profile and contact page. By the end of part one, you'll have learned how to use Dreamweaver for design, layout, structure, typography, and site maintenance. The book's second half shows how to make the content dynamic (by creating a **content management system**).

# Brainstorming

One thing that people sometimes forget is that you should do plenty of work and preparation before even turning on your computer and fiddling around with Dreamweaver. The worst websites—those that are unfocused, unusable, or just plain bad—are usually the product of poor planning. In most cases, such problems can be overcome by taking the time to work out what's best for your site. Luckily, the majority of questions you need to ask are generic and can be applied to most projects:

- What is the purpose of the website?
- Who will the site's visitors be?
- How will this target audience affect your approach?
- Is there a client involved, and if so, what are his or her needs?
- What content will the site contain?
- From where will the content be sourced?
- How will the site be structured?
- What will the site look like?
- When is your deadline?

Of course, these aren't the only questions you should ask yourself, and brainstorming will change from project to project, but this is a good place to start. Also bear in mind that there are rarely any wrong answers, but whatever you discover may help consolidate ideas, so let's take a look at some answers for the case study website.

**What is the purpose of the website?** A site's purpose is often reflected in its design—this is particularly obvious when looking at successful websites. For instance, Amazon.com's (see Figure 2-1) essential goal is to sell as many books, DVDs, and other products, as possible to as wide a range of customers ("users") as available. Therefore, the structure and navigation—if you'll pardon the expression—is *idiot-proof*. The navigation is intuitive, and searches that enable you to get deep into the site are easily available. The visual design of this highly usable site is effectively inoffensive, so although it might not excite anyone, it won't annoy them either.

**Figure 2-1.** Amazon.com

Typically, successful content-oriented sites have a similar approach: `Wired.com` and `http://news.bbc.co.uk` both have thousands of pages, and yet all information can easily be found. However, although both sites partially adhere to their corporate branding, neither would be considered "exciting" design.

At the other end of the spectrum you'll find the likes of `http://Yugop.com`, as shown in Figure 2-2. Although it is a Flash-based website, it highlights the experimental nature of many arts and personal sites. The interface does make sense, but you have to learn how to use it. This is fine for a site that people want to explore, but it would be a death knell for most commercially oriented sites.

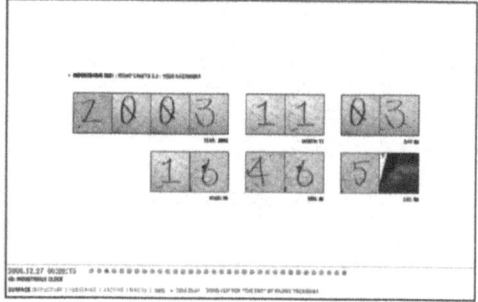

**Figure 2-2.** Yugop.com

Your site will be a showcase for photography taken in Iceland. As such, the images should be the focus of the site. In many ways, we want to combine the examples just shown—a site that has a contemporary and exciting design, but that keeps the straightforward structure and navigation evident in the likes of Amazon.com.

**Who will visit the site?** There will be a number of types of visitors to the site. These are listed below in order of importance:

- **Commissioning editors**: Having seen the images beautifully displayed on the Web, commissioning editors should be able to make contact in order to commission new work.
- **The general public**: Anyone interested in Iceland may visit the site in order to view the photographs. None of the work is confidential, so it should be accessible to all.
- **Designers**: Both print and web designers may want to use digital copies of the photographs in their own projects.

Although the first two groups are most important and most likely to visit, consideration needs to be made to all. The potential age range is fairly large, which will have a bearing on the site's visual design.

**How will this target audience affect your approach?** Because the most important visitors are those who just want to see the photographs, you'll start with a flat, gallery-oriented site. Later, you'll make dynamic content to satisfy the other two types of visitors.

The wide age range will most affect usability. Because there will be a number of non-technically savvy users, the site needs to be simple to use and navigate, and it needs to be obvious where each type of information is to be found. In fact, this rule is true for most sites, but its implementation needs to be more stringent here. In all cases, the photography must be the site's main focus—not whiz-bang effects or unrelated copy and images. Because you want the visitors to contact you, it's essential to include a very obvious way of enabling them to do so.

**Is there a client involved, and what are their needs?** In this case, the de facto client is you! There's no one to please except yourself...or is there? Of course, in some ways, the end users—the audience—are also clients of sorts. They will expect to see great-quality images and readable copy, all contained within a usable site. If they don't get it, they'll go elsewhere. If that happens, the site is a failure, so you need to ensure that won't happen.

Ideas often need to be changed and tweaked along the way, often because of external factors. You might have a preference for certain colors or layouts, but if 99 percent of your audience disagrees, you may need to rethink. Be flexible: just because clients are not artists, you shouldn't disregard their opinions. Of course, the dynamic nature of the Web potentially makes such changes relatively quick and cost-effective to put into practice, especially when using the techniques you'll learn in this book. After all, if a print brochure needs to be changed, the whole thing must be reprinted, or a supplement bolted on. Such a print job won't be any cheaper the second time around if changes are made because a new set of plates will be needed. However, for a website, this isn't the case—the site's already there and the content can be edited easily. To put a fine point on it: correcting a major typo on the introductory page of a catalog may costs thousands, or have to be ignored (due to cost); correcting the same thing on a website may only take a few minutes and effectively cost nothing. Also, the time needed to make corrections is potentially much less. If the site is your own, you can make edits and changes almost immediately.

The process of making a website changes a lot when working for a client other than yourself. You must be even more organized—after all, you'll either be wasting your time or their money, neither of which is acceptable. Perhaps the best advice we can offer when working with clients is to constantly communicate. Never assume you know what a client wants, or that they know exactly what you mean, unless things are explicit. Write everything down, get written specifications, and draw up a contract, saying exactly what the client can expect and when.

Set milestones in the project that the client will have to approve (and maybe pay a percentage of the overall costs for). Such milestones might be the completion of the visual design, the completion of site design, and content addition and upload. Make it clear that if the client changes the brief at any point, he or she may have to pay for alterations if they're substantial. Continue communicating throughout; websites usually fail because those involved didn't talk to each other about their needs and those of the end users. Finally, always ensure you get the go-ahead prior to doing any work.

**What content will the site contain?** The bulk of the site will be composed of photographic images of Iceland, although there will be supplementary information, such as titles. Furthermore, as mentioned, there will be an obvious way to contact you.

**From where will the content be sourced?** When sites aren't for personal or self-promotional use, this question must be answered in some detail. When working for or with a company, find out who is responsible for supplying you with information, and set dates (well before your final deadline) when it should be sent. Also, ensure that you specify specific file types and settings (such as image resolution)—there's little worse in the world of web design than having to rapidly produce a website after receiving a CD full of images that you cannot open or use.

For the case study, you'll use images that already exist (and are for the most part already in a digital format) and copy that you'll write yourselves.

*We should point out here that **copyright** exists on the Web the same as everywhere else, despite what some people might think. Do not just grab a load of images or text from other websites unless you have written permission from the copyright holder to do so. Failure to do so could mean anything from a harsh email to a lawsuit.*

**How will the site be structured?** Most sites have some sort of **home/news/introduction** page, an **about** page describing the site, a **contact** page so users can get in touch, and any number of pages that contain the majority of the site's content (typically **products** or **services** for a commercial site).

Overly complicated structures tend to wreck websites, so keep everything as simple and logical as possible, grouping categories and pages in a consistent and coherent manner. Wherever possible, make all top-level category pages accessible from a central location (such as a **navigation bar**) and keep sub-pages to a minimum. In some cases, this can be achieved via the clever use of layout.

For your site, which is centered around images, there obviously needs to be a **gallery**. This may contain a number of pages, perhaps accessible via **thumbnails**. The home page can double as an area for news about the site, which leaves the aforementioned **about** and **contact** pages. Anything else would probably be superfluous.

**What will the site look like, and how will it work?** Due to the wide age range of people expected to visit the site, the design should be contemporary but welcoming, and not overly fussy. Because this is a site to promote photography, the photographs should be the main focus, and the general page design should not distract from them. However, the site's design will sell the product, too, and must be suitably stylish; if it does a bad job of presenting the product, people will go elsewhere. After all, five-star food is less appealing if it's served in a bucket.

As mentioned, the site should be straightforward to use, which means stripping back the navigation area to the bare essentials, and making good use of succinct copy. Icons should be avoided—after all, the word "contact" is unambiguous, but a picture of an envelope could mean "mail," "email," or several other things.

**When is the deadline?** This is an important question to answer for any project. A wonderful masterpiece of design with a beautiful, highly animated interface is no use to a client if you've only had time to create the home page. If deadlines are too tight for what's been asked of you, talk to the client about it. If the client is you, give yourself a good talking to, and try to be more realistic about deadlines in future.

Always avoid "under construction" pages. They look shoddy and unprofessional at best; if an area of a site is not going to be ready for the launch date, remove the navigation to get to it (which is relatively simple when using the technologies outlined in this book). Even better, if the site is new, delay its launch and put up a holding page containing contact information and a small message saying when the completed site will be online. It should go without saying that you must stick firmly to whatever deadline you've published for all the world to see.

In any case, you should be able to make reasonable deadline estimates based on previous jobs. If in doubt, try to deal with the content (sourcing, structure, and formatting) first, and then the design. You can spend an age messing around with visual design, but if there's no content, any such fiddling is academic.

*A good rule of thumb is to add 50 percent to the amount of time you think you'll need for a job. Small problems always crop up, no matter how careful you and the client are. Even things like your ISP going down for a day can cause huge problems if the deadline is too tight, so always give yourself some leeway.*

## Gathering and organizing content

Gathering content is one thing, but keeping it organized is something else entirely. There are plenty of people who think they work better in a jumbled mess, but this doesn't really work with computers, even when taking into account the Search functions built into Windows and the Mac OS. After all, you may not remember the file name of something you're searching for, especially when working with images from digital cameras, which may have such "useful" file names as 02032045023450.jpg. Logical organization and naming of all your files means you should be able to easily find what you need at any point during a project.

Before getting any content, set up a folder structure on your hard drive to store everything. The structure we suggest (as shown in Figure 2-3) isn't in any way set in stone, but is a general guide that you can adapt to each project as you see fit.

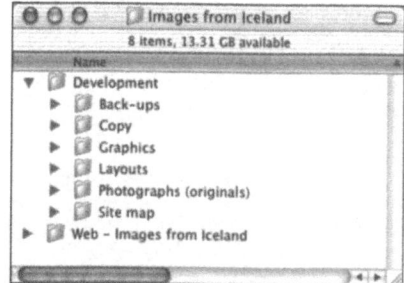

**Figure 2-3.** A tidy file structure

As you can see, the project folder has two folders in it. The second of these is the local copy of the website. We've called it Web – Images from Iceland rather than just web for a good reason. It soon becomes difficult to find a specific web folder when you have dozens of folders called web on your hard drive—even when trying to use any kind of search or "recent folders" function. You'll add more folders inside this later.

The other folder is called Development, and it houses all the files you might need to complete the website, including original copy (perhaps in the form of Word, text, or RTF documents), graphics (such as logos), layouts (which you'll create later), photographs, and the site map. The final item is only really of use for larger projects when you might need instant access to your original site structure. The photographs folder is very useful, though; it enables you to keep full-quality copies of your photos, so if you need to resize one at a later date, you can do so from the original.

Finally, note the back-ups folder. Web design can be a tricky business sometimes, so it's a good idea to make back-ups of your local web folder on a regular basis. If you suddenly find that something stops working, you can revert to (or at least make a comparison with) your most recently working version.

## Creating a site map

A site map is essentially a diagram that provides a structural overview of a website. You can use applications such as Adobe Illustrator, Macromedia Freehand, Microsoft PowerPoint, and others to make them (or if you want, good old squared paper and a pencil). Most site maps are structured in a similar fashion to the diagram shown in Figure 2-4.

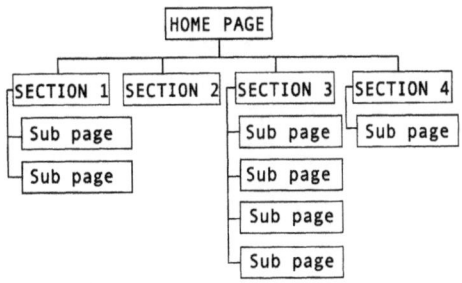

**Figure 2-4.** Site map diagram

The home page is the initial page you access, hence it is at the top of the tree. Main sections are then listed horizontally underneath. Perhaps in tandem with the home page, these will form the basis for the site's navigation bar (or at least the most prominent parts of it). Underneath each section, the pages found in that section are listed. For larger sites, these may actually be sub-sections, with more pages listed under them.

> As is often the case within this book, we provide ideas rather than concrete guidelines. This definitely isn't the only way to create a site map, but whatever method you use, ensure that you understand it well, and that it's easy to explain to a potential client.

As we said, your case study will have a simple structure with four sections; sub-pages are only likely to appear in the gallery. This means the site map looks something like Figure 2-5.

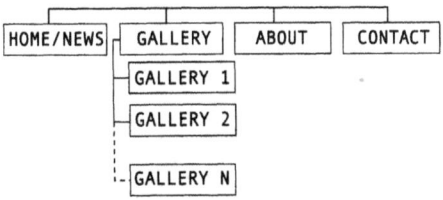

**Figure 2-5.** Case study site map

You might argue that the Home/News page should be at the top, like in the previous site map example. This site's structure is so simple that it doesn't really matter. In any case, this diagram is easy to decipher: to begin with, there will be four pages, one of which (the gallery) will contain a number of sub-pages.

## Summary

During this chapter, you mapped out a website, beginning with brainstorming, and concluding with a structure that you can begin designing around. You also set up a folder structure on your hard drive, and put in all the relevant folders, so you can easily retrieve items at a later date.

Your site is to be primarily based around the photography, but will also contain supplementary information, such as a profile, some news items, and a method to enable visitors to contact us. Said visitors are likely to be the general public and commissioning editors, but perhaps also designers and people who want to buy prints. All must be catered for, and the potential age range means that the visual design shouldn't conform to any temporary trends and fads, and that the site must be easy to use.

In the next chapter, you're going to pause from your case study to look at Dreamweaver in a little more depth, before designing a page layout in Chapter 4.

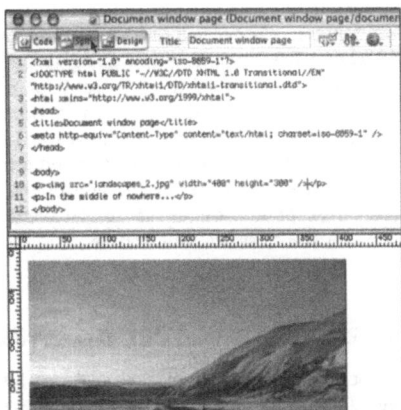

# Chapter 3

# WORKING
# WITH DREAMWEAVER

---

**What we'll cover in this chapter**

- Using the Dreamweaver interface
- Setting important preferences
- Setting up your website

In Chapter 2, you decided how your website was going to work, what its content was going to be, and the basics of how it would look. To continue building a solid foundation for your project, you're now going to spend some time exploring Dreamweaver MX 2004's interface so you'll be able to understand terminology in the rest of the book. By the end of this chapter, you'll have set up Dreamweaver so that everything is in place for you to create your website.

## The Dreamweaver interface

To borrow a phrase from a well-known book/radio show/towel: *don't panic!* Yes, the Dreamweaver interface may look complex at first, but once you know where everything is located and you've used it for a while, you'll soon find that Dreamweaver is flexible and intuitive. Select File ➤ New ➤ Create and you'll see something like Figure 3-1. Note how similar the interfaces for the Windows and Mac versions now are.

Figure 3-2 is the Mac interface, this time showing Split view.

The interface is essentially made up of five elements, each of which will be explained in more detail later on in this chapter.

- **Menus**: These are at the top of the screen. They provide access to the bulk of Dreamweaver's features and list keyboard shortcuts.

- **Insert bar**: By default, this is at the top of the screen just below the menus. It contains icon-based shortcuts to common web page items and functions. A drop-down menu provides access to various technology-specific items.

- **Document window**: This is where you spend most of your time when working with Dreamweaver MX 2004. Depending on your settings, it shows your work in **Design** (visual) view, **Code** view, or a combination of the two, referred to as **Split** view. The top of the document window has a toolbar that

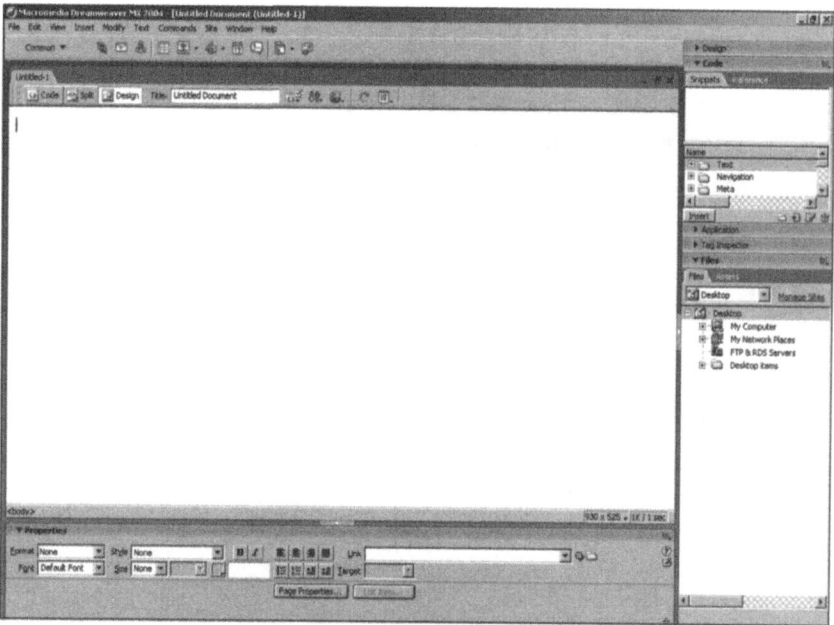

**Figure 3-1.** Design view in the Windows UI

houses various icons and icon-based drop-down menus, most of which enable you to customize the aforementioned views.

- **Properties panel**: This is a dynamic panel that enables you to change settings related to the currently selected item in any view.

- **Other panels**: These supplementary panels have a number of functions relating to Design view, Code view, storage of information, file management, and much more. The relevant ones will be explored in more detail later in the book, although salient information is also included within this chapter.

Upon reading through the description of these elements, you may have noticed some repetition. This is because Macromedia understands that different people approach projects in different ways, depending on applications they've used previously, whether they're more comfortable with visual design or coding, and how much experience with computers and software they have. Furthermore, changes in the industry (mostly due to economic downturn) and expectations from both employers and clients mean that the roles of designer and developer are merging. Also, even if you're a visual designer, there are certain things that can only be achieved in code.

Therefore, Dreamweaver MX 2004 enables designers to get used to coding, and coders to learn how to work with a WYSIWYG (What You See Is What You Get) interface, so it provides several ways of doing the same thing. Within this book, alternatives will often be mentioned, but our methods are just *one* way of achieving our goals. As with all software, you should spend some time experimenting with the interface prior to working on any projects, in order to discover your preferred methods. For instance, you may initially spend lots of time using the menus, then begin using the Insert bar more, and then learn to favor a combination of keyboard shortcuts and panels once you become more familiar with the application.

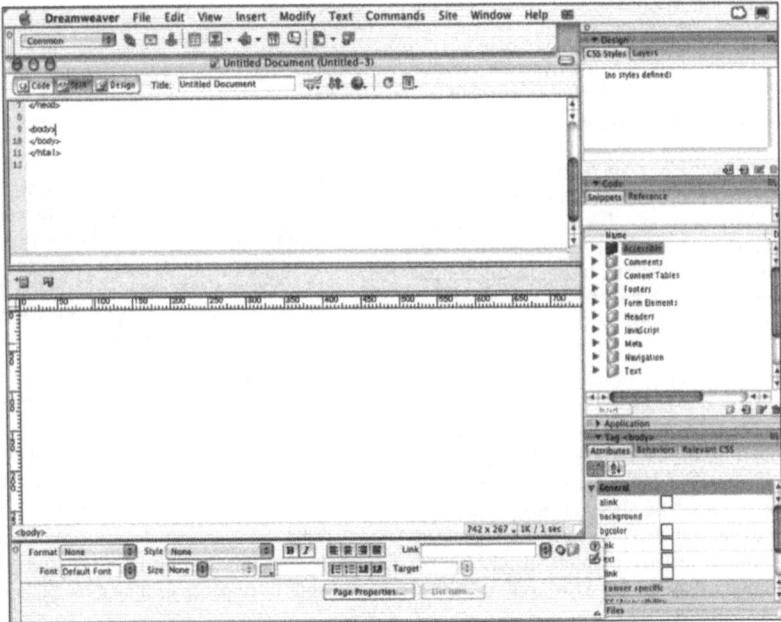

**Figure 3-2.** The Mac interface

After a quick overview of the new features in this version of Dreamweaver, we'll take you through each aspect of the interface, and explain how each element is used.

# What's new?

As with any major application that gets updated (or at least updated well), Dreamweaver MX 2004 contains a number of improvements over previous versions. Interface-oriented changes from the previous edition (Dreamweaver MX) include:

- The interface is standardized across the Windows and Macintosh versions (most notable in the Sites panel)

- Several elements of the interface, such as the Insert bar, have been streamlined

- Workflow improvements to the Tag inspector

- No support for legacy tags—that is, obsolete tags that are no longer part of the (X)HTML specifications. This is most obvious when checking out the new-look Properties panel

- The default Preferences are more geared to accessible, cutting-edge websites than legacy coding

- Development is centered around CSS

If you've used Dreamweaver MX before, you'll be glad to know that Macromedia stayed with the combination of tabs and collapsible panels, thereby making a seemingly complex user interface fairly easy to use. If you've never used Dreamweaver before, take time to get used to the interface—not only where things are stored, but also how the various elements work.

## Menus

Let's first look at the menus, which are located at the top of the screen, as shown in Figure 3-3. Upon opening each of these, some familiar options will be apparent. Of course, there will be plenty of things you don't recognize, but as we said, don't worry; we'll be covering most of the options in later chapters. In fact, some Dreamweaver users may go for years without using many of the menu items.

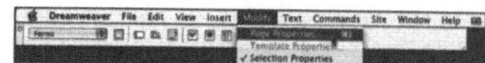

**Figure 3-3.** Dreamweaver's menus

Macromedia tried to make the barrage of menus as user friendly as possible, and items are logically categorized:

- **File**: As with most other applications, this menu deals with opening, saving, closing, and testing your files, along with importing and exporting items. File ➤ Print Code enables you to print HTML, CSS, or other code, script, or mark-up, so you can check things offline. Dreamweaver-specific options within this menu include being able to check your web page against various standards, preview pages in predefined web browsers, and add design notes.

> Design notes enable you to leave notes for other members of a project team if you are working in a collaborative environment. This book concentrates on making a site on your own, so we won't cover them in this book—but design notes are certainly worth looking into if you plan to work on collaborative projects.

- **Edit**: This menu includes the usual Cut, Copy, and Paste commands, commands to copy and paste HTML code via different keyboard shortcuts, and commands used for making changes to your work, notably in Code view. This menu also provides access to Dreamweaver's preferences and keyboard shortcuts (in case you don't like the built-in ones and want to change them).

- **View**: This menu deals with how Dreamweaver displays your work. You can use the commands on this menu to customize various aspects of the document window. (Most of these options are available via the document window icons and menus, too.)

- **Insert**: This menu is used to insert new items into your documents, including template objects.

- **Modify**: This menu enables you to edit items that have been inserted via the previous menu's commands. The Modify menu also houses extensive table-editing tools.
- **Text**: This menu enables you to style text-based elements in your web pages.
- **Commands**: This menu deals with HTML cleaning, extensions, and the creation and replay of automated tasks.
- **Site**: This menu contains the various options relating to site and file management.
- **Window**: This menu enables you to toggle panels on and off, and provides access to other documents that you may have open.

*Remember that when working with multiple documents, Windows users can also switch between documents via the tabs at the top of the document window, or by pressing CTRL+TAB. Mac users can move between open documents via the keyboard shortcut CMD+~.*

- **Help:** This menu enables you to access tutorials, reference guides, Dreamweaver Exchange, and Dreamweaver's activation menu.

Depending on the type of sites you want to create, you may find yourself regularly using all these menus, or perhaps very few of them. In most cases, there's a quicker and easier method to doing things than rummaging through menus, but if you end up looking for something, the menu titles should make it easy to find.

## Insert bar

The Insert bar (shown in Figure 3-4) is usually located above the document window. If you can't see it, go to Window ➤ Insert.

**Figure 3-4.** The Insert bar

The Insert bar may come as something of a shock to long-time Dreamweaver users because it's been massively streamlined. By default, the numerous tabs are gone, replaced by a drop-down menu (shown in Figure 3-5) that contains far fewer sets. This means that the Insert bar takes up less room, leaving you with more space for the document window.

**Figure 3-5.** The Insert bar's drop-down menu

*Should you want to use a tabbed Insert bar akin to that of Dreamweaver MX, you can choose Show as Tabs from the drop-down menu, which results in the interface shown in Figure 3-6. However, we won't be using that interface during the course of this book. Choosing Show as Menu from the Insert bar returns the panel to its default state.*

**Figure 3-6.** The Insert bar set to show as tabs

Choosing one of the options from the drop-down menu changes the icons on the panel, as shown in Figure 3-7.

**Figure 3-7.** The Insert bar with the HTML icon set activated

Some of the icons are actually lists, which contain drop-down menus themselves (as shown in Figure 3-8). These are denoted by a small black triangle. (This interface device exists throughout Dreamweaver MX 2004.)

**29**

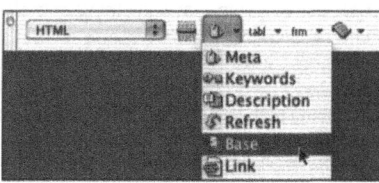

**Figure 3-8.** The Insert bar showing the Meta drop-down menu within the HTML icon set

Although we're not going to go over each individual icon, the following is a brief outline regarding what each set contains:

- **Common**: This set is used to insert the most common web page elements, such as links, images and other media, template regions, tables, and comments (as shown in Figure 3-9.)

**Figure 3-9.** The Insert bar with the Common set activated

- **Layout**: This set is used to add and edit tables, web page divisions and layers, frames, and tabular content (as shown in Figure 3-10).

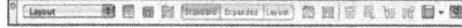

**Figure 3-10.** The Insert bar with the Layout set activated

- **Forms**: This set is used to add form elements (as shown in Figure 3-11).

**Figure 3-11.** The Insert bar with the Forms set activated

- **Text**: This set is used to format text on your web pages (as shown in Figure 3-12).

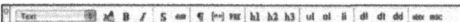

**Figure 3-12.** The Insert bar with the Text set activated

- **HTML**: This set provides easy access to things like horizontal rules, head elements (most of which aid search engines in finding and indexing your site), and table and frame elements (as shown in Figure 3-13).

**Figure 3-13.** The Insert bar with the HTML set activated

- **Application**: This set is used to insert various elements when creating database-driven websites (as shown in Figure 3-14). This will be fully explored in the second half of this book.

**Figure 3-14.** The Insert bar with the Application set activated

- **Flash elements**: This set is used to store any pre-built Flash elements that you may want to include within your designs (as shown in Figure 3-15). For example, by default Dreamweaver MX 2004 ships with a Flash image viewer that you can use as a web photo album.

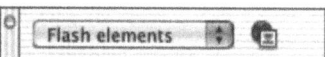

**Figure 3-15.** The Insert bar with the Flash set activated

- **Favorites**: This set is customizable and can be used to store your most commonly used elements (as shown in Figure 3-16). Once set up, this can be a massive time saver. See the following exercise for information regarding how to customize this set.

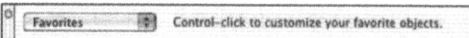

**Figure 3-16.** The Insert bar with the Favorites set activated

> *Although most of the icons on the Insert bar are fairly obvious, some are a little cryptic. To help out, tool tips appear if you hold the mouse over an icon for a couple of seconds.*

### Customizing favorite objects

**1.** To customize the Favorites set, right-click (or *CTRL*-click on Mac) the panel and choose Customize Favorites. In the Customize Favorite Objects dialog, select objects from the list on the left and use the >> button to add them to your Favorite objects list (as shown in Figure 3-17). Note that the Available objects list is context-sensitive, and it can be made more specific by making a selection from the drop-down menu.

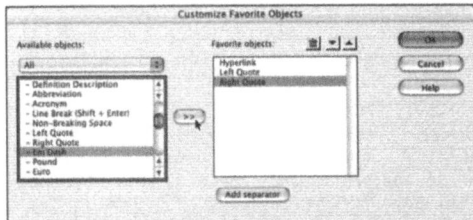

**Figure 3-17.** The Customize Favorite Objects dialog box

2. You can edit the Favorite objects list by using the other icons in the dialog box: the up and down arrows move the currently selected item up and down in the list; the wastebasket removes the current item; and Add separator adds a separator (as shown in Figure 3-18). Click OK once you're done.

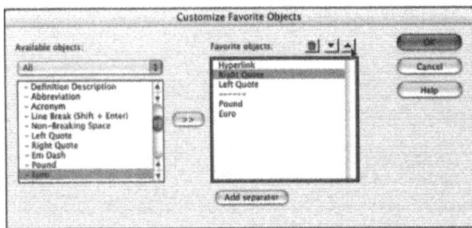

**Figure 3-18.** Sorting favorite objects

And here's the result (as shown in Figure 3-19). The Favorites set now includes everything selected in the previous step. Note that the Text set in the Available objects menu seen in step 1 has some particularly useful elements, including curly quotes and other text symbols that are otherwise only accessible via awkward and hard-to-remember system-level key combinations.

**Figure 3-19.** The Insert bar's Favorites set, as edited in this exercise

## Document window

This is where you see your work take form. Dreamweaver offers several ways to display work-in-progress web pages, so let's take a look at them by going through a quick tutorial.

1. On the friends of ED website, navigate to the download files for this book and find the folder called Document window page. Open the file called document_window.html (via File ➤ Open). You'll see a simple page that contains an image and a single line of copy (as shown in Figure 3-20).

**Figure 3-20.** The file document_window.html, as downloaded from the friends of ED website

2. As we've said, Dreamweaver offers three ways to view your work. The icons in the top-left corner of the document window enable you to toggle between them. For now, ensure that Design is selected (as shown in Figure 3-21).

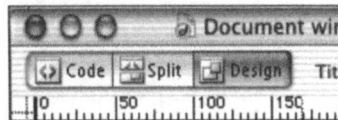

**Figure 3-21.** Selecting Design view

This view provides you with a visual representation of your work, approximating how it appears in a web browser.

Depending on your operating system, document windows can be maximized and resized by using the minimize/maximize buttons, or by dragging the bottom-right corner of the window. Dreamweaver also provides a menu on the document window's Status bar (shown in Figure 3-22) to approximate how your page will look in various monitor resolutions.

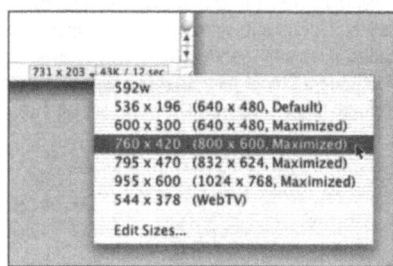

**Figure 3-22.** The Window Size drop-down menu on the Status bar

Choosing one of these options immediately snaps the document window to the desired size. You can add your own sizes via Dreamweaver's preferences, too, which we'll show later in this book. Using this menu helps you to avoid designing pages that force users with smaller monitors to do an excessive amount of scrolling. Although vertical scrolling isn't a huge problem, horizontal scrolling is annoying.

The numbers on the left are an approximation of available screen space (once browser interfaces are taken into account), and the numbers on the right are the actual monitor resolution. Therefore, in the example shown, we're approximating an 800 x 600 resolution, which leaves only 760 x 420 pixels once browser toolbars are taken into account. You should always ensure your sites work well in this size and above.

> *On Windows, you may have to go to* Window ➤ Cascade, *in order to use this function. Alternatively, for individual windows that you want to resize, click the minimize/maximize button to ensure the window isn't full size.*

Next to this menu is another measurement, which shows the **page weight**, measured in kilobytes, along with an estimate of how long the page will take to download (shown in Figure 3-23). Note that this estimate is based on the speed you set within Edit ➤ Preferences ➤ Status Bar. As a rule, it's best to keep this to the common 56K speed—*you* may have broadband, but many web users don't; try to keep loading speeds as small as possible.

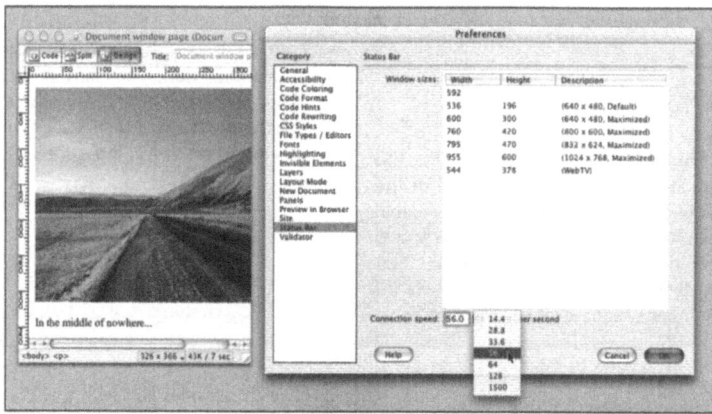

**Figure 3-23.** Changing the Status bar's connection speed in the Dreamweaver preferences

3. Regardless of the content of your web page, it's held in place by code (mainly HTML). In step 2, you chose Design view, so now click the Code button. Your document window will now look something like Figure 3-24.

**Figure 3-24.** Our open document, displayed in Code view

If you haven't worked with HTML before, this display might seem confusing. Don't worry—you'll explore HTML in later chapters. By using Dreamweaver, you can avoid typing most HTML by hand, and even when you do there are several ways of speeding up the process.

HTML stands for HyperText Mark-up Language, and is composed of various start and end tags—for instance <p> denotes the start of a paragraph and </p> the end of that paragraph. These tags are **parsed**, or interpreted, by web browsers, which then lay out web pages as intended by the author. The onset of visual design packages such as Dreamweaver means that many people no longer even look at HTML. However, we're going to be working with code throughout the book, which is the reason for mentioning such things early on. Don't say we don't look out for you!

The final view is **Split** (formerly called Design and Code view), and it's simply a useful mixture of the two views we've already explored (as shown in Figure 3-25).

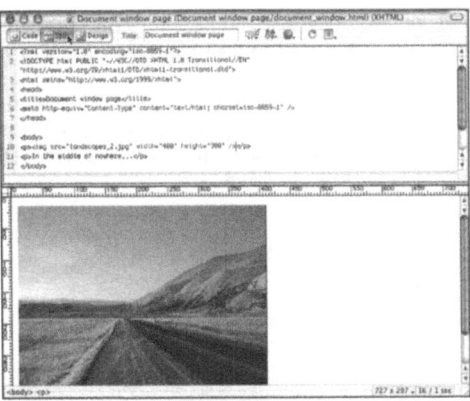

**Figure 3-25.** Dreamweaver's Split view, showing Design and Code views

Note that by dragging the bar between the two views (as shown in Figure 3-26), you can set the proportion of available space that the design and code areas use.

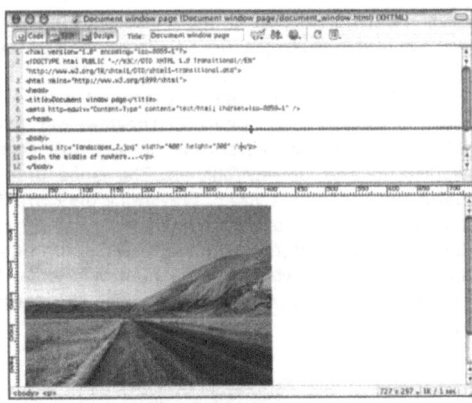

**Figure 3-26.** Customizing Split view

As you can see, this can prove to be very practical. Highlighting something in one view highlights it in the other—for instance, if you click the image in Design view, the relevant HTML will be highlighted in Code view. This enables you to tweak and streamline your code. For those of you who are new to HTML, Split view can help you learn faster, because you do things visually and can see how your actions affects the code.

**33**

**4.** You may find that you have to scroll across the code window to find the highlighted code. If that's the case, go to View ➤ Code View Options and ensure Word Wrap is active. You can also alter various other items relating to both views via the View Options button at the top of the document window, as shown in Figure 3-27.

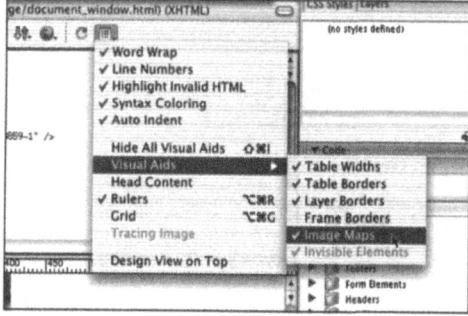

**Figure 3-27.** The View Options button

Several other icons exist on the toolbar, but for now we're only going to look at the ones to the right of the Title field. The first icon (shown in Figure 3-28) checks how well the current document is supported in various web browsers (a new feature in Dreamweaver MX 2004). The next icon checks files in and out when working in a group environment. The globe dropdown menu is another way of previewing the current document in the web browsers defined earlier; and the circular arrow icon next to the View Options button refreshes the document view. This is only active if you make changes in Code view and need to refresh Design view.

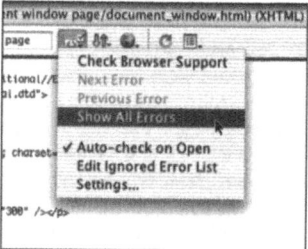

**Figure 3-28.** The Browser Check menu

## Properties panel

The Properties panel (shown in Figure 3-29) is usually situated at the bottom of the screen, below the document window. If you can't see it, go to Window ➤ Properties.

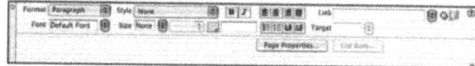

**Figure 3-29.** The Properties panel

The Properties panel is very important, and a Dreamweaver interface element on which most designers come to rely.

Figure 3-29 shows the panel in its default state, which provides the user with various options for formatting text. Across the top half of the panel you can see dropdown menus for formatting, font sets, size, and color, and there are various icons for making text bold or italic, and for justifying it. This panel is also the main one used to add styles to web page items (via the Style menu) and links (via the Link field, as you did in the previous chapter).

When you click the web page's image in Design view the panel should change to look like Figure 3-30.

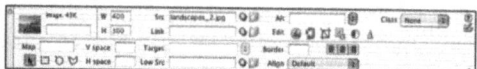

**Figure 3-30.** The Properties panel when an image is selected in Design view

As you can see, this panel is context sensitive, providing the options you need for a specific element and no more. This saves space and helps you work more efficiently.

> If you're only seeing a half-size Properties panel, click the arrow at its bottom right to expand the panel to full size. We suggest leaving the panel at full size at all times.

## Other panels

A quick look at the Window menu will show you just how many panels Dreamweaver has. With the exception of the Insert and Properties panels, these usually sit at the right side of your screen.

Dreamweaver intelligently stacks panels and panel groups, giving priority to ones that are open, so you can get at the controls. Clicking the triangles opens and collapses each panel/panel group. Note that on Windows, closed panels are differentiated by their title appearing in plain text (open panels are bold). On the Mac, closed panels' titles have a white background, and open ones have a blue background.

The following images show the panels. Figure 3-31 shows the Design panel collapsed, and Figure 3-32 shows it expanded.

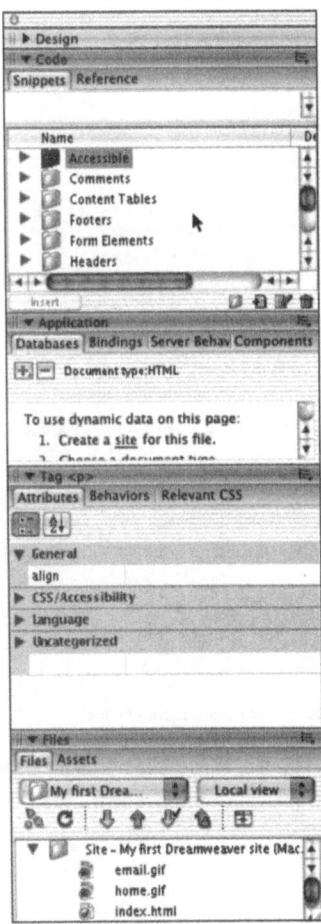

**Figure 3-31.** The panels group with the Design panel closed

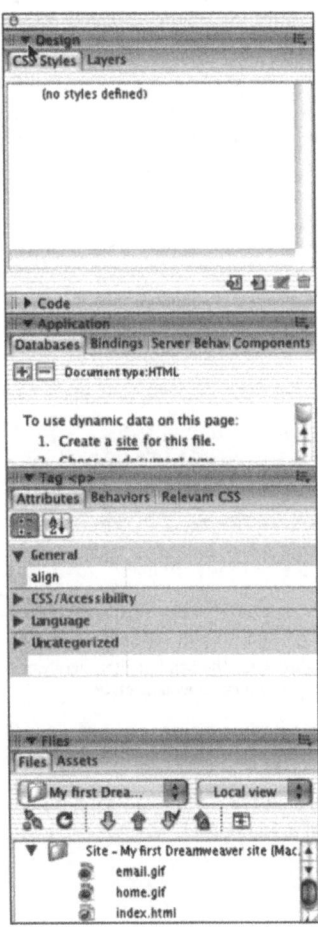

**Figure 3-32.** The Design panel expanded

**35**

*If your monitor has a maximum resolution of 800 x 600, now would be the time to upgrade. At the very least, we would recommend a resolution of 1024 x 768 when working with Dreamweaver, and even higher, if possible.*

To close a panel entirely:

**1.** Position the mouse pointer over the top left of the panel until the pointer changes into a hand, as shown in Figure 3-33.

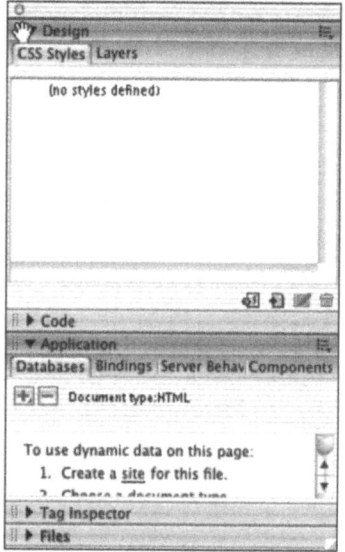

**Figure 3-33.** The hand pointer, signifying that a drag action can now take place

**2.** Drag the panel away from the group, as shown in Figure 3-34.

**3.** Use the standard Close box to close the panel, as shown in Figure 3-35.

You can also separate panels from the panel groups instead of closing them, but you'll soon find your screen getting cluttered. Macromedia created the dynamic collapsible system for good reason, and the alternatives simply don't cut it.

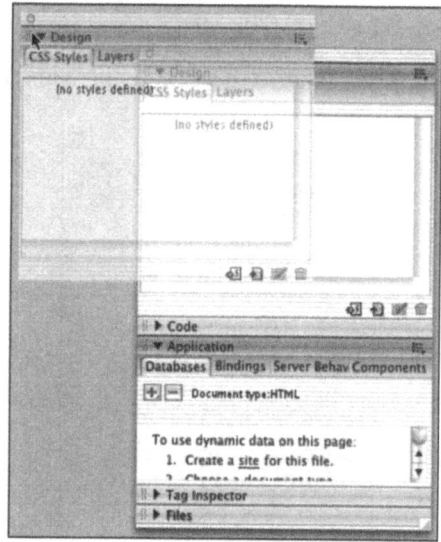

**Figure 3-34.** Dragging a panel from the group

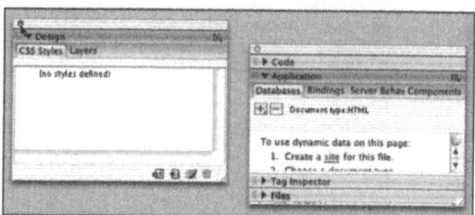

**Figure 3-35.** Closing the separated panel

Panels can be reopened via the Window menu whereupon you can drag them back in the main panels group, as shown in Figure 3-36.

**Figure 3-36.** Dragging a panel back to the group

## Panel groups

As previously mentioned, panels are organized into groups, which is apparent if you note the spacing in the Window menu (as shown in Figure 3-37). However, some panels within the menu don't entirely appear where you'd expect.

| Window | Help |
|---|---|
| Insert | ⌘F2 |
| Properties | ⌘F3 |
| CSS Styles | ⇧F11 |
| Layers | F2 |
| Behaviors | ⇧F3 |
| Snippets | ⇧F9 |
| Reference | ⇧F1 |
| Databases | ⇧⌘F10 |
| Bindings | ⌘F10 |
| Server Behaviors | ⌘F9 |
| Components | ⌘F7 |
| Files | F8 |
| Assets | F11 |
| Tag Inspector | F9 |
| Results | F7 |
| History | ⇧F10 |
| Frames | ⇧F2 |
| Code Inspector | F10 |
| Arrange Panels | |
| Hide Panels | F4 |
| Next Document | ⌘` |
| Previous Document | ⇧⌘` |
| document_window.html | |

**Figure 3-37.** The Window menu

**Design** The Design panel group includes the following:

- **CSS Styles**: This panel enables you to work with styles and add them to web page elements.
- **Layers**: This panel enables you to manage web page layers and toggle a checkbox to prevent overlapping.

**Code** The Code panel group includes the following:

- **Snippets**: This panel enables you to store and reuse small chunks of code, thereby speeding up workflow. We look at these in a later chapter.
- **Reference**: One of Dreamweaver's most overlooked features, this panel is effectively a number of reference books for when you forget how that all-important web page element works (as shown in Figure 3-38).

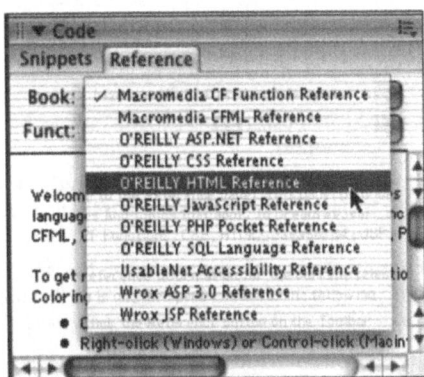

**Figure 3-38.** The Reference panel

**Application** The Application panel group includes the following:

- This group contains four panels to assist in creating database-driven websites. The panels are Databases, Bindings, Server Behaviors, and Components.

**37**

**Tag inspector** The Tag Inspector panel group includes the following:

- **Attributes**: This panel outlines the various attributes for the selected web page items via a number of collapsible menus. .

- **Behaviors**: This panel enables you to add a number of built-in JavaScript behaviors to your web pages.

- **Relevant CSS**: This panel lists relevant CSS for the currently selected item.

**Files** The Files panel group includes the following:

- **Files**: This panel enables you to manage your website's files, and in its expanded form can be used to upload files to a web server.

- **Assets**: This panel lists site assets (such as images, Flash files, and so on).

**Others** Dreamweaver has several other panels that are independent of any groups:

- **Frames**: This panel enables you to manage frames on your website.

- **History**: This panel lists recent steps, enabling you to backtrack, or even save a selection as a **Command** (macro).

- **Results**: This panel appears docked by default on Windows, but it is freestanding on Mac. It contains a number of tabs relating to web page validation, link checking, and other site reports.

- **Code Inspector**: This panel works in a similar way to Code view. By default, it appears undocked on Windows and Mac.

## Arranging panels

When a panel is open you'll see a menu icon at its top-right corner. This is a drop-down menu that enables you to access panel-specific functions, as shown in Figure 3-39. However, these menus also have some generic options, enabling you to customize the arrangement of your panels and panel groups.

As you can see, you can group a panel with a different group, rename a group, or create an entirely new group—it's up to you. Suffice to say that in this book we're working with the default settings, because they're pretty good to start with, but don't be afraid to experiment, particularly if you think a new panel group will help you work better and faster.

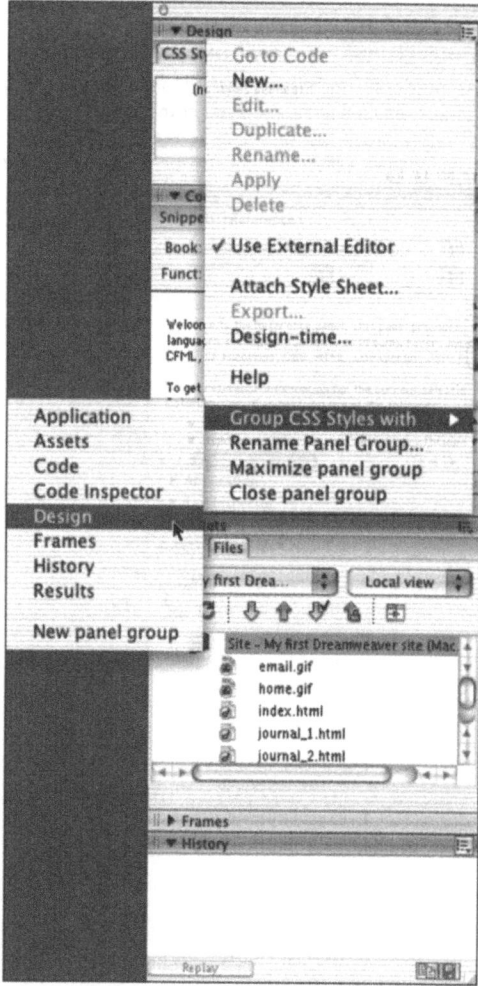

**Figure 3-39.** The Design panel's drop-down menu

Figure 3-40 shows a portion of the Window menu, which deals with arranging panels.

**Figure 3-40.** The Hide Panels option in the Window menu

The first option, Arrange Panels, does exactly what it says. In the initial release of Dreamweaver MX 2004 this option is only available to Mac users. If your panels are strewn around the screen, this option will tidy them up. Hide Panels is a useful feature for those of you with smaller monitors, enabling you to hide all on-screen panels. This acts as a toggle—activating this menu (or using the keyboard shortcut, F4) for a second time will show all the panels that were hidden. (At this point, the menu option is, logically enough, called Show Panels.)

### The Files panel

Long-time Dreamweaver users—particularly those on the Mac—might be surprised to see the Files panel tiny and hidden within the groups on the right side of the screen. However, you can expand it by using the Expand/Collapse icon, which is the furthest icon to the right in its toolbar. (Note that this icon is only displayed if you're working on a site.) This provides you with the familiar two-pane interface, seen in Figure 3-41.

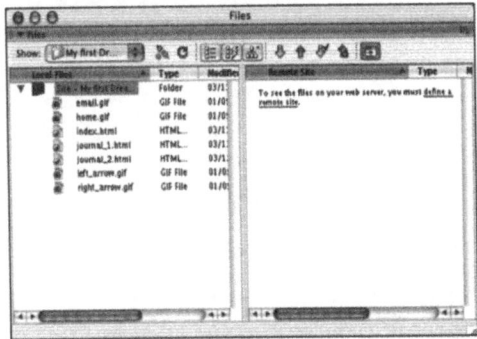

**Figure 3-41.** The expanded Files panel

Clicking the Expand/Collapse icon again returns the panel to its panel group. Generally, you won't need to expand it very often, but it can come in useful sometimes, as you'll see later in the book.

## Preferences

Dreamweaver is a complex but flexible application, so it should come as no surprise that there are a lot of preferences that can be tweaked (by going to Edit ➤ Preferences on PC or Dreamweaver ➤ Preferences on Mac). Categories are selected by highlighting options in the Category menu, whereupon associated options appear on the right, as shown in Figure 3-42.

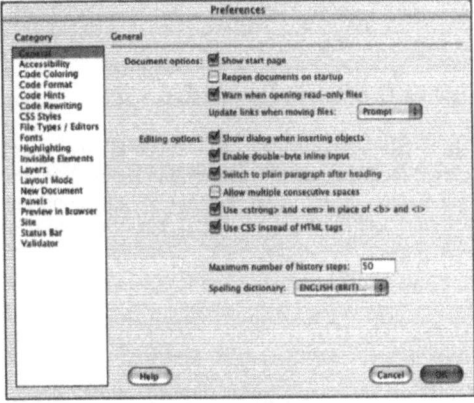

**Figure 3-42.** Dreamweaver's preferences

Most of Dreamweaver's default settings are fine, and we'll let you know when anything needs to be changed. Note that Dreamweaver's dictionary settings can be changed via General ➤ Spelling dictionary, depending on what you have installed. We've already shown you how to change the browsers you can preview sites in via Preview in Browser, so we're only going to check out a couple of things now.

Select Code Format and ensure that Automatic Wrapping is turned off (the default setting), as shown in Figure 3-43. At this point, this won't actually make a great deal of difference to you, but it helps behind the scenes. Turning Automatic Wrapping on forces line wrapping in your **HTML**, which can often make it

**39**

trickier to edit files at a later date (even when using Dreamweaver's visually oriented Design view).

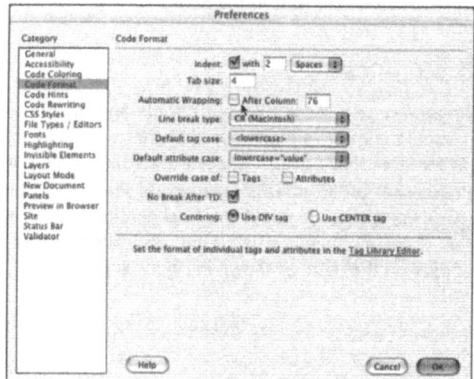

**Figure 3-43.** Code Format preferences

Next, select Accessibility, and check all the boxes, except for Form objects, as shown in Figure 3-44. This will display dialog boxes for you to add important attribute values when you add certain things to your web pages.

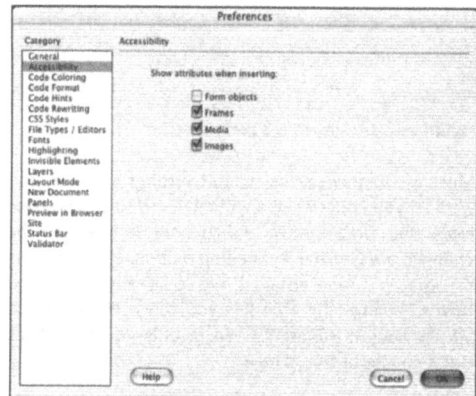

**Figure 3-44.** Accessibility preferences

The other category we're going to look at is Status Bar, shown in Figure 3-45.

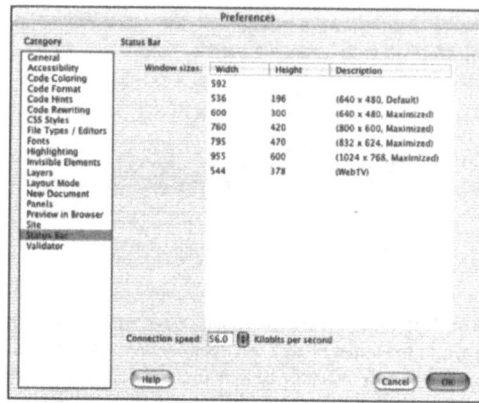

**Figure 3-45.** Status bar preferences

This is where you can change the connection speed we referred to earlier. This is used to predict how long a page will take to download. You can also add new window sizes, although the most common sizes are already built in.

## Setting up your website

We've outlined this already in the previous chapters, so setting up your site should be problem-free. You should have a folder structure on your hard drive, as shown in Figure 3-46.

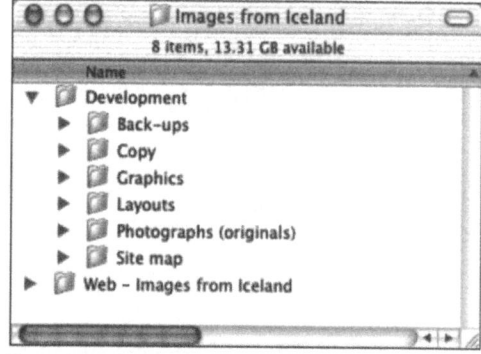

**Figure 3-46.** The folder structure for the website

**1.** Go to Site ➤ Manage Sites and then New ➤ New Site, as shown in Figure 3-47.

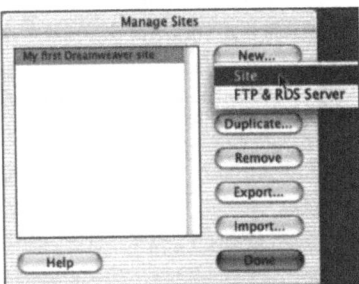

**Figure 3-47.** The Manage Sites dialog box

**2.** Click the Advanced tab when the Site Definition window appears, and select Local Info, as shown in Figure 3-48. These are settings for your hard drive, as opposed to Remote Info, which deals with setting up your web server, which is what serves your site to the general public.

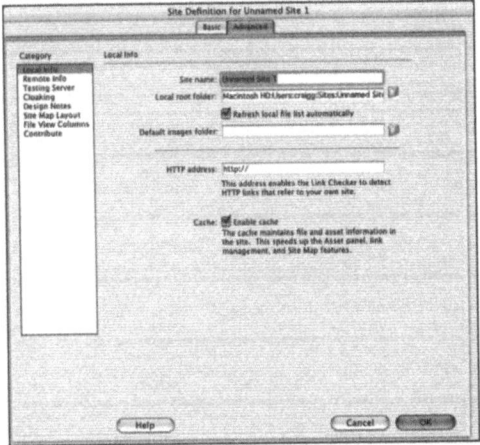

**Figure 3-48.** The Site Definition dialog box

**3.** Enter a site name (such as Images in Iceland) and then define the local root folder by clicking the folder icon, and then navigating to and selecting the folder set up earlier (Web - Images from Iceland). Note that if you move this folder later, you may have to add this information to Dreamweaver again.

> You're given more options, but these, like those we've already defined, can be changed later, if you need to.

**4.** Select the Testing Server category. Under Access, choose Local/Network. This means that when you want to test your site with working links, your root folder will simulate the web experience in your default browser. Dreamweaver automatically fills in the Testing Server Folder and URL Prefix fields with the details you provided earlier, as shown in Figure 3-49.

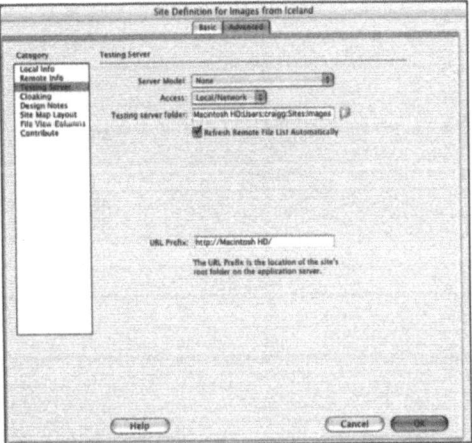

**Figure 3-49.** Testing server settings

> The alternative option is FTP, which stands for **File Transfer Protocol**. This is the standard way of transferring files across the Web, but to use it you'd need an FTP client to upload the files for each test, and you would also have to be online while working.

**5.** Click OK and Done to finish. Notice that the Files panel displays the root folder of your site, and you're now ready to start work.

**41**

## Summary

Well, that wasn't too scary, was it? And look how much you've learned during this chapter. You have:

- Explored Dreamweaver's menus
- Worked with the Insert bar and new Favorites set
- Used the document window in both Design and Split views
- Investigated Dreamweaver's panels—both their contents and how to organize them
- Looked at some of Dreamweaver's preferences
- Set up your site so it is ready for work in the following chapters

Of course, feel free to come back to this chapter if you forget where something is located. (Although we'll make references to panels later in the book, we'll gradually reduce the number of explanations, in order to avoid too much repetition.)

Now it's time to move on to the exciting part of the process, where your ideas begin to take shape, and your plans are put into practice.

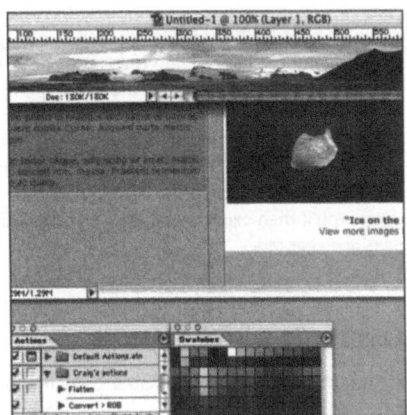

## Chapter 4
# CREATING A LAYOUT

---

**What we'll cover in this chapter**

- Designing a layout
- Sketches and planning for visuals
- Web limitations
- Building a layout overview
- Web file formats

You now have an idea of what your site's going to contain and how the information is going to be structured. The next step is to decide how the site is going to look. In this chapter, you'll design your layout, bearing in mind the limitations of online design. You'll work first offline, and then in a graphics editor, where the design will be optimized for ease of export (more on that later). You'll then export relevant images for use in the next few chapters.

# Designing the layout

At the end of Chapter 2, you had the site map shown in Figure 4-1.

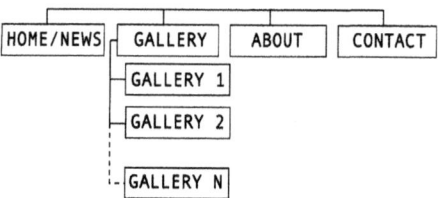

**Figure 4-1.** Site map

> This site is structurally simple, but if you're working on a larger site, it's sometimes good at this point to just bash together some **very** basic HTML pages to test that the structure works. These only need the navigation links and page title to test whether the organization is logical. As this is a rough draft, use whatever method you find quickest and keep things as simple as possible.

## Initial layout ideas

First, some quick tips when it comes to design. Keep an open mind when approaching a project, but always ensure that you keep your client's brand in mind, even if that client is *you*. For instance, if designing a site for an insurance company, you don't want to use colors and shapes that look more at home on a children's toy. With regards to the case study, Iceland is a beautiful but somewhat barren and chilly place, so the interface

can build upon those ideas, being clean and stylish but spacious and done in cool colors, such as light grays and blues.

Also, be aware that design evolves both during and after a project. Don't be afraid to change things when you need to. In fact, you'll find that certain aspects of the site will change during the course of this book. That's not because of poor editing, but because we're presenting what it's like to create a website, and not some rigid, unrealistic tome that claims you can get from A to B with no problems, changes of heart, or tangents.

### Don't touch that computer

Our final tip for now is to wrench yourself away from your computer screen for a while. When using design software, you can easily get locked into a specific way of working and using only certain tools. The output can end up looking influenced by those tools, which is why many web designers use a traditional method when planning and designing sites: drawing. That's right, with a pencil and paper.

At this stage, it's pointless being precise and precious with your work—just get a great big notepad and some pencils and start scribbling. Draw as many ideas for page layouts, parts of pages, navigation systems, and so on, as you can. Work quickly, and don't stop to think too much; we'll rationalize things later on. Go with gut instinct, and never stay on one idea for very long.

> At this point, some of you may be screaming "I can't draw!" If you can hold a pencil to paper and make some marks, you can draw. Remember, what we're trying to work on here are basic layout ideas. Nothing from these initial doodles will make it into a public forum, but these doodles eventually consolidate design ideas and make everything more obvious for you.

Here are some initial doodles for the Images in Iceland site. Note how key words and phrases are dotted around the page. These are reminders not only of what the images represent, but also denote ideas relating to content and functionality.

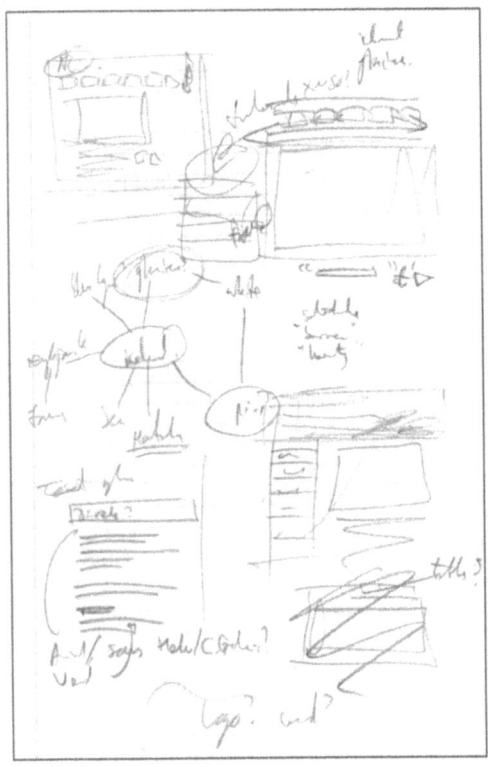

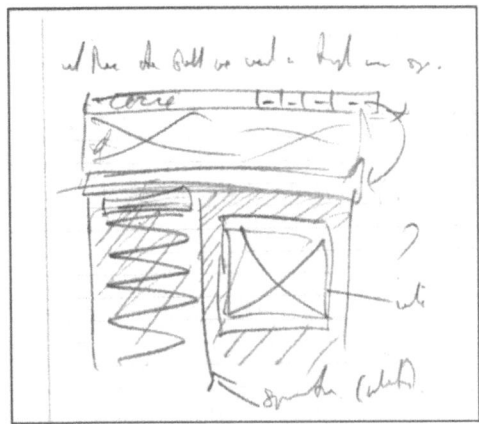

As you can see, these aren't supposed to be works of art; instead, this is a way of getting ideas down very quickly, without restricting yourself by using software. In these sketches, there are the beginnings of logos, navigation systems, page layouts, and more—try it yourself and see how quickly the ideas arrive.

### Getting inspired

Of course, sometimes the web equivalent of writer's block hangs over you and your blank sheets of paper. When this occurs, resist the temptation to turn on your computer. You'll only end up going to sites similar to your work-in-progress one and plundering ideas. Instead, find inspiration elsewhere: check out magazines, books, DVDs, and other digital media. Go to art galleries or even shopping centers and check out everything you see. Get into the habit of carrying a small notepad and pencil so you can jot down ideas. If you can, get a cheap, small digital camera and grab images of anything that strikes your fancy.

After you have done all this, you can at last use the Web to help spark or clarify ideas. Keep a favorites/bookmarks folder in your favored browser for a collection of sites you like the look of. Research sites in the same genre as yours, check out how others have approached the subject, and think about how you can improve on what's already out there.

You may find you dislike how a site's navigation works, or how certain layouts are presented, so you can steer clear of using such things. Conversely, you may happen upon novel uses of shapes and colors, which help you on your way with your own designs. Along with adding such sites to your browser's bookmarks, you might want to take screenshots (*Print Scrn* on Windows or *cmd+Shift+3* on Mac) and save the resulting files on your hard drive somewhere.

> *Please bear in mind that copyright exists on the Web the same as everywhere else. Not only is it morally wrong to copy or clone someone else's design, it's also illegal. Don't do it. Getting inspired by someone else's work is fine, but you should always end up with something distinctly different than the original. Check* www.pirated-sites.com *for examples of those who **didn't** heed this advice.*

At this point, you have three distinct sets of research to work from:

- Notes from brainstorming
- Initial doodles and sketches
- Research, such as print designs and websites

## Organization and structure

Now start taking elements from the initial sketches and organizing them. Photocopy and cut out parts of the sketches and set them against each other to build a basic layout. Try organizing them under a plainly colored cardboard frame (preferably black or gray, so it doesn't distract from your work) to see how they work within a window, and add more doodles as necessary.

**Web limitations** As this point, we need to start taking into account the limitations of the Web, even though we're not yet working with software. The most obvious of these is the screen resolution of your users' monitors. Unfortunately, unlike television, this is a variable:

at the time of writing, most web users are running monitors with resolutions of 800×600 or 1024×768, but some are using larger monitors still. Also, not everyone surfs at full screen. Therefore, you either have to build a **fixed** website, which has a set number of pixels that will work for the bulk of your users, or a **liquid** design, which stretches to fill the size of the browser window. An example of the latter sort of site is www.wireviews.com, which is depicted in Figure 4-2—note how the content shifts depending on the browser window size.

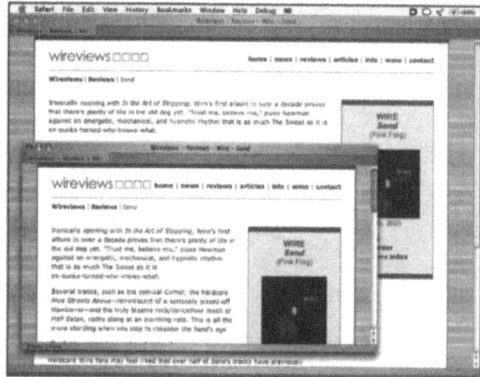

**Figure 4-2.** An example of liquid design

For sites like this, which are mostly text-based, a liquid layout is suitable. However, most of the case study site's content is photographic, which cannot stretch with the browser, so a fixed design is more suitable.

Another important thing to bear in mind is that web design is largely centered around boxes. Whether you're going to use tables or CSS, think in rectangular sections when organizing your sketches into designs, and try to simplify things whenever possible. On a similar theme, avoid flashy gimmicks and effects. This is particularly important if you're a relative newcomer to the Web—all those whiz-bang effects, fades, and tricks have been done to death, and should only be used if they are essential to the site being created. Design is probably the greatest factor in whether someone will stay on your site or go elsewhere, and just like in other media, overly flashy and gaudy sites will put people off.

**Structuring a page** Here are some more sketches for page layout designs. Of course, these are still open to interpretation, but with Dreamweaver you can continue to edit and alter designs right up until the last minute, so there's no need to worry about getting things 100 percent rock solid for the moment. Right now we just need something to work with.

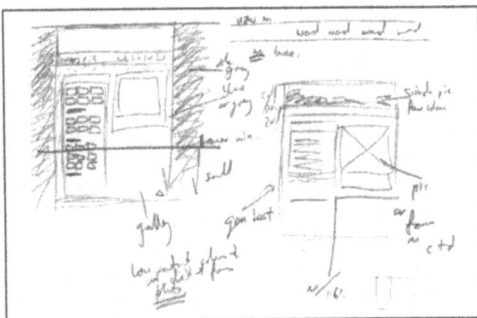

As you'll see, elements of the initial rough doodles have been combined, and the design now includes a space for a brand or logo, some navigation, and the page content. The following are some things to bear in mind when working on page structure:

- Navigation should be easily accessible as soon as you open a page. Therefore, it's best to place this fairly near the top of your design (although not necessarily right at the top). Whether it is more to the left or right or aligned vertically or horizontally is entirely up to you. Putting additional navigation at the foot of the page can also be useful because it allows users who've read through a page to access a different part of the site without scrolling back to the top.

- White space is a *good* thing. Although you don't want acres of space between each element on your web page, don't try to cram everything into a tiny space.

- Make effective use of space. Unlike with a newspaper, people may only be able to see part of your page upon entering the site. Therefore, ensure that the most important information is accessible right away.

- If your site has a brand (such as a logo) it needs to be apparent and immediately visible.

- Columned text doesn't work well on the Web because you have to scroll to the bottom of the page and then back up and down again for each column. Furthermore, there's no way of ensuring column lengths are the same. The only real use for columned text online is if the content of each column is *unique*. For instance, you could have a three-column front page, with news in the left column, features in the middle column, and some site and contact information in the right column. Generally, though, stick to a single column of text. However, one aspect of columns can be used well online: a narrow text column. The human eye finds it tricky to read very wide text columns, so when working online, ensure your text doesn't stretch to, say, 800 pixels wide.

- Simple graphical effects, such as flat boxes, borders, and colors, can be done with CSS—use this wherever possible.

- With a site this small and focused, there's little point in creating several different designs, one for each page. For the sake of speed, usability, and ease of updating, stick with a single page design that can be used throughout.

*Even when creating larger sites, important page elements, such as navigation and branding, should not fly all over the place. Users need to be able to find things instinctively and easily; therefore some consistency is required—both in terms of structure and visual style. A good example of such a site is www.wired.com, whose internal article layout sometimes changes, but it always remains within the same navigation/branding "shell."*

- *Photoshop 7 Zero to Hero* (© 2003 Gavin Cromhout et al., friends of ED, ISBN 1-90434-432-1)
- *Paint Shop Pro 8 Zero to Hero* (© 2003 Sally Beacham and Ron Lacey, friends of ED, ISBN 1-59059-238-7)
- *Fireworks MX 2004 Zero to Hero* (© 2004 Joyce Evans and Charles Brown, friends of ED, ISBN 1-59059-306-5)

It's also perhaps worth mentioning that the process is never as straightforward as going from A to B—there will always be tweaks and reiterations. In this chapter, we've merely streamlined the process somewhat to provide you with an idea of an ideal layout build.

## Creating the layout

Now that you've got a handle on the site's visual structure, you can start working on screen. At this point you might be wondering what software to use, and the answer is simply whatever you prefer. When working with bitmaps, professionals tend to favor one of the following two packages:

- **Macromedia Fireworks**: Now upgraded to MX 2004, it provides some useful integration with Dreamweaver.
- **Adobe Photoshop**: All-powerful bitmap graphics workhorse, which is perhaps not as suited to the Web as Fireworks, but is arguably more powerful overall.

As we said, the choice comes down to personal preference, and if you're on a small budget, you could use the likes of **Paint Shop Pro** or **Photoshop Elements**. We'll use Photoshop because it's the tool that we're most familiar with.

What follows is an overview of the process of creating the layout in Photoshop, although the principle for most elements is more or less the same regardless of the graphics package you use. Doing a de-facto walkthrough and showing how the layout was created is way beyond the scope of this book, as would any very specific tutorials on graphics applications. Therefore, our advice is rather general. For a more in-depth insight into the most popular graphics packages, check out one or more of the following titles:

## Building the layout

By this point, you've been thinking about and visualizing your site for some time. If you're getting fed up, go and do something else for a while, and come back to it later, when you're raring to go again. It might seem like a headache to spend so much time preparing the design, structure, and content, but it's essential in the long run. As we said, Dreamweaver provides plenty of scope for adjusting things later on, but if you have a solid base to work from, you're on to a winner.

Before we begin working on the layout document, remember these two quick tips:

- Save often—you never know if your computer or software is going to crash. Losing two minutes' work is a slight inconvenience. Losing five hours' work is likely to put your project behind schedule.
- Save incrementally with different file names when you make major changes, perhaps including the time and date. Call your first document something like `layout_25_09_11am.psd` and the next `layout_25_09_1pm.psd`. That way, you can return to a previous version if you suddenly add a bunch of stuff that you then decide against including.

Also, remember that all the graphics files for this website are included in the files you can download from the friends of ED website. Therefore, don't worry about creating these graphics yourself—the rest of this chapter is intended as a guide for when you create graphics for your own site.

And now, here's how we created the layout for the website.

We decided which sketch to base the design on. We thought this one worked pretty well—it's simple, but not overly so, and differentiates between the images and text. It also places the navigation horizontally, maximizing the on-screen area for the photographs.

We opened a new document in my image editor, Photoshop. This is to be a fixed website and must cater to users browsing at 800×600—so the site itself will be under 750 pixels wide. This is because web browser elements, such as scroll bars, take up space on the screen—the 50-pixel difference takes this into account. For the new layout document, we choose a size larger than that—around 900 pixels. This is so we could design the area *around* the layout, too—even if that only means applying a background color. The height isn't too important, so we used 500 pixels. If your graphics package enables you to set a resolution for your image, choose 72 pixels/inch, as we have done. Finally, if using Photoshop, ensure the Mode is set to **RGB** (as shown in Figure 4-3) and not CMYK, which is used for print work.

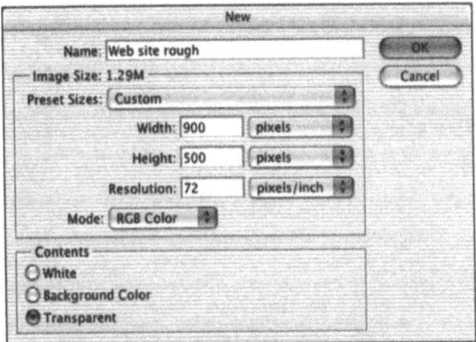

**Figure 4-3.** Setting document defaults in Photoshop

We added some guides in the center of the document to set the width of the site as shown in Figure 4-4. Because we had to take into account browser interfaces and scroll bars, a fairly safe size is 740 pixels wide.

**Figure 4-4.** A blank document in Photoshop

We then filled the document background with a dark gray so that the content would stand out. Next, we added a new layer and filled the area defined in the previous step with white, as shown in Figure 4-5. At this point, you can now clearly differentiate the main web page area. When adding new layers you should name them; otherwise you will end up with many layers called Untitled. Also, if your graphics editor enables you to create layer sets, do so, to keep together like areas of the layout.

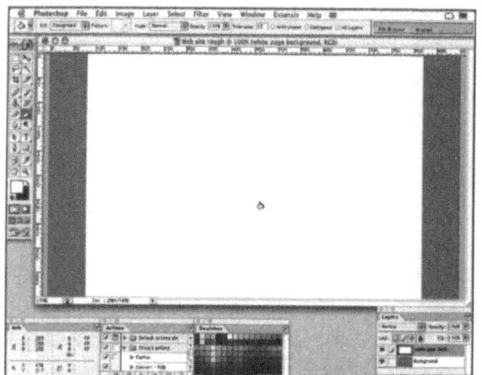

**Figure 4-5.** Adding guidelines

*Almost all image editors enable you to work with layers or objects that don't affect other elements on the document. If you don't have such an editor, go and buy one; otherwise you'll find yourself incrementally saving after pretty much every step, just in case you make a mistake. Not only that, but you'll find creating any sort of flexible layout a total nightmare.*

We added an image for the masthead graphic that was representative of the site's theme. This had to get across the nature of the site, and also be visually appealing. However, it also had to be a photograph that wouldn't distract too much when other images were on the screen. We checked out a number of photographs before choosing the image shown in Figure 4-6.

*It's very important to experiment when working with web design, to ensure you get the right feel. While your first instincts may often present the best result, still try alternatives just to make sure. As mentioned, this was one of several images we looked at for the masthead.*

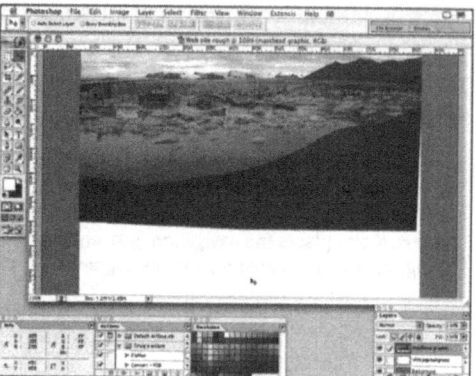

**Figure 4-6.** Adding a masthead graphic

We added a layer mask to screen out the bulk of the photo, and the photo was moved within until the composition worked best, as shown in Figure 4-7.

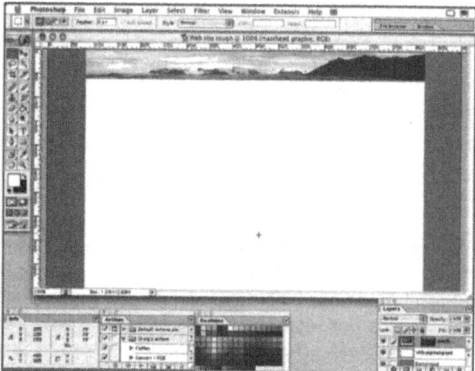

**Figure 4-7.** Adding a layer mask to screen out most of the photo

More guides were added to define the navigation area; the area under that was colored gray, so it would act as the background for the content area, as shown in Figure 4-8.

**Figure 4-8.** Differentiating the content area

We next added text for the site title and navigation. The font used was a stylish but fairly simple one (Century Gothic) in a similar gray to the main page background. More guides were added to ready the page for adding the content areas, as shown in Figure 4-9.

**Figure 4-9.** Adding more guides

Using a combination of new layers, border effects, and an imported graphic, the main text area and photo area were constructed, as shown in Figure 4-10. The white outlines on the elements were made via Photoshop's **Layer Effects**, which meant they could easily be adjusted later.

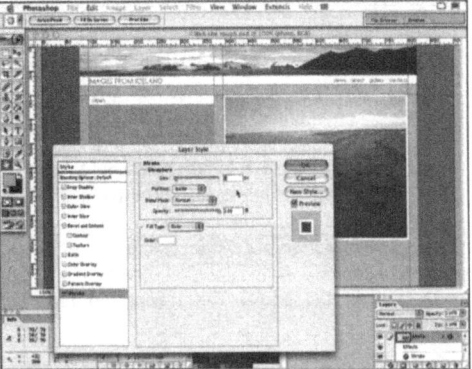

**Figure 4-10.** Adding the photo area

We added some dummy text to the text area to check how it would look, and a caption underneath the image, as shown in Figure 4-11. Because this layout is mostly composed of flat colored areas, it's easy to tweak.

**Figure 4-11.** Adding dummy copy

*Remember to incrementally save your layout often!*

If we were doing web design the old-fashioned way, we'd use Photoshop's export function to slice the layout into loads of images and an HTML document with a complex table, but obsolete methods are not used in this book. As mentioned earlier, anything with flat color can easily be reproduced with HTML and CSS, so we only needed to export elements that couldn't be created with those technologies. Essentially, the only things exported were the masthead image and the masthead/navigation/page title text because it's in a non-web-standard font. (Internal graphics are dealt with later in the book.) This meant ten files were exported:

- The masthead image
- The site title
- The site navigation (four images: news, about, gallery, contact)
- The page titles (four images: news, about, gallery, contact)

## Exporting images

Depending on what package you use for designing layouts, you may need to flatten your layout to export graphics. (You need to in Photoshop, but not in Fireworks.) One mistake designers often make is to save their layered document, flatten it, and then accidentally save it over the layered file. Save the final version of your layered document, save it *again* with a new file name (such as my_layout_flat.psd), flatten it, and then save it a third time. It might seem convoluted, but you'll regret not doing this when you have to edit your layout later and only find a flat version of the file.

### File formats

Although **PNG (portable network graphics)** has long been touted as a great format for the Web, the fact remains that Internet Explorer for Windows doesn't support many of its best features, such as transparency. Therefore, most web designers tend to stick to the tried and tested JPEG and GIF formats for web graphics.

**JPEG (joint photographic experts group)** is a **lossy** format, which means that as the compression increases, the detail decreases. It can handle millions of colors, and images still look pretty good at 60 percent

quality (40 percent compression), so it is best used for photographs.

**GIF (Graphics Interchange Format)** is a **lossless** format, which means that detail is never lost. However, it is restricted to a maximum of 256 colors, so it is really only used for line-art, vector-based logos, and graphics-based text.

*Some web designers go on and on about the so-called color-safe web palette, but not us. The vast majority of web users these days have monitors capable of displaying thousands or millions of colors, and if truth be known, the original color-safe palette wasn't all that safe anyway. It's effectively obsolete now, so ignore it.*

From the final layout, it's obvious what formats to use. The masthead image should be a JPEG, and the text-based elements (the titles and navigation text) should be GIFs.

### Using software

There are various methods for exporting images, but if you're only exporting a few choice elements, it's easy enough to whack a load of guides on your flattened layout document, use them to copy the relevant part of each element to a new file, and export that (see Figure 4-12).

**Figure 4-12.** Copying a layout section to a new file

Some graphics editors enable you to see variations on a graphic when exporting it. Figure 4-13 shows Photoshop's Save for Web dialog box, accessed via File ► Save for Web in Photoshop. Here, you can see the masthead graphic with four levels of JPEG compression side by side, along with approximate download times.

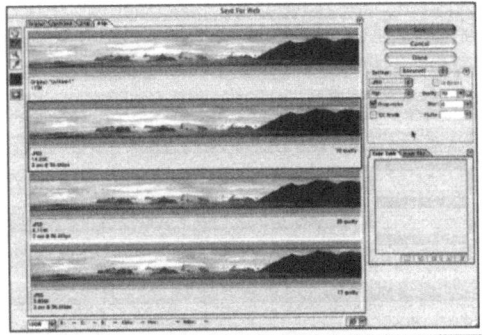

**Figure 4-13.** Photoshop's Save for Web dialog box

Sometimes you want less compression and more quality. A few extra kilobytes (which amounts to a single second of download time) can make all the difference and create a clearer and more detailed JPEG image. This is especially true for elements that will be on every page—after all, they'll only be downloaded once, then they'll be stored in the browser's cache.

### Saving the files

Although Dreamweaver can copy exported files into the correct location, you may as well put them in the correct place right away. In the Web - Images from Iceland folder, we created a new folder called assets. This is where we saved all exported files.

The masthead graphic is a photograph, so it was exported as a JPEG. It will be cached, so we could push the quality up somewhat. At 80 percent quality (20 percent compression) it weighs in at around 18k, which is about a four-second download—perfectly acceptable considering that there will be only one other large

graphic on the page at any time (the main photograph). The file was saved as masthead.jpg.

The text-based elements were exported in a similar way, but because they are gray text on a plain white background, they were exported as GIFs, as shown in Figure 4-14.

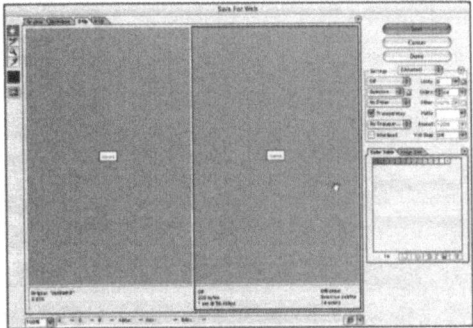

**Figure 4-14.** Exporting text elements as GIFs

Always name image files in a way that will enable you to easily recognize them later (such as nav_news.gif and title_about.gif).

Everything's now ready to start working on the basic page layout in Dreamweaver.

## Summary

Not a great deal of Dreamweaver in this chapter, but you now have everything you need to start working: the site's structure has been nailed down, the layout is designed, and the relevant graphics have been exported. You saw how to avoid the age-old method of slicing up Photoshop or Fireworks layouts into hundreds of different graphics files; doing it this way will pay dividends over the course of the site's development and enable you to build and tweak the site more rapidly.

## Chapter 5

# BEGINNING PAGE LAYOUT IN DREAMWEAVER

**What we'll cover in this chapter**

- Types of web page layout
- How to create frames with Dreamweaver
- How to create and edit tables
- How to work with Cascading Style Sheets
- How to set page defaults

The layout has been designed, and all the images have been exported, so now you need to start building the site itself. However, before you start working on your case study website, we're going to run through the various types of website that you can create, and briefly go over how to create them.

# Layout types

People often forget just how young the Web is. In fact, it was "invented" in the early 1990s and became popular several years later. Despite this, things have moved swiftly with regards to what you can do with web page layout, so much so that browsers and web design tools have had a hard job keeping up. Such problems are now largely a thing of the past. Dreamweaver MX 2004 can cope with complex layouts driven by **Cascading Style Sheets (CSS)**, but it's just as at home if you use **tables**, **frames**, or **layers**. (Note that Dreamweaver layers are actually absolutely positioned CSS divisions, and they shouldn't be confused with the proprietary Netscape Navigator layer tag.)

> *Cascading Style Sheets are documents external to your HTML pages that enable you to define design and visual elements site-wide, including font sizes and styles, element borders and positioning, and more. We'll be introducing these later in this chapter and working with them extensively in this book.*

Web browsers have also improved dramatically since the late 1990s, when each was promoting proprietary technology in the hope of usurping rivals' territory. Although the odd problem still remains, all major browsers can now handle CSS layouts while retaining support for older technology, such as tables. You can work around most quirks easily, and we'll show you how as you go through the site.

Each of the types of layout technology has its own strengths and weaknesses, and each is useful in particular circumstances. Later in this chapter, we'll explore which is the best for your case study, but first let's take a look at all the options available to you.

## Plain text

The Web was originally a repository for technical documents, so no flamboyance was needed. Documents were marked up simply in basic HTML, and the only formatting that took place was headings, lists, and paragraphs in text, along with the odd table, as shown in Figure 5-1.

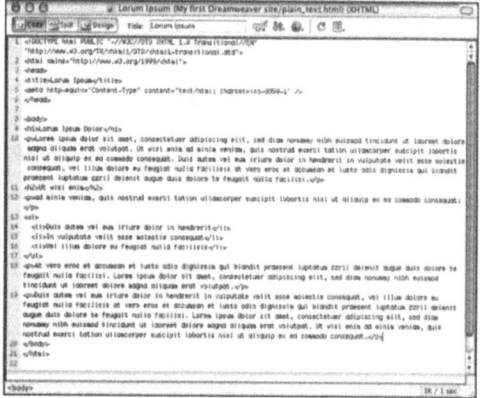

**Figure 5-1.** A basic web page's HTML in Code view

Most of you have seen HTML like Figure 5-1, and the idea of making text bold by putting <b> and </b> either side of it shouldn't be too taxing for those of you who haven't.

The obvious advantage of this method is that such pages can be displayed across a range of browsers and platforms, and they download rapidly. However, as you can see from Figure 5-2, plain text pages aren't visually appealing. There's also little control regarding the text itself: the fonts and sizes render according to the user's settings (or those of the manufacturer, if the user has left the defaults alone). If you want your page to have more impact, you need to check out some alternatives.

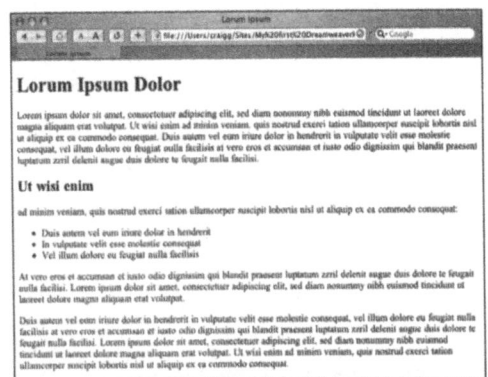

**Figure 5-2.** A plain text web page in a browser

## Frames

Now in a state of terminal decline, frames were once immensely popular. Therefore, this section is only really here for completeness—if you have no intention of using frames, feel free to skip this section. It's not hard to see why they were so popular: they enable you to split the browser window into a number of sections, some of which can remain in a static location. This method was often used to create a navigation area that did not move while the site's content, in another frame, could be scrolled.

However, you won't use frames in your case study because they have several inherent problems:

- Unless you include some fairly hefty scripting, you cannot bookmark individual pages of frames-based sites. Browsers simply bookmark the **frameset** (that is, the document that contains the frames). Therefore, users can bookmark only the pages seen upon first entering the site, which often confuses and annoys people.

- Frames can be awkward to update when dealing with template-based sites; in fact, few of the biggest online brands use frames for this very reason.

- Frames-based sites don't work particularly well with search engines. Typically, the frameset and all its pages are **spidered** individually. This means that web users often end up clicking links to "orphaned" pages, which only show part of the site, and therefore may lack navigation, footers, and so on.

> **Spidering** is a term given to the method a search engine uses to work its way through a website and save all the page details to a database.

You can get around the search engine problem by employing a "framebuster" JavaScript, which forces the entire frameset to load if one of its parts is loaded individually. However, this is a clunky workaround that causes nearly as many problems as it solves, and can choke some browsers—not a great start to any site.

There are some reasons to use frames, though. For example, they are put to good use on www.newstoday.com (shown in Figure 5-3). On this site, the frames enable a large amount of news content to be immediately accessible, along with providing a way of updating forum posts without reloading the entire site (or, for that matter, losing something you were reading elsewhere on the page).

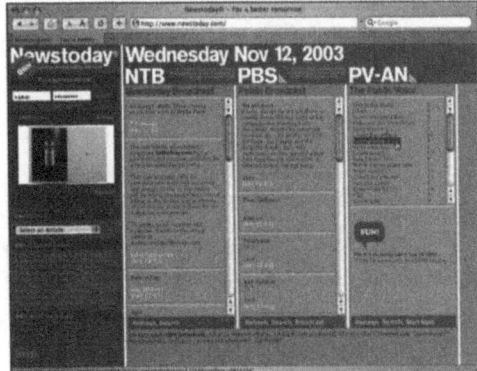

**Figure 5-3.** Newstoday.com—one of the few good uses of frames on the Internet

As previously mentioned, many sites use frames for a static navigation area, which may also include the corporate identity. This can be advantageous, but more often you end up with a jarring design split where the frame with the navigation bar meets the frame containing the rest of the content—something you'll want to avoid in your design-led site.

## Creating frames in Dreamweaver

In most cases, it's better to use CSS for layout, include navigation at the top and foot of the page, and avoid frames entirely. But if you decide that frames are for you, you'll be glad to know that Dreamweaver handles them with little fuss. This exercise shows you how to rapidly set up frames.

1. Open the My first Dreamweaver site by selecting it from the drop-down menu in the Files panel, as shown in Figure 5-4.

**Figure 5-4.** Opening a website via the Files panel

2. Go to File ➤ New, click the General tab, and select Framesets from the left column as shown in Figure 5-5.

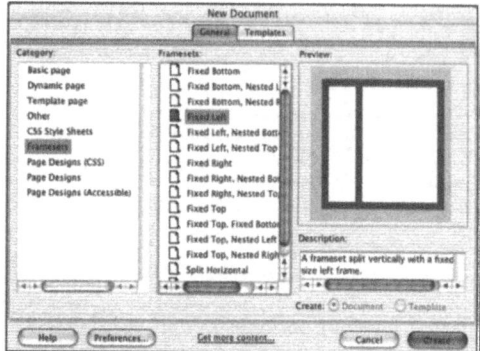

**Figure 5-5.** The New Document dialog box

3. In the middle column (Framesets), you'll see a number of options, and on the right side, there is a visual preview of your selection, along with a short description of how the selected frameset works. It's best to stick with two-frame set-ups because nesting—creating framesets within framesets—can become complicated. We've chosen the Fixed Left option.

*Any framesets referred to as "fixed" remain static, whereas content in the others stretch to take up all available space in the browser window. Therefore, "Fixed left" means that the left frame has a set width, and the right frame fills the browser window.*

4. Click Create to display your choice onscreen. Dreamweaver prompts you to name each of your frames, as shown in Figure 5-6. Keep things simple—even go with the defaults if you like because they can always be changed later. However, ensure the names have no white space in them. Click OK when you're done.

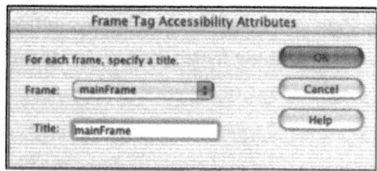

**Figure 5-6.** Adding titles to frames

*If Dreamweaver doesn't prompt you to title your frames, change the preferences, as outlined in Chapter 3. Open the* Preferences *panel, go to the* Accessibility *section, and check the* Frames *option.*

5. Save the frameset by selecting File ➤ Save Frameset as and choosing a name. We've called our document `frameset.html`.

6. Click the frame's edge in Design view and the edges are displayed as dotted lines rather than solid ones, as shown in Figure 5-7. The Properties panel also changes to provide access to various frame properties, which can be edited. Clicking the diagram at the bottom-right enables you to access properties for the individual frames. You can also change the size of the left frame in Design view by dragging the border. Note how the value in the Properties panel is updated once you release the mouse button.

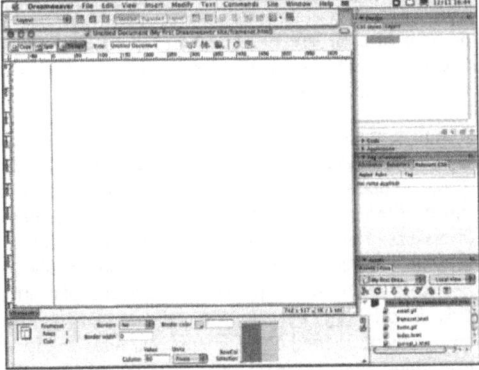

**Figure 5-7.** Selecting the edge of a frame

7. You can also use the Frames panel to choose frames or the frameset, and then edit details in the Properties panel as shown in Figure 5-8. To access the Frames panel, go to Windows ➤ Frame or press *SHIFT+F2*.

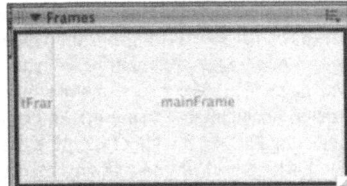

**Figure 5-8.** The Frames panel

8. Use Design view to add some content in the right frame, and then save it as `frame_right.html`. Then add some text to the left frame, including a link as shown in Figure 5-9. Save this frame as `frame_nav.html`.

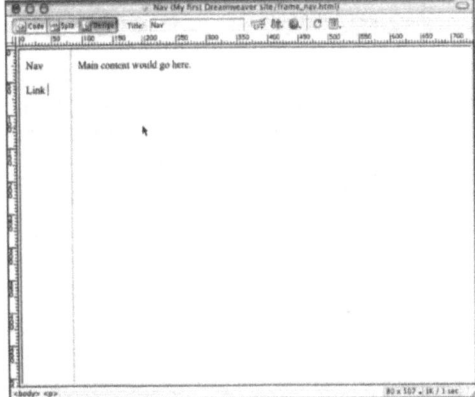

**Figure 5-9.** Adding content to the frame web pages

9. Select the link text you just typed and in the Properties panel, type `a_new_page.html` in the Link field. Then choose mainFrame from the Target drop-down menu as shown in Figure 5-10.

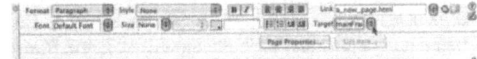

**Figure 5-10.** Defining Link and Target values via the Properties panel

**10.** Select File ➤ New and create a new HTML document (Basic Page ➤ HTML from the General tab). Type A new page and then save your file as a_new_page.html. Make sure all your other pages are saved (including the frameset). You can do this by selecting File ➤ Save All, or by using the Frames panel, clicking each frame (clicking the border to highlight the frameset), and then pressing *CTRL+S/CMD+S*. Then click the frameset border to make it the active document (or select it in the Frames panel), and press *F12* to preview it in a browser. You'll see a simple, two-frame page, and when you click the link, a_new_page.html will open in the right frame. If this preview doesn't work properly on the Mac, try changing the frameset (such as by adding and then deleting a space from the page's title), and then re-saving it.

> *Note that when working with frames, the target step is very important. The value of the target, defined in step 9, is the name of the frame in which a linked page will open. By default, links open in the frame that contains the link. Imagine, then, an expanded version of what we've just created. If you didn't define the target for the links in the navigation frame, all the pages would open in that frame rather than the main frame!*

**11.** Select Modify ➤ Frameset ➤ Edit NoFrames Content. This enables you to add content for display in non-frames compatible web browsers. Enter a bit of text explaining that this type of site requires a frames-compatible browser, and create a set of links back to the site's main pages.

It's important to remember that although Dreamweaver often displays all frames at once, each frame is an individual HTML document, as is the frameset itself. This means that you have to save each document within the frameset, and also the frameset itself. So, for this exercise, you end up with three documents (as shown in Figure 5-11).

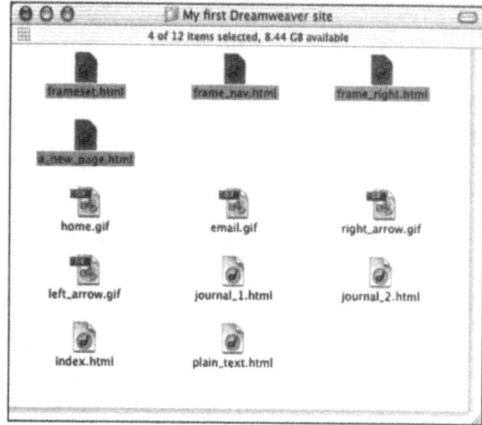

**Figure 5-11.** Typical documents that comprise a frameset

## Layers

Those of you who've worked with image-manipulation packages will already be familiar with the principle of layers. For those of you who aren't, think of layers as a number of clear sheets that sit on top of each other. The content of one sheet doesn't affect another and they can easily be rearranged.

Although graphic designers will no doubt be excited by layers and imagine them to be a web version of Quark XPress, Adobe InDesign, or Photoshop, the reality is much different. Although it's easy to build a complex layers-based page, such sites are often tricky to maintain. In addition, the results often fare badly in browsers, failing to work cross-browser and platform. This is primarily because Dreamweaver layers are absolutely positioned CSS elements that float on top of everything else, and are therefore removed from the flow of the rest of the page.

However, they can still be useful at times, particularly when used sparingly, so let's take a quick look.

## Creating layers in Dreamweaver

**1.** In the My first Dreamweaver site, create a new HTML document and save it as `layers_test.html`. Select Layout from the Insert bar, and then click the Draw Layer icon. Note that you should stay in Standard mode, as shown in Figure 5-12.

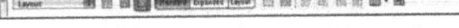

**Figure 5-12.** The Draw Layer icon active on the Insert bar

**2.** When you move the mouse pointer to Design view, it changes to a crosshair. Click the top-left of the area where you want your layer to begin and drag out a rectangle. Once satisfied with its size, release the mouse button.

*Once the layer is drawn, the mouse pointer and Insert bar return to their defaults (the Draw Layer icon will no longer be active), so you must click the Draw Layer icon each time you want to draw a layer.*

**3.** In the My first Dreamweaver site, within the files downloaded from the friends of ED website, you should find a file called `ice_grass.jpg`. Copy this file to your My first Dreamweaver site folder. In Design view, click inside the layer created in the previous step. Then choose Common from the Insert drop-down menu, and choose Image from the Images drop-down menu, as shown in Figure 5-13.

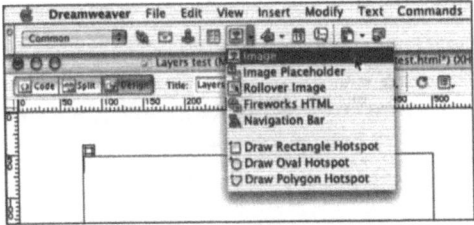

**Figure 5-13.** Using the Insert bar to attach an image

**4.** Select `ice_grass.jpg` from the dialog box, and click OK/Choose. Provide some alt text in the next dialog box, and click OK. Don't enter anything in the Long description field, and don't worry about the http:// in this field.

*This dialog box only appears if you've set the preferences as we outlined earlier. If you did not set these preferences, go to the Accessibility section of the Preferences panel and check the Images box.*

**5.** Draw another layer and enter some text. You can move text by selecting it and grabbing the top-left handle, as shown in Figure 5-14.

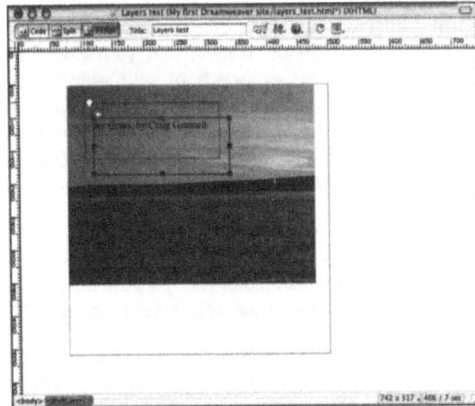

**Figure 5-14.** Dragging a Dreamweaver layer

**6.** Clicking the handle also updates the Properties panel, as shown in Figure 5-15. From here you can fine-tune your settings for the selected layer. Note that the number in the Z-Index field indicates where the selected layer rests within the stack—the higher the number, the closer to the top the layer is.

**Figure 5-15.** Layer attributes in the Properties panel

**7.** Unfortunately, the more layers you have stacked on top of each other, the more likely the page is to slow browsers to a crawl or even crash them. To help stop this, you can select Modify ➤ Arrange ➤ Prevent Layer Overlaps. However, this only affects layers created after the option is invoked.

You might also use layers to work out your basic layout, and then use Dreamweaver's conversion function to turn them into tables (Modify ➤ Convert ➤ Layers to Tables). The results can be erratic, though (converting layers to tables usually creates horrendously complex code that is a nightmare to edit), so you're often better off working with CSS (as you will see later on) or starting with tables in the first place. Speaking of which...

## Tables

Cutting-edge web designers often pour scorn on those using tables for layout, arguing that you should be using CSS for all design aspects of your websites. To some extent, they are correct: ideally, tables should be used solely for presenting tabular data rather than graphical layouts, and they can cause messy HTML if you're not careful. Although messy HTML may not seem problematic on the surface, it increases download times and causes problems for people using screen readers to surf the Web. The latter issue arises because content within tables is often positioned arbitrarily within the HTML document, rather than logically.

Furthermore, table-based layouts can be a pain to edit and often require ugly hacks, such as invisible GIFs to stretch cells. They are easy to understand, however, and designers continue to use them for all manner of tasks, including layout. They often have the additional advantage of working identically across legacy browsers, unlike CSS-based layouts, which require more modern browsers in order to be displayed as intended. However, the browser issue is disappearing, and many major websites, including Wired.com, ESPN.com, and alltheweb.com, have switched to CSS-only layouts. CSS also enables you to tweak many aspects of a site's design to pixel-perfect precision via an external document. There's no longer much risk associated with CSS designs, meaning tables are more often being used as they should be: for tabular data.

Whatever you use tables for, the golden rule is still: keep things simple. Don't nest them too heavily (or at

all, if you can help it). Not only does this cause havoc for the aforementioned screen readers, but nested tables are a pain to edit and update. Also, many browsers load an entire table's content prior to displaying anything, so the more complex your tables, the longer your pages will take to download and appear.

### Creating tables in Dreamweaver

Dreamweaver MX 2004 adds some useful enhancements to its already highly advanced table-editing tools. Dreamweaver MX 2004 also includes built-in support for rudimentary accessibility, which assists those using screen readers.

> *Note that although Dreamweaver helps with accessibility, it doesn't ensure that your site will be accessible. If you're planning on complying with legislation for accessible websites, you're probably better off avoiding tables for layout.*

**1.** In the My first Dreamweaver site (which is fast becoming a rather eclectic mix of pages and styles!) create a new HTML document and save it as `tables_test.html`.

**2.** Choose Layout on the Insert bar and click the Table icon. You'll be prompted to enter the number of rows and columns of your table, along with various other attributes, as shown in Figure 5-16.

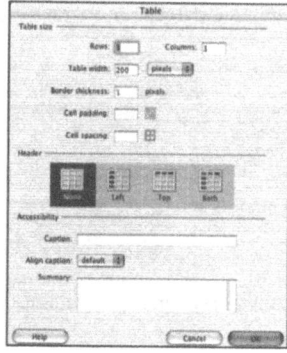

**Figure 5-16.** Defining a table in the Table dialog box

**3.** The table's width can be defined in pixels or as a percentage of the browser window width (for now, set this to 600 pixels). **Cell padding** refers to the space (in pixels) between the content and the edge of the cell (shown in Figure 5-17). This is set to 0 when positioning graphical elements in a layout. It is set to a higher number when working with text. For now, set it to 2.

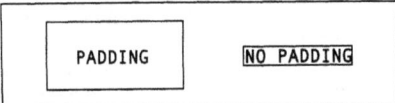

**Figure 5-17.** Example of cell padding

**4.** Cell spacing refers to the space (in pixels) between the cells—set this to 0. Accessibility options are at the bottom of the dialog box. The most important of these is Summary, which is used to provide an overview of the table's content for screen readers. Click OK and Dreamweaver will set up the table in Design view, as shown in Figure 5-18.

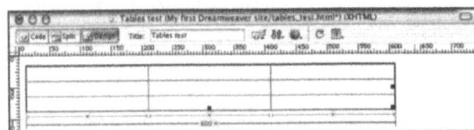

**Figure 5-18.** A table, as shown in Design view

## Editing a table

**1.** If they're not already on, activate the Table Widths visual aids via the View Options button, or via the View ➤ Visual Aids menu, as shown in Figure 5-19.

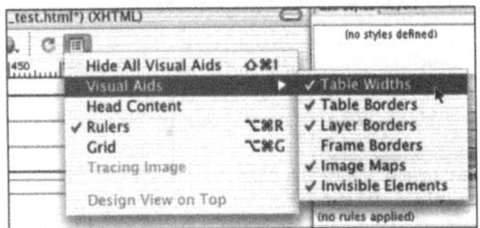

**Figure 5-19.** Activating visual aids via the View Options button

**2.** With this option selected, small drop-down menus appear when any part of the table is selected, or when you click inside it. These menus can be used to select columns, as shown in Figure 5-20, or the entire table, as shown in Figure 5-21, in order to edit various elements via the Properties panel. Menus are accessed via the small inverted triangles at the foot of each column (or the whole table).

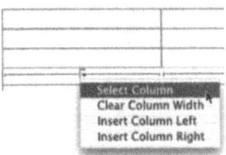

**Figure 5-20.** Selecting a table column

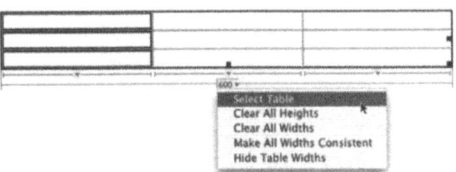

**Figure 5-21.** Selecting the entire table

*Pressing F6 or clicking* Expanded *in the* Layout *section of the* Insert *bar activates Expanded Tables mode, which makes selecting table elements even easier. However, when this mode is on, the page's layout differs from how it looks in a web browser. Press F6 again or select* Standard *to return to the Standard mode, which you'll be using from this point on.*

For instance, you can use the Properties panel to convert table widths from set measurements to percentages and back (effectively switching between "fixed" and "liquid" tables), as shown in Figure 5-22.

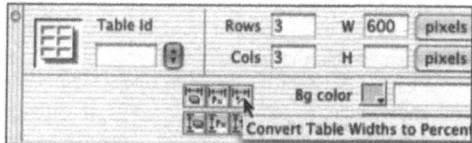

**Figure 5-22.** Table attributes in the Properties panel

In Design view, you can drag edges to resize cells, and you can merge cells by selecting them, right/*Ctrl*-clicking, and selecting Table ➤ Merge Cells, as shown in Figure 5-23.

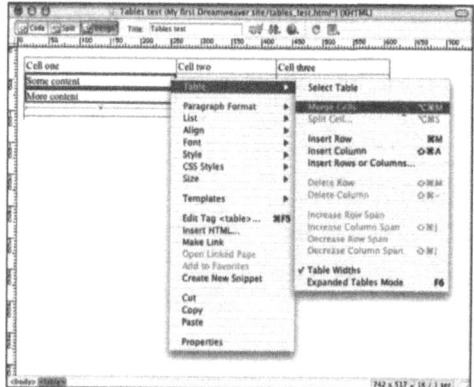

**Figure 5-23.** Merging table cells

Using either this menu or the small drop-down menus in Design view, you can insert rows, columns, and more.

## Cascading Style Sheets

HTML is a mark-up language that is intended to deal only with information *structure*, not with the *appearance* of that information. This might seem like a small distinction, but it's an important one. Unfortunately, there are numerous obsolete, design-oriented HTML tags that are superfluous to requirements because what they do can be achieved by more modern means. Using legacy tags means your web pages won't be future proof because support for legacy code is gradually being removed from browsers. Also, adding

unnecessary code leads to bloated web page sizes and a lack of cross-platform/browser consistency.

Because modern browsers support key CSS standards, it's now feasible to use CSS extensively when building web page layouts. Of course, there are still some inconsistencies. Although most browsers released over the past few years support almost all the CSS1 specification from the W3C, and parts of CSS2, Internet Explorer 5.5 for Windows has incomplete support for the box model, which affects borders and padding on page elements. This sort of issue slowed acceptance of CSS, but there are simple workarounds to get around such bugs.

> Legacy browsers are another issue that arises when people consider CSS. Some older browsers, such as Netscape Navigator 4, have such shoddy CSS support that they might as well not have any at all. The market for such browsers is tiny and diminishing, though, and there is a method of "hiding" the CSS from them (we'll show you how later in this book). This method can allow the users of these browsers to at least access your site's content, if not the design.

A CSS document is a separate, external file that enables you to format much of your site's design. This means that if you want to change fonts site-wide at a later date, you only need to edit and upload a single file. Likewise, if you decide to change the background color of your web pages, or increase the size of an element's border, you can do this via the CSS file. Therefore, as shown in Figure 5-24, the final result that's seen in your web browser relies on two files: an HTML document containing content and structure, and a CSS document, defining design and styling information.

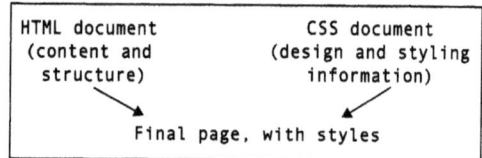

**Figure 5-24.** A web page displayed in a browser relies on both HTML and CSS documents

Generally, it's easier to allow for a cross-browser audience using CSS. Yes, there are problems that require hacks and workarounds, but it's far easier to hack a single CSS document than every HTML file on your website.

Many web designers are accustomed to using CSS in place of the deprecated <font> tag, but we will go further than that and use CSS for the entire layout. This provides you with more opportunities in the future, including "skinning" your site by using multiple style sheets (see www.csszengarden.com for an excellent example of this).

> *Many well-known HTML tags are marked as "deprecated" in the current W3C specifications. This means that these tags are marked for removal and shouldn't be used. Common examples include <font> and <center>. Some browsers have already dropped support for many deprecated tags, so CSS not only offers a feasible alternative to these tags, but it is future proof.*

Dreamweaver MX 2004 finally brings CSS into the world of visual web design. Although you'll be working with CSS in Code view later in the book, it's now also possible to work on a CSS-based layout in Design view. There are a number of methods of working with CSS in Dreamweaver, the basics of which are outlined over the next few pages.

### Creating and attaching a style sheet

1. Select File ➤ New and under the General tab, select CSS Style Sheets. From the list in the middle column, choose Basic: Verdana, as shown in Figure 5-25, and then click Create.

2. A new CSS document is created. Because these documents are code-based, you can view such files only in Code view. Save the file as css_test.css and close the document.

3. Create a new HTML document, save it as css_test.html, and then type some text into it, as shown in Figure 5-26.

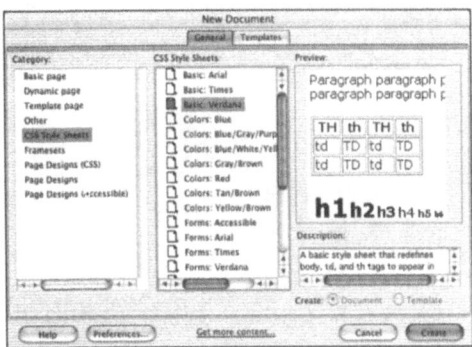

**Figure 5-25.** Choosing a predefined CSS file from the New Document dialog box

**Figure 5-26.** Adding some text to an HTML file

4. Preview css_test.html in a web browser (press *F12*) and you'll see something like Figure 5-27. The text is formatted per the browser's default settings, so it won't be consistent across browsers and platforms.

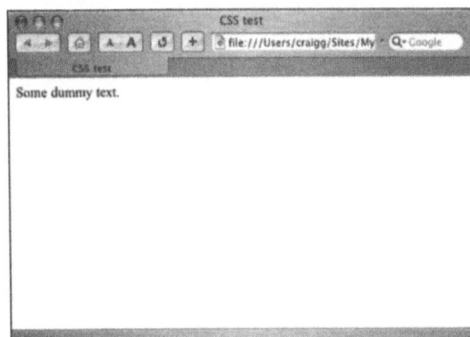

**Figure 5-27.** A preview of the HTML file in a web browser

**67**

**5.** Back in Dreamweaver, select your text, and then use the Properties panel's Format drop-down menu to define it as a Paragraph, as shown in Figure 5-28.

**Figure 5-28.** Formatting text using the Properties panel

**6.** Select Style ➤ Manage Styles on the Properties panel to display the Edit Style Sheet dialog box. Click Attach to open the Attach External Style Sheet dialog box, browse to and select css_test.css, click OK, and then click Done, as shown in Figure 5-29.

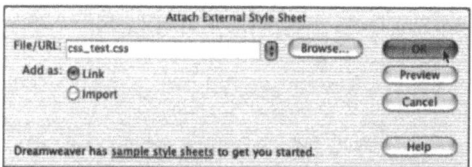

**Figure 5-29.** The Attach External Style Sheet dialog box

**7.** Save your HTML document and refresh it in your web browser to confirm that the text in Design view is Verdana, as shown in Figure 5-30.

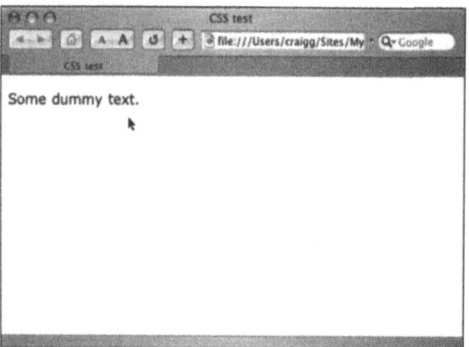

**Figure 5-30.** Previewing the HTML file after attaching a style sheet

So, how does all this work? After all, you didn't use any font tags. A quick look at the CSS reveals the following code:

```
body {
    font-family: Verdana, Geneva, Arial,
helvetica, sans-serif;
}

td {
    font-family: Verdana, Geneva, Arial,
helvetica, sans-serif;
}

th {
    font-family: Verdana, Geneva, Arial,
helvetica, sans-serif;
}
```

This is the simple, built-in style sheet chosen in step 1. Although this may look complicated, the style sheet simply defines attributes and values within curly brackets for each HTML element. Therefore, in the first case, the body tag's font-family has been defined as a list of fonts, in order of preference. This is just one of many great things about CSS: its flexibility. You can list your font preferences in case a user doesn't have your first choice installed. If the user doesn't have Verdana, the browser works its way through the list until it happens upon one that is installed; if none of the named fonts are there, a generic alternative is used.

The advantage over the old <font> tag is clear: whatever you define in the body declaration will be the default for your *entire* website. Should you decide to change this later, you just edit the CSS file and upload it. The same is more or less true for all aspects of CSS.

## CSS classes

You can add variations to the defaults, which can be used by multiple HTML elements. These variations are called **classes**. In the following exercise, you're going to create a class that turns any elements it's attached to blue.

### Creating a class

1. Type another line in your HTML document, and format it as a paragraph. On the Properties panel, go to Style ➤ Manage Styles and click New. Give the class a name (which must be preceded by a period)—.blue will do just fine, as shown in Figure 5-31. Although you can use Define In ➤ This Document Only for single-use styles, they take up space and download time. Therefore, it's best to define them in the global CSS file, just in case you decide to use them elsewhere later.

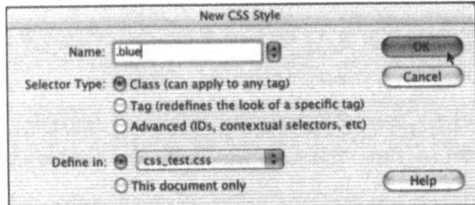

**Figure 5-31.** The New CSS Style dialog box

2. The next dialog box enables you to define your style. Right now you only want to define the color as blue. Note that the Color setting specifies the color of text, even when it is applied to the body style. This is roughly equivalent to the deprecated HTML body attribute <text>. Use the Color menu in the Type category to select a blue color as shown in Figure 5-32 and then click OK.

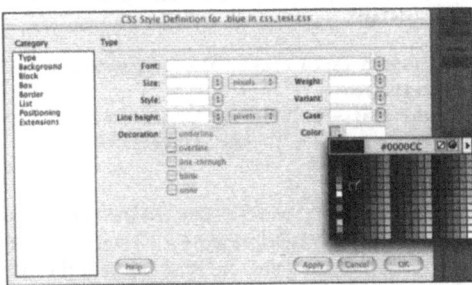

**Figure 5-32.** The CSS Style Definition dialog box

3. Click Done a couple of times, and then select your line of text in Design view. To add your style use one of the following methods:

- Select the Relevant CSS tab and then use the Tag Inspector panel's drop-down menu to select Set Class ➤ blue as shown in Figure 5-33.

**Figure 5-33.** Applying a style using the Tag Inspector

- Select the relevant style from the Properties panel's Style menu as shown in Figure 5-34.

**Figure 5-34.** Applying a style using the Properties panel

- Right/CTRL-click the relevant style in the CSS Styles panel, and then choose Apply from the context menu as shown in Figure 5-35.

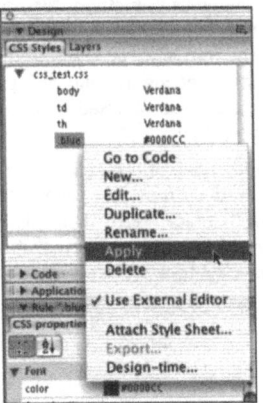

**Figure 5-35.** Applying a style using the CSS Styles panel

**69**

■ Right/*CTRL*-click the relevant tag at the bottom of the document window and select Set Class ➤ blue as shown in Figure 5-36.

**Figure 5-36.** Applying a style using the Status bar

4. Save your file and preview it in a browser. The second paragraph should now be blue. Note that the text should also appear in blue in Dreamweaver's Design view. If the dialog box shown in Figure 5-37 appears when you save the file, don't worry—this just refers to the style sheet—click Yes to ensure all files are saved properly.

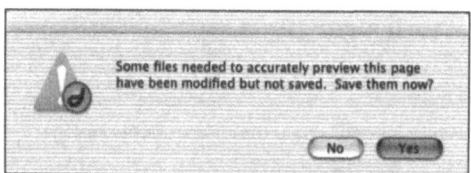

**Figure 5-37.** A prompt to save files to preview you work

5. To remove the style from your element, simply use one of the previous methods for adding a style, as detailed in step 3, but select None for the CSS Style. You can also add and remove styles by selecting something in your web page and using the context menu, accessed via right/*CTRL*-clicking, as shown in Figure 5-38.

6. Add another line of text and use the Format dropdown in the Properties panel to define it as Heading 1 (which means "heading, level 1"). Then use one of the aforementioned methods to add the blue class to it.

**Figure 5-38.** Changing a style using a context menu

You can add classes to specific characters, such as partial sentences. Select one word in the first line and add the blue class to it, as shown in Figure 5-39.

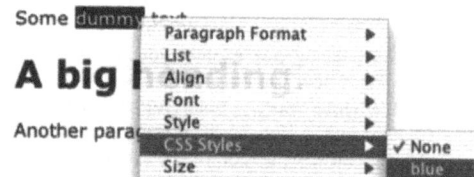

**Figure 5-39.** Applying a style to an inline element

For the curious, the steps just shown result in the following HTML:

```
<p>Some <span class="blue">dummy</span>
text.</p>
<h1 class="blue">A big heading</h1>
<p class="blue">A new paragraph of
text.</p>
```

For anyone who's worked with HTML before, this should be fairly straightforward. Even if you haven't, it's easy to see what's going on. Anything with the class applied has class="blue" appended to its opening tag. When the class is applied only to a few characters, said characters are wrapped in a <span> tag, also with the class applied.

To show how flexible CSS is, you're now going to make everything with the blue class bold and red.

## Editing a class

1. In the CSS Styles panel, select .blue—the style you're going to edit. The Tag inspector then lists its properties as shown in Figure 5-40. On Windows, you may have to first deselect any selected items in your HTML document.

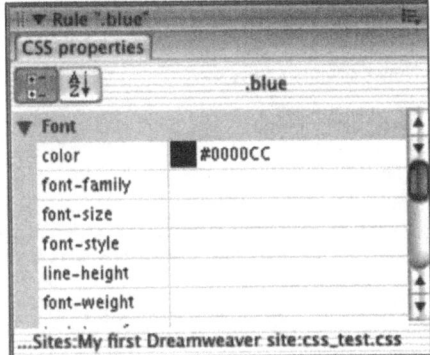

**Figure 5-40.** Style properties in the Tag inspector

Bear in mind that Dreamweaver MX 2004 is extremely context-sensitive, and this is noticeable even in certain panels. For instance, the Tag inspector's title changes depending on context. For example, when clicking something in Design view, the Tag inspector panel is called Tag <x>, with <x> being the tag you are working on. When you start working with CSS, the Tag inspector's title changes to Rule ".x", with ".x" being the rule you're working on.

2. Use the menus in the Tag inspector to change the color setting to red and the font-weight setting to bold, as shown in Figure 5-41.

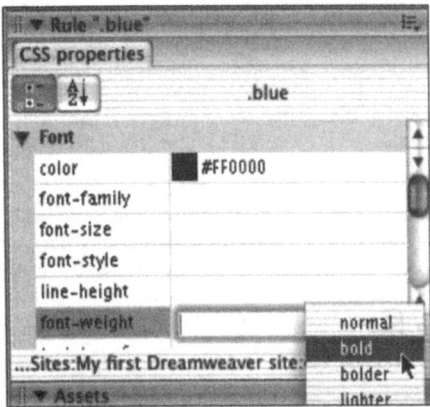

**Figure 5-41.** Editing rule property values in the Tag inspector

3. Right/*CTRL*-click .blue in the CSS Styles panel, choose Rename, and in the subsequent dialog box, type .red as shown in Figure 5-42. Dreamweaver then tells you that the style is in use, and with your authorization, it will find and replace the style in all documents in the current site (not just the open page). Clicking Replace All in the dialog box will update the HTML document you created earlier (where all the elements were affected by .blue, not the renamed class, .red). Changes made when pages are not open cannot be undone.

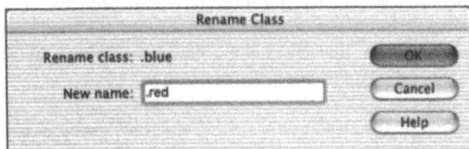

**Figure 5-42.** The Rename Class dialog box

4. Save both your HTML document and your CSS file (which Dreamweaver automatically opens when changes are made to it). Preview the page in a web browser and you'll see all elements affected by the style are now red and bold.

Now consider the time you would have saved if your site was several hundred pages long and each page used the blue style several times. What if you had updated 20 styles? What if the styles affected all aspects of the design? *That* is why you'll use CSS in the case study.

Arguably, this is also a case for careful naming of CSS styles. You used .blue, which was logical enough, as was .red. However, if you have dozens of styles, you're generally better off choosing names related to what the styles are actually intended for, rather than their general appearance (for example, .boxoutHeading rather than .blueAndBig).

> Remember that Dreamweaver MX 2004 comes with plenty of reference guides, one of which is for CSS. Select Window ➤ Reference and then select O'Reilly CSS Reference from the drop-down menu.

## The case study

Now you've had a crash course in CSS, we're going to return to the case study, whose layout is going to be driven solely by CSS. For the remainder of this chapter you're going to concentrate on the general page defaults; we'll leave the internal layout until the next chapter. In Chapter 7, you'll make a template from your page layout, thereby making content addition much easier later in the book.

Much of the next exercise contains things people forget when creating web pages—especially when doing so visually. Use it as a checklist whenever creating new websites in the future.

### The first page

1. Use the Files panel to switch to the Images from Iceland site. Then select File ➤ New and from the General tab, and select Basic Page ➤ HTML. Also ensure you check Make document XHTML compliant as shown in Figure 5-43. Save this new file as work_page.html.

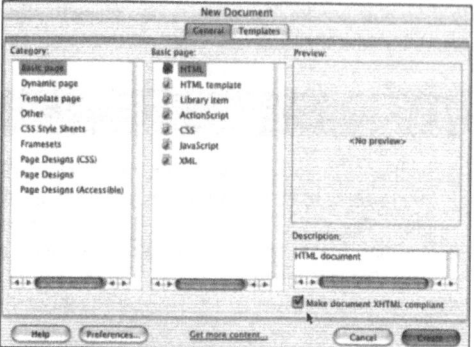

**Figure 5-43.** Creating a new XHTML-compliant document via the New Document dialog box

> XHTML is the reformulation of HTML 4.x as an application of XML. If that makes no sense to you, don't worry about it. All you need to know is that XHTML is more likely to create cleaner code that's more compatible with the current crop of web browsers.

2. Use the document window's Title field to give your page a title. For now, use "Images from Iceland – temporary" as shown in Figure 5-44. In pages you'll create later, the last word will be replaced with something to denote the page's content.

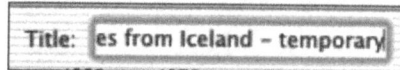

**Figure 5-44.** Editing a web page's title

> The title is what's displayed at the top of browser windows. Leave it blank and your site will proudly display "Untitled Document"—very unprofessional-looking.

3. Select HTML from the Insert bar drop-down menu and click the Head drop-down menu to see a number of options for things that can be added to your

page. Use this to add **Keywords** and **Description** to your page, as shown in Figure 5-45. These provide search words and a short description respectively, which aids search engines in indexing it. The description should be succinct; otherwise it gets cropped on search engine results pages. (We used "Images from Iceland – photographs from the land of fire and ice.") Keywords should be restricted to around 30 non-generic keywords or short phrases—putting in too many or repeating them too often could get your site penalized. Make sure they're relevant to your content.

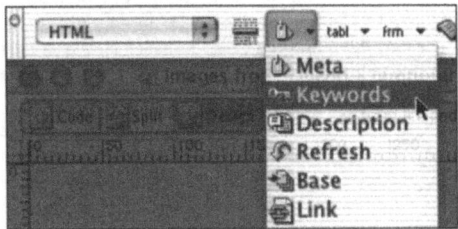

**Figure 5-45.** Adding meta tags using the Insert bar

*Go to* View ➤ Head Content *to be able to access each of these tag's properties via icons that appear in the document window*

### Creating and attaching external files

The next step is to add a couple of external files to your page in order to create global CSS and JavaScript documents.

1. Create a new document, and choose CSS from the Basic page category. Save this file as `iceland.css`. Create another new document, this time choosing JavaScript and save it as `iceland.js`.

*Unless stated otherwise, you should always save files in your* Images from Iceland – web *folder.*

2. To link to the JavaScript file, display Code view (or the code part of Split view). Click after the last `<meta>` tag and press *ENTER*. Select Insert ➤ HTML ➤ Script Objects ➤ Script as shown in Figure 5-46 (or select HTML ➤ Script ➤ Script in the Insert bar as shown in Figure 5-47) and click OK in the dialog box. You'll see a `<script>` tag appear within the `<head>` section.

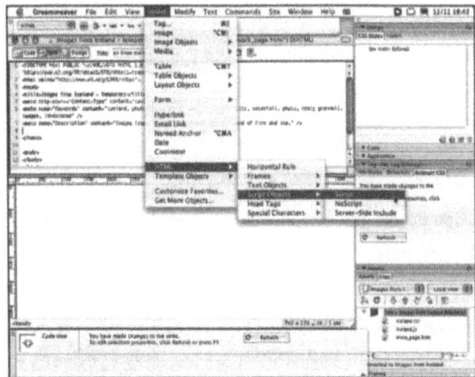

**Figure 5-46.** Inserting a Script object using Dreamweaver's menus

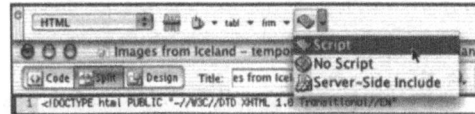

**Figure 5-47.** Inserting a Script object using the Insert bar

3. Right/*CTRL*-click anywhere within the tag and select Edit Tag from the context menu. The Tag Editor will appear and you can use the Browse button to navigate to and select `iceland.js` as shown in Figure 5-48.

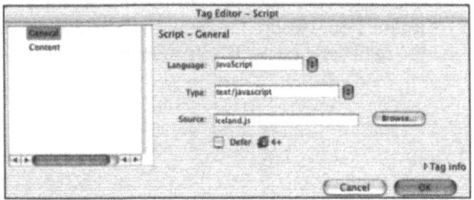

**Figure 5-48.** The Tag Editor

**4.** Thankfully, attaching the CSS file is easier—and you've already done it once. If you've forgotten how, don't worry: click anywhere in Design view and select Style ➤ Manage Styles via the Properties panel. Click Attach and use Browse to navigate to and select iceland.css as shown in Figure 5-49. However, this time select Add as ➤ Import, not Link. Click Done to finish and save your HTML file.

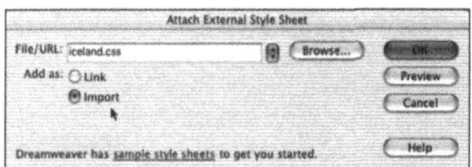

**Figure 5-49.** The Attach External Style Sheet dialog box

*If you check out your code now, you'll see the CSS is attached using the @import method, rather than the <link> method used earlier in the book. The former "hides" the CSS from obsolete and alternate browsers, meaning users of these browsers can see your content but not the design, which would otherwise be formatted incorrectly for their browsers.*

## Setting page defaults with CSS

The final thing you're going to do in this chapter is set up the page defaults.

**1.** Open the New CSS Style dialog box via the Properties panel (Style ➤ Manage Styles ➤ New). Choose Tag from the Selector Type options and body from the Tag drop-down menu as shown in Figure 5-50. (Ensure Define in has iceland.css as the selection.) Click OK to continue.

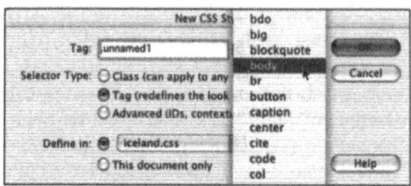

**Figure 5-50.** Selecting the body tag in the New CSS Style dialog box

**2.** From the Font menu, choose Verdana, Arial, Helvetica, sans-serif as shown in Figure 5-51. Remember, you can easily change this later. Set the Size to 11 pixels (by typing 11 directly into the relevant field) and the Color to #666666. We've taken this color from our Photoshop document created earlier.

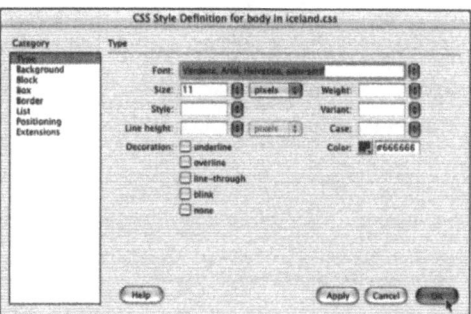

**Figure 5-51.** Defining fonts in the CSS Style Definition dialog box

Don't forget the pound sign (#) prior to color values. Although Dreamweaver will still display colors if you forget the pound sign, its omission will create invalid CSS that won't render correctly in browsers.

**3.** Choose Background from the Category menu, and type #929194 into the Background color field. Again, this color is taken from our Photoshop document.

**4.** In the Box category (which deals with margins, padding, borders, dimensions, and "floating"—more on the last one later in this book) set Padding and Margin both to 0, ensuring Same for all is checked in both cases as shown in Figure 5-52. These settings ensure your content will hug the edge of the browser window (some browsers put arbitrary space there by default).

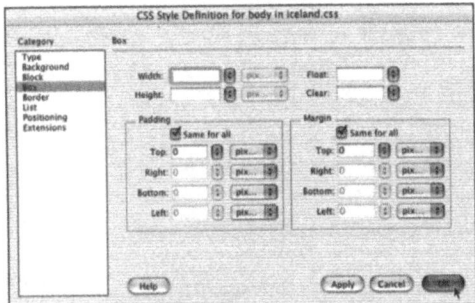

**Figure 5-52.** Defining padding and margin settings

**5.** Click OK and Done a couple of times and save both your HTML and CSS documents.

> Note that when changes are made to your CSS file, Dreamweaver opens it. However, it might be behind the currently open document, so make sure you bring it to the front and save it before moving on to other things. Alternatively, make a habit of regularly visiting File ➤ Save All.

## Summary

During this chapter you've learned plenty about how to work with Dreamweaver and use various methods to create web pages. You saw how to work with plain text, frames, and tables, and have begun to delve into CSS, first via layers, and then by using Dreamweaver's CSS tools and the Tag inspector.

You also started work on your case study, and although the page doesn't look like much just yet, you've created a solid foundation on which to build your first page. The site's default settings have been defined, including page background, font family, color and size, and padding, and margin settings. You also defined important meta tags, which will aid search engines in finding and correctly indexing your site. In the next chapter, you start working on internal page layout.

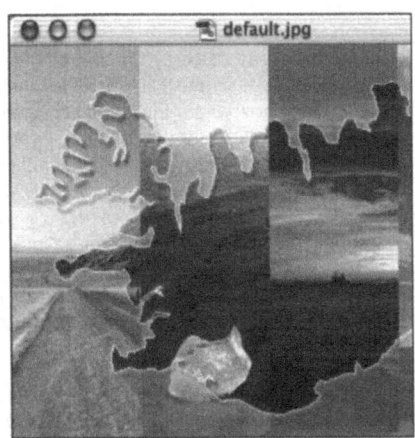

## Chapter 6

# INTERNAL
# PAGE LAYOUT

**What we'll cover in this chapter**

- How to structure a web page
- How to create a masthead, navigation area, content area, and page footer
- How to style copy, images, and links

Now the fun really starts. By the end of this chapter, you'll have a page layout that resembles the original mock-up. Note how we say the layout will *resemble* the mock-up. Web design is an ongoing process that requires compromise and slight changes throughout the course of a project. Also, remember that the original mock-up was just that: a way of working out more or less how the final design was going to look. For the final site, you should always aim for something that looks good, that's close to your original design, and that works well, but don't bust a gut trying to get it 100 percent exact.

You might wonder about the difference between page layouts and *internal* page layouts. By internal page layout, we mean the structure of the page. If you like, you can think of the process in three building stages: in the previous chapter, you sorted the foundation; in this one, you're building the walls; and in the next, you're moving in and adding all your stuff.

## Working on the layout

You're now going to start work on the internal (structural) page layout, using the graphics exported earlier. Let's open the Photoshop layout document (shown in Figure 6-1) to check how the page should look once it's completed.

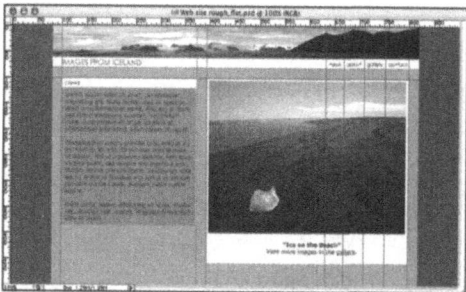

**Figure 6-1.** The original Photoshop mock-up of the site

From this document (and with the help of the guides), you can visualize the web page's structure, and work out what page sections you're going to create. The whole page is centered on the screen and contained within a fixed area. In web terms, this sort of containing area is often referred to as a **wrapper**. Within the wrapper, there is a **masthead** at the top of the page that contains an image and the site's **navigation**.

Below the navigation is the **content** area, which is composed of two parts—one contains the text, and another contains an image and caption. Although it's not depicted here, most sites also contain a **footer**, in which users can access navigation if they've scrolled to the bottom of the page. Footers often contain copyright information and a method of jumping to the top of the page.

### Wrapping up your site

1. If it's not still open, open work_page.html, and then go to Layout in the Insert bar as shown in Figure 6-2. Click the Insert Div Tag icon and a dialog box will appear. Within the dialog box, type wrapper into the ID field as shown in Figure 6-3. Leave the Insert option in its default state (At insertion point).

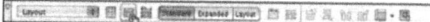

**Figure 6-2.** Clicking the Insert Div Tag icon

**Figure 6-3.** The Insert Div Tag dialog box

2. You now need to style this new division. Via the Properties panel, go to Style ➤ Manage Styles, select iceland.css, and click New. The New CSS Style dialog box will appear. Type #wrapper into the Selector field, ensuring that you don't omit the pound sign, and then choose Advanced from the Selector Type options, as shown in Figure 6-4.

*Assigning an ID to a page element is similar to assigning one to a class. However, an ID can only be attached to a single page element (unlike a class, which can be attached to as many as you like). We're using IDs with main page elements because there will only be one of each; furthermore (and more importantly) IDs can be targeted later on, in JavaScript, should you need to do such a thing. Using IDs for these page elements therefore makes for a more flexible site later on.*

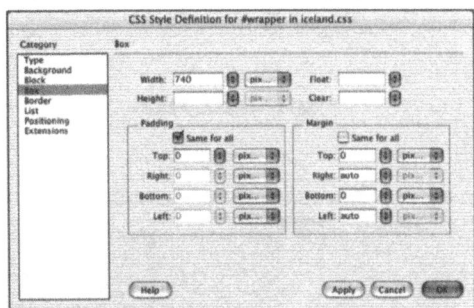

**Figure 6-5.** Defining box properties in the CSS Style Definition dialog box

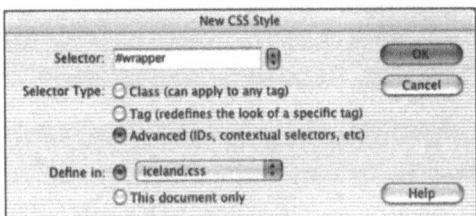

**Figure 6-4.** The New CSS Style dialog box

*Note that in the New CSS Style dialog box, you precede your ID's name with a pound sign (#). This is because the pound sign signifies an ID selector within a CSS file (just as a period signifies a class). However, as seen in step 1, you do not use pound signs and periods when typing ID and class names in HTML documents.*

3. Clicking OK displays the familiar CSS Style Definition box. Measuring the layout document confirms the design's width as 740 pixels, so in the Box category, add that measurement to the Width field as shown in Figure 6-5. Padding is set to Same for all, with 0 in the Top box, but for Margin, set Top and Bottom to 0, and Left and Right to auto. This has the effect of centering the layout. (Note that this won't center the layout in Internet Explorer 5.5 for Windows because that browser has bugs relating to CSS—we'll deal with this later in the book.)

4. Finally, use Background to set the Background color to #d5d6d5. Remember to not omit the pound sign—although Dreamweaver still displays your chosen colors, the omission means invalid CSS is created, so the site may not display correctly in web browsers. Click OK and Done until you're back in Design or Split view (depending on what you're using) and then go to File ➤ Save All to save both work_page.html and iceland.css.

*Remember this sequence. From this point on, we'll tell you how to style each element, but not how to access each of the dialog boxes.*

## Adding the masthead and navigation

Next, you will add the top section of the page, which houses the banner image and the navigation. During this exercise you'll add the images you exported in Chapter 4. First you will copy the assets folder found in the Web - Images from Iceland folder, which is in the site files you downloaded from the friends of ED website. Place the copy in your work-in-progress Web - Images from Iceland folder.

1. Select all the content from the wrapper div and delete it, but do not delete the div itself. Working in Split view so you can see both the site and underlying code helps prevent that error (see Figure 6-6).

**79**

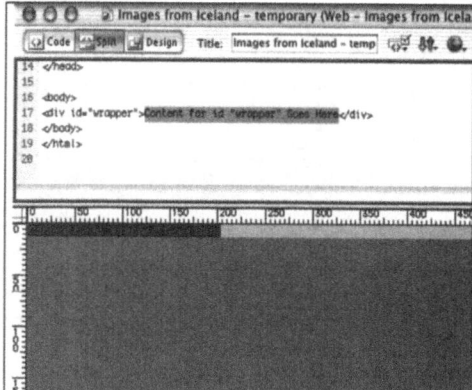

**Figure 6-6.** Deleting div content in Split view

2. Use the Insert bar to add another div, as you did for the wrapper. This time type masthead into the ID field.

3. Styling this division is simple—use the Box category of the CSS Style Definition dialog box to set Padding and Margin to 0. Then use the Background category to set the Background color to #ffffff (which is white in hexadecimal).

> Remember, when in the New CSS Style *dialog box the selector must be preceded by a pound sign (#), so you should type #masthead, not masthead. (This is not the case when adding attribute values to div tags, so add the pound sign when working on CSS, but not on XHTML.)*

4. Delete all the content from the masthead div, like you did in step 1.

5. Ensure that Design view is in focus by clicking in the div you just created. Go to Common in the Insert bar, click the Image button, and in the subsequent dialog box, choose masthead.jpg, saved earlier to the assets folder, as shown in Figure 6-7. Type some descriptive alt text, such as distant glacier photo. This task is performed in Design view because the height and width attributes are omitted if the images are inserted in Code view. Although browsers don't technically require height

and width attributes for images in order to render sites, including them speeds a web page's display.

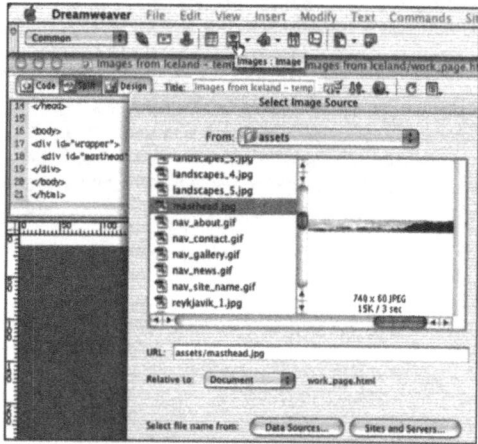

**Figure 6-7.** Choosing an image to add to the web page

> *Remember that you can download all the final images for this website from www.friendsofed.com.*

6. Move the mouse pointer to the right side of the new image, hold down the *SHIFT* key, and press *ENTER*. This creates a **carriage return** (<br /> in Code view). Then insert the following images (in order): nav_site_name.gif, nav_news.gif, nav_about.gif, nav_gallery.gif, and nav_contact.gif. Ensure that there are no gaps between these images and that you add relevant alt text for each. For the navigation images, simply type their content names—news, about, gallery, and contact.

7. In Code view, delete any spaces before the closing masthead div tag (as seen in Figure 6-8).

**Figure 6-8.** Checking for and deleting spaces in Code view

*White space in HTML documents can be problematic, as you'll see later in this book. Some browsers, such as Internet Explorer 6 for Windows, sometimes display white space incorrectly, which messes up perfectly valid layouts. If your website isn't working in a browser, the problem may go away if you delete the white space around the affected elements. Note that despite what some people claim, it is not necessary to remove all white space from a web page's code. To do so makes everything harder to edit, and although the affected page will download faster, the increase in speed is insignificant.*

8. To turn your navigation images into links, click each image, and use the Properties panel's Link field to link it to index.html, about.html, gallery.html, and contact.html respectively, as shown in Figure 6-9. These pages will be created from a template you'll make in Chapter 7.

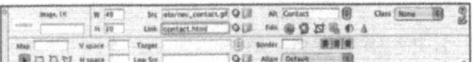

**Figure 6-9.** Turning images into links via the Properties panel

*The News page will double as the home page, and* index.html *is usually the default name for a website's home page. That is why you are using* index.html *instead of* news.html *for that link. Also note that web page file names are case sensitive, so stick to lower-case throughout.*

## Creating the content area

The next step is the trickiest—dealing with the content area. As you can see from the Photoshop layout, it has a gray background with two boxes—one for text, and the other for an image and caption, as shown in Figure 6-10.

**Figure 6-10.** The website's content area from the Photoshop mock-up

For a tables-based site, you'd most likely create a two-column table, and then nest others within it, but CSS has a number of different ways of achieving the desired effect, most of which create less code and are simpler to edit later. You will create a **boxout** for the photo and caption, and **float** it. Although this isn't the only way of getting the desired layout, it's a technique you'll be able to use in other sites for various tasks, such as positioning inline images, pull quotes, and more.

*Boxout is a term often used in magazine production, referring to boxes on the page that are supplementary to the main page content.*

Your page will look something like Figure 6-11.

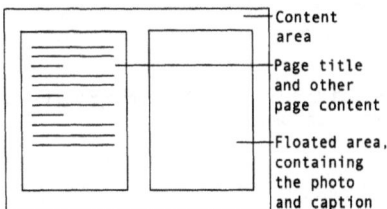

**Figure 6-11.** The content area's structure: (A) the content area, (B) the boxout (C) the text area

To create this layout, you have to nest div tags, but unlike nesting tables, this doesn't affect the structural integrity of the site or information. The following exercises lead you through the process of setting everything up.

## Setting up the content area

1. Add another div to the layout, this time with an ID of content. Note that the content area comes after the masthead, so in terms of code, after the masthead div. In the Insert Div Tag dialog box, you can ensure the div is correctly positioned by setting Insert to After tag and selecting <div id="masthead"> from the drop-down menu, as shown in Figure 6-12. Click OK and check Code view—the div is placed after the masthead tag but still within the wrapper.

**Figure 6-12.** Using the Insert Div Tag dialog box to add a div after a specific tag

2. Delete the content of the new div (but not the div itself). Then add another div, this time inside the one you just created. Call this one photoArea, and ensure Insert is set to At insertion point, as shown in Figure 6-13.

**Figure 6-13.** Using the Insert Div Tag dialog box to add a div at the insertion point

*Note that everything here is case sensitive, so photoarea is not the same as photoArea. This is a convention used by many web designers when creating multiple-word IDs and classes. It's best to avoid hyphens, underscores, and spaces in class and ID names because certain browsers choke on them.*

3. Create the third div, and give it an ID of copyArea because it will hold the copy (text). Because this comes *after* the floated element in the structure, it must sit in the correct place in the code. Therefore, it should be inserted after <div id="photoArea">, as shown in Figure 6-14.

**Figure 6-14.** Adding the copyArea div

## Styling the content area

Now you have to style the div tags you created. As before, all styles are defined in iceland.css, and created by going to Style ➤ Manage Styles ➤ New via the Properties panel.

1. The name of the content div should be #content, and set the Selector Type to Advanced. In Box, set Padding to 20 pixels and Margin to 0. Click OK and then Done a couple of times, and you'll see padding appear around the content in the content area, as shown in Figure 6-15.

**Figure 6-15.** The content area in Design view

**2.** To define property values for #photoArea, in the Box category of the CSS Style Definition dialog box, set the width value to 400; add 5 pixels of padding at the top, left, and right edges; and add 10 pixels at the bottom. These measurements are all based on those within the Photoshop mock-up. Then set the float definition to right as shown in Figure 6-16.

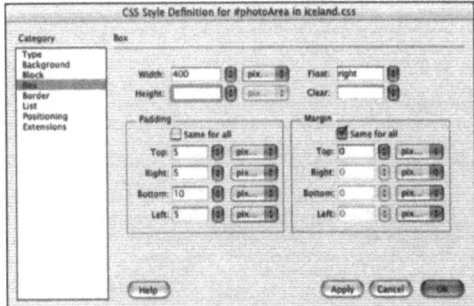

**Figure 6-16.** Setting box property values for #photoArea

*Uncheck* Same for all *to put in individual settings for* Padding *or* Margin.

**3.** While you are still in this dialog box, set Background ➤ Background color to #ffffff.

Click the Block category, which deals with white space, word and letter spacing, and alignment. Set text-align to center to make all content within this div align center, rather like the deprecated <center> tag, but in a nice, web standards-compliant way.

**4.** To specify the settings for #copyArea, in Background, set Background color to #c1c1c1. In Box, set Width to 274 pixels (a measurement taken from the mock-up) and set Padding to 0 pixels for Top, Right, and Left, and 9 pixels for Bottom. In Border, set Style to solid, Width to 1 pixel, and Color to #ffffff, as shown in Figure 6-17.

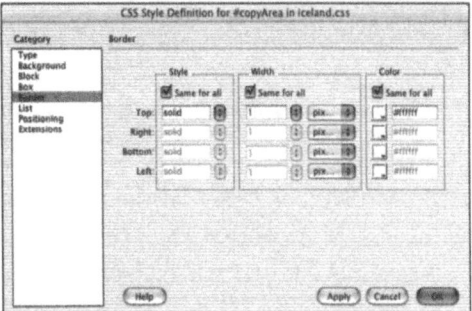

**Figure 6-17.** Defining property values for #copyArea

*If you find that Dreamweaver "forgets" some value sets, click* Apply *after finishing each category of the* CSS Style Definition *dialog box.*

**5.** Click Done to see something like Figure 6-18.

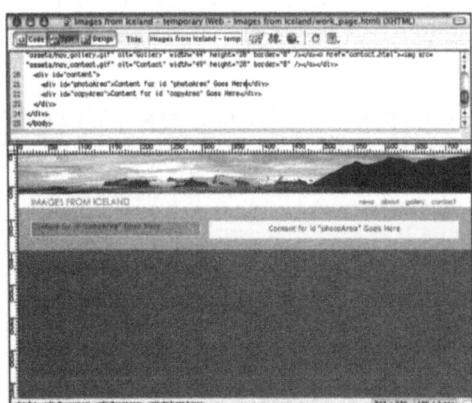

**Figure 6-18.** The site in Split view after completing this exercise

*Don't forget to include pound signs when inputting color values in the* CSS Style Definition *dialog box.*

## Adding a footer

**1.** Add another div, this time with an ID of footer. The footer comes after the content div, so set Insert to After tag and choose <div id="content"> as shown in Figure 6-19.

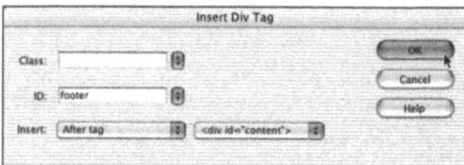

**Figure 6-19.** Adding a footer via the Insert Div Tag dialog box

> If you're wondering why the footer div comes after the content div, and not the most recent div created (copyArea), look back at the structure again. The photoArea and copyArea divs are nested within the content div. Putting the footer after either photoArea or copyArea would put it inside the content area, not after (underneath) it.

**2.** Display the New CSS Style dialog box, and add a new Selector called #footer, with Selector Type set to Advanced, as shown in Figure 6-20.

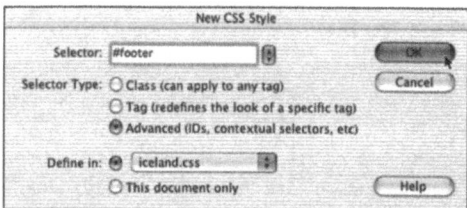

**Figure 6-20.** Adding a new selector in the New CSS Style dialog box

> If you can't remember how to display this dialog box, look back earlier in the chapter. (See step 2 of "Wrapping up your site," earlier in this chapter.)

**3.** In the CSS Style Definition dialog box, go to Box and set Clear to both as shown in Figure 6-21. Save your web page and CSS file via File ➤ Save All.

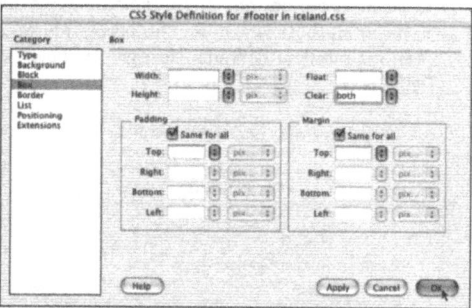

**Figure 6-21.** Defining box property values for #footer

> Setting Clear to both *effectively positions the associated element underneath any floating elements. This is required because as far as a web browser is concerned, floating elements take up no physical space. Leaving the* Clear *property out of your footer would create a page in which the floated area overlaps the footer.*

## Adding copy and images

Figure 6-22 shows the page, as previewed in a web browser:

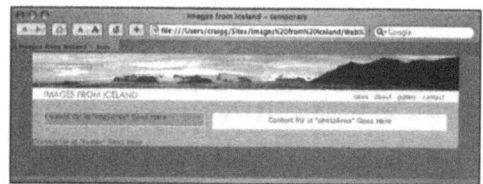

**Figure 6-22.** The page so far, previewed in a web browser

This contains all the structural elements for your web page, but you're still not ready to make a template—

you need to add some "dummy" text and images, including the page header.

## Finishing the copy area

1. The section heading is going to be a graphic, but you still need to ensure the structural integrity of the site. Select the current content of the textArea div and use the Properties panel to format it as Heading 1 as shown in Figure 6-23. This is because even though this heading will be an image, it's still the main heading on the web page. Because you'll use CSS to set margins around various HTML elements, it makes sense to mark it up in this manner. (Also if we later decide to use text-based headings, there'll be less work to do when making such amendments.)

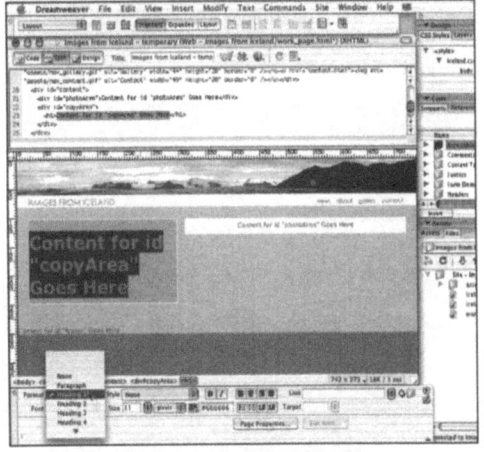

**Figure 6-23.** Formatting content as Heading 1

2. Delete this content, taking care not to delete the <h1> tag itself (check in Code view to ensure that just the content is selected). Then use the Insert panel to insert one of the title graphics from the assets folder, such as title_news.gif (it doesn't matter which one). Figure 6-24 shows the result. In Code view, you should see the following:

```
<h1><img src="assets/title_news.gif"
alt="News" width="274" height="20" /></h1>
```

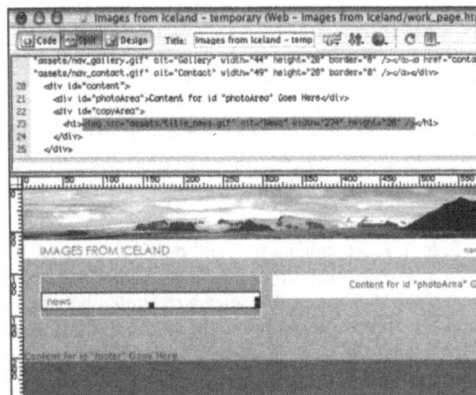

**Figure 6-24.** Inserting the heading graphic

3. At the moment, there's a gap above the graphic you just added. This is because browsers put margins above and below block elements, such as headings and paragraphs. You can get rid of it by using CSS. Display the now familiar New CSS Style dialog box. Note that because Dreamweaver's Properties panel is context-sensitive, it will display properties relating to images. However, you can still access the New CSS Style dialog box via the Class drop-down menu (choose Manage Styles as shown in Figure 6-25).

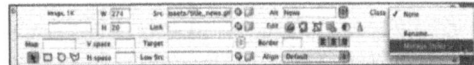

**Figure 6-25.** Accessing the Manage Styles command via the Properties panel

4. Choose Tag as the Selector Type. In the Tag field, type h1 as shown in Figure 6-26.

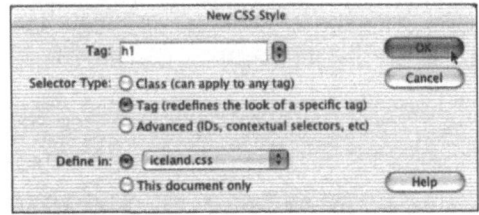

**Figure 6-26.** A tag selector type in the New CSS Style dialog box

**85**

> *You're using Tag as the selector type because you want the style definition to affect all HTML elements of this type by default. This is another great thing about CSS: default properties of HTML elements can be controlled directly by CSS.*

> *Remember to keep saving both your HTML and CSS files after making changes. When looking at changes in a browser, you won't see any difference until both files have been saved.*

**5.** In Box, set Padding to 0 and deselect Same for All in Margin, as shown in Figure 6-27. Then set everything to 0 except Bottom, which should be 10 pixels. This sets a gap below the heading. If you want to adjust it, you can always change it later by editing the CSS.

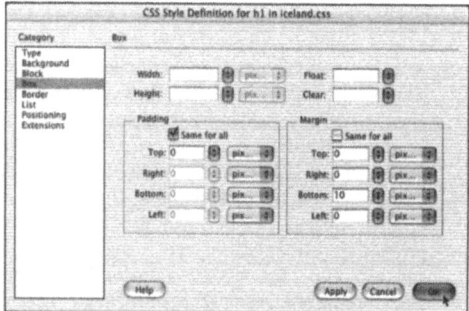

**Figure 6-27.** Defining box property values for <h1>

**6.** Back in Design view, the heading should now fit snuggly into the top of the copyArea div as shown in Figure 6-28.

**Figure 6-28.** The heading graphic is now placed at the top of the copyArea div

**7.** The dummy text you will add to the area under the heading graphic will be formatted as a series of paragraphs via the Properties panel, except for a few words, which will be on a separate line, formatted as Heading 2. (This represents any **crossheads** in your website's text. Crossheads are words or short phrases used to break up large amounts or defined sections of text.) Your cursor should still be located within the <h1> tag to the right of the recently placed image, so press *ENTER* to move it to the right place, or use Code or Split view to do so as shown in Figure 6-29. Don't just press the right arrow key or your cursor will end up in the footer!

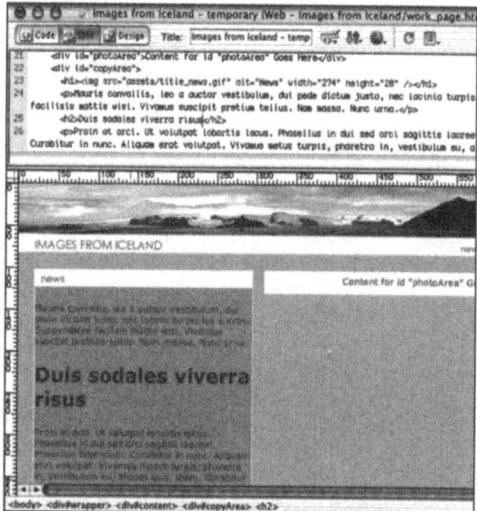

**Figure 6-29.** The web page with added dummy copy

**8.** Redisplay the New CSS Style dialog box. This time we're styling the <p> tag (paragraph tag) as shown in Figure 6-30.

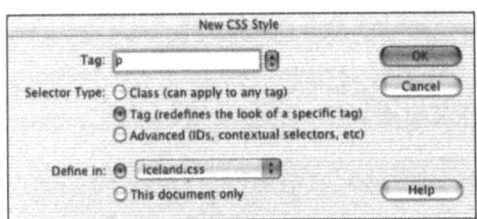

**Figure 6-30.** The New CSS Style dialog box

**9.** In Type, set Font to Verdana, Arial, Helvetica, sans serif, by using the drop-down menu. Set Size to 11 pixels and Line height to 14 pixels as shown in Figure 6-31. Line height enables you to change the **leading** on your page for the relevant element—in this case, the measurement between lines of text within paragraphs. Using the aforementioned settings makes this spacing slightly greater, therefore increasing readability.

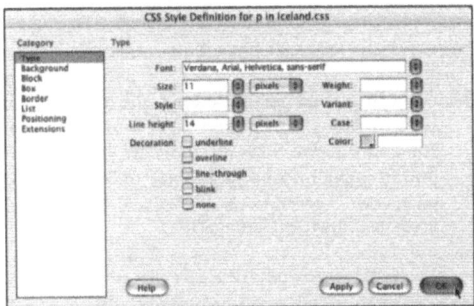

**Figure 6-31.** Defining type property values for the <p> tag

> *The reason a number of fonts are selected is that users may not have your specified one installed. Here, Verdana is specified—a very readable sans-serif font—as the first choice. If this is not installed on a user's machine, Arial will be displayed, then Helvetica, and then the generic sans-serif font for their system.*

**10.** Set Padding in the Box category. You don't want padding at the top and bottom of your paragraphs, so those settings should be 0. However, you do want some space to the left and right; otherwise the paragraph text is too close to the edges of the box it's contained in. Therefore, Right and Left are set to 7 pixels as shown in Figure 6-32. Again, this measurement is based roughly on the Photoshop mock-up. For the Margin settings, everything except Bottom should be set to 0, and Bottom should be set to 1 ems. This creates a margin at the bottom of each paragraph that is the height of one full character of the chosen font.

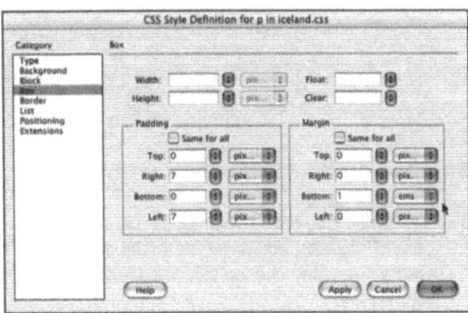

**Figure 6-32.** Defining box property values for the <p> tag

> *Note that you don't need a margin at the top because you've already set a bottom margin on the heading. This is good practice for CSS-based text—consistently control spacing via the bottom margin of elements.*

**11.** Click OK and Done until you return to the web page. You should see the paragraph text correctly formatted, as shown in Figure 6-33.

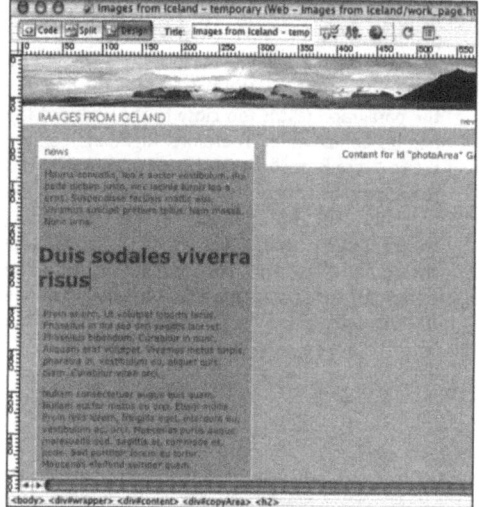

**Figure 6-33.** Newly formatted paragraphs in Design view

**12.** To format the <h2> (heading 2) tag, in the New CSS Style dialog box, type h2 in the Tag field and ensure Tag is the chosen selector type as shown in Figure 6-34.

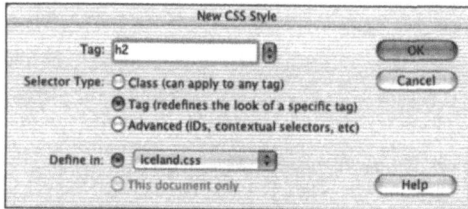

**Figure 6-34.** The New CSS Style dialog box

**13.** In Type, select Arial, Helvetica, sans serif for the Font and 12 pixels for the Size. Choose bold for the Weight and uppercase for the Case as shown in Figure 6-35. The last option means that regardless of what you type for the heading, it will always be displayed in uppercase—useful for site-wide consistency.

> We've chosen Arial for our primary heading font instead of Verdana because the latter's bubbly curves make it rather suspect for headings. Although Arial isn't great for body copy, its bold styling makes it suitable for headings.

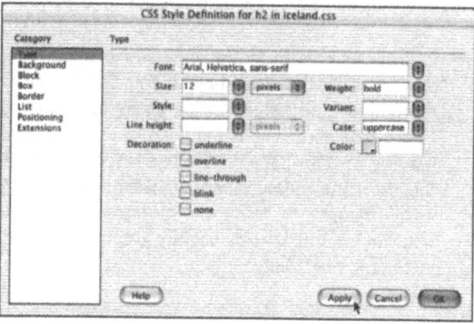

**Figure 6-35.** Defining type property values for <h2>

**14.** Like with the paragraph settings, the h2 Padding is set to 7 pixels for Left and Right, and 0 pixels for Top and Bottom. However, this time you want the bottom margin to be fairly close to the following paragraph. Therefore, set Bottom in Margin to 3 pixels as shown in Figure 6-36.

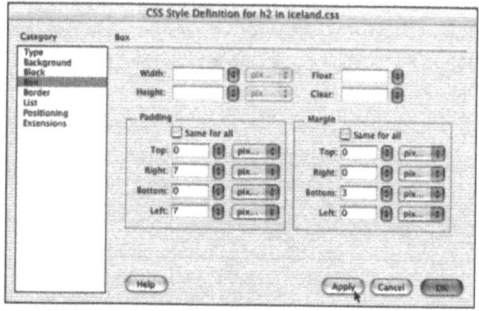

**Figure 6-36.** Defining box property values for <h2>

**15.** Back in Design view, the final text should look something like Figure 6-37. The heading stands out and the body copy is readable—just how it should be.

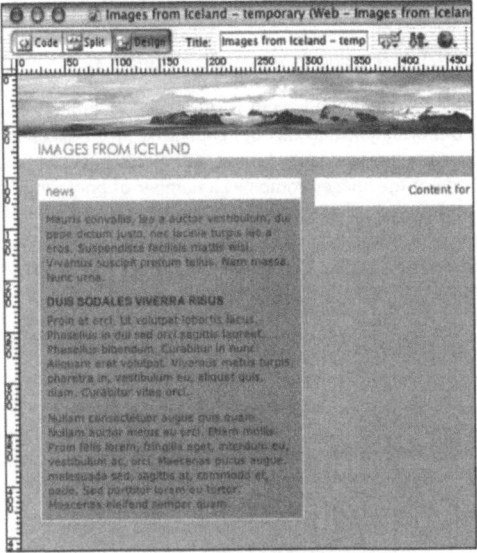

**Figure 6-37.** All text is now formatted.

**16.** In Code view look at how simple the HTML has remained.

```
<h1>
<img src="assets/title_news.gif"
alt="News" width="274" height="20" />
</h1>
<p>Mauris convallis, leo a auctor
vestibulum, dui pede dictum justo, nec
lacinia turpis leo a eros. Suspendisse
facilisis mattis wisi. Vivamus suscipit
pretium tellus. Nam massa. Nunc urna.</p>
<h2>Duis sodales viverra risus</h2>
<p>Proin at orci. Ut volutpat lobortis
lacus. Phasellus in dui sed orci sagittis
laoreet. Phasellus bibendum. Curabitur in
nunc. Aliquam erat volutpat. Vivamus metus
turpis, pharetra in, vestibulum eu,
aliquet quis, diam. Curabitur vitae
orci.</p><p>Nullam consectetuer augue
quis quam. Nullam auctor metus eu orci.
Etiam mollis. Proin felis lorem,
```

fringilla eget, interdum eu, vestibulum ac, orci. Maecenas purus augue, malesuada sed, sagittis at, commodo et, pede. Sed porttitor lorem eu tortor. Maecenas eleifend semper quam.</p>

Again, this shows the power of CSS. The fonts have been defined and spacing set to the nearest pixel, yet the HTML is untouched by decorative tags. Should you want to change the spacing, fonts, or case of any element at a later date, all you have to do is edit the CSS.

# Semantic mark-up explanation

Before we go any further, we're going to talk a little more about the idea of **semantic mark-up**. The process you've followed so far has enabled you to create mark-up of this type. That means elements are marked up according to what they represent. This is something you should get used to doing in *every* website you create, regardless of whether you use Design or Code view. The most important heading on a page should be marked up as h1 (heading 1 in Dreamweaver's Properties panel), and secondary headings should be marked up as h2 (heading 2). Paragraphs should be marked up as such, avoiding the use of double carriage returns to separate paragraphs of text.

Therefore, you should *never* end up with something like the following:

```
<p class="mainPageHeading">Main heading</p>

<p>Lorem ipsum dolor sit amet,
consectetuer adipiscing elit.  Integer
pretium, augue et condimentum gravida,
ipsum nulla porta libero, non pharetra
odio leo a purus.<br /><br />
Nullam non odio. Proin nulla sem,
consequat non, congue id, posuere non,
dui. Pellentesque malesuada elit at massa
volutpat sollicitudin. Aenean odio risus,
venenatis eu, semper et, elementum ut,
quam.</p>

<p class="secondaryHeading">Secondary
heading</p>
```

```
<p>Duis ut nulla. Sed vitae purus eu
sapien elementum iaculis. Suspendisse id
justo.<br /><br />
Nulla et dui et purus facilisis hendrerit.
Ut molestie, turpis eget venenatis
eleifend, pede wisi posuere velit, a
feugiat diam odio eu turpis. Proin
fringilla egestas mauris.</p>
```

Instead, code should look like this.

```
<h1>Main heading</h1>

<p>Lorem ipsum dolor sit amet,
consectetuer adipiscing elit.  Integer
pretium, augue et condimentum gravida,
ipsum nulla porta libero, non pharetra
odio leo a purus.</p>

<p>Nullam non odio. Proin nulla sem,
consequat non, congue id, posuere non,
dui. Pellentesque malesuada elit at massa
volutpat sollicitudin. Aenean odio risus,
venenatis eu, semper et, elementum ut,
quam.</p>

<h2>Secondary heading</h2>

<p>Duis ut nulla. Sed vitae purus eu
sapien elementum iaculis. Suspendisse
id justo.<br /><br />
Nulla et dui et purus facilisis hendrerit.
Ut molestie, turpis eget venenatis
eleifend, pede wisi posuere velit, a
feugiat diam odio eu turpis. Proin
fringilla egestas mauris.</p>
```

As you can see, headings have been marked up with the proper tags, and double carriage returns replaced with *de-facto* paragraphs.

A further point worth making is that the content itself should be in a logical order. A lot of people who have used nothing but visual web design editing packages seem blissfully unaware of what's going on in their code, particularly if they use Dreamweaver layers.

A web page should still make sense—both in terms of structure and content—if all CSS, tables, layers, and other presentational elements are stripped out. Local

placing of content and semantic mark-up makes this more likely to happen.

## Completing the photo area

Now you're going to work on the photo area.

The first thing you need is an image. In order to fit comfortably within this design, all the final images for this site are landscape format, 400 X 300 pixels in size. One of the images combines a number of photographs and a map of Iceland (see Figure 6-38). As with all other images, this can be found in the files downloaded from the friends of ED website (in the assets folder of Web - Images from Iceland).

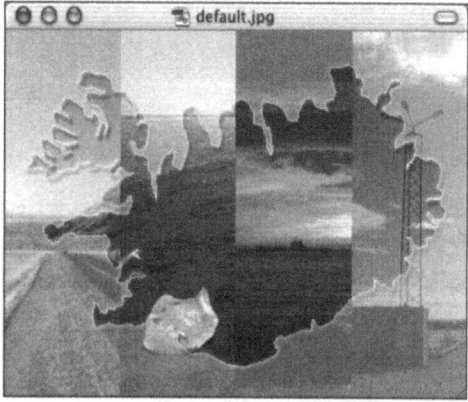

**Figure 6-38.** A default image for the photo area

1. Delete the current content in the photoArea div and press *ENTER* to create two blank paragraphs. (To check this, use Split or Code view, and you should see the following code:

```
<p> </p>
<p> </p>
```

2. Press the up arrow key to move the cursor into the first paragraph, and then add the image default.jpg via the usual means. Then move the cursor into the second paragraph and add a caption for the photograph. In Design view, notice that the layout is slightly wrong after adding these elements, as shown in Figure 6-39. The photo area

and text area are joined, but there should be a gap between them. This is because they both have the same paragraph padding that you set for the copyArea div. You now have to override this for paragraphs within the photoArea div.

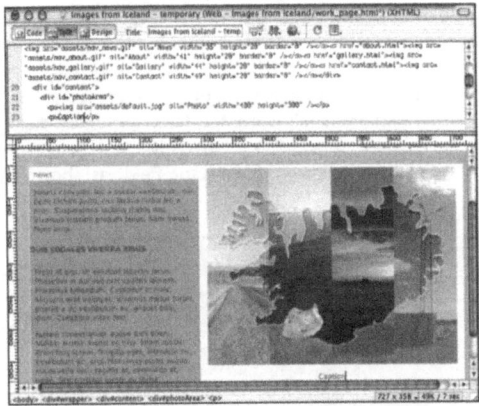

**Figure 6-39.** The site's photo area and text area are joined.

There are a couple of ways you can go about this. One way would be to add a class to each paragraph in the photo area and set that class's horizontal (that is, left and right) padding to 0. However, there is an easier method. Using CSS, you can effectively set all paragraphs within the photoArea div to have no horizontal padding. This is called a **contextual selector** and in this case, it is composed of the selector followed by the relevant HTML tag, with a space in between: **#photoArea p**. Place this in the Selector field in the New CSS Style dialog box, ensuring that Selector Type is set to Advanced as shown in Figure 6-40.

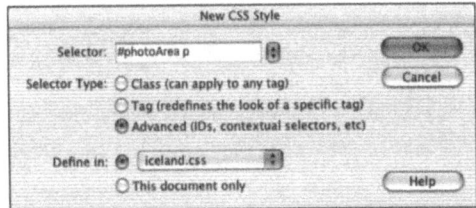

**Figure 6-40.** A contextual selector within the New CSS Style dialog box

**3.** All you have to edit is the setting you want to override. Therefore, in Box, check Same for all under Padding and set Top to 0 as shown in Figure 6-41.

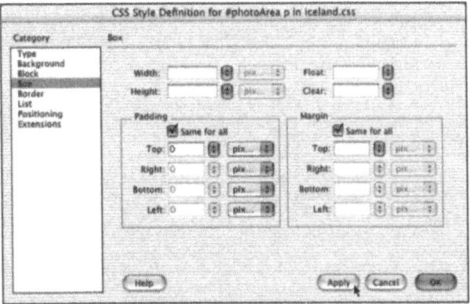

**Figure 6-41.** Defining the padding setting for #photoArea p

**4.** Return to Design view and the layout appears as shown in Figure 6-42. There is a gap between the photo area and text area, as per the original mock-up.

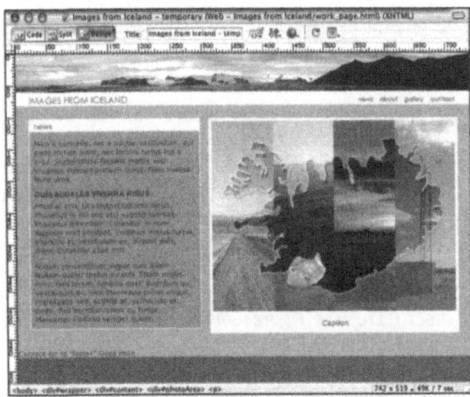

**Figure 6-42.** The page in Design view, with a gap between the photo area and text area

## Building and styling the footer

The footer is relatively simple to deal with, and you can add the final content at this stage because we know what's required.

1. Add some alternate navigation so visitors with small monitors don't have to scroll to the top of the screen to change pages. This is done in plain text, and the Link field in the Properties panel is used to create links to the relevant pages, as shown in Figure 6-43. See earlier in this chapter for the correct file names.

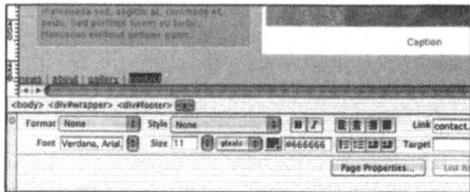

**Figure 6-43.** Adding alternate navigation

> Sometimes Dreamweaver adds spaces inside links that you don't want. Use Code view to remove these whenever necessary. (For example, if you see something like `<a href="link.html">link </a>`, use Code view to remove the space prior to `</a>`.)

2. Add another common feature—a "top of page" link. The old method of linking to #top fails in some browsers, so you will use some simple JavaScript. Typing `javascript: scrollTo (0,0);` in the Link field means the browser scrolls to coordinates 0,0 (the top-left corner) when the link is clicked, sending the user back to the top of the page. Note that the capitalization of the T in scrollTo (see Figure 6-44) is vital—do not write scrollto instead.

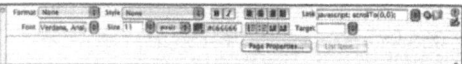

**Figure 6-44.** Adding a top of page link

> Something to bear in mind for commonly used items such as the code just shown is Dreamweaver's Snippets feature. We'll cover Snippets in Chapter 9, and creating one for this piece of code is simplicity itself.

3. Format the footer content as Paragraph via the Properties panel, open the New CSS Style dialog box, set Selector Type to Advanced, and type #footer p into the Selector field, as shown in Figure 6-45.

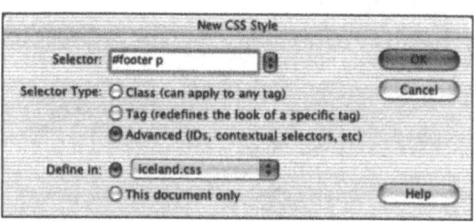

**Figure 6-45.** The New CSS Style dialog box

> This is similar to what you did earlier for the paragraphs in the photo area. In this case, #footer p is used to define styles for paragraphs in the footer only.

4. Align the footer copy to the right by setting Block ➤ Text-align to right as shown in Figure 6-46. Simple.

> You might be used to aligning things directly in HTML, but that method is deprecated. Anyway, doing it in CSS means you can easily edit it later on.

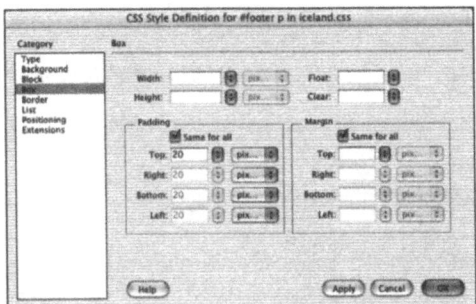

**Figure 6-46.** Defining block property values for #footer p

**5.** Set Box ➤ Padding to 20 pixels as shown in Figure 6-47. This means the footer text will more or less line up with the photo area because the content area that the photo area is within has identical padding settings.

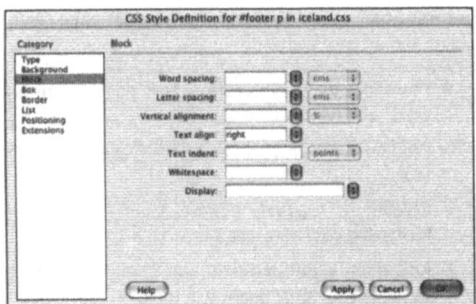

**Figure 6-47.** Defining box property values for #footer p

The result looks like Figure 6-48.

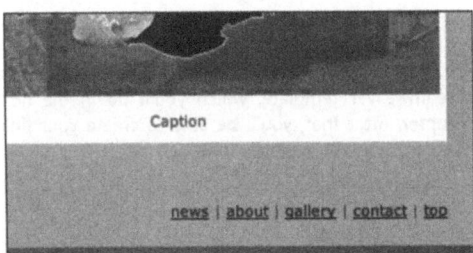

**Figure 6-48.** How the footer now looks in Design view

Of course, although the links have the correct font, they still have the default coloring, so they clash somewhat with the web page. Therefore it's now time to style the website's links.

## Styling website links

**1.** Open the New CSS Style dialog box, select Advanced under Selector Type, and click the Selector drop-down menu to see the choices shown in Figure 6-49. These are all the states of web links: link (the default/standard), visited (for links you've already clicked), hover (for when the mouse pointer is over a link), and active (for while the link is being clicked). These should be added in the order shown in the drop-down menu. This is because things that are placed later in a CSS file can override previous settings, which can cause problems if link states are styled out of order.

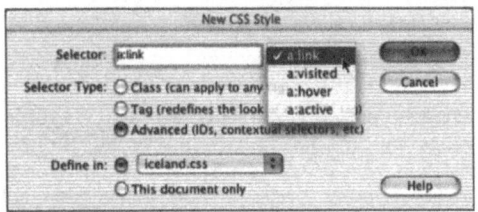

**Figure 6-49.** Accessing anchor pseudo-classes via the New CSS Style dialog box

*A good way of remembering the correct order: Link, Visited, Hover, Active, is to use the words LoVe, HAte.*

**2.** In all but the hover state, set Color to #444444, Weight to bold, and Decoration to none as shown in Figure 6-50. This makes links slightly darker than the body copy, bold to make them stand out more, and have no underline. If they still don't stand out enough, you can always amend these settings later.

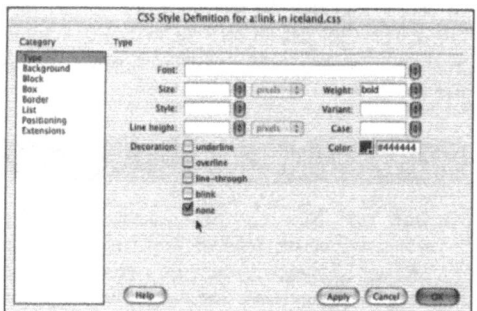

**Figure 6-50.** Defining type property values for a link

**3.** For the hover state, make the color slightly darker still (#222222), and set Decoration to underline as shown in Figure 6-51. This means users get a reaction when the mouse pointer is positioned over a link.

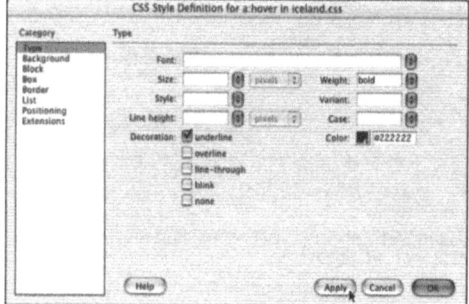

**Figure 6-51.** Defining type property values for the hover state

**4.** Figure 6-52 shown the page with the links styled, as previewed in a web browser.

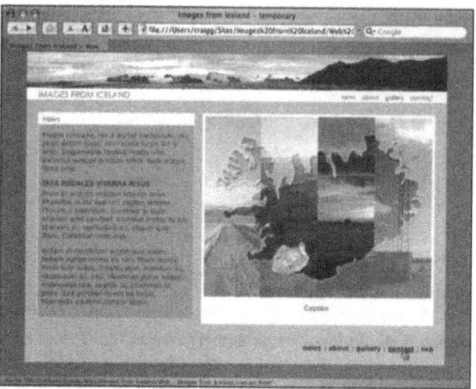

**Figure 6-52.** The styled links, as previewed in a web browser

## Summary

At this point you should now have a web page resembling the original mock-up. In this chapter, you have:

- Learned how to structure a web page layout and work with semantic mark-up
- Worked with CSS, using Dreamweaver's new CSS tools
- Created a wrapper, boxout, content area, and footer for your web page
- Added and styled some dummy content in order to see how your final pages will look
- Styled page elements with CSS rather than tables and ugly workarounds
- Used advanced CSS, such as contextual selectors, for maximum flexibility
- Styled links with CSS

You're now in a position to turn this initial work into a Dreamweaver template, which you'll do in the next chapter. After that, you'll be able to create your final web pages, complete with content.

# Chapter 7

# CREATING TEMPLATES

---

**What we'll cover in this chapter**

- Creating and editing templates
- Working with editable regions
- Creating pages based on templates
- Working with embedded templates

Templates are one of Dreamweaver's best features. Instead of duplicating files and changing the content of the new page, common elements can be defined in a template and locked to ensure site-wide consistency. Dreamweaver notices when templates are updated and asks whether you want all associated pages based on the template to be updated—a process that typically takes only a few seconds for each page.

However, this sort of template is fairly common in web design applications, so Dreamweaver takes things a step further, enabling you to create repeatable regions for repeated page elements that need to be consistent; optional regions for elements that aren't required for all pages; and embedded templates for a main template that needs only a few changes, perhaps the addition of a few sub-pages.

The case study site is simple, and you'll only need a basic template. Therefore, before you get down to work, you're going to create a standard template and then an embedded template so you can use the latter in your own projects.

## Creating a template

1. Using the Files panel, open My first Dreamweaver site, as shown in Figure 7-1. You're going to work in this test site for your practice templates, in order to avoid putting unused files in the Images from Iceland site.

**Figure 7-1.** Opening My first Dreamweaver site in the Files panel

2. You're first going to create a simple table-based HTML page with a masthead at the top, footer at the bottom, navigation to the left, and content area to the right. Add a new table, using Layout ➤ Table from the Insert bar, as shown in Figure 7-2.

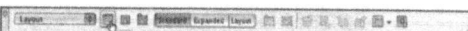

**Figure 7-2.** Adding a table using the Insert bar

3. The structure calls for three rows and a maximum of two columns (for the navigation and content area). We've set an arbitrary width of 90 percent, as shown in Figure 7-3, although because you're just doing a quick practice page, this setting matters little.

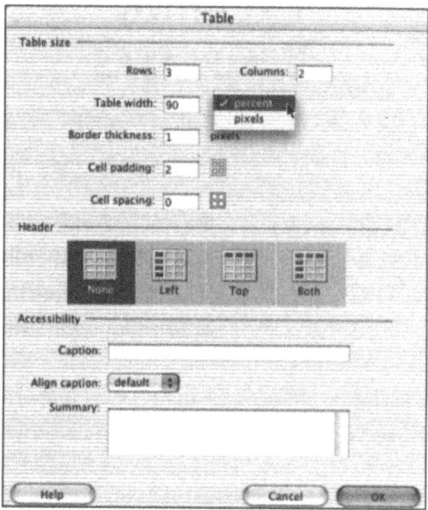

**Figure 7-3.** Defining table attribute values in the Table dialog box

*With the design and layout focus of this book centering on CSS, you may wonder why you're using a table for this exercise's layout. The reason is that it's quicker to rapidly get a table up and running for this sort of exercise; however, we still advocate using CSS for actual site designs.*

**4.** Merge the cells on the top and bottom row, as shown in Figure 7-4. You do this by selecting the cells you want to merge and then right/*CTRL*-clicking and choosing Table ➤ Merge Cells.

You could also use the Merge selected cells using spans button in the Properties panel to do this, as shown in Figure 7-5.

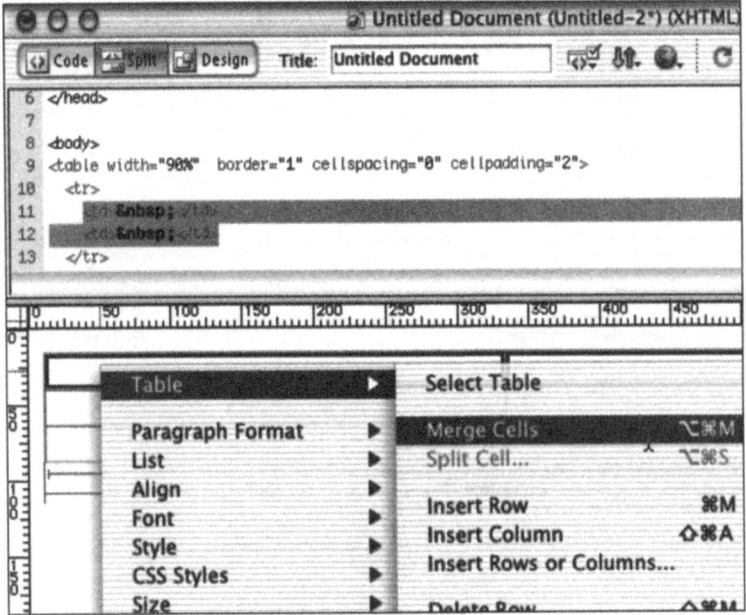

**Figure 7-4.** Merging cells in Design view using the context menu

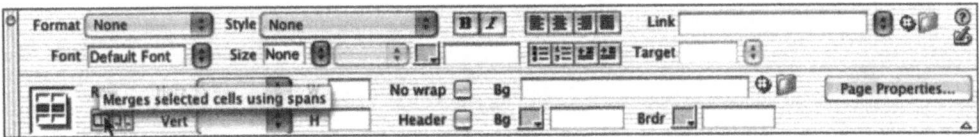

**Figure 7-5.** Merging cells using the Properties panel

5. Add some dummy content to each of the cells, and then select the navigation and content cells. In the Properties panel, set Vert to top, as shown in Figure 7-6. This sets the vertical alignment of these two columns to top.

6. The principle behind Dreamweaver templates is to define **editable regions**. In pages based on the template, these are the areas that will be editable (as their name suggests)—all other areas of the page will be locked. For a site such as this, the masthead, footer, and navigation would most likely be locked, and just the content area editable. Therefore, select the content in the right cell, and right/*CTRL*-click it, and choose Templates ➤ New Editable Region, as shown in Figure 7-7.

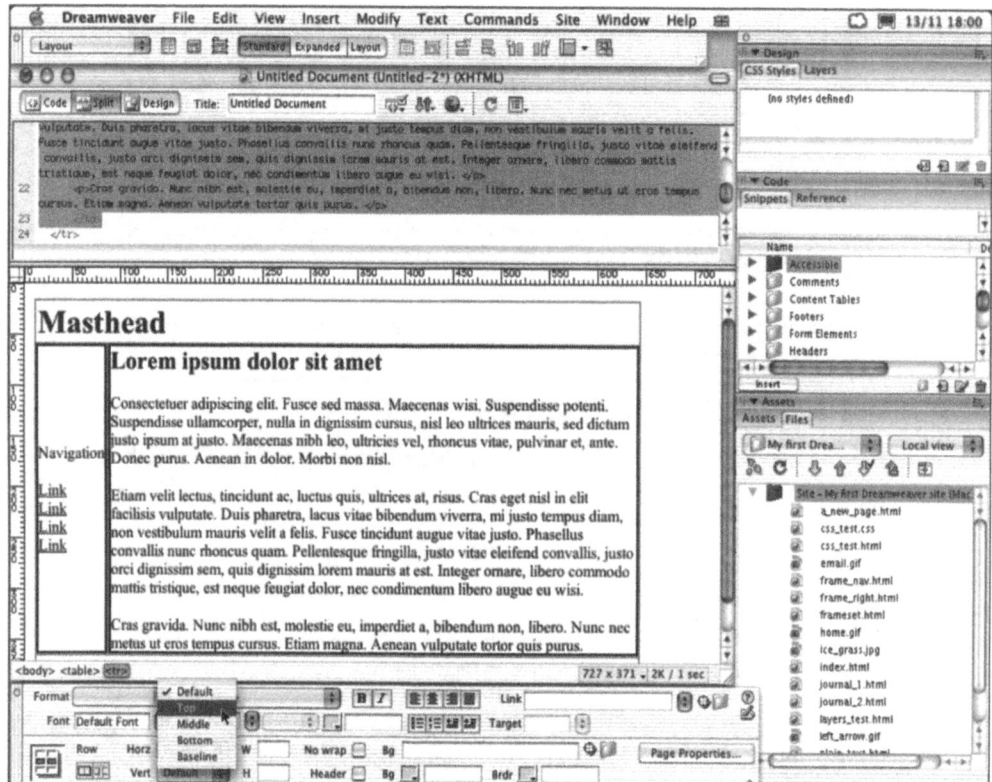

**Figure 7-6.** Setting vertical alignment of table cells using the Properties panel

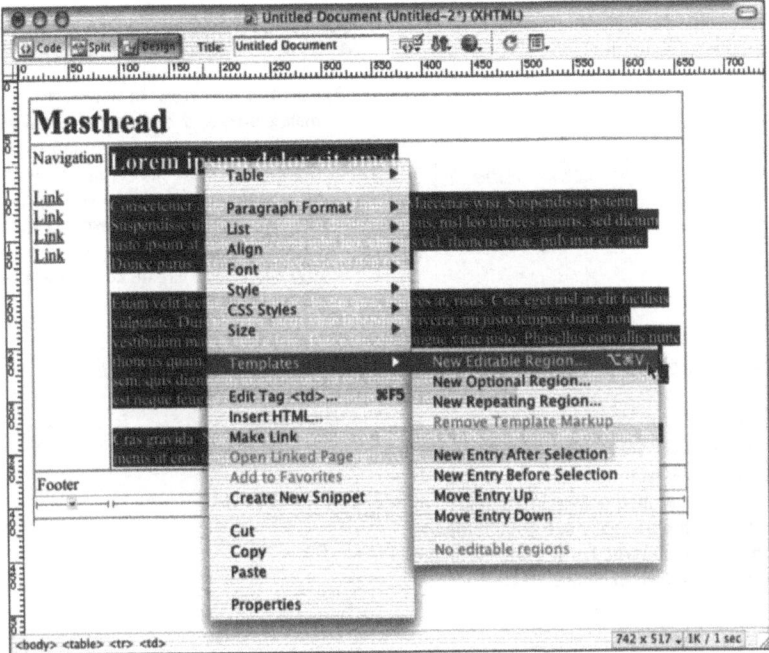

**Figure 7-7.** Defining a new editable region

**7.** Dreamweaver warns you that the document will be converted into a template. Feel free to turn this warning off via the check box, and then click OK, as shown in Figure 7-8.

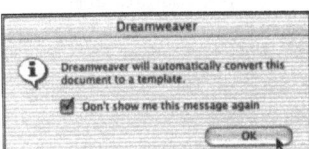

**Figure 7-8.** Dreamweaver's convert to template alert

**8.** In the Name field of the New Editable Region dialog box, type the name of your editable region, omitting spaces, underscores, and hyphens. Something like contentArea is fine, as shown in Figure 7-9 (thereby following the same convention for multiple-word naming that you used in your CSS).

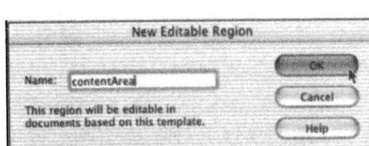

**Figure 7-9.** Naming an editable region

**101**

**9.** Select File ➤ Save as Template to save your file. Choose a sensible, memorable file name, as shown in Figure 7-10.

**Figure 7-10.** Saving the template

**10.** Dreamweaver automatically saves templates in a template folder in your site's root folder. Templates have a file extension of .dwt (as you can see, main.dwt is now in the Templates folder of your site). If you don't initially see your template folder in the Files panel, refresh it using *F5* or the Refresh button, as shown in Figure 7-11.

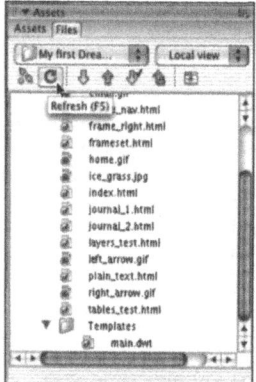

**Figure 7-11.** The Files panel with the Refresh button highlighted

*Do **not** move template files out of the Templates folder—they must stay there in order for them to work properly.*

**Creating a page based on a template**

**1.** Go to File ➤ New to access the New Document dialog box, and choose the Templates tab. Select My first Dreamweaver site and in the second column, you'll see the template you just created. Select the template and a visual preview appears in the right column, as shown in Figure 7-12. Ensure Update page when template changes is checked, and then click Create to create a new document based on the template.

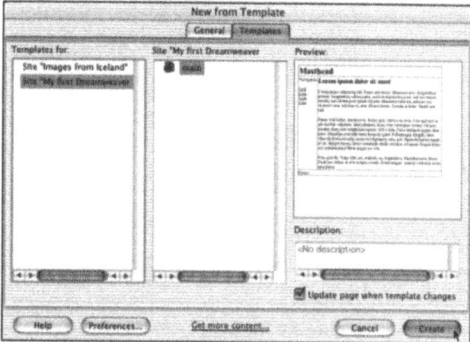

**Figure 7-12.** Choosing a template

**2.** Moving over any of the locked areas changes the mouse pointer to a "no entry" pointer, as shown in Figure 7-13, signifying you can't change any content in these areas. Save this new document as first_page_from_template.html.

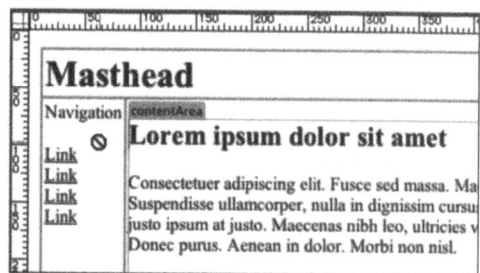

**Figure 7-13.** The no entry pointer, signifying locked regions

**3.** The area with a blue tab is the editable region. This is populated with whatever was left in the template. Many designers remove all content from template, but it can be useful as a reminder, and you can often simply change bits of content, like we did with the title, as shown in Figure 7-14.

*Note that templates are the basic building blocks from which actual pages are made, and shouldn't themselves be published on a live site. Furthermore, if anything needs changing in a locked area, you must change the template or detach the relevant page from the template.*

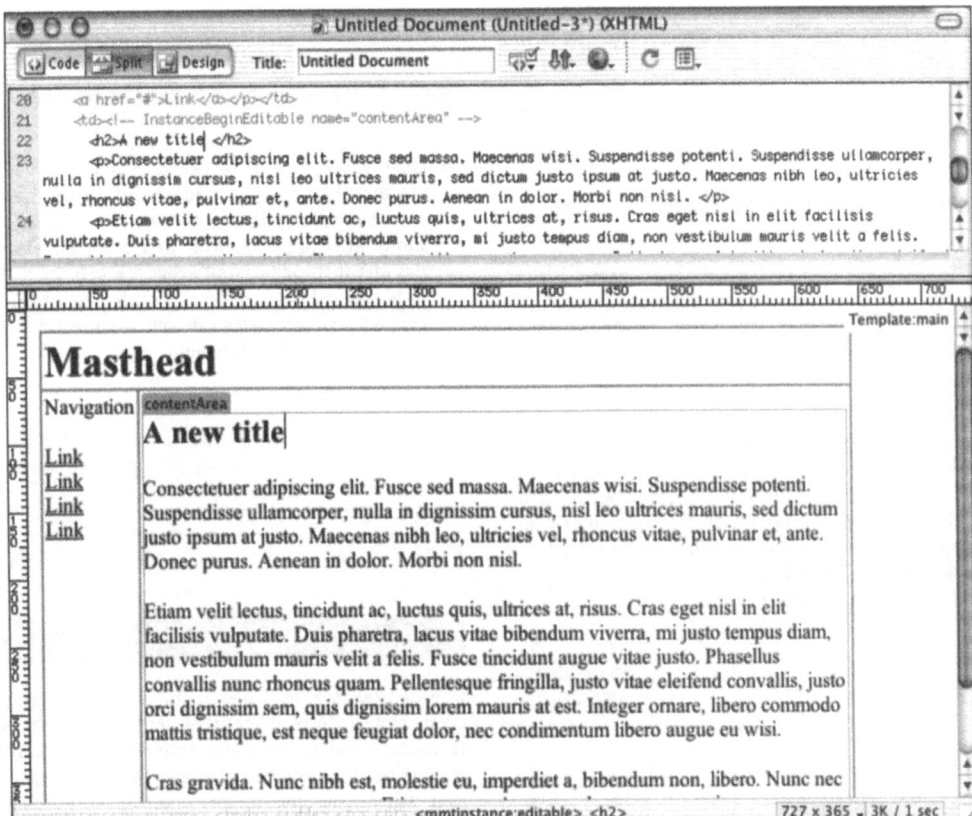

**Figure 7-14.** Adding a new template within the editable region

1. Close any open files and open main.dwt **again**. Change some of the locked content, such as the name of the masthead, as shown in Figure 7-15.

**Figure 7-15.** Changing the main title of the main.dwt file

---

*If you don't close template-based files prior to editing the template, Dreamweaver can't update those files as thoroughly.*

---

2. Save the template (via the usual *CTRL/CMD+S*) and you'll see the Update Template Files dialog box, as shown in Figure 7-16. Click Update and Dreamweaver will update all the pages based on the template, providing a report when it's done so, as shown in Figure 7-17.

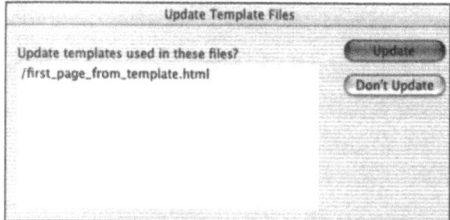

**Figure 7-16.** The Update Template Files dialog box

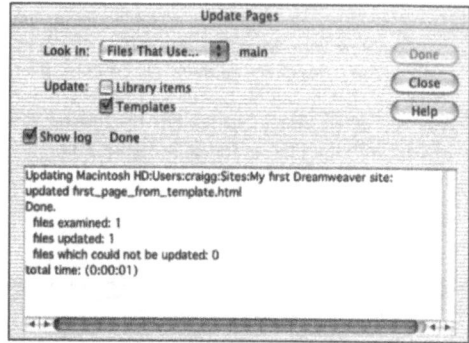

**Figure 7-17.** The Update Pages dialog box showing the report

3. Open first_page_from_template.html and you'll see that the page you made based on your template has been updated with the new masthead, as shown in Figure 7-18. With your one-page effort, this isn't that exciting, but imagine if you had a 50-page site and needed to make such a change. CSS coupled with templates can save massive amounts of time for any web designer.

---

*Remember, of course, that when you update your pages, this is initially only done locally. For anyone on the Web to see the changes to your site's template, you'll have to upload the affected pages.*

---

Working with embedded templates

One of Dreamweaver's best features is the ability to create embedded templates (also referred to as nested templates—that is, templates within templates). The great thing about embedded templates is that they cascade when you update them, providing you with incredible flexibility for your site designs.

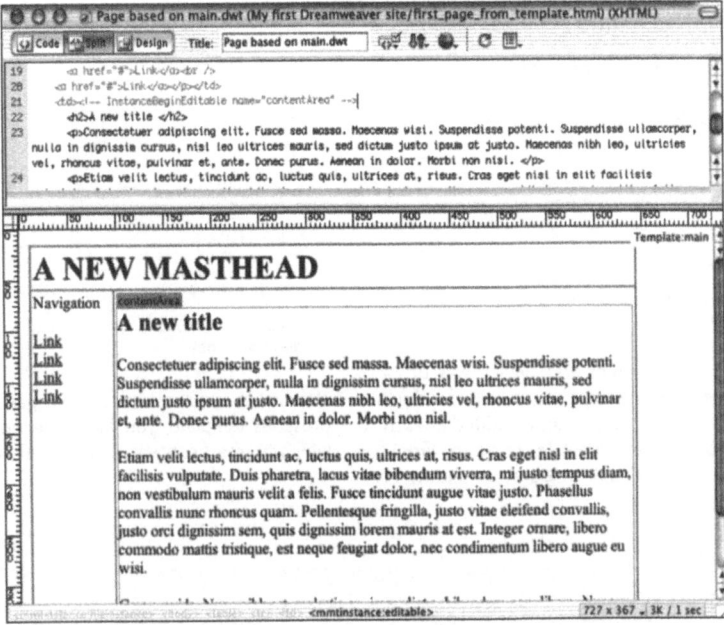

**Figure 7-18.** The web page created earlier, automatically updated by Dreamweaver

For instance, you may have a site based around a template (say, `main.dwt`), which contains a number of almost identical product pages. You could create an embedded template (say, `products.dwt`) for the product pages; updating this template would only update the product pages based on it. However, updating `main.dwt` would update all of the site's pages *and* the product template.

In some ways this is a small distinction from using one standard template, but as the following exercise shows, it's an important one. In this exercise, you will augment your page with a "pros and cons" table.

1. Create another new page based on the template. Place the new table inside the editable region and define editable regions within it, as shown in Figure 7-19.

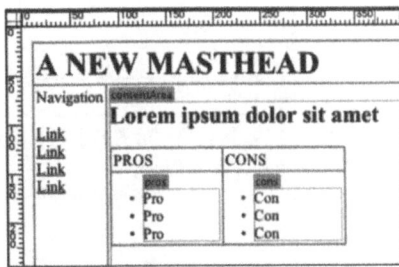

**Figure 7-19.** Adding a pros and cons table and defining editable regions

2. Save the template via File ➤ Save as Template (we named our file proscons). Note how in Design view that the old editable region's tab has turned yellow, as shown in Figure 7-20. This means that this region is locked.

**105**

**Figure 7-20.** Locked and editable regions within the embedded template

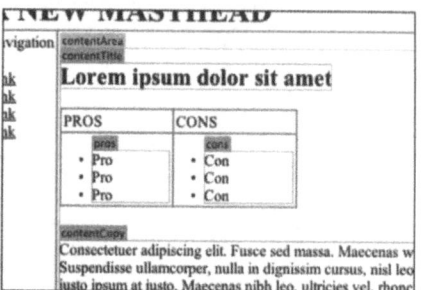

**Figure 7-21.** Editable regions added for the page title and body copy

3. Because the main content area, which was originally editable, is now locked, you need to unlock the title and body copy so it can be edited in each page based on this new template. To do so, simply make some more editable regions, as shown in Figure 7-21.

Now when you create a new page based on the proscons template, you have four editable regions in which to insert content, as shown in Figure 7-22.

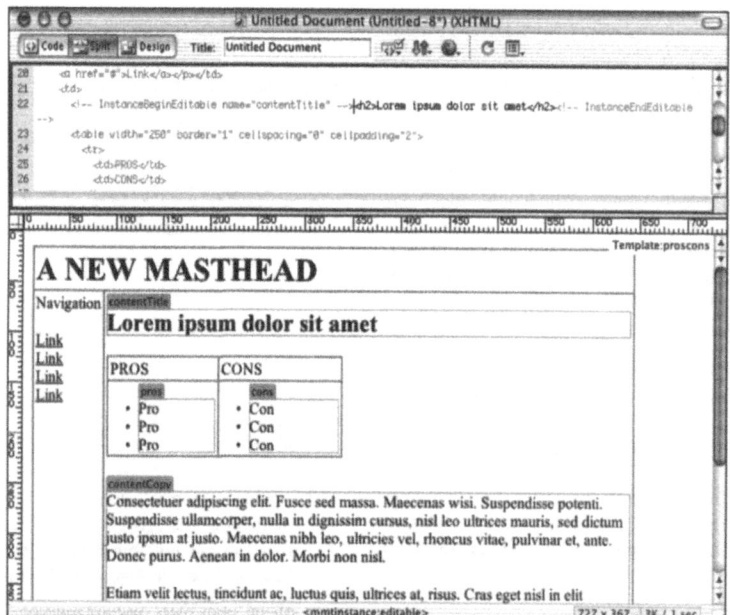

**Figure 7-22.** All four editable regions within a document based on `proscons.dwt`

> Note that in this exercise we only showed you how to create the template elements. This was not meant as a complete walkthrough for making a web page. Observant readers will have noticed we didn't give the page a title or meta tags—things that are essential to any public web page.

## A template for your case study

The main page layout for the case study has already been created, as shown in Figure 7-23. What you need to do now is decide which elements will be locked and which will be editable.

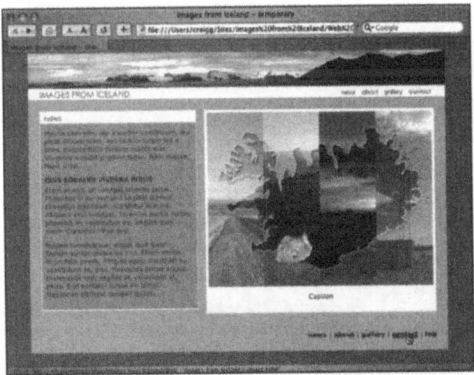

**Figure 7-23.** The website's layout, as completed in Chapter 6

From Figure 7-23, it's obvious that the masthead, navigation, and footer need to be locked. Dreamweaver also automatically creates an editable region in the <head> section of each page so you can add scripts or unique meta tags to individual pages.

All the editable regions will be in the content area. The most obvious of these is the entire photo area. Although most pages are going to have images in that section, the contact area will most likely contain a form, so this entire area needs to be flexible.

You could make the entire copy area editable. However, to ensure consistency regarding the format-

ting of the page's title graphic at the top of the copy area, you can make just the image itself an editable region, leaving the remaining copy as the final editable region on your page.

1. In the Images from Iceland site, open work_page.html and go to File ➤ Save as Template. In Save as, give the template a sensible name, such as main, as shown in Figure 7-24.

**Figure 7-24.** The Save As Template dialog box

2. Dreamweaver prompts you to update your links. Click Yes, as shown in Figure 7-25.

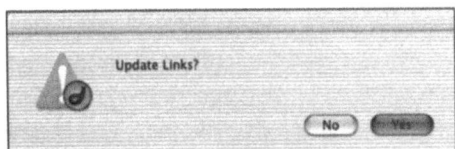

**Figure 7-25.** Dreamweaver's Update Links alert

3. Go to the Files panel and you'll see a new folder in your site: Templates, as shown in Figure 7-26. This is where Dreamweaver stores template files.

**Figure 7-26.** Note the Templates folder in the Files panel

> *You may have to refresh the panel (press F5) for the* Templates *folder to be displayed.*

**4.** You're now going to create your first editable region—the page title at the top of the copy area. Select the image, checking in Code view that just the ⟨img⟩ tag is selected, and not the ⟨h1⟩ tag. Right/*CTRL*-click and use the context menu to go to Templates ➤ New Editable Region, as shown in Figure 7-27.

> *You can also go to* Insert ➤ Template Objects ➤ Editable Region *to choose the same option.*

**5.** When the New Editable Region dialog box appears, give your new region a name and click OK, as shown in Figure 7-28. When choosing names, try keeping the same conventions used in the CSS files, that is, wordWord. Do not use underscores, spaces, or hyphens. In this case, use the name pageheading.

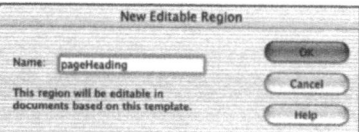

**Figure 7-28.** Naming the editable region

**6.** For the second editable region, select the page's copy and follow the same procedure, as shown in Figure 7-29. When you see the New Editable Region dialog box, type the name pageCopy.

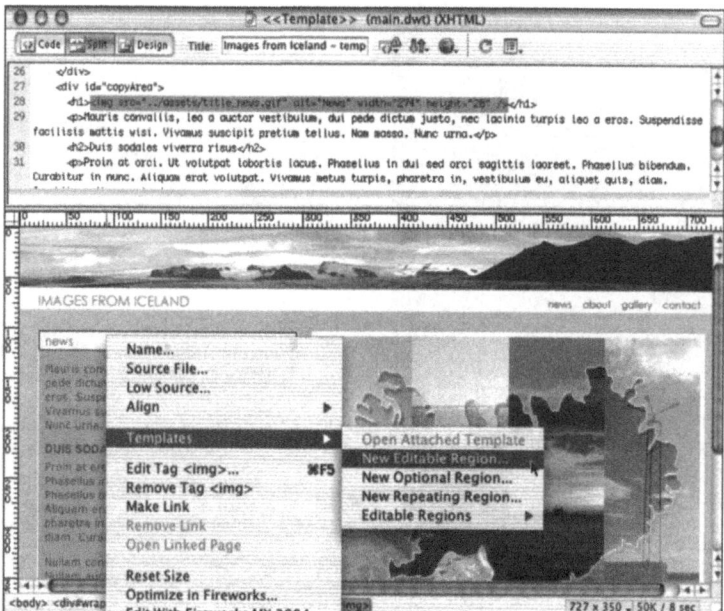

**Figure 7-27.** Making the heading graphic an editable region

**Figure 7-29.** Turning the page's body copy into an editable region

**7.** Select everything within the photo area and then open the New Editable Region dialog box, as shown in Figure 7-30. This time, type photoArea as the name. Don't worry about trying to select the opening and closing <p> tags if working in Design view—Dreamweaver automatically and intelligently wraps the editable region around the selection. However, check in Code or Split view to ensure the relevant template code is wrapped around both paragraphs.

> *Note that because in Chapter 6 you created a contextual selector to define how paragraphs within the photo area should look (#photoArea p), you won't have to remember to add classes to each element within the* photoArea *editable region when pages are added in the future.*

**8.** Save your template. You'll see the error shown in Figure 7-31. This is an irritation, and you'll see it again in the future. This is due to your having made the web page title an editable region *within* the <h1> tag, instead of including the tag in the editable region, too. You put up with this because it prevents you from having to reapply the Heading 1 formatting to the element each time it's changed.

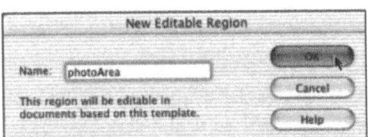

**Figure 7-30.** Naming the editable region

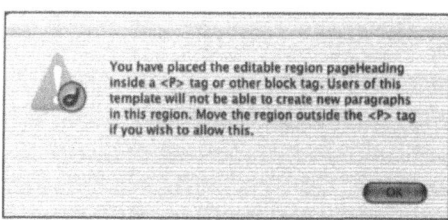

**Figure 7-31.** Dreamweaver's alert about editable regions being placed within HTML tags

9. If you want to change this, find the following code in Code view:

```
<div id="copyArea">
       <h1><!-- TemplateBeginEditable
name="pageHeading" --><img src="../
assets/title_news.gif" alt="News"
width="274" height="20" /><!--
TemplateEndEditable --></h1>
```

Move the template code, changing it to the following:

```
<div id="copyArea">
       <!-- TemplateBeginEditable
name="pageHeading" --><h1><img src="
../assets/title_news.gif" alt="News"
width="274" height="20" /></h1><!--
TemplateEndEditable -->
```

Be very sure to surround entire tags with the template code; otherwise the template will not work properly. For instance, the following creates an error:

```
<div id="copyArea">
       <!-- TemplateBeginEditable
name="pageHeading" --><h1><img src="
../assets/title_news.gif" alt="News"
width="274" height="20" /><!--
TemplateEndEditable --></h1>
```

Remember that if you do change this to get rid of the alert box, you must take care when editing the title image. Changing its formatting from heading 1 to anything else will alter the way the page looks.

## Summary

In this chapter, you worked with editable regions and created a Dreamweaver template. You then made a page based on the template, updated the template, and updated the page based on it. We briefly touched on Dreamweaver's advanced template capabilities, and you worked on an embedded template.

Finally, you worked through creating a Dreamweaver template based on your case study work page, as created in the previous chapter. This means you can now create your website pages based on this template and add content to them, which is precisely what you're going to do in the next chapter.

# Chapter 8

# ADDING
# CONTENT

**What we'll cover in this chapter**

- Adding content to web pages
- Advanced contextual selectors in CSS
- Adding a form to your web page

You now have your site designed and template sorted, so the next stage is to add content. Although content can easily be changed, you should still think long and hard about what content to use, and make sure that it's high quality.

A major challenge when creating content for the Web is that people using it don't tend to hang around for long—unless something grabs their attention and keeps it, they'll go elsewhere. This issue is compounded by the fact that reading on screen is much harder on the eyes than reading printed publications, due to the lower resolution of the text and glare of the screen. In fact, studies suggest that reading text on screen can take twice as long as reading text in print. People tend to skim online rather than reading from beginning to end, so you should make good use of headings and crossheads, and ensure all text is succinct. Furthermore, if you want to make it look professional, ensure everything is spell-checked and proofread. It's always a good idea to have at least one other person look over it because they'll be more likely to spot errors in text that you've been looking at for days.

If you or your clients can't write decent copy, hire someone to do it. People don't think twice about hiring sales staff, operations people, IT technicians, or, for that matter, designers, but for some reason people think they can write their own words. However, poor copy is as likely to turn someone off as anything else. Common problems include inconsistent and poor spelling and formatting, and poorly constructed and wordy sentences.

A similar level of care needs to be taken with any images you add to your site. Don't include graphics just for the sake of it—all images should be relevant, appropriate, and enhance your site. In addition, don't just stick images online as is—if an image looks better cropped, crop it. Also, take care with compression; strike a balance between detail and keeping file size down. Common mistakes with graphics tend to fall into two camps: the first is designers who refuse to sacrifice a little detail and compress the images, thereby inflicting massive download times on site visitors, who

ultimately go elsewhere. The second is designers who want everything to download as rapidly as possible, set JPEG compression to 90 percent, and wind up presenting a muddy mess. Strike a balance that is geared toward your target market. For instance, our site is about photography, so it makes sense that the images—and particularly those in the gallery, where users *choose* to download them—are not compressed too much.

Finally, take care to not infringe upon other people's copyright: only use what you or your clients have express permission to use. Do *not* just take things from other sites or scan in images for which you don't own the rights—you may get a warning, or even get sued.

## The news page

The news page doubles as the introduction to your site. It will therefore contain a brief introduction and some news items. Because this is primarily a portfolio-based site with a few pages, there's little point in having a news archive—just the most recent two or three items is enough. The graphic for this page will contain a mix of images, and underneath it will be a link to the gallery.

> *Something many designers miss is the opportunity to lead visitors around the site. The use of multiple paths to the same point can be useful, if everything's logical. Better is the use of links within body copy, where appropriate.*

**1.** Go to File ➤ New and click the Templates tab to see a list of templates for whatever sites you have set up. Selecting a site shows all related templates in the second column. Selecting a template then presents a visual preview in the third column. Therefore, choose main and click Create, as shown in Figure 8-1.

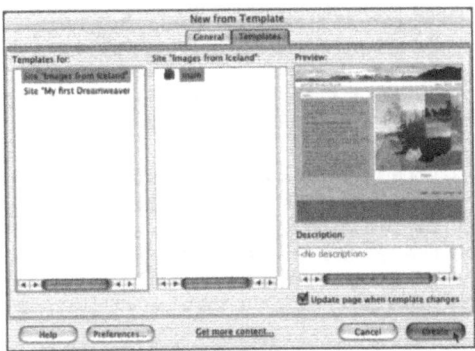

**Figure 8-1.** Choosing a template

**2.** When the template opens, you'll see something like Figure 8-2. Note that whatever content you left in your template file will be displayed by default in each new page based on the template. The "dummy" content provides you with a reminder, which is useful because you can often just select this dummy content and replace it. Note the tabbed areas—these are your editable regions. Everything else is locked and cannot be edited unless you do so by opening the template itself.

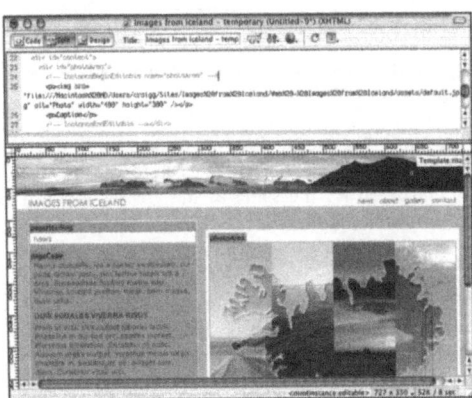

**Figure 8-2.** An unaltered page created from the template

**3.** Save this new page as index.html. Use the document window's Title field to change the page's title, amending temporary to news.

*Remember, Dreamweaver uses .htm as the default file extension, but you want .html, so you must change this manually.*

**4.** Add some succinct introductory copy (a few lines or so). Underneath this is the space for news items. In each case, add a date and brief title on its own line, and add the news item underneath. Click the line or select it and use the Properties panel's Format menu to define the line as Heading 2, as shown in Figure 8-3. Remember that you defined this style earlier in the CSS. Merely changing the format of these lines means they are styled automatically (and because their case is set, you can write September, SEPTEMBER, september, or sePtEmbEr, and the words will be rendered in uppercase—this is useful for site-wide consistency with regards to headings).

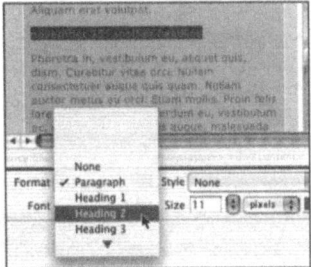

**Figure 8-3.** Formatting text as Heading 2

**115**

**5.** Add the next image to the photo area, and then add a caption. After the caption, press *SHIFT+ENTER* to produce a carriage return, and type View more images in the gallery. Select the word gallery and use the Properties panel to link it to gallery.html. This then makes that word an additional pull-in, making it obvious to site visitors what they're going to find in the gallery, as shown in Figure 8-4.

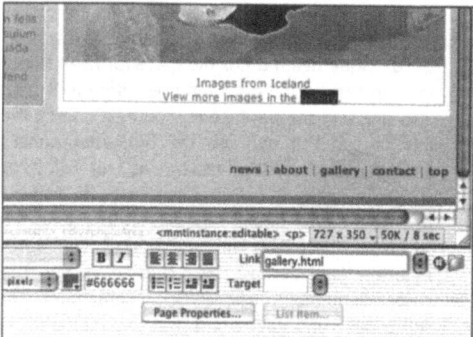

**Figure 8-4.** Adding an internal page link

*Because everything under the photo is effectively a caption, you can get away with deviating slightly from semantic mark-up in order to make the page look better.*

### The about page

In many ways, the about page is the same as the one you just created—it will just have different copy and a different image. Because of this, you can open index.html and change the content.

**1.** Open index.html and save it as about.html. Doing this right away means you won't accidentally overwrite index.html with new (and wrong) content. Once again, change the page's title, using the Title field, as shown in Figure 8-5.

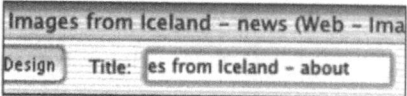

**Figure 8-5.** Changing the about page's title

**2.** Double-click the page heading graphic within the pageHeading editable area. The Select Image Source dialog box appears, enabling you to select a new graphic (choose title_about.gif). Click OK/Choose to insert the graphic, as shown in Figure 8-6.

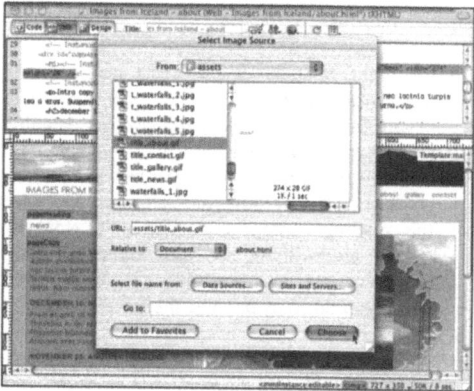

**Figure 8-6.** Choosing a new page heading graphic for the pageHeading editable area

**3.** Select the newly inserted image, and use the Properties panel to change its alt text (using the Alt field), so it's the same as the graphic (about), as shown in Figure 8-7.

**Figure 8-7.** Amending the alt text of the page heading graphic

*Remember to update your alt text every time you change the page heading graphic.*

4. Change the content in the pageCopy editable area, too. Again, general copy should be formatted as Paragraph, and any crossheads as Heading 2.

5. Change the image in the photo area. Again, this can be done by double-clicking it and selecting a different image from the assets folder, as shown in Figure 8-8. As this already has relevant alt text, that doesn't need to be changed.

6. Change the caption to reflect the new photo, as shown in Figure 8-9.

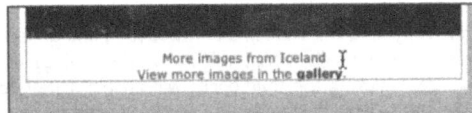

**Figure 8-9.** Editing the caption in the photoArea editable region

**Figure 8-8.** Changing the image in the photoArea editable region

# The gallery

The gallery will be different than the pages you created so far. Although the photo area won't change per se, the copy area will contain an introduction and a number of thumbnails, which will be previews of gallery images. Clicking the thumbnails will enable a user to see the full-size image and its accompanying caption. The images are all taken from digital photos and have been resized to 400 x 300. Again, when working with web images, never forget the power available to you with regards to digital tools. Sometimes cropping an image and focusing on a small portion of it can turn a mundane image into a masterpiece.

All the images required can be found in the assets folder, along with **thumbnail** versions. These are the same images shrunk down to 44 by 33 pixels. These dimensions were settled upon when working on the original layout in Photoshop, and enables us to fit five images horizontally in the copy area. A good tip to remember when creating thumbnail images from originals is: after shrinking them, use an Unsharp Mask filter to bring back some of the detail. Despite its name, it's the tool of choice for intelligently sharpening photographic images, and it works by evaluating the level of contrast between adjacent pixels, increasing this level when it's high, because large changes in contrast usually represent an edge. It's also worth differentiating your thumbnail images when you save them in your assets folder, which you can do by giving them a t_ prefix. Thus, for the case study site, the thumbnail for glaciers_1.jpg is t_glaciers_1.jpg.

## Creating the initial gallery page

1. Open one of the previously created pages, save it as gallery.html, and update its title via the Title field.

2. Update the graphical heading found in the pageHeading editable area to title_gallery.gif, as shown in Figure 8-10, and change its alt text accordingly.

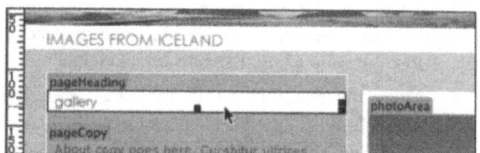

**Figure 8-10.** The updated graphic within the pageHeading editable region

3. Enter some introductory copy in the pageCopy editable region and then add the thumbnails. These should be organized into groups of five, and each group should have a heading, formatted as Heading 2. After each group of thumbnails, add a carriage return and insert another group (see Figure 8-11). Ensure these thumbnails have *no* formatting by using the Properties panel (you'll deal with margins around them later, so using the standard paragraph padding would interfere with this). Remember to provide alt text for each image, too.

4. Use the Properties panel to link each of the thumbnail images to an as-yet nonexistent HTML file. Each HTML file should be sensibly named, so the t_glacier_1.jpg thumbnail image should link to gallery_glacier_1.html, t_glacier_2.jpg should link to gallery_glacier_2.html, and so on.

> This is tedious work, but there is an alternative: insert one image, add the link, copy and paste it a number of times, and edit the copies. Of course, there's the possibility for error here, so ensure that if you use a lot of copy and paste, you thoroughly check the results. Also, note that you can often edit properties faster in Code view, rather than selecting each element and using the Properties panel.

5. As you can see, spacing is currently a problem, so you need to fix that. To do so, you'll use another contextual selector, which will affect all images within the copyArea div. In the New CSS Style dialog box, select Advanced for the Selector Type and name the Selector #copyArea img, as shown in Figure 8-12.

**Figure 8-11.** Groups of thumbnails added to the pageCopy editable region

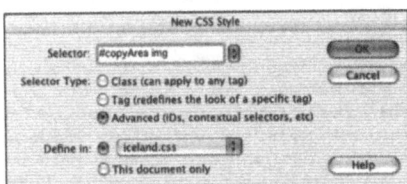

**Figure 8-12.** The New CSS Style dialog box

**6.** In the Box category, set the top margin to 0 pixels, the right margin to 0 pixels, the bottom margin to 10 pixels, and the left margin to 7 pixels, as shown in Figure 8-13. This means each image within copyArea will have a 10-pixel margin underneath and a 7-pixel margin to its left.

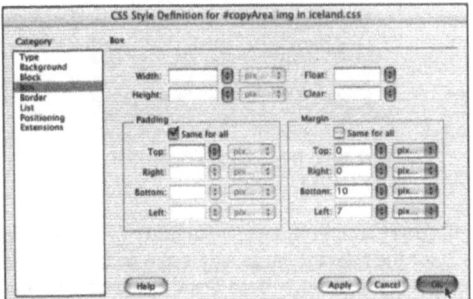

**Figure 8-13.** Defining box property values

**7.** In the Border category, set Style to solid, Width to 1 pixel, and Color to #929194, as shown in Figure 8-14.

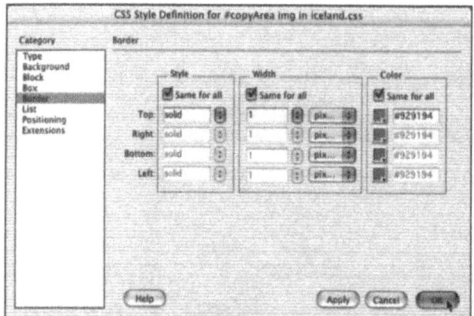

**Figure 8-14.** Defining border property values

8. As you can see, this correctly spaces the thumb-nails, but it moves the page heading graphic into the wrong place, as shown in Figure 8-15. This is because the page heading graphic is also an image within the copyArea div.

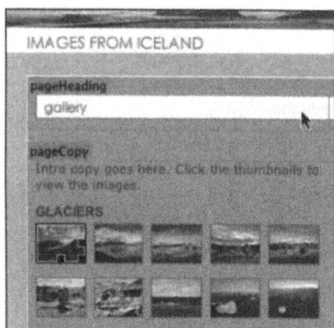

**Figure 8-15.** The web page, updated due to the newly created CSS styles

9. To get around this, create another new style, just for the relevant image, and use it to override the settings created in steps 6 and 7, but only for our page heading. So you don't have to edit any HTML, use another contextual selector named #copyArea h1 img, as shown in Figure 8-16. As you might have guessed, any styles attached to this selector will affect only images within h1 tags inside the copyArea div (the graphical page headings).

10. To override the border settings, set Style to none and Width to 0, as shown in Figure 8-17.

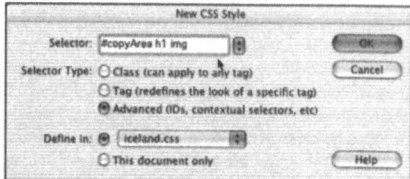

**Figure 8-16.** Creating another contextual selector

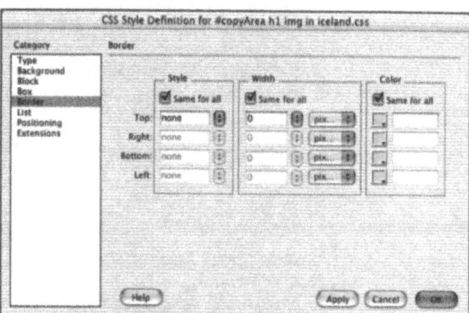

**Figure 8-17.** Defining border property values

11. To override the margin settings, check Same for all, and set Top to 0, as shown in Figure 8-18.

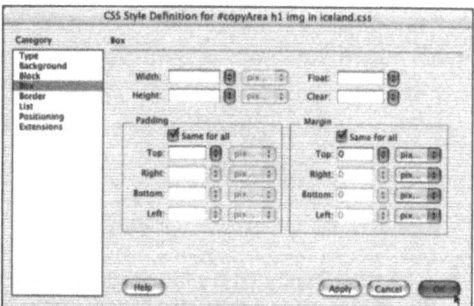

**Figure 8-18.** Defining box property values

Here's the result: the thumbnails are correctly spaced *and* the title is no longer misplaced, as shown in Figure 8-19.

12. Change the main photo and caption to the image associated with the first thumbnail image (the large version of which is glaciers_1.jpg), as shown in Figure 8-20.

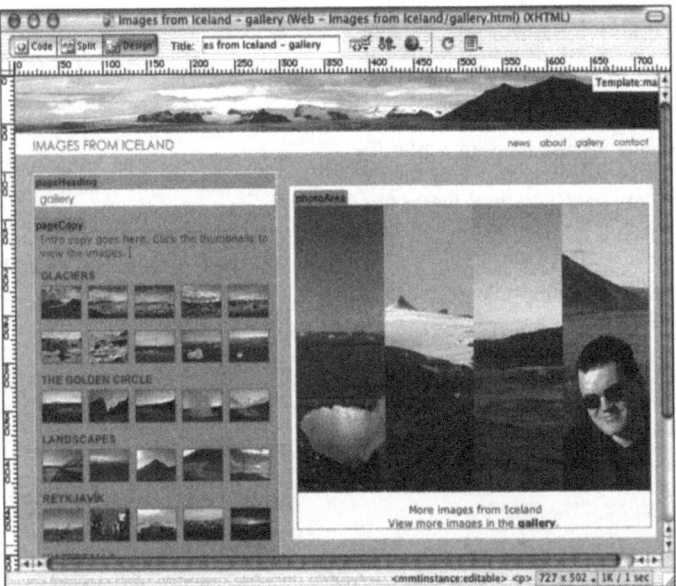

**Figure 8-19.** The resulting page—all images now have correct margins and borders

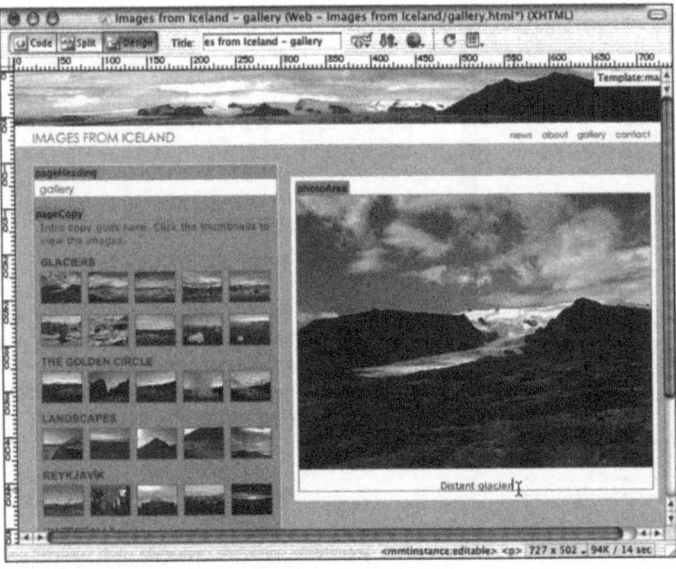

**Figure 8-20.** Changing the main photo and caption

### Creating the gallery pages

For each page of the gallery, do the following:

1. Save the previously created file with a new file name, as per those defined in step 4 of the last exercise (so, gallery_gaclier_1.html for the first, gallery_glacier_2.html for the second, and so on).

2. Change the image and caption, as shown in step 12 of the previous exercise.

3. After doing this for all files, you'll end up with something like what is shown in Figure 8-21. This is a bit messy in terms of file structure, so it would be good to move these gallery files to their own folder.

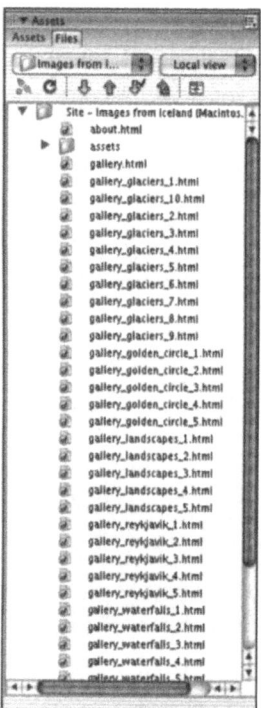

**Figure 8-21.** All the gallery files, as shown in the Files panel

> Like images, HTML *files can be organized into folders.*

4. Save and close all files before doing any file management. If you require more space in which to work, expand the Files panel via the Expand/Collapse button, as shown in Figure 8-22. Go to File ➤ New Folder in the Files panel drop-down menu (the one at the top right), as shown in Figure 8-23. Name the new folder gallery.

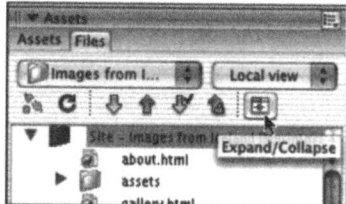

**Figure 8-22.** Expanding the Files panel

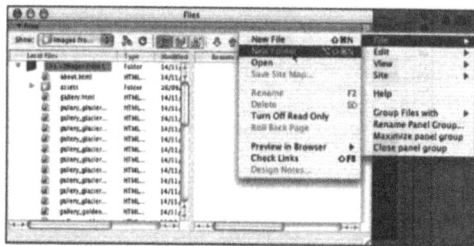

**Figure 8-23.** Creating a new folder using the Files panel

5. Drag all the gallery files except gallery.html (which is effectively the front page of the gallery, and can therefore stay in the site root) into the folder created in the previous step. Dreamweaver prompts you to update the files. Unless you want hundreds of broken links, click Update, as shown in Figure 8-24.

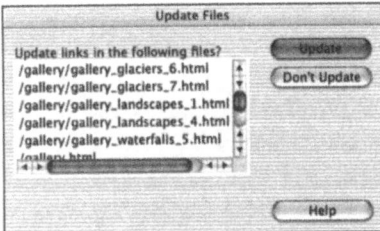

**Figure 8-24.** The Update Files dialog box

You're done!

*And yes, this was a **very** long-winded way of creating a gallery, but it's the simplest. However, adding a new image means editing all the pages. There are two solutions to this: the first is to use an embedded template and lock the thumbnails. A much better solution is outlined in the next chapter (in the "A better gallery" section).*

## Creating the contact page

The final page will enable visitors to contact us. What you include here will depend on the nature of your site. If it's business-oriented, be sure that you provide as many means of contact as possible. Supplying only e-mail addresses will both frustrate your visitors and make your organization look extremely suspicious. However, for a personal site, supplying just an e-mail address or a basic contact form is fine.

For your case study, there is the possibility of commissions, so you need to provide a range of contact details. Use the copy area for written details: your address, phone number, and e-mail address. The photo area will be repurposed for a contact form.

*Contact forms are a great way of getting specific information from site visitors, but beware: do not create massive forms that take a long time to fill in—people simply won't bother. Ask for the bare minimum of details and ensure that your privacy policy is within easy reach. If you don't have a privacy policy, tell visitors that you will not use their details for any means other than to contact them. Furthermore, do not use the fact that someone emailed you as an excuse to add them to a mailing list.*

1. Open `index.html`, save the new file as `contact.html`, change the page's title via the Title field, change the graphic within the pageHeading editable region (to `title_contact.gif`) as shown in Figure 8-25, and change its alt text, as you've done with the pages created previously.

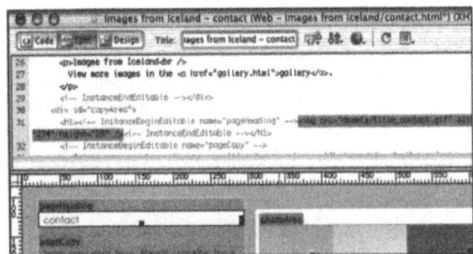

**Figure 8-25.** Changing the page heading graphic within the pageHeading editable region

2. Use the copy area on the left for text-based content. Format it as paragraphs, and separate it by crossheads formatted as Heading 2, as shown in Figure 8-26.

**123**

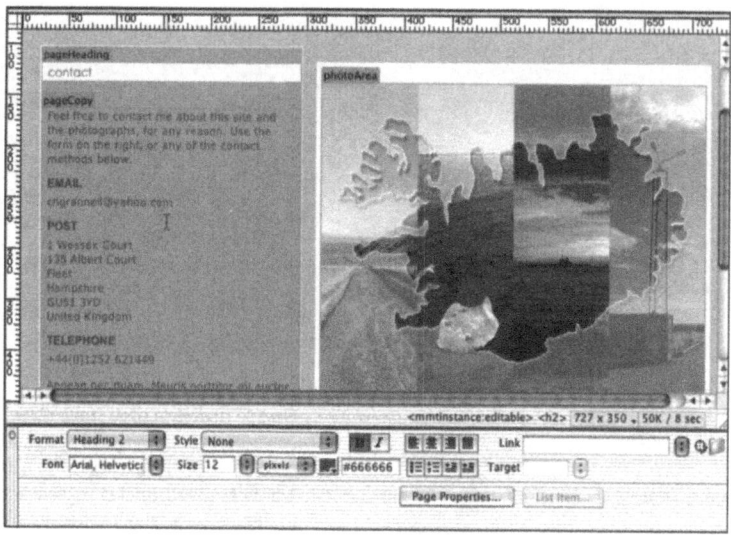

**Figure 8-26.** Formatting text as paragraphs and headings

**3.** For the e-mail address, select the relevant text and use the Link field in the Properties panel to add your address. This must be preceded by mailto: (for example, `mailto:youraddress@yourdomain.com`), as shown in Figure 8-27.

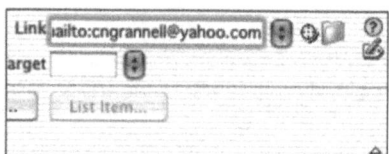

**Figure 8-27.** Defining some text as a mailto: link

**4.** To build an e-mail form, first remove all the content from the photo area.

For personal sites, we use a Yahoo! e-mail address because it handles the inevitable spam that comes in droves once your e-mail address is seen online pretty well. If you want to cut down on spam—particularly if you're using a personal e-mail account—try encoding the e-mail address. A good place for this is www.hiveware.com/enkoder_form.php (see Figure 8-28), whose online form enables you to create an output for XHTML or HTML, depending on your site's other mark-up. The output is complex enough to fool the majority of spidering software that surfs the Web, harvesting e-mail addresses, although it is a little weighty. Once the form has done its thing, simply copy the results and paste it into Code view, in place of `<a href="mailto:youremailaddress@yourdomain.com">youremailaddress@yourdomain.com</a>`.

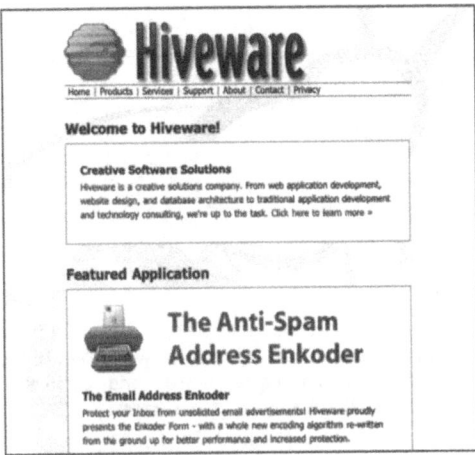

Figure 8-28. The Hiveware website, home of Enkoder

5. To override the automatic centering of content, add another div within the photo area, set text-align for all paragraphs to left, and give it an ID of formArea, as shown in Figure 8-29.

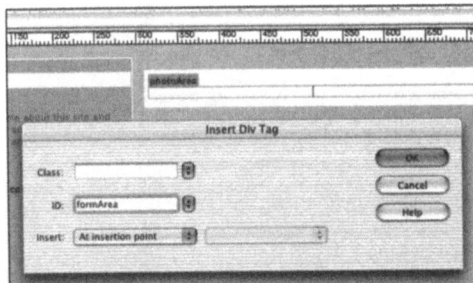

Figure 8-29. Adding a div within the photoArea editable region

6. Open the New CSS Style dialog box, set Selector Type to Advanced, and Selector to #formArea p, as shown in Figure 8-30.

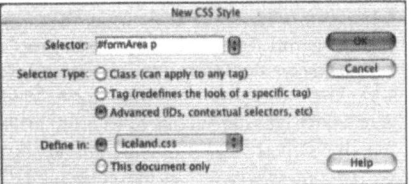

Figure 8-30. The New CSS Style dialog box

Note that we called this div formArea and not merely form. This is because "form" is an HTML element. Naming the div directly after an HTML element could cause problems with regards to browsers rendering the page properly. In fact, you should **never** use an HTML element name for any CSS class or ID.

7. In the CSS Style Definition dialog box, set Block ➤ Text align to left and Box ➤ Padding ➤ Left to 20 pixels.

8. Use Code view to check for a superfluous paragraph under the newly created div tag. If there's one there, as shown in Figure 8-31, remove it.

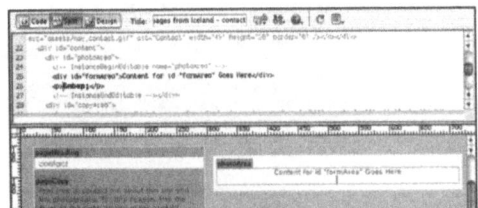

Figure 8-31. A superfluous paragraph tag under the div tag

9. Select and delete all content from formArea div. Choose Forms from the Insert bar drop-down menu and click the Form button, as shown in Figure 8-32. Then, using the Properties panel, find the Action field, type the full URL to your CGI mailform, and choose post as your Method and application/x-www-form-urlencoded as the Encoding type, as shown in Figure 8-33.

**Figure 8-32.** The Form button in the Insert bar

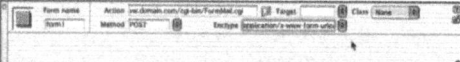

**Figure 8-33.** Defining form attribute values using the Properties panel

> *If you're creating a site for yourself, ask your ISP whether you have access to a mailform script on your hosting space. Alternatively, check your* cgi-bin *for* FormMail.pl, FormMail.cgi, *or a similar sounding name. Likewise when creating sites for clients. If you don't have access to a mailform script, we'll show you how to set one up later in the chapter.*

10. Add text to denote what each of your form fields will be, as shown in Figure 8-34. We've kept to the bare minimum: name, e-mail, and comments, although this is enough in most cases.

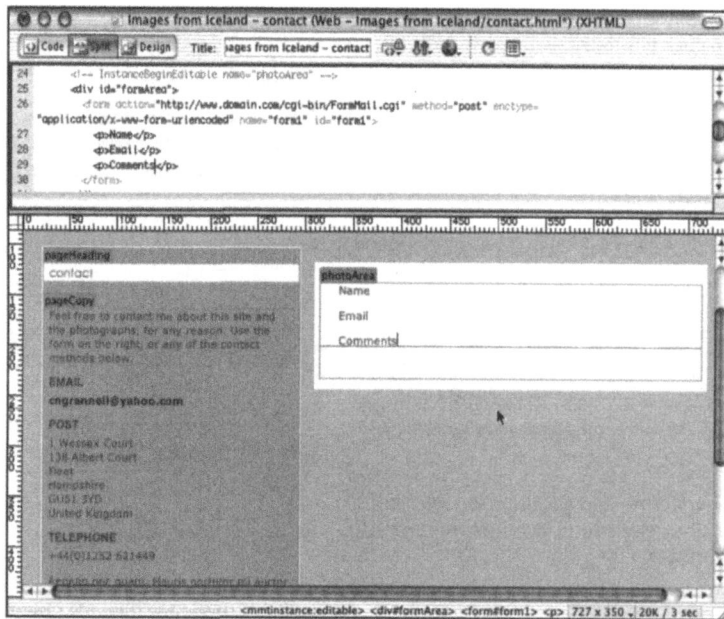

**Figure 8-34.** Adding form field titles

One slight problem with this method of laying out a form is that paragraphs within forms can cause problems with some versions of Netscape Navigator 4, a dated browser that's still fairly common in some educational establishments. Because your site won't be displayed correctly in that browser anyway, and because it's primarily aimed at people using relatively modern browsers, we'll carry on using paragraphs for form field layout. However, it's perfectly possible to lay out form fields within a table, which all versions of Netscape Navigator 4 have no problems with.

**11.** The process for setting up the name and e-mail fields are identical. Click after the end of the relevant word inserted in step 8 and press *SHIFT+ENTER* to enter a carriage return. Then go to Forms on the Insert bar and click the Text Field button, as shown in Figure 8-35.

**Figure 8-35.** The Text Field button on the Insert bar

**12.** Note that if you have the form accessibility option turned on (via Preferences ➤ Accessibility), you may see the dialog box shown in Figure 8-36 when inserting form fields. The idea behind labels and access keys is to provide keyboard access to various form elements, although support for this is not consistent in browsers. An explanation of these elements is beyond the scope of this book. However, there is a nasty little gotcha for those of you who come across this dialog box. By default, the Style radio button is set to Wrap with label tag, and clicking OK will mean your page's HTML ends up with empty label tags. Therefore, select No label, and Dreamweaver remembers your selection for next time. Click OK to continue.

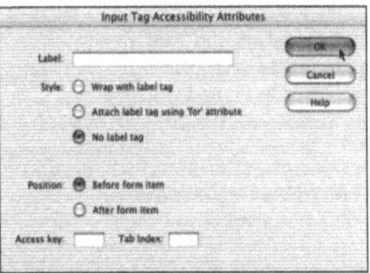

**Figure 8-36.** How to set options in the Input Tag Accessibility Attributes dialog box

**13.** Click the newly inserted field in Design view. At the bottom left of the Properties panel is an empty field where you can enter a name for the field. What you put here will depend on the requirements of your mailform script. For the popular FormMail, this needs to be realname, as shown in Figure 8-37.

**Figure 8-37.** Defining the name/id attribute of a text field

**14.** Do the same for the e-mail field, naming it email.

**15.** Add a field for the comments, but not a straight text field, which is only one line high. Instead, add a text area (inserted by using the Textarea button on the Insert bar), as shown in Figure 8-38.

**Figure 8-38.** The Textarea button on the Insert bar

**16.** Set Num Lines to however many lines high you want the text area to be—five is more than enough. Name it—we used comments, as shown in Figure 8-39.

**Figure 8-39.** Naming the text area using the Properties panel

**127**

**17.** Use the Button button to add ... a button (logical, huh?). By default, this adds the ubiquitous Submit button to your page, which you don't need to do anything to, as shown in Figure 8-40.

**Figure 8-40.** Adding a Submit button

*If you like, you can add a second button and set its Action to Reset, as seen on many websites. All this does is set a form to its default state. This is often clicked by accident, meaning the user has to start filling in the form again from scratch, and we don't really see any benefit of including such a button, so there's no need to add one to the case study site.*

**18.** Add a number of hidden fields in order to provide some added functionality to your form. Each is added via the Hidden field button, as shown in Figure 8-41.

**Figure 8-41.** The Hidden field button in the Insert bar

The names and values of these fields will depend on the script you're using. In our case, there are three name/value pairs, listed in Table 8-1.

**Table 8-1.** Name and Value Pairs for Hidden Form Fields

| Name | Value |
| --- | --- |
| recipient | An e-mail address where the results are to be sent |
| subject | Whatever you want to appear in the e-mail client's subject field when a form is received, as shown in Figure 8-42 |
| redirect | The full URL of the page where the visitor is to be sent after the form is sent. |

**Figure 8-42.** Adding hidden field values using the Properties panel

**19.** The form is now complete, but it doesn't look all that hot. You need to add some classes to your CSS via the New CSS Style dialog box. The first is to affect the Tag, form. When defining the style, set the top margin to *20 pixels.*

*By now you should know how to edit styles without us telling you how to open the dialog boxes. If unsure, look back at some previous exercises you've worked on.*

**20.** Add a class called .formField, which has a solid, 1-pixel border, with the color #929194, padding of 2 pixels, and a width of 300 pixels.

**21.** Add another class, .formFieldSubmit, which has a solid, 2-pixel border, also with a color of #929194, a width of 80 pixels, padding of 3 pixels at the top and bottom, and 7 pixels at the left and right.

**22.** Add the classes to the relevant fields. Click each in Design view and use the Class drop-down menu in the Properties panel to add the formField class to the text fields and text area, as shown in Figure 8-43, and formFieldSumbit to the Submit button.

**Figure 8-43.** Adding classes to form fields

*Note that the styling of form fields does not work consistently across all browsers. Some, such as Safari, ignore border settings. However, all current browsers recognize the width and padding settings, providing you with more layout control over your form fields.*

**23.** To create the redirect page linked to in step 15, save `contact.html`, duplicate it, and provide it with the name written in step 15 (in our case, `contact_thanks.html`). Then make a small change to the page, perhaps putting a "thank you for emailing us" message above the form.

> *Remember to save each page again once you've completed each exercise!*

### Setting up FormMail

Most hosting companies now include a preconfigured mailform by default as part of a hosting package. In fact, even free web space often comes with a shared form, so check with your hosting provider or ISP prior to trying to set one up for yourself. In order to set one up, you need access to a **cgi-bin**. We're going to work with FormMail, a free script that you can download from Matt's Script Archive: `www.scriptarchive.com/formmail.html`. You may want to use a newer alternative, nms FormMail, available from `www.scriptarchive.com/nms.html` and `http://nms-cgi.sourceforge.net/`.

**1.** Unzip the downloaded file and open `FormMail.pl` in a text editor (such as Notepad on Windows or BBEdit on Mac). This must be a plain text editor that doesn't interfere with the file in any way; otherwise the script may fail when it's uploaded.

**2.** Change the first line to match the location of Perl on your server. Initially, this is `#!/usr/bin/perl`. You can get this from your web host.

**3.** If necessary, change the line `$mailprog = '/usr/lib/sendmail -i -t';` to match the location of sendmail on the server. Again, this is information you can get from your web host.

**4.** Change the referrers line (`@referers = ('scriptarchive.com','209.196.21.3');`) to include the domain and IP address of the site that will be using the form.

**5.** If e-mail responses need to be sent to a domain other than that on which the website is hosted, populate the recipients line (`@recipients = &fill_recipients(@referers);`) with the relevant domains (such as `@recipients = ('domain.com', 'anotherdomain.com');`). This stops your copy of FormMail from being used by people on any server.

**6.** Depending on your server's preference, you may have to rename the file `FormMail.cgi` prior to uploading it.

**7.** Upload the file to your cgi-bin and update its permissions, as shown in Figure 8-44. Your FTP client may display this information in a different format. To bring up this option, you can usually right/*Ctrl*-click the `FormMail.cgi` file and choose information from a context menu. Some FTP clients have an option that refers to the Unix command to change file permissions: CHMOD. If so, the setting should be 755.

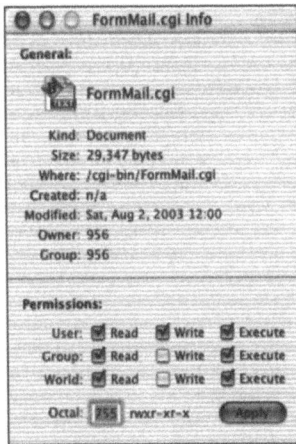

**Figure 8-44.** Setting permissions for `FormMail.cgi`

> *If you get errors when trying to use your form, once your site is uploaded, thoroughly check all links and permissions, along with the settings in the mailform itself.*

## Summary

In this chapter, you worked on a number of things relating to the content of your web pages. You learned about best practice for text and images, created all your pages for your site, and then populated them with relevant content. You worked with more advanced CSS, and also added a form to your contact page.

So, the site done ... or is it? It's true that you could stop right now—after all, the pages are built and the content has been added—but there are numerous things still to do. The most important is testing the site in a range of web browsers and fixing any major problems. Furthermore, you can also make a number of improvements to what you've done so far, most notably on the gallery page. And that's exactly what you're going to do in the next chapter.

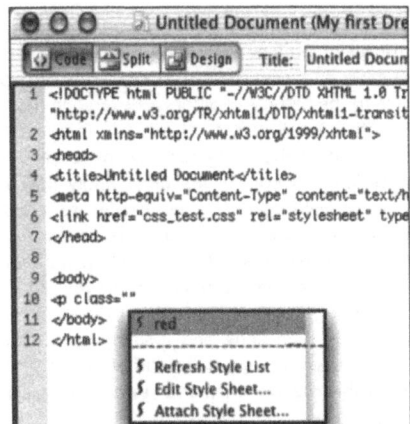

## Chapter 9

# WORKING WITH CODE

**What we'll cover in this chapter**

- Setting Dreamweaver preferences
- Exploring Code view
- Working with Code Hints
- Enhancing web pages by adding JavaScript
- Checking the compatibility of your site

The prospect of working with **code** often scares new web designers and even some seasoned pros. Perhaps this is due to the barrage of acronyms everyone has to contend with—ASP, PHP, XML, HTML, JSP, CSS, and so on—or it could be that using code seems so alien to *graphic* design. However, if you don't know how to directly manipulate code, it's far harder to create cutting-edge sites, and near impossible to optimize them. Code also enables you to create a bunch of cool things that would otherwise be impossible (or at least very tricky) using visual design tools. In the long run, working directly with code and creating such "cool things" can actually save you time and effort, as you'll see later in this chapter when you rework the gallery into a single page.

You're already familiar with Code view—you used it in earlier exercises to make a few adjustments to your HTML. Now you're going to look at it in depth, checking out the available preferences and working through some code-centric exercises.

## A different view

As mentioned this earlier in the book, Dreamweaver has three views: Code, Split, and Design, as shown in Figure 9-1. In this chapter, you should be working either in Code view, or Split, which shows both Code and Design at the same time.

**Figure 9-1.** Click these buttons to switch between views.

## Code preferences

As you might expect, Dreamweaver has a number of preferences relating to Code view. It's worth taking the time to familiarize yourself with these options— although they may sometimes seem decorative or intrusive, most make your job far easier. Note that the vast majority of Dreamweaver's default settings are fine, but we'll mention preferred ones nonetheless, just

in case you've adjusted certain settings. Selecting Edit ➤ Preferences (Dreamweaver ➤ Preferences on Mac) displays the pane you'll be working with in this section. You can also access the preferences via CTRL+U/CMD+U.

## General

This section of the Preferences panel enables you to fine-tune how Dreamweaver works with regards to dialog boxes, some aspects of editing your pages, and language settings. The Document options group's default settings are fine, although if you don't want an update links confirmation dialog box to appear when you move files, you can change Prompt to Always on the Update links when moving files drop-down menu, as shown in Figure 9-2. As mentioned earlier in the book, this panel is also where you toggle the start page.

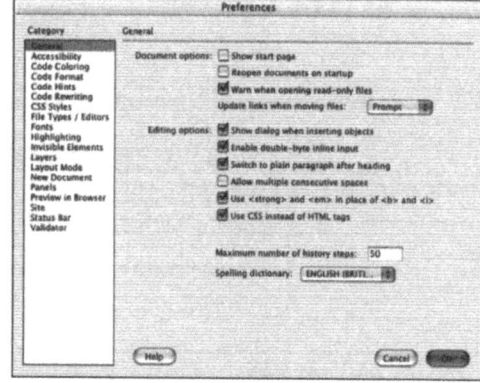

**Figure 9-2.** General preferences

Editing options deals with options related to editing your web pages. Again, the default settings are fine for general use, and are geared to a more modern way of working—for instance, the use of **logical** font styles (such as <strong> and <em>) instead of **physical** font styles (<b> and <i>) is recommended because it assists people using screen readers.

The most likely options to be changed in this section are Maximum number of history steps and Spelling dictionary. Both are pretty self-explanatory. Setting the former to a lower number may speed Dreamweaver up on slower systems, whereas the latter should obviously be set to whatever language you're working with. Take care when using English, as there are several versions, including American English and British English, so ensure you choose the right one for your target market.

## Accessibility

Remember, by default, the accessibility options are turned off, but some are very useful in assisting you in tailoring your pages to those with disabilities. For instance, checking the Images box, as shown in Figure 9-3, means Dreamweaver always prompts you for alt text when images are inserted. Leaving this option unchecked means you'll most likely forget to add alt text much of the time. Accessibility for forms is somewhat more complex and beyond the scope of this book, so we've left that unchecked.

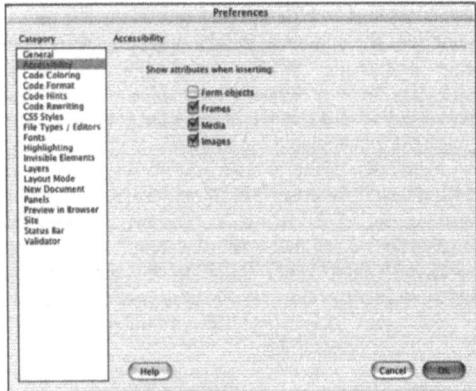

**Figure 9-3.** Accessibility preferences

## Code coloring

By default, Dreamweaver assigns certain colors to specific tags, CSS values, and so on. This enables you to pick things out from a soup of code quickly, such as links and image tags.

To modify the colors for a particular language (such as HTML), just click the relevant language in the Document Type pane, and then click Edit Coloring Scheme. You can edit the settings via the Text Color drop-down menu on the right side of the dialog box, as well as make specific tags bold, italic, and underlined, as shown in Figure 9-4. However, it's best to avoid such text decoration because it usually makes things confusing when working in Code view.

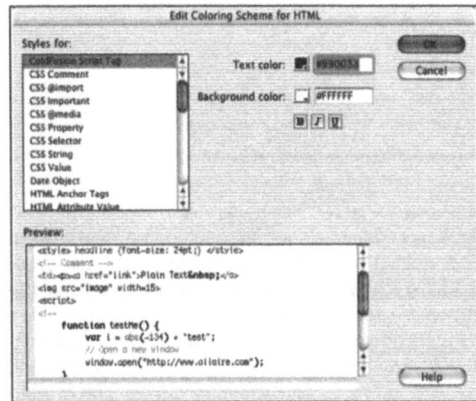

**Figure 9-4.** Editing the coloring scheme for HTML

Although you'll probably never need to edit these colors, people used to working with code in another application might want to change the colors to suit whatever they're used to.

## Code Format

The Code Format preferences are more important because using certain settings can sometimes affect how your page is displayed in web browsers, and make your code harder to edit. Although several of these settings can be ignored or changed to your own personal preference, *always* turn off Automatic Wrapping, as shown in Figure 9-5.

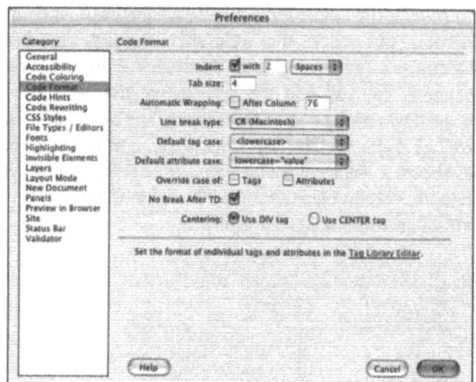

**Figure 9-5.** Code format preferences

Enabling Automatic Wrapping might make your code look nicer when viewing the source in a web browser that doesn't support line wrapping, but it can cause errors in your site. This is because some browsers parse the white space created by Automatic Wrapping, which causes odd gaps to appear in your pages. Admittedly, this is rare but it's infuriating when it happens, and deleting the automatic-wrapping spaces out of your pages is a tedious task, especially when they're placed within large amounts of copy. Note that you can get code to soft wrap (which is non-destructive) by selecting Word Wrap from the View Options menu, as shown in Figure 9-6.

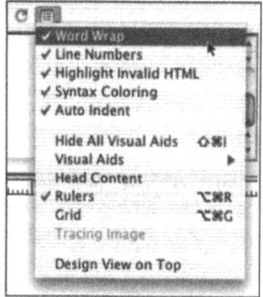

**Figure 9-6.** Selecting Word Wrap from the View Options menu

Line wrapping means that lines of code fit within the current window. Some browsers, such as Internet Explorer for Windows, use source code editors (in this case, Notepad) that don't initially display line wrapping. The upshot is that you have to scroll horizontally when perusing code. However, this won't affect you as a designer so you shouldn't worry about it. After all, you'll always use Dreamweaver for viewing your source code, not a browser.

There are also very important options in this section with which you specify tag and attribute cases. Dreamweaver's default settings for tags and attributes are both lowercase and you should leave this alone, even if it's often easier to make out tags in uppercase. This is because XHTML calls for lowercase for all tags and attributes. Using uppercase tags in XHTML creates invalid web pages.

Other settings include the ability to indent code—a good idea if you want to be able to edit anything with ease—and change the Line Break type to a specific operating system's default. Mucking about with line breaks won't make a lot of difference to your sites unless you're sending them to someone who's working on a different platform than you. It's usually best to ensure Line break type is set to whatever system you're working on, be it Macintosh, Windows, or Unix. No Break After TD should remain selected. It ensures that whatever content goes inside table cells won't be indented, and therefore no odd little spaces will appear in your layout. Again, some browsers will present a gap if you have code like this:

```
<td> <img src="an_image.jpg" height="100"
width="100" alt="Image" /></td>
```

Other browsers won't. It's never a good idea to leave these things to chance.

The final option concerns centering, and seeing as the <center> tag is now deprecated, you should set Dreamweaver to use the div tag (although, as we've shown, centering is better controlled via CSS).

## Code Hints

Code Hints will be explained in depth later in the chapter. They are one of Dreamweaver's greatest innovations, and Dreamweaver MX 2004 extends them to incorporate CSS. Essentially, they enable you to quickly insert tags and attributes when working in Code view. Unless you have a photographic memory or a fetish for typing HTML and CSS attributes, it's best to leave them on. The same goes for Auto Tag Completion. Setting Delay to 0, as shown in Figure 9-7, is also a good idea because it enables you to write code rapidly by using the arrow and ENTER keys on your keyboard rather than directly typing out code or portions of code.

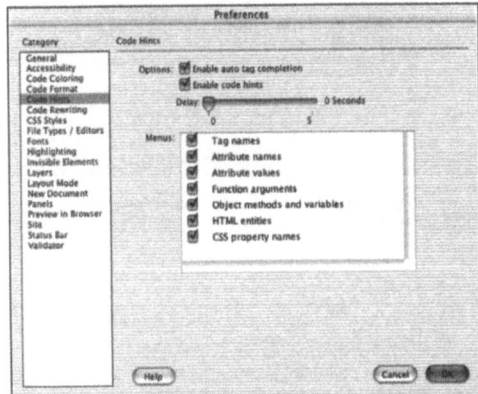

**Figure 9-7.** Code Hints preferences

## Code Rewriting

This area determines what Dreamweaver does when opening documents. After you've worked with code for a while, you'll be the best judge of which of these options to enable and disable. Dreamweaver sometimes gets confused with regards to nested tags, so the first option is usually best left disabled, as shown in Figure 9-8.

However, if you're using Code Hints and continually getting extra closing tags, such as

```
<p>I am a paragraph.</p></p>
```

then you should enable Remove Extra Closing Tags.

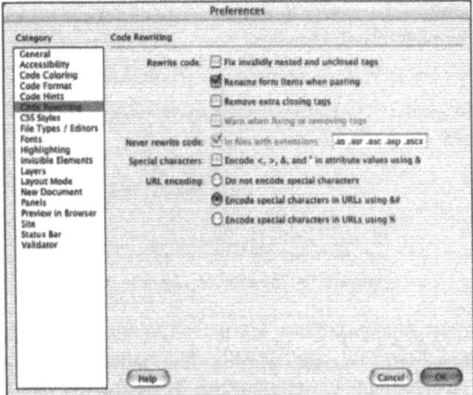

**Figure 9-8.** Code rewriting preferences

## View Options

The next set of definable options you're going to look at aren't in the Preferences panel. Instead, they're found in the View Options button's menu, shown in Figure 9-9 (the button is located at the top of your document windows).

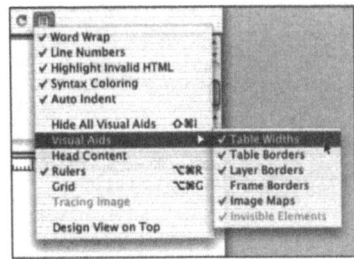

**Figure 9-9.** Setting visual aids via the View Options menu

To make your life easier, select everything on the main menu. Word Wrap soft wraps lines of code to the window width so you don't have to scroll to view long lines of code. Line Numbers are useful when debugging, as is Highlight Invalid HTML. Syntax Coloring should only be disabled if you enjoy looking at a sea of black characters.

If you open a page that immediately displays errors, you may have ventured into the Browser Check menu, as shown in Figure 9-10. This menu enables you to

**137**

dynamically check the compatibility of pages against a number of web browsers.

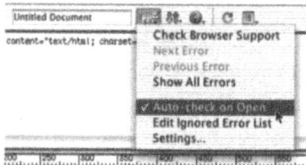

**Figure 9-10.** The Browser Check button's menu

Clicking Settings brings up the Target Browsers dialog box. Here, you can fine-tune the settings to taste. When working to web standards, as we are, you should ensure Netscape Navigator is set to version 6 or above, as shown in Figure 9-11, because version 4 has poor support for these standards and will therefore cause Dreamweaver to find plenty of browser errors, when there are no de facto errors in the page.

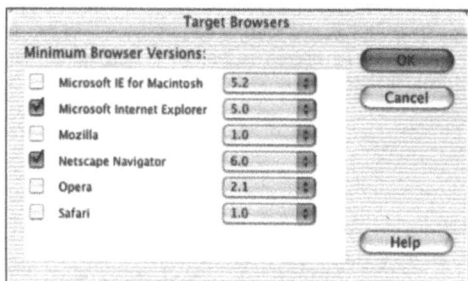

**Figure 9-11.** The Target Browsers dialog box

# Working with code

First, don't panic. Make regular backups of your pages and store them in a safe place, which is *outside* your website folder. At the very least, you should take backups on a daily basis. If you're working on a particularly complex piece of code and slightly unsure of what you're doing, save milestones when you get specific things working. Then, if you make an error that causes problems, you can just revert to the previous version.

One major Dreamweaver feature that is often overlooked is the Reference panel, shown in Figure 9-12.

Pressing *SHIFT+F1* displays this panel and makes various guides accessible via a drop-down menu. Along with being a great way to check on specifics regarding HTML, CSS, JavaScript, and more, this panel is also a good way to learn. For instance, the HTML reference guide includes a brief description of each tag, lists all the attributes, and points out anything that is deprecated (removed from the official HTML specification, as drawn up by W3C).

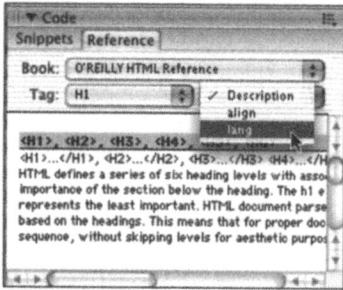

**Figure 9-12.** The Reference panel contains helpful guides.

The reason you should store backups elsewhere is that if you don't, template changes will affect the backed-up pages along with the ones you are working on. But remember, if you're trying to test code that you've saved elsewhere and it has direct links to other things in your site, those links may not work because you've changed the location of the file. All relative links must be tested from the website folder.

### Adding HTML tags and elements

Although raw coding usually gives you a greater degree of control—at least if you know what you're doing—it can be dull and time consuming. Dreamweaver enables you to do away with the bulk of the tedium by using Code Hints. This simple concept is basically a context-sensitive drop-down menu that appears under any given element that you're adding. By using the arrow keys, you can key in tags and attributes remarkably quickly. Code Hints works with HTML, CSS, and JavaScript, and it can even point out things you may have forgotten, as you'll see in the following exercise. Note that in this exercise, you're once again working in your My first Dreamweaver site test site.

1. Select My first Dreamweaver site from the Files panel, and open a new XHTML document. As yet this isn't attached to any site, and it uses no templates. It's just the most basic XHTML document you can get, as set up by default in Dreamweaver (shown in Figure 9-13).

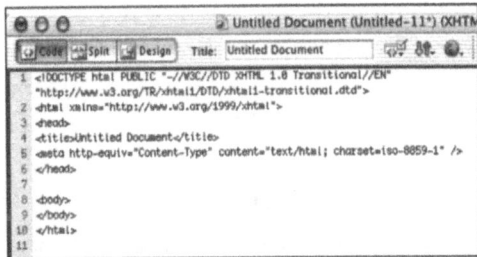

**Figure 9-13.** The default Dreamweaver XHTML document

As you've likely noticed, **HTML tags** are enclosed within less than (<) and greater than (>) symbols, also referred to as **angle brackets**. An **opening** or **start** tag looks like this: <tag>. The closing or **end** tag looks the same, but with a forward slash added, like this: </tag>. Tags are used to mark up HTML elements.

*All elements, including those without any content, must have a closing tag in XHTML. Whereas in HTML, you can get away with: <p><img src="my_image,jpg">, in XHTML you need to do this: <p><img src="my_image.jpg" /></p>. Note the addition of the end tag, and the trailing slash for the image tag. The same is true for meta tags, line breaks/carriage returns (<br> in HTML, but <br /> in XHTML), and several other tags. If in doubt, check the guidelines in the Reference panel. Also, note that when closing tags that have no content, you should leave a space prior to the trailing slash; otherwise older browsers, notably Netscape Navigator 4, won't display the tag accurately, or in some cases, at all.*

2. In your new document, type the very first character of an opening tag (<). The Code Hints menu appears, as shown in Figure 9-14, providing you with a list of all available tags. Of course, scrolling through the list would be somewhat tedious, so type a letter, such as P.

**Figure 9-14.** Activating the Code Hints menu

*If this isn't working, you need to turn Code Hints on—see how earlier in the chapter.*

The list immediately snaps to the first tag that starts with the letter you just typed. In this case, it's scrolled to <> p, indicating a paragraph tag. At this point, you can move up or down the list, select a different option, and press *Enter* to insert it. Once you've got the hang of where tags appear, you can choose how to work. The menu is context-sensitive, so for instance, to access the <option> tag, you only need to type <*op* for the menu to display it. Alternatively, because this is the last tag that begins with the letter O, you could start by typing P, press the up arrow, and then press *Enter* to choose it, as shown in Figure 9-15. Try experimenting with different methods, and see which is fastest for you.

**139**

**Figure 9-15.** Type a letter and the Code Hints menu snaps to the relevant selection.

3. Type a space after the p. The drop-down menu changes, showing a number of attributes associated with the tag, as shown in Figure 9-16. Again, you can use the arrow keys to move through the list, or start typing the first characters of an attribute to display it in the menu.

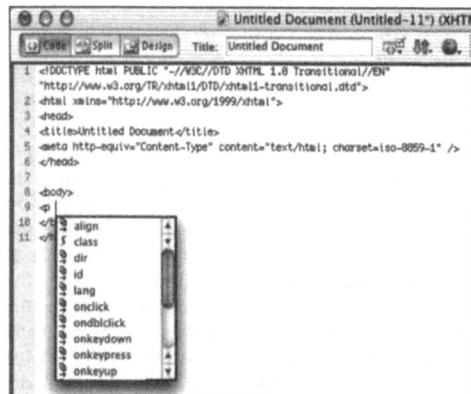

**Figure 9-16.** A Code Hints attribute list

4. Choose class in order to utilize some styling from your CSS. However, this is a totally new page and you've not yet attached a style sheet. As you can see, Dreamweaver not only reminds you of this fact, but additionally provides options to Refresh,

Edit, or Attach a style sheet via the menu, as shown in Figure 9-17. Because attaching a style sheet at this point would create a full link to the file on your hard drive, you should save this document before going any further (we used the file name working_with_code.html). Should you forget to do this, Dreamweaver will update all links when you finally save the file.

**Figure 9-17.** Working with style sheets using the Code Hints menu

5. Attach the CSS created earlier in the book (css_test.css) via Attach Style Sheet. Note that going back to the tag won't always bring back the drop-down menu right away. A workaround for this is simply to delete and reenter the attribute. Upon selecting class once again you see the class you defined way back at the start of this book (red), as shown in Figure 9-18.

**Figure 9-18.** Applying styles using the Code Hints menu

6. Press *ENTER* to add the class and close the attribute with a second quote mark. If you add another space after the class attribute, you can add more attributes to the tag. When typing a > symbol, Dreamweaver automatically closes the tag (in this case adding </p>). The cursor is then positioned for you to add content, as shown in Figure 9-19.

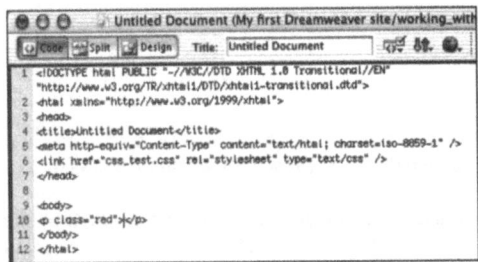

**Figure 9-19.** Complete an element by pressing *ENTER*.

7. While undoubtedly useful, this feature can be slightly awkward when trying to add code around information already in your document. Add some content intended to go in a table, as shown in Figure 9-20.

**Figure 9-20.** Some content intended for table cells

8. Use the Code Hints menu to add a table and its associated attributes, and note how the tag closes prior to the content, as shown in Figure 9-21.

**Figure 9-21.** The table element, closed prior to the content intended to go within it

9. Rather than constantly deleting and entering tags, it's usually simpler to set up the entire table and then select and drag content into it once you're done. Therefore, set up a table with a single row and two columns, as shown in Figure 9-22.

**Figure 9-22.** A row and two cells within the table element

10. For both pieces of text, select the content, as shown in Figure 9-23.

**141**

**Figure 9-23.** Selecting content in Code view

**11.** Place the content within the correct tag, as shown in Figure 9-24.

**Figure 9-24.** Dropping content within a table cell

Remember that if all this viewing of code is becoming a bit eye-boggling, you can switch to Design or Split view to check out an approximation of how things look, as shown in Figure 9-25.

> Note that when you change code in Code view, the Design view usually has to be refreshed using the options that appear on the Properties panel.

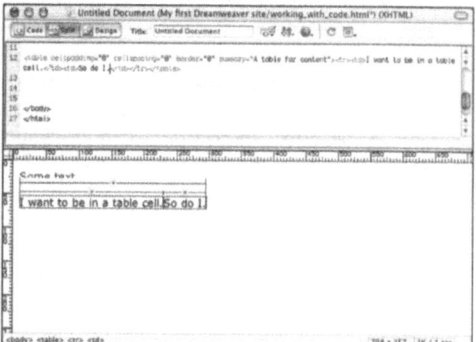

**Figure 9-25.** Checking how the page looks in Split view

Because Dreamweaver automatically closes tags and then assumes you're going to add content, take care to not end up with something like the following, which has incorrectly nested two table cells within each other rather than placing them next to each other:

<table><tr><td><td></td></td></tr></table>

Although this may not look like a huge mistake, something along these lines can mess up an entire web page layout. What you should have is something like this:

<table><tr>**<td></td><td></td>**</tr></table>

## The Tag Editor

If you're relatively new to HTML, there's going to be some trial and error when playing around with various tag attributes. Therefore, check out Dreamweaver's Tag Editor, shown in Figure 9-26. To access this, click a tag in Code view and go to Modify ➤ Edit Tag, or right/CONTROL-click an item in Code or Design view and choose Edit Tag.

In the Tag Editor, almost every aspect of any tag can be edited, and attributes are logically grouped in order to make it clear whether, for instance, they are specific to browsers, tie into the CSS, and so on. Generally, browser-specific items should be ignored unless authoring for a corporate Intranet, where all the users have the same browser.

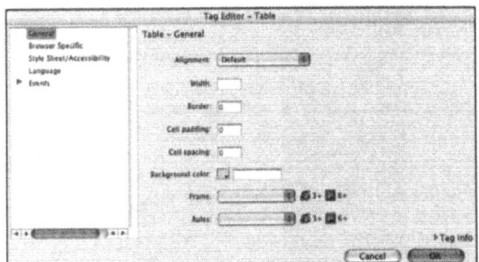

**Figure 9-26.** Editing a tag using the Tag Editor

Two additional areas of information are available: Tag Info (shown in Figure 9-27) displays information about the tag you're editing (this information is also shown in the Reference panel), and Events enables you to add JavaScript events (although you have to type the contents yourself).

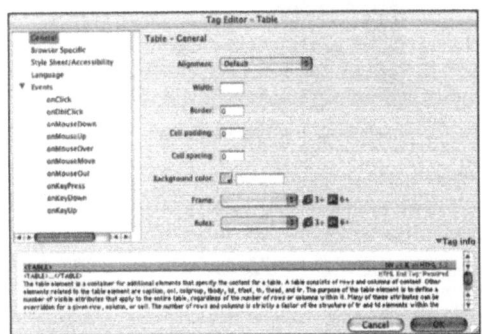

**Figure 9-27.** Viewing tag information via the Tag Editor dialog box

Once you click OK, you return to the Code view with all your changes in place.

## JavaScript

Working in Code view means you have more control over client-side scripting. As with any computer language, JavaScript can be very complicated, but there are many ways in which it can greatly benefit your sites. Once again, Dreamweaver enables you to rapidly add scripts even if you don't have scripting experience via a combination of panels and menu items.

There are various methods of achieving this. Designers used to working visually might want to start with the Behaviors panel. This is accessed via Window ➤ Behaviors, or *SHIFT+F3*. If you already have the Tag Inspector panel group active, Behaviors is one of the tabs in it, as shown in Figure 9-28.

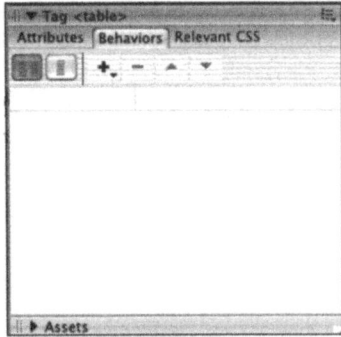

**Figure 9-28.** The Behaviors panel

Adding a behavior is a simple process: click inside a tag in Code view and use the drop-down menu under the [+] sign to add JavaScript events, such as the ever-popular "text in the status bar," pop-up windows, and so on.

> *Remember when working with JavaScript that it is case sensitive.*

If you venture into writing your own JavaScript, you must pay particular attention to syntax. Missing a semicolon might make the script fail in any number of browsers. Some are more lenient than others, though, strengthening the reasoning behind testing your site in numerous web browsers. For now, you're going to begin working with behaviors, and later in the chapter you'll integrate some "cut and paste" scripts into your case study website.

**143**

## Using a simple JavaScript behavior

In this exercise, you'll create the text that appears in the browser's status area when you position the mouse pointer over a link.

1. Add a paragraph to your web page that contains a link. Do this by using Code Hints until you have the line of code that's highlighted in Figure 9-29.

**Figure 9-29.** Code view displaying an HTML link within a paragraph

> The HTML element for a link (or, more accurately, an **anchor**) is <a>. Here, the href attribute's value is simply a pound (#) sign, which makes a "dummy" link.

2. Click inside the anchor tag (<a href...), and use the Behaviors panel's drop-down menu to go to Set Text ➤ Set Text of Status Bar, as shown in Figure 9-30. You may have to refresh the panel before doing this—if that's the case, the Behaviors panel will prompt you to do so.

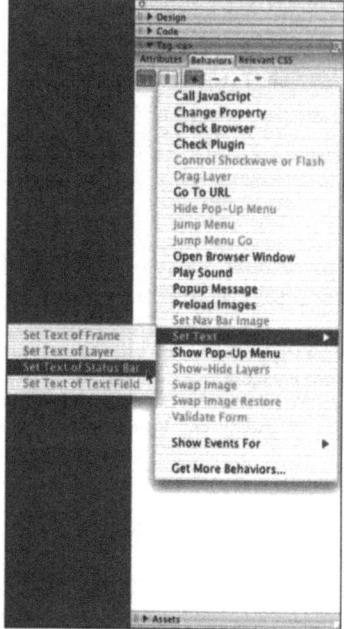

**Figure 9-30.** Selecting a behavior

3. In the dialog box, add your text, keeping it succinct, as shown in Figure 9-31.

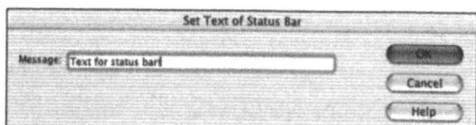

**Figure 9-31.** The Set Text of Status Bar dialog box

4. The behavior will be added in the <body> part of your document, and in the <head> section, you'll see some JavaScript that Dreamweaver created automatically, as shown in Figure 9-32.

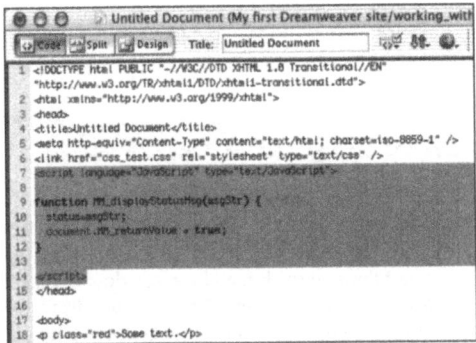

**Figure 9-32.** Dreamweaver-created JavaScript in the document's <head> section

5. To edit the text, you can either amend the words within the anchor tag, or double-click the behavior in the Behaviors panel, which redisplays the dialog box, as shown in Figure 9-33.

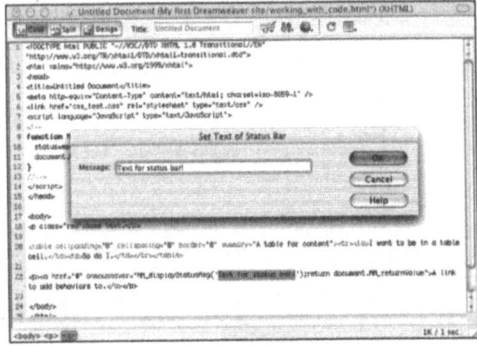

**Figure 9-33.** Editing the status bar text

*Although it's complicated, Dreamweaver's JavaScript output is modular and quite efficient. Avoid editing what it places in the <head> of your document unless you know exactly what you are doing.*

Some characters have special meanings in JavaScript, including:

- #
- %
- &
- =
- ,
- ?

- *
- '
- "
- []
- {}

These may cause conflicts with Dreamweaver-generated code. On the whole, Dreamweaver adds a backslash before each of these characters, which enables them to be displayed. This is called "escaping" the characters.

*Dreamweaver is not consistent in this area, though, ignoring the plus sign (+), equal sign (=), and colon (:) on the basis that they rarely cause problems. Curly brackets ({ }) are converted to a standard parenthesis, so to display one, you must manually escape it yourself. Therefore, take care when working with such characters.*

6. Open the Set Text of Status Bar dialog box again, as shown in Figure 9-34, and add an apostrophe to the text.

**Figure 9-34.** Including an apostrophe in the status bar text

7. Check your code and you'll see the following:

```
<p><a href="#" onmouseover="MM_display
StatusMsg('I\'m very happy! ');return
document.MM_returnValue">A link to add
behaviors to.</a></p>
```

**145**

As we mentioned before, Dreamweaver places a back-slash (\) before the special characters, ensuring that the JavaScript continues to work and that your text can be shown. In layman's terms, when you escape a character, a browser displays the character itself rather than trying to work out what it means in JavaScript, and terminates the tag when it comes across the apostrophe. Figure 9-35 shows how the status bar text typically appears in a web browser.

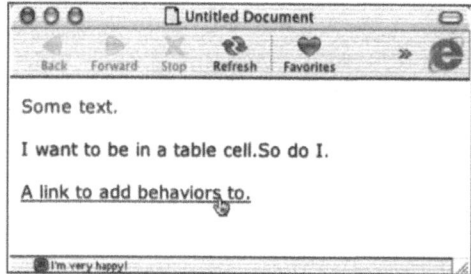

**Figure 9-35.** Status bar text displayed in Internet Explorer.

Although useful, this script isn't perfect. In practice, the behavior won't work if double quotation marks are added to your text. However, there is a workaround: replace all escaped double quotation marks (\") with their HTML entity name, and add the escape prior to it (\&quot;).

This behavior also fails entirely in some web browsers, although it won't cause them any problems. In addition, the status bar text sits there until you mouse over something else. We'll deal with the first problem later by creating a script via the use of **snippets**. With regards to the status bar text, you need to return it to blank once the mouse moves off the link. This is done by adding another behavior.

8. Repeat step 2, but this time don't add any text in the Set Text of Status Bar dialog box, as shown in Figure 9-36.

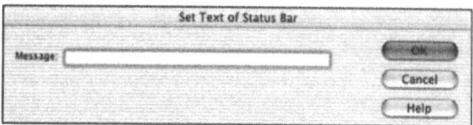

**Figure 9-36.** Leaving the Set Text of Status Bar dialog box blank

9. Again, this behavior appears in the Behaviors panel. The most recently added event will be the lowest down in the list, and you can double-click it to make sure (you'll see the dialog box from the previous step with a blank Message area). Click OK to close the dialog box, and use the drop-down menu next to the behavior in the Behaviors panel to change the **event** that triggers the behavior. Choose onMouseOut, as shown in Figure 9-37.

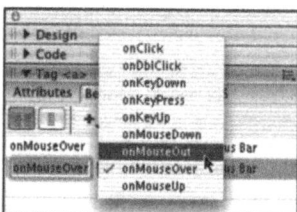

**Figure 9-37.** Changing the event that triggers the behavior

Although this menu shows a mix of uppercase and lowercase in these events, Dreamweaver automatically makes them all lowercase when adding them to any web pages defined as XHTML compliant, thereby making them accurate to current standards.

10. Note that if the options are not available to you, use the [+] menu, go to Show Events For, and select 4.0 and Later Browsers, as shown in Figure 9-38.

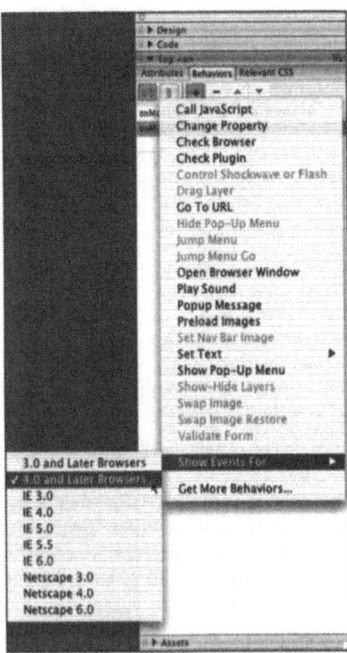

**Figure 9-38.** The Show Events For menu

11. Save and test your page in a browser to ensure everything's gone to plan. (Of course, this page is included in the files you can download from the friends of ED website, too, so you can check your work against ours.)

As mentioned earlier, when using behaviors it's important to test your work in as many browsers as you can. This is one reason why Dreamweaver enables you to set a number of browsers in which to preview your site.

You can add as many behaviors to each link as you like, but avoid using too many or you might end up confusing your site's visitors (or yourself). To delete a behavior, simply select it in the Behaviors panel and click the [-] icon. Don't try to remove behaviors using Code or Design view or you may end up with loads of redundant code in the head section of your web pages. Removing unwanted behaviors correctly becomes even more important later in the book because the underlying code can rapidly become a mess and frequently cause scripting conflicts.

## Raw coding

Using Code view, you can add your own code instead of using the built-in behaviors. In some cases, this is beneficial. Although the bulk of Macromedia's code is streamlined, some, such as the JavaScript for displaying status bar text, can be reduced in size and complexity.

This is what Dreamweaver produces from the built-in behavior (along with some additional scripting in the <head> of the document).

```
<a href="#" onmouseover="MM_display
StatusMsg('Explanation of
link');return document.MM_returnValue"
onmouseout="MM_displayStatusMsg('');  return
document.MM_returnValue">This is a link</a>
```

If you hand-code this, you end up with the following:

```
<a href="#" onmouseover="window.status=
'Explanation oflink');return true"
onmouseout="window.status='';">This
is a link.</a>
```

This is one third shorter than when using the built-in behaviors, but this isn't always the case. For instance, Macromedia's built-in JavaScript for image rollovers is excellent, and although complex, it's extremely streamlined. As always, try various methods, work out which suits you, and balance that with trying to make streamlined code and reducing download times.

The main problem of working with code is that it takes time, and isn't nearly as convenient as working with drag-and-drop behaviors. If you want to add something like the code just shown to dozens of links, you don't want to have to type it in every single time. Dreamweaver has this covered—you can use **snippets**. These are small pieces of HTML, CSS, or JavaScript that can be stored and organized in folders and then used an unlimited number of times.

## Snippets

A snippet is a Dreamweaver feature that enables you to collect and manage sections of code, thereby saving you time when adding it to your pages. You access the Snippets panel via *SHIFT+F9*, as shown in Figure 9-39. However, if you have the Code panel group active, it's

**147**

displayed within it by default. Dreamweaver comes with plenty of built-in examples, but you're going to create two new ones that will replace the need to type in the JavaScript to create the status bar text.

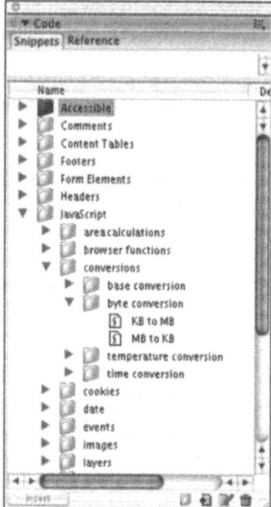

**Figure 9-39.** The Snippets panel

You're going to create a new snippet from scratch in the following exercise, but you might also want to visit the Snippets Exchange at www.dwfaq.com/snippets/, which has many ready-made examples.

## Creating and using snippets

1. Unselect everything in Code view. Open the Snippets panel and select the location to save your snippet (this can always be changed later via drag and drop). Use the panel's drop-down menu to select New Snippet, as shown in Figure 9-40.

2. In the Snippet dialog box, give your snippet a name and a description. The Snippet Type options include Wrap Selection, which enables you to wrap the snippet around an object such as a piece of text, and Insert Block, which treats it as a block element (such as a paragraph tag).

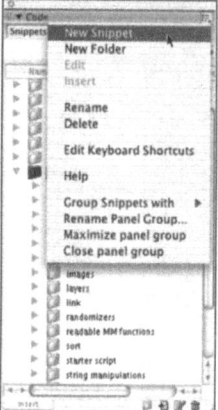

**Figure 9-40.** Creating a new snippet

Anything placed in the Insert Before field is inserted in Code view prior to your selection point, and anything in the Insert After field is inserted after your selection point. Because you're creating something to wrap around browser status text, Insert Before contains everything up to and including the first window.status quote (onmouseover="window.status='), whereas Insert After contains the second quote and what follows thereafter (';return true"), as shown in Figure 9-41.

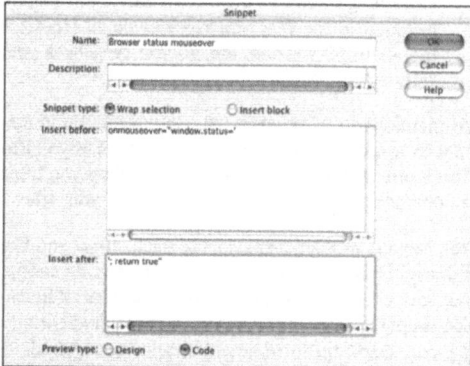

**Figure 9-41.** The Snippet dialog box

Take care not to mix up your quotation marks. This JavaScript contains a mix of single and double quotation marks, and using the wrong one in any case breaks the script.

**3.** Click OK to save the snippet and return to your page in Code view. Add another link, enter the text that you want to appear in the status bar *inside* the anchor tag, and then select it, as shown in Figure 9-42.

**Figure 9-42.** Selecting the text that will become status bar text

**4.** Either double-click the snippet you made in step 2 (that is, click its name in the Snippets panel), or drag it onto your selected text. The snippet code will wrap itself around the selected text, as shown in Figure 9-43.

**Figure 9-43.** Double-clicking a snippet to apply it to the selection

**5.** Now you have to deal with the mouseout code because the previous steps only deal with the mouseover code. Create a new snippet, as shown in Figure 9-44. Because this snippet doesn't need to be wrapped around anything in Code view, everything goes in the Insert Before field. Enter onmouseout="window.status='';". Note that after status= are two single quotes, not one double quote.

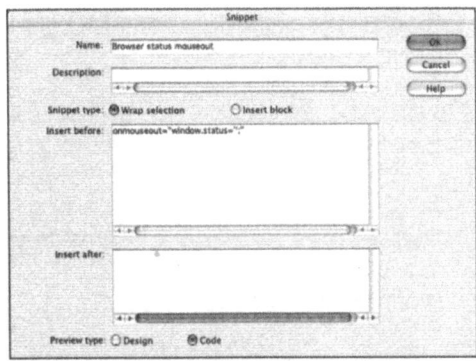

**Figure 9-44.** A new snippet for an onmouseout event

**6.** Click inside the anchor tag in Code view and then either drag the snippet across or double-click it. After it's been added to your code, ensure there's a space between it and the previously added snippet:

```
<p><a href="#" onmouseover="window.status=
'This will become browser status text';
return true" onmouseout="window.
status='';"></a></p>
```

*Snippets can include anything you want, so you can add huge chunks of HTML, JavaScript, and even inline CSS. They can be created as start and end blocks, and can be used to surround other tags and content. Therefore, they're useful for inserting special formatting, links, navigation elements, and script blocks. If you want a break after all this coding, take a trip through the various folders in the Snippets panel, where you'll find everything from browser detection to cookies and ready-made drop-down menus.*

**149**

## Getting your <head> checked

After adding one or more JavaScript behaviors, you'll notice that the <head> section of your HTML document contains a bunch of code. Figure 9-45 shows the page you've been working with during this chapter.

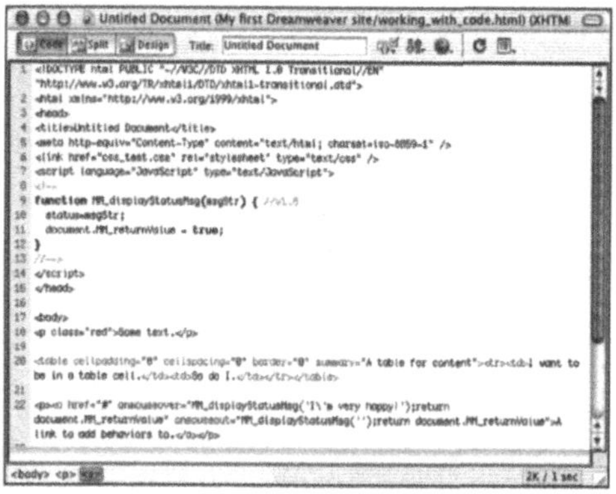

**Figure 9-45.** JavaScript code in the <head> section of an HTML document

Like CSS, JavaScript can be driven via external files, as we've already shown you how to do. Therefore, if you use Dreamweaver JavaScript behaviors, remember to copy the function to your external JavaScript file so you can reuse it on any page of your website. This also reduces page weight, meaning slightly faster download times.

> Note that you should only copy the function itself, and not the HTML comments surrounding the function (<!– and //–>) or the HTML script tags. Also, don't miss the final curly bracket of any functions, or they may not work. Finally, Dreamweaver is smart enough to know if you've already added a built-in function to an external JavaScript file, so the only time it will add another to the head of an HTML document is if the behavior has been upgraded to a higher version number.

# Upgrading page elements

Now that you've gone through various elements of Code view, you should be more comfortable with it. You're now going to use your newfound knowledge to upgrade various aspects of your website using Code view.

### Front page random image

The image you've used on your front page is all well and good, but it might look boring after a while. Therefore, you're going to replace it with a random image from a selection. When visitors enter the site, they'll see one from a selection of images, and when the page is refreshed, a new random choice from the selection will be displayed. Random content can make pages look like they're updated more often than they are, and provide immediate access to a selection of content that otherwise wouldn't be seen until later. It also enables a designer to show a selection of items rather than limiting the choice to one.

1. Open `iceland.js` in Dreamweaver, and type the following.

```
// random splash generator

function randomSplash()

{
// subsequent code goes here

}
```

The double forward slash is a comment in JavaScript. In this case, the first is used to note what the following subsequent function is for. The second one is to show you where the code in subsequent steps should be placed, and it can be omitted.

> For more on JavaScript, check out *Practical JavaScript for the Usable Web* (www.glasshaus .com/BookInfo.asp?bookId=45) and also *Foundation Web Design* (www.friendsofed.com/ books/1590591526/index.html).

**2.** Inside the curly brackets, type the following:

```
var splashImage=new Array()

// location of images in this array
splashImage[1]="assets/glaciers_1.jpg";
splashImage[2]="assets/glaciers_10.jpg";
splashImage[3]="assets/golden_circle_1
➥.jpg";
splashImage[4]="assets/landscapes_1.jpg";
➥splashImage[5]="assets/landscapes_5.jpg";
splashImage[6]="assets/reykjavik_1.jpg";
splashImage[7]="assets/reykjavik_5.jpg";
splashImage[8]="assets/waterfalls_5.jpg";
```

This sets up an **array**, essentially providing you with a list of items from which you can later choose. Note that the value of each item is simply the path from the JavaScript file to various images. Therefore, if you later place your JavaScript file in a folder, you'd need to update these links to ../assets/image.jpg. Note that Dreamweaver *won't* do this for you when working with custom JavaScript functions such as this.

> As we said, put the above script **inside** the curly brackets, and not after them. If in doubt, check out the downloadable example site.

**3.** Add another array for the image captions:

```
var splashCaption=new Array()

// captions
splashCaption[1]="Distant glacier";
splashCaption[2]="Ice on the beach";
splashCaption[3]="&THORN;ingvellir in
➥winter";
splashCaption[4]="Snow road";
splashCaption[5]="The harbour";
splashCaption[6]="Sun voyager";
splashCaption[7]="Summer at midnight";
splashCaption[8]="Black falls";
```

**4.** Place the following underneath what you've just typed. This is the part of the script that creates a random number. Don't worry about understanding the script—you can just copy it!

```
var getRan=Math.floor(Math.random()
➥*splashImage.length);
if (getRan==0)
getRan=1;
```

**5.** Add the following JavaScript—this writes the HTML back to the web page:

```
document.write('<p><img src="'+splashImage
➥[getRan]+'" alt="Images from Iceland."
➥title="Images from Iceland." width="400"
➥height="300" \/><\/a><\/p>');

document.write('<p>'+splashCaption[getRan]+
➥'<br \/>');
document.write('View more images in the <a
➥href="gallery.html">gallery<\/a><\/p>');
```

Note that you can easily adapt this to your own needs. Instead of images and captions, you could have HTML in your array, which can then be written back to the HTML page via as many Document.Write lines as you choose. However, bear in mind that certain characters can cause a string to terminate unexpectedly in JavaScript, which is why we escaped quotes by using backward slashes. Removing these would terminate the string early, causing the script to fail or at least not work correctly.

> We've also escaped forward slashes. This isn't strictly necessary in external scripts, but is required when writing embedded JavaScript, otherwise a page won't validate correctly. Therefore, it's a good habit to get into in order to prevent unexpected problems when working on embedded scripts.

**6.** Replace the content of the photoArea editable region with the following script (also shown in Figure 9-46):

```
<script type="text/javascript"
➥language="JavaScript">
<!--
randomSplash();
//-->
</script>
```

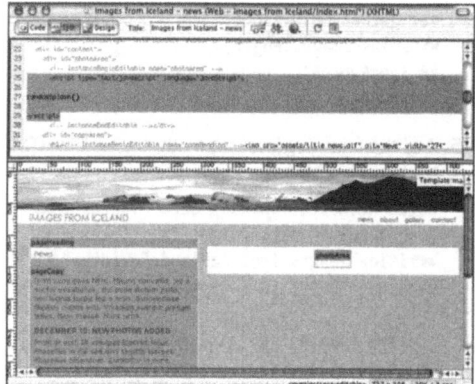

**Figure 9-46.** JavaScript within the photoArea editable region

> Note that this script should have no formatting—it should **not** be surrounded by paragraph tags. This is because formatting is taken care of in the script.

Figure 9-47 shows the result: the same page, refreshed in a browser, randomly showing three of the images.

**Figure 9-47.** The same web page in three different browser windows

## A better gallery

To say the current gallery is unwieldy would be putting it mildly. Updating it would be a nightmare because you'd have to update each of the 30 pages. Even if you were using an embedded template, you'd still be outputting these pages, which seems a little over the top. Surely there's an easier way? There sure is, again involving JavaScript. You can provide your images and captions with unique IDs (as you've done with things like the site's masthead and footer) and then use JavaScript to swap them for new content when a thumbnail is clicked. The process of doing this is remarkably straightforward, too.

> There is a downside to this method: not only does the script fail in obsolete browsers such as Netscape Navigator 4, but the gallery fails to work if you have JavaScript turned off. Arguments rage as to how many people will fall into one of the above groups, and estimates vary from a scant few up to around ten percent. However, for our target markets, we're happy to take the risk. If you're not in such a position, you'll have to stick with one of the other methods outlined in this book.

1. Duplicate `gallery.html` because you're going to be making major changes to it. Rename the copy `gallery_old.html` and open `gallery.html`.

2. Open `iceland.js` and type the following underneath the previously entered script:

```
// swap image and caption

function swapPhoto(photoSRC,theCaption) {

  var displayedCaption = document.
➥getElementById("caption");

  displayedCaption.firstChild.
➥nodeValue = theCaption;

    document.images.imgPhoto.src =
➥"assets/" + photoSRC;
}
```

**152**

Note that the final line is the path to wherever your images are stored, so if you've put your gallery images in a subfolder, this line must reflect that.

3. The code for the photo and caption needs to be changed in order for the script to work. As we said, you're essentially adding unique IDs to both the image tag and the caption paragraph. The original code looks like this:

```
<p><img src="assets/glaciers_1.jpg"
alt="Photo" width="400" height="300"
/></p><p>Distant glacier</p>
```

It needs to be changed to this:

```
<p><img src="assets/default.jpg"
width="400" height="300" id="imgPhoto"
name="imgPhoto" alt="Main photo" /></p>
<p id="caption">Images from Iceland</p>
```

> The ID attribute in the image tag should suffice, but the name attribute is also added as a backup for unruly web browsers.

4. Now you must amend all your links on this page. The first link looks like this:

```
<a href="gallery/gallery_glaciers_1.html">
<img src="assets/t_glaciers_1.jpg"
alt="Thumbnail" width="44" height="33"
border="0" /></a>
```

All you change is the value of the href attribute, to what's shown here.

```
<a href="javascript:swapPhoto
('glaciers_1.jpg','Distant glacier')
"><img src="assets/t_glaciers_1.jpg"
alt="Thumbnail" width="44" height="33"
border="0" /></a>
```

Inside the first set of single quotation marks is the file name of the image that should be shown when this thumbnail is clicked. Inside the second set of quotation marks is the associated caption.

A deft bit of copying and pasting will keep this process from taking too long; however, once the page is done, it's the only one that will need amending when new photos are added, rather than editing and checking numerous gallery pages. The final page is shown in Figure 9-48.

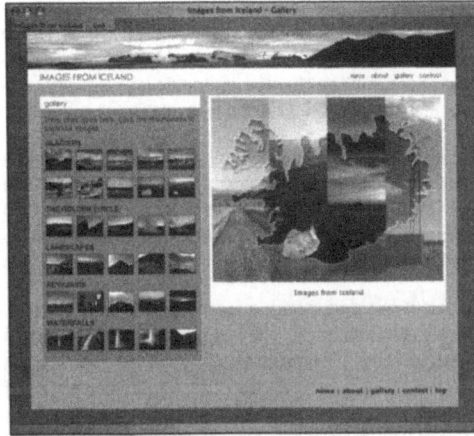

**Figure 9-48.** The updated gallery page

After clicking a thumbnail, the page looks as shown in Figure 9-49.

**Figure 9-49.** Clicking a thumbnail to update the main image and associated caption

**153**

## Enhancing the navigation bar

The final site upgrade is to the navigation bar. It's a bit lifeless and it doesn't provide any feedback to the visitor. Let's create a stylish rollover, but avoiding the hassle of using JavaScript rollovers because preloading graphics is a tricky business that doesn't work in many browsers. This means sites with rollover graphics can look shoddy for those brief seconds that they're loading; more importantly, the visitor doesn't get immediate feedback on the first rollover.

Therefore, you're instead going to use CSS, and the mouseover effect will be a simple gray underline. You can use the New CSS Style dialog box for this, but it's just as simple to open iceland.css and type it in by hand.

If you've avoided anything regarding CSS code thus far, here's a quick recap. CSS rules are made up of a **selector** and a **declaration**. The former is usually an ID, class, or tag, whereas the latter can be composed of one or several property/value pairs. The declaration is placed within curly brackets, and property/value pairs are separated by semicolons. Then there are **contextual selectors**, which you've used several times already. These define a style for an element in a particular page area or in specific circumstances.

1. Open the file iceland.css. The masthead is in a div named masthead. In CSS, IDs must be preceded by a pound sign, so add a new rule like this:

   **#masthead {**

   **}**

2. The elements you want to affect with this style are images (<img>) within links (<a>) in the masthead, so turn the selector into a contextual selector, like this:

   #masthead **a img** {

   }

3. The link state you want to affect is the **hover** state. As you saw earlier, when defining links, this is written a:hover in CSS, so this needs to be added, too:

   #masthead a:**hover** img {

   }

4. Next, add the property/value pair, which defines a gray, solid, two-pixel border:

   #masthead a:**hover** img {
   **border-bottom: 2px solid #c1c1c1;**
   }

5. Test the site in a Gecko-based browser (Mozilla, Netscape Navigator) and the layout might "jump" because the border is added only on the hover state. In Internet Explorer, no border at all is displayed. You therefore need to add the border on the default link state, too, and to standard images (i.e., non-linked ones) in the masthead, so everything's the same height. This is done by adding the following rule:

   #masthead a img, #masthead img {
   border-bottom: 2px solid #fff;
   }

As you can see, this defines any images in the masthead, including linked images, as having a two-pixel white border, which is the same as the background color of the masthead, and therefore (for all intents and purposes) invisible, as shown in Figure 9-50.

**Figure 9-50.** The updated navigation bar

So there you have it: rollover behavior without JavaScript and preloaders.

# Testing and validation

Although you should test in numerous browsers while building your site, it goes without saying that you *must* test in plenty of them before it goes live. We're not expecting many problems with our site—after all, we've used web standards throughout, and little deprecated or legacy mark-up. Because of this, we're first going to outline some common issues that arise with certain browsers, and tell you how to get around them.

## Centering a site in IE 5.5 on Windows

You'll remember that the website was centered by using CSS margins on the wrapper, as seen in the first property/value pair of the following CSS rule:

```
#wrapper {
  margin: 0px auto;
  padding: 0px;
  width: 740px;
  background: #d5d6d5;
}
```

Although current browsers deal with this correctly, Internet Explorer 5.5 for Windows doesn't understand the auto setting for the margin, and therefore aligns the wrapper to the left of the browser window. If you want to cater to IE 5.5 users, there is a simple workaround that involves centering the entire site and then overriding this definition in the wrapper div. First add the text-align property/value pair to the body declaration:

```
body {
  text-align: center;
  font: 11px Verdana, Arial,
  ➥Helvetica, sans-serif;
  color: #666666;
  background-color: #929194;
  margin: 0px;
  padding: 0px;

}
```

Then override this setting in the wrapper tag, as follows:

```
#wrapper {
  text-align: left;
  margin: 0px auto;
  padding: 0px;
  width: 740px;
  background: #d5d6d5;
}
```

## White space bugs

For something that isn't actually anything, white space can be a royal pain in the backside when it comes to developing websites. In theory, the only white space that browsers should notice is single spaces between words or elements. However, in practice, some browsers display far more than that, and pixel-perfect layouts are often thrown off by white space. The thing is, most web design tools introduce white space into your code, as can web validation tools, in order to make it easier to read.

```
<td>
  <img src="image.jpg />
</td>

<td><img src="image.jpg" /></td>
```

The two examples just shown are effectively the same, but might be displayed differently depending on the browser. So what's the solution? If you have a layout that's not rendering properly even though your measurements are perfect, try deleting the white space around the offending elements. In our experience, the Windows version of Internet Explorer seems most affected by white space problems, but we've seen such things occur in all major web browsers, right back into the 1990s.

> Note that you shouldn't use tools to delete all white space from your code—only delete the white space that is messing up your layout. Despite claims to the contrary, deleting all the white space from your pages won't make a significant difference in download times.

## The XML prolog

This is an easily missed problem that often has web designers tearing their hair out with frustration and then feeling rather foolish when they find it. Some design tools, including Dreamweaver on occasion, will add an XML prolog to the very start of your HTML pages. It looks something like this.

```
<?xml version="1.0" encoding="UTF-8"?>
```

It's part of the web standards, but optional. This is just as well because an XML prolog throws both Internet Explorer 6 and Opera 7 into quirks mode, making them lay out a site as though it's based on old-fashioned, deprecated mark-up, even if it isn't. Sometimes the effects are even worse—the tripped-up browser rendering all the mark-up as text. The solution is simple: if you see the prolog at the start of your page, delete it. However, when doing so, it's important to include a meta tag that details the character set used. Dreamweaver adds the following appropriate line by default:

```
<meta http-equiv="Content-Type"
content="text/html; charset=iso-8859-1" />
```

## Opera padding

These days, web browsers tend to add no padding by default to a web page. Opera does, though, which can (slightly) affect your layout. To get around this, set a specific padding in your CSS file's body declaration. We usually use 0.

## The box model

Perhaps the most infamous browser problem of them all is the one concerning the box model. As you might know, CSS elements generate a rectangular box called the element box. Although it may not be particularly intuitive, web standards dictate that padding appears *outside* the defined element width, followed by the border and margin settings, as shown in Figure 9-51. Backgrounds extend to the edge of the borders, thereby being included within the padding, but not the margin.

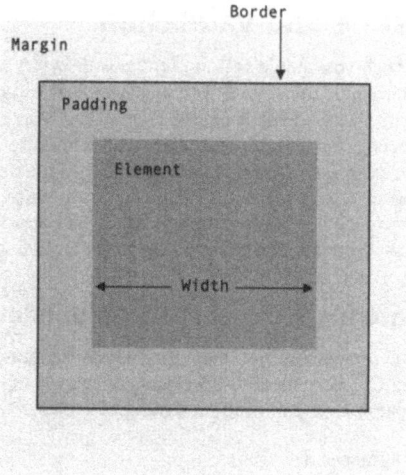

**Figure 9-51.** How compliant web browsers interpret the box model

Versions of Internet Explorer earlier than 6.0 on Windows misinterprets the box model, placing padding and borders *inside* an element, instead of *outside*, as shown in Figure 9-52.

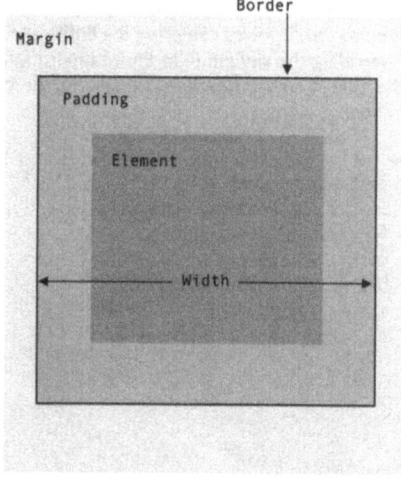

**Figure 9-52.** How versions of Internet Explorer before 6.0 for Windows misinterprets the box model

**156**

For instance, say we want to create a 300-pixel area on our page, with 20 pixels of padding around it and a 5-pixel border. For compliant browsers, the defined width is 300px, the padding set to 20px, and the border to 5px. Effectively, this takes up 350 pixels of space on the web page (5+20+300+20+5).

Because Internet Explorer 5.5 and below gets the box model wrong, placing the padding and borders inside the element width, you end up with 300-(2 × 5) - (2 × 20) = 250 pixels for content, instead of 300 pixels. As you can imagine, this can cause major problems when laying out websites.

The way around this is to exploit a bug in these browsers, developed by Tantek Çelik, and explained in full at http://tantek.com/CSS/Examples/boxmodelhack.html. The "box model hack" works as follows: you first set a width for IE 5.5, which adds together the element width, padding, and border (in this case, 350 pixels):

```
#element {
padding: 20px; border: 5px;
width: 350px;
```

Next, you add the following, which causes IE 5.5 to terminate reading the rule:

```
voice-family: "\"}\"";
voice-family:inherit;
```

You then add the "correct" width for compliant web browsers.

```
width: 300px;
}
```

Because some browsers, such as Opera 5, are standards compliant but have the same parsing bug that we're exploiting in IE 5.5, we add a further rule, containing the correct element width:

```
html>body #element {
width: 300px;
}
```

Because a large number of web users are sticking with IE 5.5 for Windows, this is one hack that we advocate using when you have to. And after all, we're only hacking the odd rule here and there in our CSS, not on every page on our website.

> *Unfortunately, this widely used hack may soon no longer validate in the W3 validator because the validator will likely move to the CSS 2.1 draft spec, which deprecates all aural styles. Therefore, use it with caution.*

## The case study site

As we thought, no major problems occurred when testing the site. The layout is thrown very slightly in IE 5.5 for Windows due to the borders on the boxed areas. However, it's not enough of a problem to use the box model hack. Internet Explorer 5 for Mac had problems with HTML entities in the gallery swap script (which were used to display "smart" quotes), so they were removed. Further testing in Safari, Mozilla, and Opera presented no further problems.

Note that because we attached our CSS via the @import method, the site's design won't be accessible to obsolete and alternate browsers, such as Netscape Navigator 4, which simply displays all the content areas one under another. This isn't a bug—it's intentional. Use of such browsers continues to fall, and we shouldn't be compromising our site for a buggy browser that's not been significantly updated in over four years, not least because there are plenty of free and affordable alternatives available.

However, you should be aware that the updated gallery fails completely because it uses JavaScript that Netscape Navigator 4 cannot interpret. There is a way of warning such users—add the following to the gallery page:

```
<p class="hidden">To view the gallery,
you need to be using a version 5 or
newer web browser.</p>
```

And then add this rule to your CSS:

```
.hidden {
display: none;
}
```

This means compliant browsers won't display the warning.

**157**

# Checking compatibility

The final step is to check the site's compatibility. Press *SHIFT+F6* or select File ➤ Check Page ➤ Validate Markup to do this in Dreamweaver. Alternatively, you can go to http://validator.w3.org/ and use the service of the company who defines the standards. Either way, you'll be presented with warnings or errors concerning your mark-up, if any are to be found.

In testing our site's pages, we found only one error, in contact.html:

Dreamweaver said:

Line: 33; Description: in tag: textarea the following required attributes are missing: cols

W3's validator concurred:

Line 33, column 76 :required attribute "cols" not specified

We'd forgotten about defining columns for our text area because we defined the width in CSS. However, cols is a mandatory attribute, so we opened contact.html and added a cols attribute by using the Properties panel's Char width field, as shown in Figure 9-53.

**Figure 9-53.** Adding a textarea cols attribute using Char width in the Properties panel

## Validating CSS

To validate CSS, upload your file to http://jigsaw.w3.org/css-validator/. Once completed, you'll be presented with errors and warnings. The former need to be fixed in order to have a valid document, whereas the latter are often things to just take on board (such as not having background color when you have a foreground color, and so on). Again, we didn't get any errors, as shown in Figure 9-54.

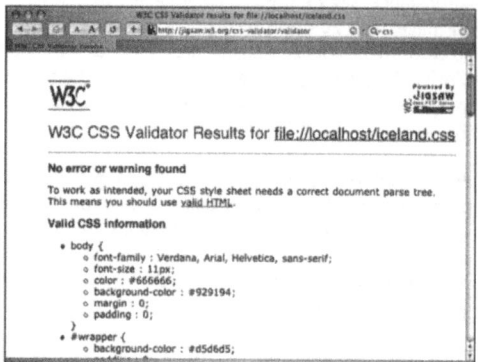

**Figure 9-54.** The CSS validator at W3C

> You might wonder why we're bothering to validate our site. It's because doing so is good for fine-tuning and ensuring that we have valid code. If we have valid code, it's more likely to work across a range of web browsers. After all, some are more lenient than others. An error may be ignored by one browser but stop the site from working in another. If our code is valid, there's less risk and no guesswork.

# Going further

Although we've now completed our website, bear in mind that it's never the end. One of the greatest things about the web is that it's dynamic. Sites can constantly be updated, and can be rapidly affected by user feedback or your own new ideas. Leaving a site alone for a few weeks and then coming back to it with fresh eyes and a fresh mind usually prompts all sort of new thoughts. For instance, perhaps the photo captions don't stand out enough, and should be rendered in bold type or uppercase. (Maybe you can have a go and see if you can do that.)

More importantly, people often use the web to get the most up-to-date information, so try to keep adding new things to any site you create. A site that never has any new content is one that ends up being ignored by everyone online.

## Summary

We thoroughly checked out Code view, tweaked the site accordingly, and upgraded various elements. Hopefully you're now at least a little more confident with regards to delving into code rather than solely relying on Design view. With a little practice and a couple of decent reference books (and the help of the excellent Code Hints) doing stuff the "hard way" often turns out to be the easy way, or at least certainly a quicker way.

Dreamweaver's visual tools do make our job easier, but familiarity with the code it generates is essential. You may not have to write code yourself, but the ability to make edits in code helps you to troubleshoot, optimize your pages, and keep everything in pristine shape.

That's the end of the book's first half. The flat site is done and dusted, complete and validated. In this half of the book you've learned how to create a cutting-edge, CSS-based website using the power of Dreamweaver. Using templates and Dreamweaver's new CSS tools, updating, tweaking, and editing sites is now faster than ever. However, you've also learned how to work directly in Code view, which is often a faster way of getting results. The final files, which you can test against your own, are available for download from the friends of ED website.

The second half of this book builds on what you've learned so far by making the website dynamic, so you can update content via a **Content Management System**. Before that, though, we provide you with a thorough introduction to dynamic content concepts, MySQL, PHP, and how to set up your machine.

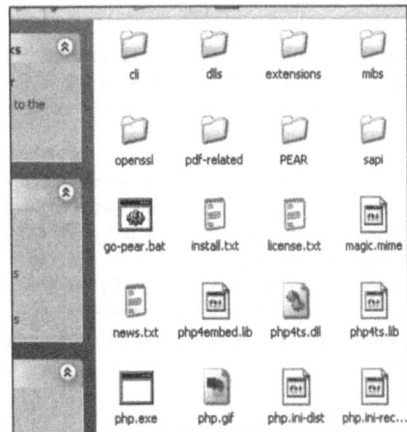

**Chapter 10**

# INTRODUCING DYNAMIC CONTENT WITH PHP

**What we'll cover in this chapter**

- What are dynamic sites?
- How dynamic sites work
- Installing Apache and PHP
- Testing your installation
- Setting up a PHP site in Dreamweaver MX 2004
- Viewing PHP output with Live Data

So far you've only built static sites in Dreamweaver MX 2004. In this chapter, we introduce the second half of this book in which we'll add dynamic content to your site.

Producing dynamic websites is probably a new experience to you. There's quite a lot involved, but MX 2004 takes much of the hard work out of it, and over the course of the next five chapters and the final case study, we'll get you up to speed. By the end, you'll not only have a solid foundation in PHP, but you will have converted Images from Iceland into a database-driven site.

## What are dynamic sites?

Have you ever visited Amazon.com and wondered what makes it tick? It remembers you between visits—you can log in and check your orders, and it even recommends books based on your previous purchases. How do they do it? Welcome to the world of dynamic websites (see Figure 10-1).

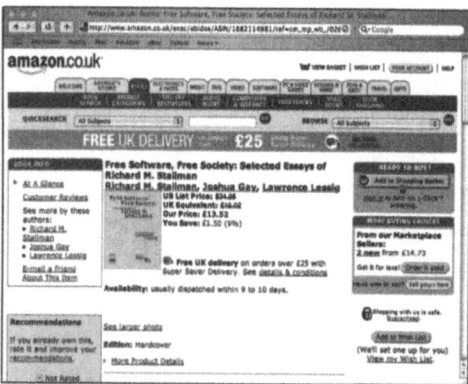

**Figure 10-1.** Quiet in the front, busy behind the scenes: a perfect example of a dynamic site

When you sign up for an account at Amazon.com, they store your information in a database. They identify you

between visits by using cookies, so the next time you visit the site, they access this data and display your own personalized page. Among other things, this page offers products based on your previous buying history. Throughout the rest of this book, you will be looking at the technology that drives this type of website, and of course, creating some of it yourself.

In the background of the website, there is a database that stores your information, and you can see this information displayed on your Amazon web page. But how do they get this information from the database to the page? They use a **server-side language**. A server-side language can be thought of as additional code that is embedded into your XHTML. This code makes certain requests upon which the computer will act. For instance, it may ask to open a connection to the database and retrieve specific information; or it may want to create files and place them on the hard drive for future use. Most importantly, server-side languages allow you to carry out fairly complex tasks with ease.

To get all of this to work, you need three things: a web server, a server-side language, and a database-management system. Normally, your ISP has these installed, but you're going to install them on your local computer as well because it's much more efficient to develop dynamic sites locally than to have to upload each page to your remote server after every single change. It's important to test your pages often while building them so that you can catch small mistakes before they turn into a major disaster. Unlike with static web pages, though, you can't just select File ➤ Preview in Browser (*F12*) in Dreamweaver MX 2004 to view the pages you're creating in a browser unless you have all three elements installed.

The three elements are

- **Web server**: Apache
- **Server-side language**: PHP
- **Database-management system**: MySQL (covered in Chapter 13)

The way the three elements work together is shown in Figure 10-2.

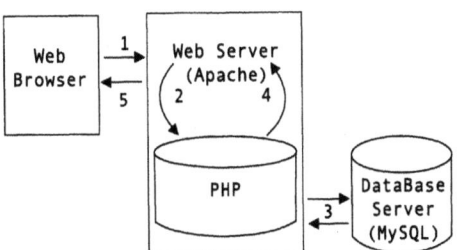

**Figure 10-2.** What happens when a browser requests a dynamic page

1. A user requests a page via his or her browser. This request is sent to the web server—in this case Apache.

2. Because the file has a .php extension, Apache knows it must be handled by the PHP preprocessor, which executes our PHP script.

3. If the script needs to get information from a database, it opens a connection to the database server and retrieves the requested data. Otherwise it skips to step 4.

4. When the PHP script has all the information it needs, it formats the data (typically into (X)HTML).

5. Finally, the resulting output is sent back to Apache, which in turn returns this information to the user's browser.

As you can see, there's a lot going on behind the scenes of a dynamic site. Static web pages do not perform steps 2, 3, and 4. It sounds complicated, but for basic scripts the process can take only microseconds. Obviously, the more complex the query and the bigger the database, the longer it takes, but both PHP and MySQL are extremely fast.

## Why use PHP?

Web developers have a bewildering selection of server-side languages at their disposal, including Microsoft's ASP and .NET solutions, Macromedia's ColdFusion, and open source alternatives like JSP, CGI, and PHP. They all serve the same basic purpose, and each has its own pros and cons that have been debated many times—there is never a winner.

We chose PHP because it has several features that make it ideal for this book.

- It's free!
- It's cross platform. It will run on most operating systems, including the most popular ones: Windows, OS X, and Linux.
- It's easy to learn compared to many other languages. However, don't confuse ease of use with loss of power. PHP offers many of the features available in other languages and more, including native connectivity to any database system.
- There are a large number of resources available—from prewritten scripts to a thriving online community—to turn to if you need help at any point.

## PHP: More than just an acronym

PHP has made giant steps forward since Rasmus Lerdorf first released PHP/FI (Personal Home Page/Forms Interpreter) in 1995. It began as just a collection of Perl scripts, but in the past few years it has grown to become one of the most popular languages for web development.

Rasmus decided early on to release the source code because he wanted others to be able to use the code he had already written, and also because he knew that by allowing other programmers to download the source, bugs would be fixed quicker and overall the code would be improved. By the time the second version was released two years later, it had a hardcore group of users, and it was estimated that one percent of all web servers had PHP/FI installed. Around that time, two students, Andi Gutmans and Zeev Suraski, decided to use it for a university project, but they soon discovered that it was woefully underpowered for what they had in mind. They decided to work with Rasmus Lerdorf to create a successor to PHP2.

**163**

In 1998, PHP3 was released. This release was rewritten from the ground up. It was renamed—Personal Home Page image was dropped, and PHP became a recursive acronym that stood for PHP: Hypertext Pre-processor.

PHP4 was released in 2000. This release included the Zend (a contraction of Zeev and Andi's first names) engine, which offered increased performance and stability as well as the ability to install PHP on a wider range of web servers.

The people at Zend haven't been resting on their laurels since 2000. PHP5 is due to be released in early 2004. What will the latest PHP release mean to you as a developer? PHP5 includes the newest Zend engine (version 2). It also includes an improved object model along with a vastly improved and simpler XML interface. Most of these improvements are of immediate interest only to advanced users. All the PHP you will learn in this book will still be valid in PHP5. It's also nice to know that you are learning a language that is constantly being improved and built upon.

If you want to find out more about the plans for the future of PHP, visit the Zend website at www.zend.com, shown in Figure 10-3. Once you get to a more advanced level, you'll also find the developer center there has lots of tutorials and other useful resources.

**Figure 10-3.** The official Zend website

## The Apache web server

Another essential ingredient for dynamic sites is a web server. Netcraft carries out a monthly survey of web servers installed worldwide, and recent figures show Apache to be the most widely used server on the Internet today. In November 2003, it found more than two thirds of all sites were running Apache. Details of the survey are shown in Table 10-1.

**Table 10-1.** Netcraft Survey Results

| Web Server | October 2003 | Market Share | November 2003 | Market Share | Change |
|------------|--------------|--------------|---------------|--------------|--------|
| Apache | 28,235,972 | 64.61% | 30,298,060 | 67.41% | +2.80% |
| Microsoft | 10,252,227 | 23.46% | 9,449,180 | 21.02% | -2.44% |
| SunONE | 1,528,090 | 3.50% | 1,525,202 | 3.39% | -0.11% |
| Zeus | 735,179 | 1.68% | 743,611 | 1.65% | -0.03% |

For the most up-to-date figures, visit http://news
.netcraft.com/archives/web_server_survey.html.

One of the most revealing things about these figures is
that Apache was the only web server to increase its
share over other server platforms—a trend that has
continued for some time.

The name Apache was adopted early on in its development. According to the Apache site, it was named out
of respect for the Native American Indian tribe "well-
known for their superior skills in warfare strategy and
their inexhaustible endurance." The more popular theory is that it was so named because it was "a patchy"
server. (You can decide for yourself which story to
believe.)

Initially the full project was unmanaged, but after a
while two programmers, Cliff Skolnick and Bob
Behlendorf, set up a centralized code base, and so the
Apache project was born. In the late 1990s, the Apache
Software Foundation, a not-for-profit organization, was
created to oversee future development.

Over the last few years, the interest in Apache has
grown, not only due to increasing awareness of open
source, but also because of the crippling security flaws
that seem to plague Microsoft's IIS, including its vulnerabilities to the Code Red and Nimda worms. What's
more, with companies like IBM now investing in the
Apache project, the future of this web server looks
good.

Don't be put off by the price tag attached to PHP and
Apache; many people wrongly assume that if something is free it must be inferior to a commercial offering. When it comes to open source software, this is
often not the case. PHP and Apache are no exception.

For further reading on the open source movement try
*The Cathedral and the Bazaar* by Eric Raymond
(O'Reilly & Associates, 2001).

# Installation

Enough theory and history—let's install the necessary
software on your local machine. We will cover how to
install Apache and PHP on both Windows and OS X.

The installation process differs greatly on these two
platforms.

You can upload the code contained in the rest of the
book to your ISP for testing, assuming it supports PHP,
but it will speed up development time considerably if
you have a local machine capable of serving up
dynamic pages. A little time spent now on installation
will save you oodles of time later.

## Installing Apache and PHP on a PC

The first step in the installation process is to download
the latest versions of PHP and Apache. At the time of
this writing, the latest version of the Apache web server
available is 2.0.48. Although this version is considered
stable enough to use on a production server, many ISPs
still run version 1.3.xx, which has a proven track record.
It is a good idea to emulate your ISP's server setup as
much as you can so you won't have any surprises when
you deploy your application. Therefore, we recommend that you download the latest version of 1.3.xx, in
this case 1.3.29.

1. Download the latest version at http://httpd
   .apache.org/download.cgi, as shown in Figure
   10-4. Scroll down to the section for Apache 1.3.xx,
   and select the file marked Win32 Binary.

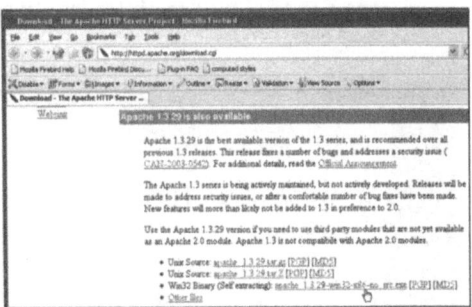

**Figure 10-4.** Selecting the Windows download

Next you need to download PHP. Two options are available: an installer package and a zip file. You are going
to use the zip file because it lets you install PHP as an
Apache API (Application Programming Interface),

which offers greater stability over the CGI version used by the installer package. You also have more installation options using the zip.

**2.** Go to the www.php.net/downloads and select the latest stable Windows binary version of PHP, shown in Figure 10-5.

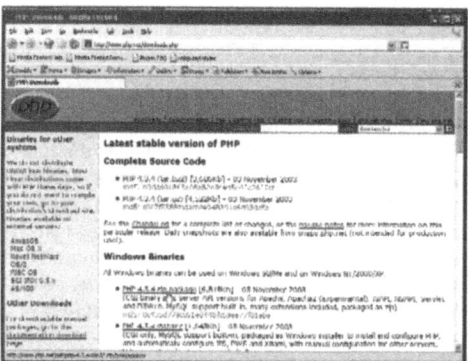

**Figure 10-5.** Selecting the zip package

Now that you have the software you require, let's begin the installation process. First, Apache.

**3.** Open the location in which you downloaded the Apache installer. Double-click the icon. A wizard will appear to take you through the installation process, as shown in Figure 10-6.

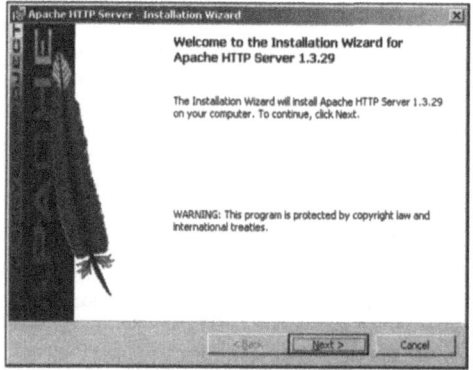

**Figure 10-6.** The Apache installation process on Windows

**4.** Click Next to continue the installation. Next is the Apache license agreement, as shown in Figure 10-7. Take some time and read the conditions and terms of use. It also contains details about the Apache documentation, which may help you should you face any problems in the future.

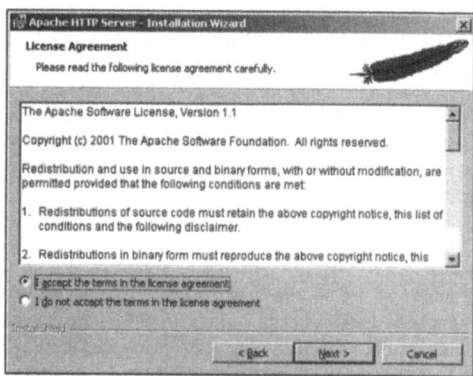

**Figure 10-7.** The license agreement

**5.** Click Next to display a screen with a warning to not use Apache as a production server on a consumer-operating environment. This is not a problem because you intend to use Apache on your local machine for testing only, not as a live server on the Internet. Read the screen and click Next.

**6.** Next is the Server Information screen, as shown in Figure 10-8. This is where you enter the default settings for your web server. In the Network Domain field, enter **127.0.0.1**. In the Server Name field, enter **localhost**, and in the last field, enter your e-mail address.

**7.** If you are running NT, 2000, or XP Professional, select the Run as a Service for All Users option. That way Apache runs as a service in the background and you don't need to worry about starting it. If you run 98, ME, or XP Home, select the Run When Started Manually option because you will be unable to run Apache as a service and must manually start it each time. Click Next.

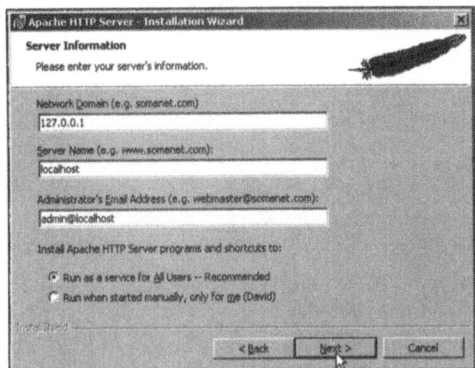

**Figure 10-8.** The Server Information screen

**8.** Select the Complete option (as shown in Figure 10-9) to install the Apache documentation, which you will almost certainly need to refer to at some point. Click Next to continue.

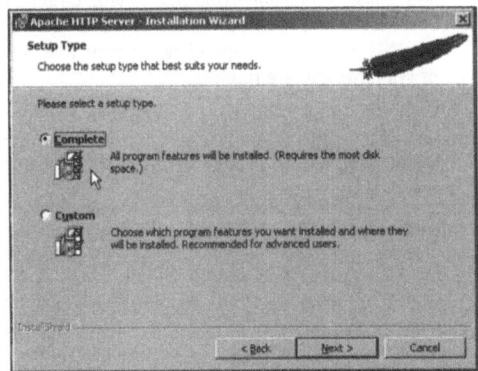

**Figure 10-9.** Choose the complete installation.

**9.** Specify the location where Apache will be installed. The default is C:\Program Files\Apache Group. This is fine. Click Next to finish the Apache installation.

**10.** Well done. You have successfully completed the Apache installation process! Finish by checking that Apache is running and ready to serve up web pages. Open your browser and enter http://localhost in the URL bar. If all went well

you should see the default Apache test page in your browser, shown in Figure 10-10.

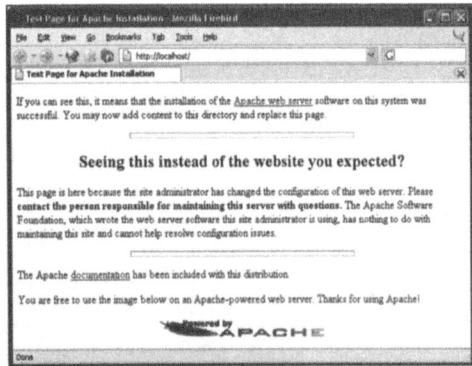

**Figure 10-10.** Congratulations! Apache is up and running.

## Troubleshooting

If you get an error message, check that the server is running. You can do this by selecting Start ➤ Program Files ➤ Apache Httpd. If you are running Win2000, Windows XP Professional, or Windows NT, you can ensure that Apache is running from the Task Manager.

## Running IIS and Apache together

If you already installed another web server, such as IIS or PWS (to run ASP pages, for example), you will need to shut the other server down to test Apache. It is possible to run two web servers on the same machine, but one must be set to listen for web page requests on port 8080, instead of the default 80. Think of a port as simply a gateway to a particular part of your computer. By using different ports, there's no danger of getting web page requests mixed up, and both servers will happily go about their own business.

To shut off IIS, open Administrative Tools from the Control Panel, and then access the Internet Services Manager. Right-click the Default Web Site in the main panel, and choose Stop from the context menu. If you want to change the port IIS listens on, open Properties from the same context menu, and change the TCP Port to 8080, as shown in Figure 10-11.

**167**

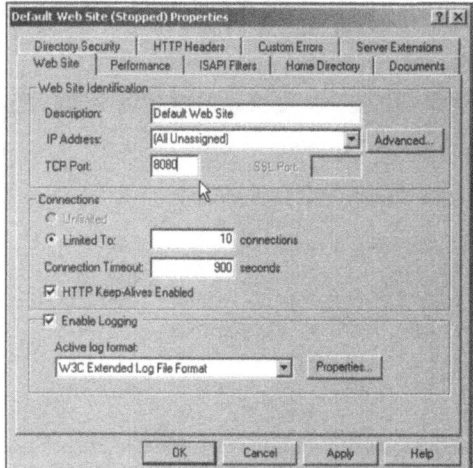

**Figure 10-11.** Changing the port IIS listens on

You can either leave IIS switched off, or if you changed the port, you can start it up again right away. To check that Apache is running correctly, you will probably have to restart it. Do so by clicking the Windows Start button and navigating to Apache on the program menu.

If you changed the IIS port number to 8080, you will need to change the URL for your ASP pages to include the port number. Instead of http://localhost/, use http://localhost:8080/. That's localhost followed by a colon and the port number. If you prefer to keep IIS running on port 80, you can easily run Apache on 8080 instead. We'll give you instructions on how to do that in the section on configuring Apache.

### Installing PHP for Windows

So far you have successfully configured Apache. Next you have to turn your attention to PHP.

1. Browse to the PHP zip file you downloaded and extract the contents directly onto your C: drive, as shown in Figure 10-12.

2. You should now have a folder called PHP-4.x.x. Rename this folder **php**. Make sure that you can access this folder at C:\php. If the folder isn't in that location move it there.

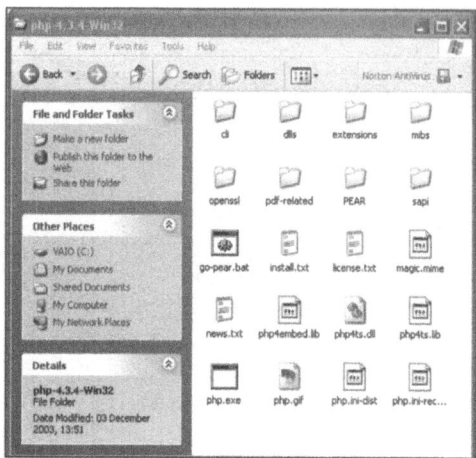

**Figure 10-12.** The contents of the PHP zip file

3. Open the folder located at C:\php. You will see a file called php4ts.dll—make a copy of this file and place it in your Windows system directory, C:\WINDOWS\SYSTEM, C:\WINDOWS\SYSTEM32, or C:\WINNT\SYSTEM32, depending on which version of Windows you are running.

4. Copy the file php.ini-dist to the main Windows directory (either C:\WINDOWS or C:\WINNT, depending on your version of Windows) and then rename it **php.ini**.

5. Open the newly renamed php.ini in a text editor. This file configures all the main settings for your installation of PHP. Although there's a lot in there that may seem incomprehensible, each section contains an explanation of what it does and the most important settings. The first thing to note is that any line that starts with a semicolon is a comment, so if you make changes to any lines that are commented out, the changes won't take effect. Also make sure not to delete any semicolons by mistake. Look for the line

   error_reporting = E_ALL & ~E_NOTICE

6. Make sure the line *doesn't* begin with a semicolon (an identical line with a semicolon appears a few lines earlier). Change the line without the semicolon to

   error_reporting = E_ALL

This will set error reporting to the highest level. As a beginner this will help you debug any mistakes in your code.

**7.** Look for the line

extension_dir = "./"

**8.** Change it to

extension_dir = "c:\php\extensions"

This simple change tells PHP where to find any extra extensions it may require. They all are stored in a sub-directory of your PHP installation directory. Extensions are covered in more detail later in this chapter.

**9.** To specify a temporary directory where PHP can store your sessions, look for the following line:

Session.save_path = /tmp

**10.** Change it to **one** of the following, depending on which version of Windows you are running.

Session.save_path = c:\windows\temp
Session.save_path = c:\WINNT\temp

This is important. By default, PHP stores information in the /tmp directory. However, this doesn't exist in Windows, so in order to correct this, you change the path to point to the equivalent folder in Windows.

**11.** Save your changes and close the file.

### Configuring PHP to work with Apache

Now you have to alter Apache's httpd.conf file that, by default, is stored in C:\Program Files\Apache Group\Apache\Conf.

**1.** Open the httpd.conf file with any text editor. Search for the line

#LoadModule ssl_module modules/mod_ssl.so

**2.** Directly underneath that line, add

LoadModule php4_module
➥c:/php/sapi/php4apache.dll

This tells Apache to load the PHP module when it starts. If the PHP module isn't loaded, you will be unable to use PHP on the web server.

**3.** Look for the following line:

#AddModule mod_perl.c

**4.** Directly under that line, add

AddModule mod_php4.c

This tells Apache to add the module at runtime.

**5.** Look for the line

AddHandler cgi-script .cgi .pl

**6.** Add this block of code a line or two below that

```
#
#To use PHP scripts
#
AddType application/x-httpd-php .php
```

This tells Apache that if a file is requested with a .php extension, it must pass it to the PHP engine in order to be parsed.

There is one last thing you need to do, and that is change the **document root**. This is where Apache looks for all your web files. By default, Apache uses C:\Program Files\Apache Group\Apache\htdocs. If you're the only person using the computer and plan to log on always as Administrator on a multiuser system like Windows XP Pro, you can leave it where it is. Storing web files, which may need constant updating, in such a sensitive part of your computer as the Program Files folder is not a good idea, though. We recommend you change it to something like C:\htdocs.

**7.** In httpd.conf, find the following line:

DocumentRoot "C:/Program Files/Apache
➥Group/Apache/htdocs"

**8.** Change it to

DocumentRoot "C:/htdocs"

Note that even though you're working on a Windows system, Apache uses forward slashes instead of the normal Windows backslashes.

**9.** About two dozen lines further down, locate this:

```
# This should be changed to whatever you
➥ set DocumentRoot to.
#<Directory "C:/Program Files/Apache
➥ Group/Apache/htdocs">
```

**10.** It should be self-explanatory, but change the final line to the following or whatever name you chose for your new document root.

```
<Directory "C:/htdocs">
```

**11.** Save the changes you made to httpd.conf and close the file.

**12.** Restart the web server by selecting Programs ➤ Apache HTTP Server ➤ Control Apache Server ➤ Restart.

That may have seemed like a lot of work, but it's all pretty straightforward if you follow the instructions carefully. You'll also need to get used to working with code if you want to build dynamic websites that do anything more than very basic things. Rolling your sleeves up and digging into the code will give you far more control over your environment than the average web designer is used to.

You are now ready to test your installation of PHP. So unless you have a Mac as well, you can skip the rest of this section and head straight to "Testing Your PHP Installation."

## Changing the Apache Port

If you want to experiment (or do serious development) with both ASP and PHP, you may want to run both IIS and Apache on the same machine. Although it's possible to install PHP on IIS, thereby avoiding the need to run two web servers, it's not something we recommend. Apache and IIS will run happily together, but they need to listen for page requests on different ports. The default is port 80, and port 8080 is recommended for the second server. Instructions were given earlier in the chapter for setting IIS to port 8080. If, for any reason, you want to set Apache (and PHP) to run on the alternative port instead, follow these steps.

**1.** Open Apache's configuration file httpd.conf (as described in the last exercise) and find the

following line (you should be able to find it with Notepad's Find feature—it's right at the beginning of Section 2 of http.conf):

```
Port 80
```

**2.** Change it to

**Port 8080**

It's as easy as that! After saving httpd.conf, restart Apache. The only thing to remember is that after making this change, you will always need to access your PHP pages by adding a colon and the port number after "localhost" (http://localhost:8080/).

# Setting up Apache and PHP in Mac OS X

The good news for Mac owners is that Apache and PHP come already installed in OS X. The bad news is that although you use the default Apache installation, you are not going to use the PHP version that comes bundled with OS X. This is because the bundled version is older, and you will use the latest version of PHP, which has improvements and additional options, which we will cover later in this chapter.

**Starting Apache**

Getting Apache up and running in OS X is a breeze. In this example we are using 10.2—if you are using an earlier version, your mileage may vary.

**1.** Open System Preferences and select Sharing, which is under the Internet & Network section, as shown in Figure 10-13.

**Figure 10-13.** The Internet & Network section

**2.** Click the Services tab, as shown in Figure 10-14.

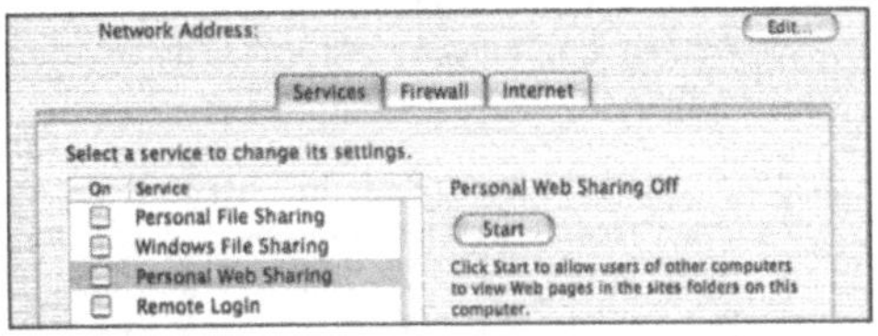


**Figure 10-14.** The Services tab

3. From the list select Personal Web Sharing, as shown in Figure 10-15, and then click the Start button on the right side of the list.

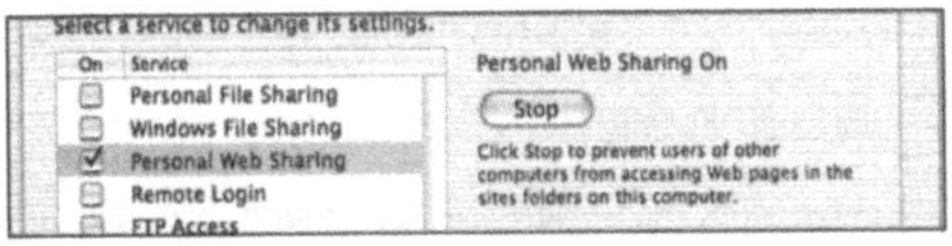


**Figure 10-15.** Selecting Personal Web Sharing

Congratulations. You have started Apache! If you are the only user of the machine, Apache will be started at boot. If this is the case, you can jump to the "Installing PHP" section.

4. If there are multiple users on your machine, you may want to start Apache from boot for all users—to do this you must alter the `hostconfig` file. Open a new terminal window by going to Applications ➤ Utilities. Drag the terminal icon to your Dock because you will need easy access to this in later chapters.
5. Before you alter any system files, let's make a backup copy. Type the following command into the terminal window:

```
sudo cp /etc/hostconfig hostconfig.
➥original
```

6. Enter your password.
7. Now you have a backup copy, so open the original. Type

```
sudo pico /etc/hostconfig
```

This will open the file in the pico editor.

8. Look for the following line:

```
WEBSERVER=-NO-
```

9. Change it to

```
WEBSERVER=-YES-
```

10. To save your changes, press CONTROL+X and select yes by pressing *Y*. Then press RETURN.

You have now configured Apache to start at boot for all users.

## Installing PHP

OS X includes with a version of the PHP module. that doesn't have many features enabled, and chances are, you will soon outgrow it. Don't worry, help is on hand in the form of Marc Liyanage, a software engineer and Mac fanatic who was kind enough to build a `.pkg` file for the latest versions of PHP. (A `.pkg` file is an executable file that installs software in a specific location.) At the time of this writing, he just released a version for PHP 4.3.4, which comes with the following extensions enabled:

- **The MySQL and PostgreSQL databases**: Although MySQL support comes enabled as standard, this version adds support for another popular open source database, PostgreSQL.
- **The PDFLib PDF library**: This allows you to create PDF files on the fly, either through user input or directly from a database.
- **Curl**: This is a library of various communications protocols.
- **The GD image creation library**: This is a powerful set of applications that allow you to create and alter images dynamically.
- **The expat XML parser and WDDX support**: These two options enable you to handle XML files and web syndication using WDDX (Web Distributed Data Exchange).
- **XSL Transformations**: This extension enables you to transform XML files into (X)HTML or other XML files.

- **LDAP access**: This enables PHP to interact with Lightweight Directory Access Protocol servers.

- **The IMAP client library**: This supplies PHP with an interface to IMAP, an alternative to the POP3 email protocol.

- **FTP client access**: This allows you to build web-based FTP applications.

- **Transparent session id propagation option**: This automatically propagates the session id transparently by adding it to the URL if cookies are not enabled on the user's computer.

- **Sockets extension**: This extension offers improved networking capabilities, allowing you to use PHP to get two machines to exchange information.

- **GNU gettext**: This extension library allows you to add multilingual support to your website.

- **XML-DOM**: This extension offers better XML support than the default libraries bundled with PHP.

- **PEAR**: This is the PHP Extension and Application Repository, a collection of open source classes that greatly simplify many complex operations.

- **CLI version**: This extension allows you to run PHP scripts outside of a browser, from the command line.

At this stage, that may seem like little more than alphabet soup, but it's a rich list of extensions that will be at your fingertips. What's more, installation is a breeze and can be done in a few steps.

1. Download the latest release from Marc's site at www.entropy.ch/software/macosx/php/.

2. Click the installer and follow the onscreen instructions.

It's that simple! Now you have Apache running and a feature-rich version of PHP installed. The only thing left to do is test it.

## PHP extensions (Windows and Mac)

None of the exercises in this book use the PHP extensions, but it's useful to know they're there. As you get more adventurous with PHP, you'll want to use them. The recommended installation for Mac OS X means you'll be able to use them right away. Windows users

shouldn't feel left out, though. They have access to all the same extensions. All you need to enable an extension is a simple change to the php.ini file.

1. Open php.ini and locate the section marked Windows Extensions. Find the extension you want and remove the semicolon from the beginning of the line. For example, say you want to create some dynamic graphics and need the GD Image Creation library.

2. Find this line

   ;extension=php_gd2.dll

3. Uncomment it by deleting the semicolon like this

   extension=php_gd2.dll

4. Save php.ini, open the command prompt, and type **net stop apache**. Once Apache has stopped, restart it by typing **net start apache**. That's it! You're ready to go.

### Testing your PHP installation

Now you will test your installation.

1. Open your favorite text editor, for example, Notepad in Windows or BBEdit in OS X. Type the following bit of code:

   ```
   <?php
   phpinfo(); //print out details about our
   ➥ PHP set up
   ?>
   ```

2. Save this file as **info.php**. Make sure that you use a .php extension.

3. Save this file in the Apache server directory. Windows users, if you changed the root directory as suggested earlier, it will be C:\htdocs. Mac users will have to go to Macintosh HD ➤ Users ➤ Username ➤ Sites.

Now it's time to see if everything went according to plan.

4. PC users, open your browser and browse to http://localhost/info.php.

**5.** Mac users, open your browser and go to `http://localhost/~username/info.php`. Replace `~username` with your system username.

If all went according to plan you should see something similar to Figure 10-16.

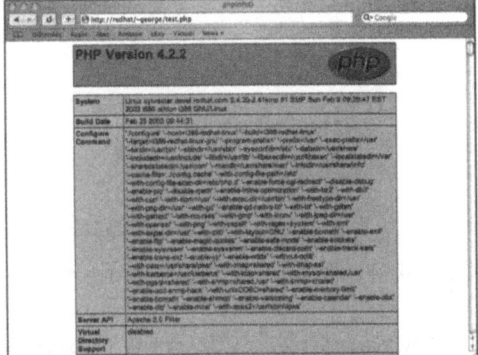

**Figure 10-16.** Testing your PHP installation

Windows users will see a slightly simplified version (without the Configure Command section). This is nothing to worry about. It's simply the different ways Windows and Mac OS X handle PHP. For all intents and purposes, they function exactly the same.

## Troubleshooting

Sometimes not everything goes to plan. The most common problem is that a user has incorrectly modified the `httpd.conf` file. If you experience difficulties, retrace your steps and check the information you entered into the file.

If you are using a Mac and encounter problems, the best place to ask a question is the forum of the man who wrote the package—www.entropy.ch/phpbb2/.

If you are a PC user and feel dejected because Mac users seemed to have it so much easier during the installation process, don't worry. There are several packages that will install it all for you, the best of which is available at www.firepages.com.au. Installing PHP and Apache separately, though, gives you much greater control and it's worth the effort. The installation should

take you only a few minutes if you follow the instructions carefully.

Now it's time to get Dreamweaver MX 2004 ready for your first dynamic pages using PHP.

**1.** From within Dreamweaver, select Site ➤ Manage Sites from the top menu to open the Manage Sites box. Click the New button. You will be presented with two options. Select the first one, Site, to open the Site Wizard, as shown in Figure 10-17.

**Figure 10-17.** Opening the Site Wizard

**2.** If your screen doesn't look like Figure 10-18, click the Basic tab at the top of the dialog box. You will notice that the text field is populated with the text Unnamed Site 1. Change this to `php_site` and then click the Next button.

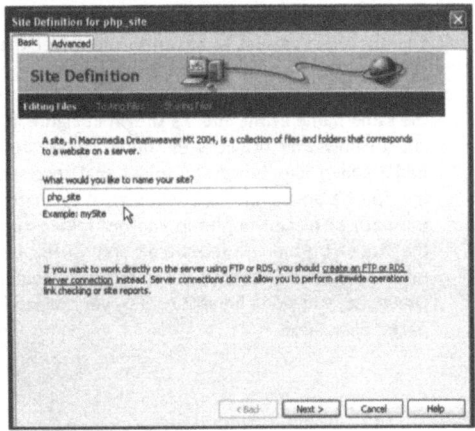

**Figure 10-18.** Choose a suitable name for your site.

**3.** In the next page, select Yes, I want to use a server technology, as shown in Figure 10-19. Once this option is selected, a drop-down menu will appear. Select PHP MySQL and then click Next.

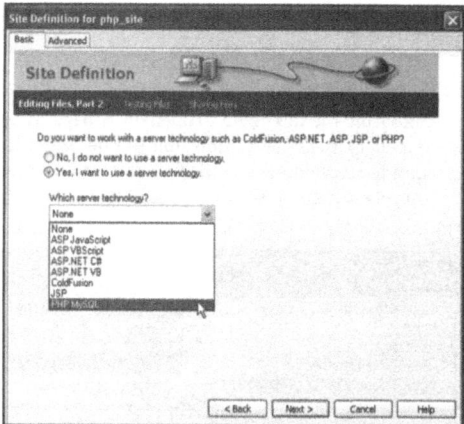

**Figure 10-19.** Choosing the PHP MySQL server-side technology

**4.** Now that you specified which server-side technology you are going to use, you need to tell Dreamweaver where to store the files it will need to create. Because Apache and PHP are running locally, select Edit and test locally (my testing server is on this computer).

**5.** You also need to specify a path to the folder that will store the files. MX 2004 tries to find the root folder of your web server and create a folder with the same name as the site. As shown in Figure 10-20, Dreamweaver provides the option to create a folder called php_site in the folder that serves as the Apache document root. If you want to change this path or place the files in another folder, click the Browse button and select a different place, but make sure it is within your server's root folder. Otherwise, you won't be able to view your dynamic pages. Click Next.

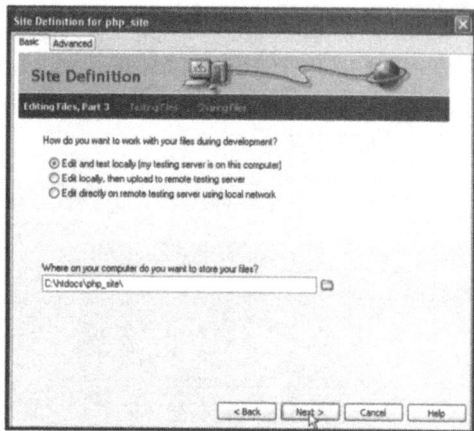

**Figure 10-20.** Selecting the folder where your files will be stored

**6.** Now you must provide a URL path to the folder you just created. If you're on Windows, this will be http://localhost/php_site/, as shown in Figure 10-21. Mac users will need to enter the username like this: http://localhost/~username/php_site/.

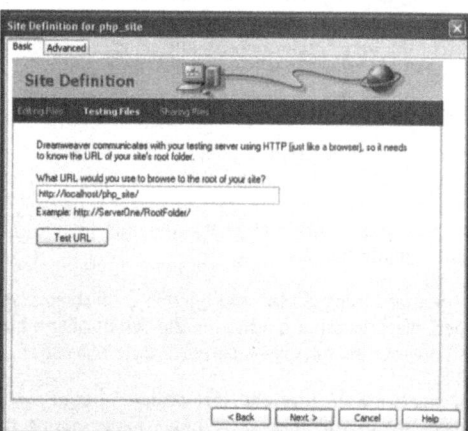

**Figure 10-21.** Specifying the local URL of your site folder

7. Click the Test URL button. If you have done everything correctly, you should get a dialog box similar to the one shown in Figure 10-22. If you get an error message instead, go back and check the URL you just entered (double-check that you've remembered the slash at the end).

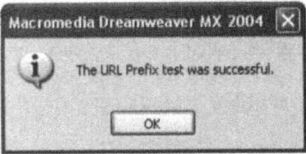

**Figure 10-22.** Congratulations! Nearly finished

8. Once you get a successful test, click OK. Then click Next.

9. MX 2004 now asks if you want to transfer your files to another server after you edit them. Click No, as shown in Figure 10-23, and click Next for the final check to make sure everything has been set up the way you want it.

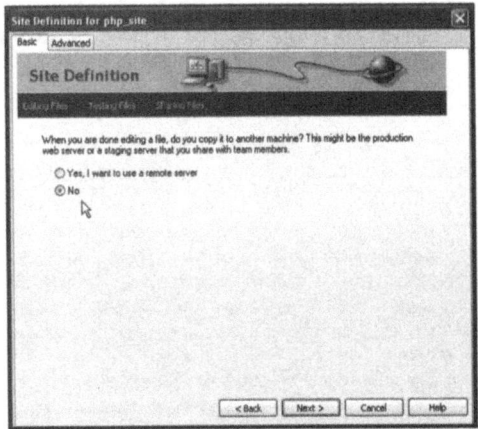

**Figure 10-23.** Choosing to not transfer your files to another computer

10. The final screen presents you with a summary of the settings for your site, as shown in Figure 10-24. Check the details, and if you're happy, click Done. If there's anything you need to change, the Back button will display the previous screens. (You can do this at any stage in the process.)

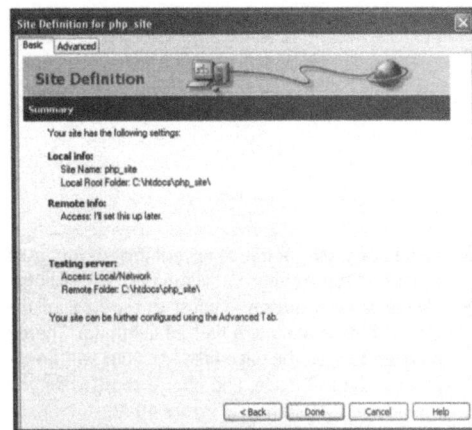

**Figure 10-24.** Checking that the details are right

11. If the Manage Sites screen is still open, click Done again. You're now in business to start creating dynamic PHP pages with Dreamweaver MX 2004. Let's just make sure it works.

12. Select File ➤ New from the top menu. Then select Dynamic Page in the Category field. When you do this, the list in the right field will change. Select PHP from that list. Although you should make sure the Make document XHTML compliant box is checked, as shown in Figure 10-25, it doesn't matter on this occasion because you're going to strip out all the code from the page.

13. With the new page open in the MX 2004 workspace, go into Split view, highlight all the code in the page, and delete it. Once you've made sure there's nothing left in the page, type

```
<?php
phpinfo();
?>
```

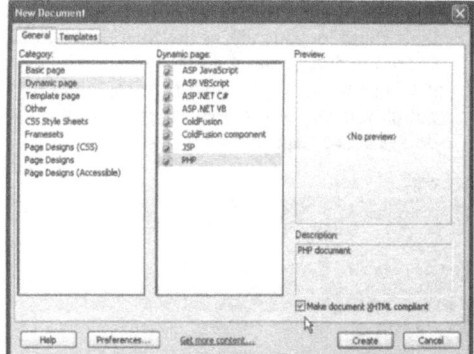

**Figure 10-25.** Creating a new PHP page in MX 2004

**14.** Remember, this is the same command you used when first testing your installation of PHP. Click the Live Data view button (it's just to the right of the Design button and has a flash of lightning). There's no need to save the page first. MX 2004 will simply process the PHP code, and after a short while you should see something like Figure 10-26.

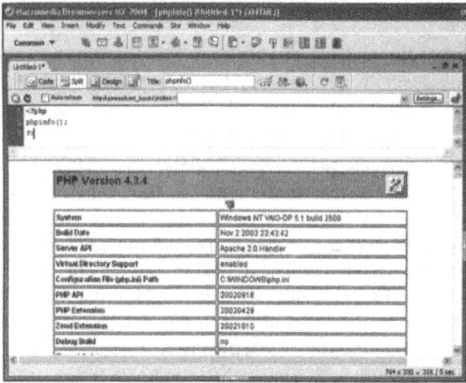

**Figure 10-26.** Live Data view showing how much PHP can generate from so little code

**15.** Not only have you proved the site is working, you've learned how to use one of Dreamweaver MX 2004's most useful tools for developing dynamic websites. Live Data view enables you to see on screen what your underlying code is generating. You shouldn't leave it switched on while you're building a page because it uses quite a lot of processor power and could slow your system down, but it's very handy for a quick check of progress. To switch it off, just click the Live Data view button again. Try it now, and all the data in the lower half of the workspace should disappear.

## Troubleshooting

If Live Data view doesn't work, try moving your mouse pointer over the Design view part of the page. If that doesn't do the trick, check the code very carefully.

- Make sure you've typed the opening <?php correctly. There should be no space between any of the characters.

- Check you've used a semicolon at the end of phpinfo(); and that the closing ?> has no spaces.

- Check all the previous steps in this chapter. If you've got everything else working, it means there's almost certainly a mistake in the way you set up your PHP site in MX 2004.

> One of the things people new to any programming language like PHP find hard to get used to is the need to make sure everything's exactly the way it should be. Browsers make up for a lot of mistakes in HTML coding, so it often doesn't matter if you miss a closing tag. If you leave out something from PHP—even something as seemingly insignificant as a comma—it can break your whole script. This is true for all other server-side languages as well. But once you've learned the simple rules, Dreamweaver MX 2004 has some useful features to help you track down problems. So don't panic!

## Summary

You may be feeling a little shell-shocked by now, but you have accomplished a lot. In this chapter, you

- Looked at the basics of dynamic sites
- Dipped into the history of PHP
- Looked at the background of Apache, the most popular web server available today

- Installed Apache web server
- Installed and configured PHP
- Set up a PHP site in Dreamweaver MX 2004
- Tested it all

Quite an achievement, and all in the space of one chapter. Have a cup of coffee and allow yourself to feel satisfied—but not for long because in the next chapter you delve into the PHP language.

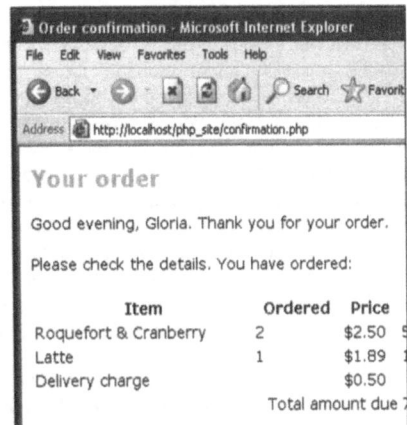

**Chapter 11**

# GETTING INTERACTIVE WITH FORMS

**What we'll cover in this chapter**

- Dreamweaver MX 2004 features that make light work of coding PHP
    - Auto-completion
    - Balance Braces
    - Code colors
    - The PHP Insert bar
- Gathering and displaying information from a form
- The basic grammar of PHP
- Handling text
- Using PHP for calculations
- Building an online order form

Now that you've put in all that hard work installing Apache and PHP, you're probably raring to create dynamic pages. The first thing most books on programming languages teach you is how to write "Hello, world" or "Hi mom, this is my first page." We're ditching that boring old tradition because you can already do that quite adequately with XHTML. Instead, we're going to show you PHP's real power right away, and by the end of this chapter, you'll have created an online form that will do calculations. In the next chapter, you'll take things further by getting the form to send any input to your e-mail inbox. Really useful stuff!

In the course of the next two chapters, you'll also learn most of the basics of PHP, giving you a solid foundation to start writing scripts of your own.

Hang on a moment...why learn about PHP? Doesn't MX 2004 create it all for you?

Certainly Dreamweaver takes a lot of the hard work out of building dynamic pages, and you can build a database-driven site with it very quickly, as you'll see when we get to the final three chapters. But if you rely entirely on MX 2004 to generate your code, you'll often find yourself stuck with a solution that doesn't quite fit your needs. You'll also be helpless when things go wrong. The PHP code generated automatically by MX 2004 does some very powerful things, such as displaying a table row only in specific circumstances, but if you mess up the code accidentally or want to make it do that little extra, the skills you learn here will make your life a lot easier. You'll also find it satisfying to create your own dynamic effects.

There's a lot of information in this chapter and the next. Read both chapters through at least once and do all the exercises, but don't try to remember everything at one sitting. Come back and use them as a reference whenever you need to refresh your memory.

Let's get on with making your first dynamic page.

### Putting PHP to work

You will be working in the site you created in Chapter 10, php_site, so make sure you create all new pages there until you get to Chapter 15. If you don't want to

type in all the code yourself, you can download the sample files from the friends of ED website. Hands-on practice is usually the best way to learn, though, so do the exercises yourself, and just use the download files to check against if anything goes wrong.

1. Create a new PHP page in MX 2004 and call it confirmation.php. If you set up your site correctly and selected PHP from File ➤ New ➤ Dynamic page, MX 2004 automatically gives your file the .php extension.

2. In Design view, type Your order and format it as a heading. Press *ENTER* to create a new paragraph. Then open Split view. When creating pages with dynamic code such as PHP, Split view enables you to move quickly between Design view, where you create the basic layout and any static content of the page, and Code view to insert server-side code. If you need more space, use your mouse pointer to drag the top half of the window wider, or simply open Code view. You'll find yourself getting used to going back and forth in no time at all. Put your mouse pointer into Code view, and highlight the   between the <p> tags, as shown in Figure 11-1.

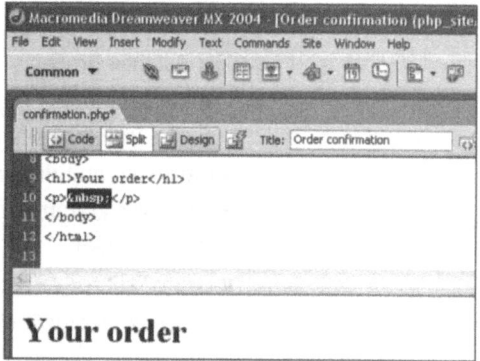

**Figure 11-1.** Working in Split view

3. Delete the   and type the following code. As soon as you get part of the way through the third line, you'll discover one of the most useful features in MX 2004 to help you with coding PHP—**auto-completion** (described in steps 4 and 5).

```php
<?php
  // Get the name from the form
  $name = $_POST['name'];

  // Find out what hour of the day it is
  $date = date('H');

  // Work out a suitable greeting
  if($date <= 11) { // if between 0 and 11
    $greeting = 'Good morning, ';
    }
  // or if after 11 and before 17 (5pm)
  elseif ($date > 11 and $date < 17) {
    $greeting = 'Good afternoon, ';
    }
  else { // otherwise
    $greeting = 'Good evening, ';
    }

  // Print out the greeting and name
  echo $greeting.$name;
?>
```

4. Type **$_** and a little menu should pop up next to your cursor, as shown in Figure 11-2.

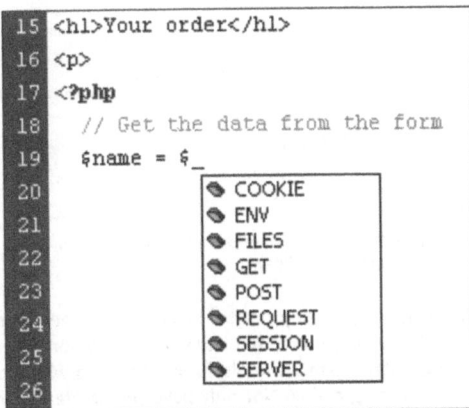

**Figure 11-2.** Begin a built-in PHP expression and MX 2004 offers to finish it for you.

5. MX 2004 realizes you probably want to use one of PHP's built-in expressions, and offers you a list of those available. Either type **p** (uppercase or lowercase—it doesn't matter), or use your down arrow key or mouse pointer to highlight POST. MX 2004 fills in the rest automatically, and creates the opening square bracket ready for you to continue: $_POST[. It may not seem worth it for just a few keystrokes, but when you're entering a lot of these, it saves time and prevents misspellings that could break your code. If the pop-up fails to materialize, go to Edit ➤ Preferences ➤ Code Hints and check the Enable auto tag completion box. If the pop-up gets in your way, that's also where to turn the option off.

6. Changes made in the Code area of Split view won't be reflected in Design view until you move your mouse pointer back into the Design view portion of the screen. When you do, instead of seeing your code, you'll see a gold PHP icon, as shown in Figure 11-3. This is an important feature about server-side languages—they remain on the server. Anybody looking at the source code of a PHP page in a browser won't be able to see your PHP code—if they can, you've made a mistake. They should only be able to see the output of that code. You can use the Live Data View button (as you did in the last chapter) to view dynamic output, but that won't work with this page because the dynamic data will always be drawn from an online form and cannot be accessed by MX 2004.

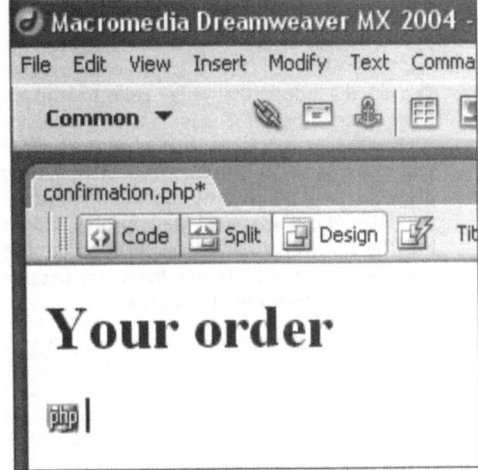

**Figure 11-3.** The location of your PHP script, marked with a gold icon

**181**

**7.** Now let's create the form to generate some input for your page to work on. Create a new XHTML page in your site. (Select File ➤ New. Last time, you chose Dynamic Page ➤ PHP; this time choose Basic Page ➤ HTML.) Call the page order.html, and insert a form in it.

---

*A lot of people get confused about which file name extension to use when first creating a dynamic site. It's perfectly normal to mix pages with .php and .html extensions on the same site, and is arguably more efficient. Just remember, though, that you should always use .php if you plan to add dynamic content to a page. Although it is possible to configure a server to treat .htm or .html as PHP, most ISPs don't do it that way. Also note there's no practical difference between using .htm and .html. We use .html in these examples because that's the way our system is configured. If MX 2004 saves your pages with an .htm extension, don't worry. Stick to one naming convention because mixing .htm and .html on the same site can lead to broken links or the wrong file being served up. For history buffs, the difference arose because early versions of Windows and DOS were unable to handle more than three characters after the period in a file name.*

---

**8.** Set the Action of the form to confirmation.php and the Method to POST, as shown in Figure 11-4. This tells the browser that you're going to send any input to confirmation.php for it to process. Using POST as the method means that when the input is sent to the server, it is hidden from view. GET, on the other hand, sends the information as part of the URL so it can be seen in the browser's Address bar. There are other differences between the two methods, but we won't go into them here because they are not relevant to this exercise.

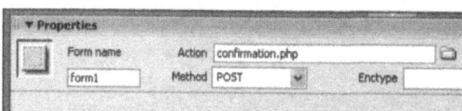

**Figure 11-4.** Setting up the form to send input to your dynamic page

**9.** You want only a text box and a Submit button in the form, as shown in Figure 11-5. Rename the text box name. (Refer back to the section "Creating the contact page" of Chapter 8 if you're not sure about naming text boxes in forms.) Save both pages, and press *F12* to preview order.html in your browser.

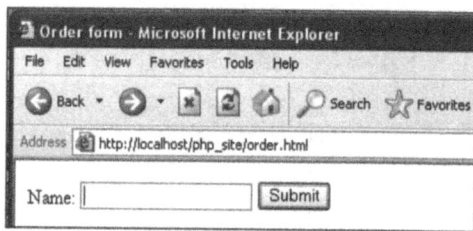

**Figure 11-5.** The simplest of forms, but you'll add more elements later.

**10.** Type your name, and click Submit. If everything has gone well, you should get something like Figure 11-6.

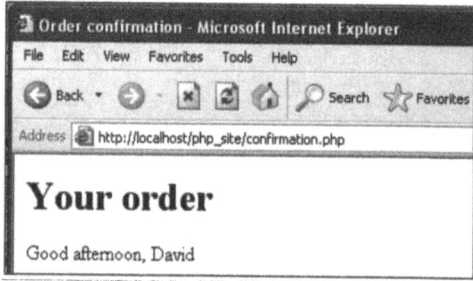

**Figure 11-6.** PHP gathered information from the form and worked out the time of day.

We made that page just after lunch, and it greeted us with "Good afternoon," but had we done it before midday or after 5 p.m., it would have responded with the appropriate greeting. Not only have you created your first interactive form, you used many of PHP's powerful features, which we'll now look at a little more closely.

## Troubleshooting

Hopefully, everything went fine with your first interactive script, but if it didn't, there are several things you should look out for. Read this section even if you had no problems because it contains a lot of important information.

- If you're used to testing files by simply opening them in a browser from your local hard disk, get out of the habit now. For PHP files to work properly, they need to be processed by a web server. Either use *F12* to launch them from a Dreamweaver site configured for PHP MySQL, or use the correct URL for your Apache server (see Chapter 10).

- Go back over the PHP script and make sure you have copied it correctly. It's easy to leave out a quotation mark, semicolon, or bracket.

- Make sure you used the right type of bracket. It's easy to confuse them. Some places require a square bracket, others a curly bracket, and yet others a parenthesis. They all have different meanings (which we'll cover later).

- Every opening bracket needs to have a matching closing bracket, although matching pairs can often be many lines apart with other brackets nested in between.

- Make sure you are consistent in your spelling, particularly with the use of uppercase and lowercase letters. PHP is case sensitive. For example, $name and $Name mean two different things to a PHP script.

- You can use either single or double quotation marks, but only in matching pairs.

Dreamweaver MX 2004 does a lot to help you avoid mistakes. As you are typing PHP code, Dreamweaver uses color coding to indicate different elements in the script. If your preferences have not been changed, the opening <?php and ?> should be in bold red; comments (lines beginning with a double slash) in orange; everything in quotes in red; and certain words and characters that have special meanings in PHP are in light blue. If suddenly something you expect to be in blue is in red, it usually means you've got a quotation mark missing somewhere.

*Keeping track of matching braces is possibly one of the most frustrating parts of code writing, not only in PHP, but in all similar languages. Fortunately, MX 2004 has a superb little tool called "Balance Braces." Click your mouse pointer just inside any type of bracket (curly, square, or parenthesis) and choose Edit ➤ Balance Braces. MX 2004 highlights all the text up to the matching bracket, as shown in Figure 11-7. If nothing is highlighted, it means you have an uneven pair. To track down the problem, find the innermost bracket and work outward using Balance Braces each time until you identify the problem. It may sound like hard work, but it's a lot faster than trying to spot a missing bracket in a lengthy piece of code. Balance Braces also has a keyboard shortcut (Ctrl/Cmd+'), but it may not work on all systems. You may need to change it using Edit ➤ Keyboard Shortcuts (see the MX 2004 Help files for details).*

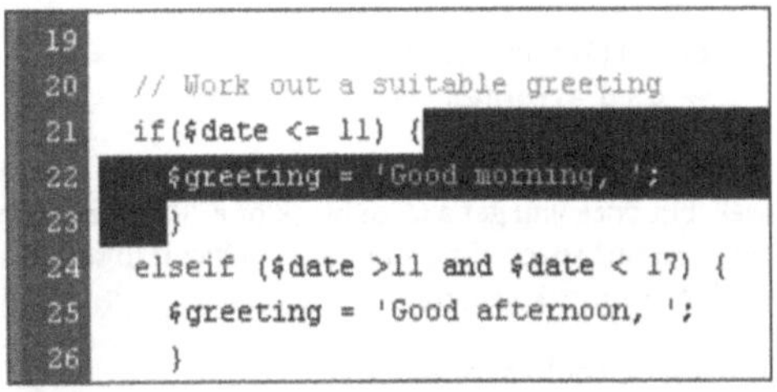

**Figure 11-7.** Using Balance Braces to check for a missing brace or bracket

# The basic grammar of PHP

You'll return to your order form later in the chapter. For now, let's move on to the grammar of PHP.

PHP lets you embed code straight into your XHTML. Anything you place within the opening tag <?php and the closing tag ?> will be interpreted by the PHP engine. Anything outside these tags will be treated as plain XHTML.

> *You may come across PHP scripts in other books or in online tutorials that use <? instead of <?php. The shorter form is perfectly legal, but it is no longer recommended. This is to prevent confusion with the XML declaration, which begins with <?xml. PHP servers generate an error when they encounter the XML declaration, so many administrators are disabling the short form. By using <?php, you are future-proofing your scripts.*

Just like HTML and XHTML, PHP ignores white space. The indenting in the code is purely to make it easier to read and maintain. Instead of

```
elseif ($date > 11 and $date < 17) {
    $greeting = 'Good afternoon, ';
    }
```

we could have written it all on one line with no spaces (although it had to be broken here because of printing limitations).

```
elseif($date>11and$date<17){$greeting=
➥'Good afternoon, ';}
```

The meaning is exactly the same, and it works just as well, but once you get a large block of PHP written with no breathing space, it becomes very difficult to sort out problems or make changes.

Equally, we could have written

```
elseif ($date >
        11 and
$date

                        < 17)                {
        $greeting

=

                                        'Good
afternoon, '                            ;
                        }
```

It wouldn't be very sensible, and it would be a nightmare to maintain, but it's perfectly legal PHP.

## The ever-elusive but oh-so-important semicolon

The reason PHP is able to ignore white space and new lines is that it expects a semicolon at the end of each **statement** (or instruction). PHP is made up of a series of statements, usually single instructions to do something.

> *Find the date;*
> *Print this message;*
> *Multiply number of items by item price;*

Single statements always end with a semicolon—forgetting this simple rule is something that constantly messes up beginners. From time to time, it affects seasoned programmers, too, so you're not alone. But if you're new to programming languages, you're in for a rude shock when you make your first mistake. If you make a mistake in HTML, most browsers will still try to display the page to the best of their ability. With PHP (or any other server-side language) you get a blunt message like the one shown in Figure 11-8.

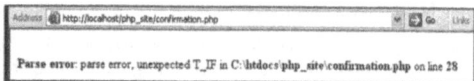

**Figure 11-8.** PHP error messages are not exactly user-friendly, especially for beginners.

All this tells you is that PHP found something it wasn't expecting and where it found it. Line 28 began with an if statement (we'll get to those in Chapter 12), which is exactly what belongs there, so that's not where the problem lies. What PHP is telling you in a roundabout way is that something is wrong *before* that point in the script. The only solution is to start going backward through the code until you find it. Fortunately, it was easy in this case: the semicolon was missing at the end of $date = date('H') on the previous line.

If only it were always that easy! Sometimes you get a message saying PHP expected a semicolon on line 548, but when you look, you discover your script is only 547 lines long. In other words, PHP hasn't the faintest idea where the problem is, and it's up to you to find it. You can end up wasting a lot of time searching for that one tiny piece of punctuation. Don't get discouraged—PHP's far too much fun for that, but it's worth drumming home at an early stage that all programming languages have strict rules you must follow. The good thing about PHP is that there are a lot fewer of them to worry about than with many other languages.

## Commenting scripts

The exercise begun earlier in this chapter contained four lines that began with double slashes (and will have been displayed in orange in MX 2004).

```
// Get the name from the form
// Find out what hour of the day it is
// Work out a suitable greeting
// Print out the greeting and name
```

These lines have no real function within the script other than to remind you what the script is for. Anything on a line following a double slash is regarded as a comment, and it will not be processed. You can also place comments to the right-hand side of script, like this.

```
if($date <= 11) { // if between 0 and 11
```

Why add comments? You add them so that in six months you are not asking yourself *why didn't I?* Even for experienced scripters, it can be hard to see at a glance what a piece of PHP is doing. By liberally sprinkling your scripts with comments in human language, you can come back to something much, much later and see at a glance what it's for and locate the portion you may need to change. In practice, you probably wouldn't use as many comments as we have in that script. The purpose here is to help you learn to read scripts that may not yet mean very much to you (but they will soon, we promise).

You can also use the pound sign (#) in place of the double slash.

```
# if between 0 and 11
```

The disadvantage of using the double slash and pound sign comment symbols is that you must put them in every line you want to be ignored by the PHP processor; otherwise it will trigger an error. Fortunately, there is another way of creating comments that stretch over several lines, and that is to sandwich them between /* and */ as shown here:

```
/* This is a long comment
   that will stretch over
   four lines, but it could go
   on for many more
*/
```

This is a very useful technique for disabling parts of a script that you think might be causing problems. MX 2004 has a convenient tool for creating quick comment tags around blocks of script. Just highlight the text or script you want to comment out, and click the Comment button on the PHP Insert bar, as shown in Figure 11-9.

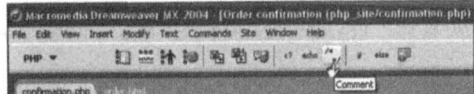

**Figure 11-9.** Commenting out sections of code via the PHP Insert bar

## Variables

Variables are the backbone of just about every programming language. They are a handy way of storing information, particularly if you don't know what that information is going to be beforehand. When creating confirmation.php, you had no idea what name users would enter in the form, nor what time of day they would submit it. By using variables—in this case $name and $greeting—you were able to create a page that would respond to any situation. In Figure 11-6, you could see that someone named David submitted the form sometime between midday and 5 p.m., but the same script would work if Craig or George had filled it in at a different time of day. A variable doesn't only hold a piece of information; it's flexible enough to change that information whenever told to do so.

One thing you'll have noticed is that both $name and $greeting begin with a dollar sign. All variables in PHP do—that's what tells you it's a variable. Forgetting the dollar sign is a common beginner's mistake. If your scripts don't work, that's one thing to look out for. Also, don't confuse the dollar sign with an uppercase S. PHP won't play ball if you use the wrong one.

Some other important things to note:

- Variables can consist only of alphanumeric characters (A-Z and 0-9) and the underscore.

- The first character after the dollar sign cannot be a number (you can use the underscore, but this is best avoided because it is normally reserved for a specific type of variable—play safe and stick with A-Z).

- No spaces are allowed.

- Although you can mix uppercase and lowercase, variables are case sensitive, so $totalPrice and $totalprice are not the same to a PHP script.

Table 11-1 lists some examples of what you can and cannot do.

**Table 11-1.** Rules for Variables

| Example | Rule |
| --- | --- |
| $first variable | illegal: contains space |
| $2ndvariable | illegal: starts with a number |
| $third&variable | illegal: contains an illegal character (&) |
| $-fourthvariable | illegal: starts with neither a legal character nor an underscore |
| $first_variable | legal |
| $secondvariable | legal |
| $thirdAndvariable | legal |
| $_fourthvariable | legal |

When choosing variable names, it's a good idea to select something that will help you understand the working of your script. In the exercise, you could have saved some typing by using $n instead of $name and $g instead of $greeting, but the savings are wiped out by the difficulty in keeping track of what everything means, particularly in a long script or when coming back even to a short script several months later.

A lot of people use camel case notation (capitalizing the first letter of second or subsequent words in variables) to make them easier to read; for example: $totalPrice. Choose whatever suits you best. And remember, although there is no limit on the length of variables, the longer they are, the more difficult they are to type—and the easier to misspell.

$totalPriceAfterDiscountButIncludingTax

It says exactly what it's for, but is probably not a good idea.

Finally, don't use $this as a variable. It has a special meaning and is only used in objects, which are beyond the scope of this book. MX 2004 provides a visual warning by highlighting $this in light blue, indicating that it is part of the PHP core language.

## Data types

PHP is what's known as a loosely typed language, which makes it a lot easier for beginners. This means variables can hold any type of data without you having to specify beforehand. For instance, in Java, which is strictly typed, you cannot create a variable to hold a number without first declaring what type of number (whole numbers or ones with a floating decimal point are treated differently). Once you decide the data type in Java, you cannot change it.

PHP doesn't care. You can assign a number to a variable and later change it to a word (or words). This can be extremely useful. If the value held in $totalPrice turns out to be 0, you could assign the word "free" to $totalPrice, and display that on the screen. This flexibility also has its dangers; you might later try to multiply a number by $totalPrice. Computers can multiply numbers, but they're not clever enough to realize five times free is still free. (Actually, the result you would get in this case is 0, so it may still work, but attempting to use a word in a mathematical calculation would normally produce a nonsensical result or stop the script from working.)

PHP has several data types, but the main three are

- **Integers**: These are whole numbers with either a positive or negative value, ranging from –2,147,483,648 to +2,147,483,647. In other words, the range for a 32-bit machine is 2^32. Note that you must never put a comma or any other punctuation in a number to separate thousands. Examples of valid integers include –734, 0, 9, 637343.

- **Doubles**: These are numbers that have a decimal place or an exponential value. Examples of valid doubles include 2.0, 2.87, 4.86495685, 3.57E-2.

- **Strings**: These are used to represent non-numerical values, such as text. They must be enclosed in either single or double quotation marks. It is also worth noting that a numerical value enclosed in quotes will be treated as a string. String examples: 'I am a string', '2 + 2 = 4', "394".

# Handling text in PHP

The whole point of creating dynamic pages is so that you can change the content, so it's important to know how PHP handles text—or strings, as you just learned they're called. It's mostly straightforward, but there are several things you need to bear in mind.

## Single or double quotation marks?

If all you're concerned about is what ends up on the screen, most of the time it doesn't matter which you use, but behind the scenes, PHP uses single and double quotes in very different ways.

- Anything between single quotation marks is treated as plain text.
- Anything between double quotation marks is processed.

A simple example will explain what that means. To display something on the screen in PHP, you use **echo**, followed by whatever it is you want displayed. If it's a

variable, you need no quotes, but if it's a string, you need to use either single or double quotes.

```php
$name = 'David';
echo $name; // displays "David"
echo 'Hi, $name'; // displays "Hi, $name"
echo "Hi, $name"; // displays "Hi, David"
```

In other words, the variable is ignored inside single quotes, but its value is displayed when you use double quotes. Another advantage of double quotes is that you can include text that uses the apostrophe. As far as PHP is concerned, an apostrophe and a single quote are the same thing, and quotes must always be in matching pairs.

```php
echo 'It's fine'; // generates an error
echo "It's fine"; // displays as expected
```

The reason the first generates an error is because PHP sees the apostrophe as the closing single quotation mark. The rest of the line is treated as illegal code. To get round this, you have to **escape** any apostrophes in single-quoted strings with a backslash. ("Escape" simply means telling PHP to ignore a character it would normally treat in a special way.)

```php
echo 'It\'s fine'; // displays "It's fine"
```

So why not use double quotes all the time? Good question. A lot of people do, but the official recommendation is to use the quoting method that uses the least processing power, and that's usually single quotes. Whenever PHP sees an opening double quote, it tries to process any variables first. If it finds none, it goes back and treats the string as plain text. On short scripts, such as the ones you're creating in this book, the difference in processing time is negligible, but it can make a difference on long, complex scripts.

Because PHP variables begin with a dollar sign, and PHP processes variables in double-quoted strings, how can you get it to display an ordinary dollar sign? Again, the answer is to escape it with a backslash.

```php
$totalPrice = 7.99;
echo "The total is \$$totalPrice";
// displays "The total is $7.99"
```

If you want double quotes within a double-quoted string? You guessed it—escape them.

```
echo "Shakespeare's \"Macbeth\"";
// displays the double quotes
```

There's one final thing to learn about strings—joining them together.

## The humble dot with a fancy name

Often, you'll want to join together two or more strings (or strings stored in variables). Every programming language uses what is called a **concatenation operator** to do this. Concatenation means "joining together one after another." In ASP, the concatenation operator is the ampersand (&); in JavaScript it's the plus sign (+); and in PHP it's a humble period (or full stop, as we like to call it in Britain). You saw it in operation in confirmation.php, where the period joins the string values together in the following line:

```
echo $greeting.$name;
```

PHP takes no notice of white space (except within a quoted string), so you could write that line

```
echo $greeting . $name;
```

It still works, but it won't add any white space to what's displayed in a browser. To get white space between concatenated string variables, you have three options.

- Include the white space in the string itself.
- Add the white space as a separate string.
- Use a double-quoted string.

You used the first technique when assigning the value to $greeting, so let's take a look at the other two.

```
$greeting = 'Hi,';
$name = 'Pat';

echo $greeting . $name; // "Hi,Pat"
echo $greeting.' '.$name.'.'; // "Hi, Pat."
echo "$greeting $name."; // "Hi, Pat."
```

Note how the second and third examples handle the period at the end of the sentence. The use of double quotes is clearly far more efficient here.

Although it may seem strange that something normally associated with bringing sentences to an end is used to join strings of text together, you soon get used to it. Perhaps the biggest drawback is that the concatenation operator can be difficult to spot in a long script in a book or on your computer screen. If seeing it becomes a problem in Dreamweaver MX 2004, go to Edit ➤ Preferences ➤ Fonts, and change the size of the font for Code view.

# Doing calculations with PHP

Take a very simple calculation:

```
33 + 27
```

You know that the plus sign in this example tells you to add the two numbers together. To get technical for a moment, the plus sign is known as an **arithmetic operator**, and 33 and 27 are the **operands**. PHP has a full range of arithmetic operators, most of which will be completely familiar to you from school days, and they work exactly as you expect. You will have noticed, though, we haven't completed the sum by adding = 60. There are several reasons for that.

- You can get PHP to do the hard work of calculating the result.
- In calculations, at least one of the numerical values is usually stored in a variable.
- Programming languages like PHP use the equal sign (=) in a different way.

## When the equal sign doesn't mean equal

Most of the arithmetic operators in PHP and similar languages mean exactly what you expect. The major exception is the equal sign. Officially, it's known as the **assignment operator**. Think of it as meaning "is set to."

In the opening exercise, the PHP script tries to work out a suitable greeting for the time of day. If it's before midday, it uses the following line to find the value assigned to the variable:

```
$greeting = 'Good morning, ';
```

You will make far fewer mistakes when writing PHP if you think of this as

```
This variable ($greeting) is
set to 'Good morning, ';
```

Programming languages have a slightly different way of saying "is equal to," and PHP is no exception. You will understand this better when we cover conditional statements in the next chapter.

## Back to school with arithmetic operators

The following table shows you how the standard operators work. To demonstrate their effect, the following variables have been set:

```
$x = 20;
$y = 10;
$z = 4.5;
```

Table 11-2 lists examples of the standard arithmetic operators in PHP.

**Table 11-2.** Arithmetic Operators in PHP

| Operation | Operator | Example | Result |
|---|---|---|---|
| Addition | + | $x + $y | 30 |
| Subtraction | - | $x – $y | 10 |
| Multiplication | * | $x * $y | 200 |
| Division | / | $x / $y | 2 |
| Modulo division | % | $x % $z | 2 |
| Increment (adds 1) | ++ | $x++ | 21 |
| Decrement (subtracts 1) | -- | $y-- | 9 |

The first four operators should need no explanation. They work exactly as you would expect. You may not be familiar, though, with the modulo operator. This returns the remainder of a division, as shown in Table 11-3.

**Table 11-3.** Using the Modulo Operator

| Modulo | Result |
|---|---|
| 26 % 5 | 1 |
| 26 % 27 | 26 |
| 10 % 2 | 0 |

This is a very useful arithmetic operator in a number of situations. One very practical use is to work out whether a number is odd or even. $number % 2 will always return 0 or 1. You'll use it later to give alternate table rows different colors.

The increment (++) and decrement (--) operators are fairly straightforward, except they can come either before or after the variable. When they come before, 1 is added or subtracted from the value held in the variable, and then any calculation is carried out. When they come after, the calculation is carried out first, and then the value in the variable is changed. This may sound confusing, but you will see this in action when you get into flow control statements and loops.

Arithmetic operators also have an order of precedence, as shown in Table 11-4. One way of remembering this order is the acronym BODMAS (Brackets of Division Multiplication Addition Subtraction).

**Table 11-4.** Order that Arithmetic Operators Are Evaluated

| Precedence | Group | Operators | Rule |
|---|---|---|---|
| Highest | Brackets | ( ) | Operations contained within brackets are evaluated first. If these expressions are nested, the innermost is evaluated first. |
| Next | Multiplication and division | * / % | These operators are evaluated next. If an expression contains two or more operators, they are evaluated from left to right. |
| Lowest | Addition and subtraction | + - | These are the final operators to be evaluated in an expression. If an expression contains two or more, they are evaluated from left to right. |

Applying the rules just shown to this complex expression

```
$result = $a*($b+($c*$d)/$e)*($f-$g%$h);
```

the calculation would be done in the following order:

1. $c * $d—because it is the most deeply nested expression in brackets.

2. The product of $c * $d divided by $e—because the leftmost expression remaining in brackets is evaluated first, and division takes precedence over addition.

3. The result of that calculation is then added to $b, thereby completing evaluation of the first set of outer brackets, which we'll call $temp1.

4. Focus then moves to the remaining set of brackets on the right—modulo takes precedence over subtraction, so $g % $h is evaluated first.

5. The remainder produced by that calculation is subtracted from $f—completing the evaluation of the last set of brackets, which we'll call $temp2.

6. Now we are left with a calculation that can be rephrased as $a * $temp1 * $temp2 because both operands have equal precedence; $a is first multiplied by $temp1 and the product of that calculation is multiplied by $temp2.

Phew! If that left your head spinning, don't worry. Unless you're a mathematical genius, you're not likely to need to do a calculation as complex as that—and if you are, you probably didn't need that explanation. Still, it's important to know the order of precedence because it will help you work out why you're getting what seems a completely nonsensical answer to your calculation.

If in doubt, break the calculation down into simpler parts. Many programmers take no chances, and apply two simple rules of thumb.

- Multiplication and division have higher precedence than addition or subtraction.
- Use brackets for everything else.

That's more than enough theory for the moment. Let's get back to your order form and put some of this new knowledge to practical use.

### Bringing the confirmation page to life

1. Open the page you made earlier, order.html, and add three new text boxes to it. We used some very basic CSS to take the really rough edges off plain XHTML, but what it looks like doesn't matter. What you're really interested in is getting information from the form to your confirmation.php page. Name the new text boxes: roqCran, latte, and address. ED's Online Deli is getting ready to take

orders. Make the page look something like Figure 11-10 or download the file from the friends of ED website. If you're building the page yourself (you are, aren't you?), make sure you get the uppercase C in the middle of roqCran.

**Figure 11-10.** Getting ready to pass an order to your PHP script

2. Open confirmation.php. You need to update the page to reflect the new information it's going to receive from the form. You need to make a slight change to the PHP script you created last time. Go into Code view or Split view and find the following line (it should be around line 13 unless you are using the download file, where it's on line 19):

```
$name = $_POST['name'];
```

3. Add three new lines of code, so the top section of your PHP code block looks like this.

```
<?php
  // Get the data from the form
  $name = $_POST['name'];
  $address = $_POST['address'];
  $roqCran = $_POST['roqCran'];
  $latte = $_POST['latte'];

  // Find out what hour of the day it is
  $date = date('H');
```

4. This gets the new details from the form and assigns them to variables. We'll explain $_POST ['formName'] in more detail later.

> If you've had any previous experience with PHP, you may be wondering why we bother creating variables using the names of form fields. Surely one of the convenient things about PHP is that it automatically creates a variable using the same name as each form field? That's the way it used to be, and a lot of scripts you may come across still make that assumption. Our advice is: Don't do it! It leaves your website vulnerable to malicious scripters—automatic assignment of variables is being disabled on many servers. Try such a script on the version of PHP we recommended you install. It won't work.

you need to create.

**Figure 11-11.** Building the static parts first

6. It's all straightforward static XHTML, apart from the PHP script that was already in the page (look back at Figure 11-2 to see what's changed). All that's been added are a couple of lines of text, formatted as paragraphs and a 5-row, 4-column table to

accommodate the parts of the page that will remain constant. Before typing the words Thank you for your order, check Figure 11-12 to make sure your cursor is in the right place.

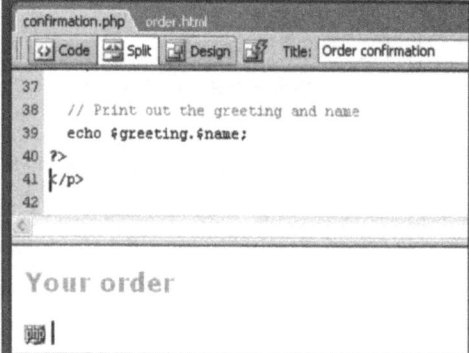

**Figure 11-12.** Make sure your cursor is not still inside the PHP closing tag.

7. It's important to make sure your cursor is placed after the closing ?> PHP tag, and just before the </p> tag. Dynamic pages can be brought crashing down by entering your code in the wrong place, so it's always a good idea to check in Split view before typing merrily away. Once you've checked the position, add the following text: . Thank you for your order. Notice that you begin with a period (full stop) and a space. That's because the name displayed by the existing PHP script doesn't include any punctuation after it.

> If you're wondering how PHP will treat the dollar signs in the price column, the answer is: it won't see them. PHP processes only what it finds between <?php and ?> tags. The dollar signs in the static XHTML are treated just like any other text in a web page. You can embed as many blocks of PHP as you like in a page.

8. Once you've got the page the way you want it, switch to the PHP category on the Insert bar (see Figure 11-13).

**Figure 11-13.** Opening the PHP category on the Insert bar

9. With your cursor in the Design side of Split view, click inside the second cell of the second row of the table (under the word "Ordered," as shown in Figure 11-14). As you do this, you'll notice that it's also moved to the relevant place in the Code side, where you're going to start working. Highlight the   immediately to the right of your cursor and delete it.

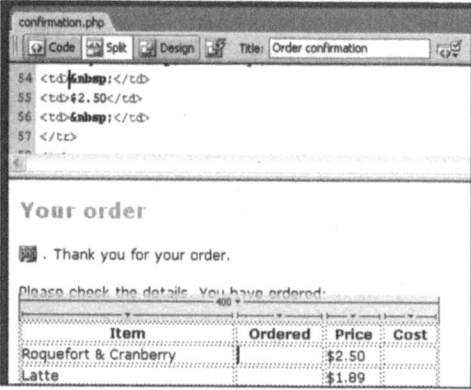

**Figure 11-14.** Use Split view to find the right place to insert dynamic text.

> Normally, when you're creating a static page, MX 2004 places   (a non-breaking space) inside table cells to stop them from collapsing or looking ugly in certain browsers. As soon as you insert any content, it automatically deletes the  . Unfortunately, it won't do that when you start inserting dynamic content, so you have to remember to take it out yourself. Otherwise, at best you'll get an unwanted space; at worst, it could prevent your dynamic script from working.

10. With your cursor still between the `<td></td>` tags in Code view, click the Echo button on the PHP Insert bar, as shown in Figure 11-15.

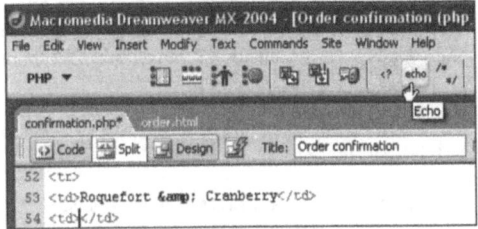

**Figure 11-15.** Clicking the Echo button on the PHP Insert bar

11. MX 2004 inserts `<?php echo   ?>` between the tags, and leaves the cursor one space to the right of echo—just where you want it. It may save only a few keystrokes, but you'll be using echo a lot when developing pages with dynamic text, and it's quite a relief not to have to keep typing those `<?php ?>` tags all the time. A word of caution, though: the shortcuts on the PHP Insert bar always use the PHP tags, even when they're not needed (such as in a block of existing PHP script). As a result, you can end up with a horrible mess that probably won't work. The Insert bar is brilliant for dropping a short piece of PHP into your XHTML—stick to using it for that, and you'll be fine.

12. Type **$roqCran;**. That entire line should now look like this.

```
<td><?php echo $roqCran; ?></td>
```

What this does is **echo** the value held in the variable $roqCran to the screen, in other words, the number of croissants being ordered.

13. Move your cursor back to the Design side of Split view, and click the cell immediately beneath the one you've just been working in. As you do so, MX 2004 inserts a PHP icon to indicate where your new script has been entered. Repeat Steps 9 to 12 in the cell you've just selected (row 3, cell 2), only this time use $latte instead of $roqCran.

```
<td><?php echo $latte; ?></td>
```

14. Move back to the Design view, and do the same at the end of the line that reads: "Your order will be delivered to:" only this time use $address as the variable. Make sure your cursor is just before the `</p>` tag because you want the address to be part of the same paragraph.

```
<p>Your order will be delivered to:
➥<?php echo $address; ?></p>
```

15. Let's check that everything's working so far. Save both pages and load order.html into your browser, using either F12 or the localhost address. Enter an order, and click Place order. Hopefully, you should get something like Figure 11-16.

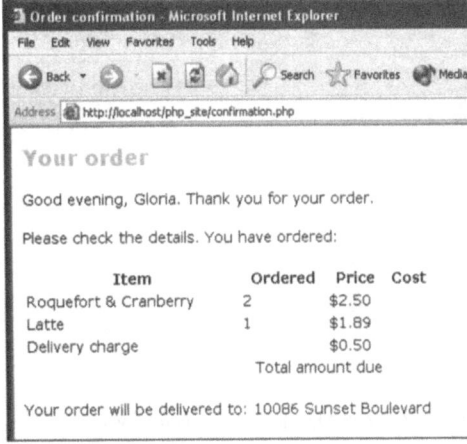

**Figure 11-16.** Adding the details from the form

**193**

**16.** If anything went wrong, check all your code again. Did you get the mixture of uppercase and lowercase right in $roqCran? Is Apache running? If you're on a system on which Apache needs to be started manually, check back in the previous chapter to see how to start it.

**17.** This is where PHP does some hard work for you—working out the bill. Click the cell where the cost of Roquefort & Cranberry is to be displayed, and repeat Steps 9 to 12 so that the resulting line of code looks like this.

```
<td><?php echo $roqCran * 2.50; ?></td>
```

**18.** Do the same in the next cell down, but use $latte as the variable, and 1.89 as the figure.

```
<td><?php echo $latte * 1.89; ?></td>
```

**19.** In the cell next to Total amount due, insert a block of PHP so that it looks like this.

```
<td><?php echo $roqCran * 2.50 + $latte *
➡1.89 + 0.50; ?></td>
```

**20.** Save `confirmation.php` and test the form again. This time, you should get something like Figure 11-17.

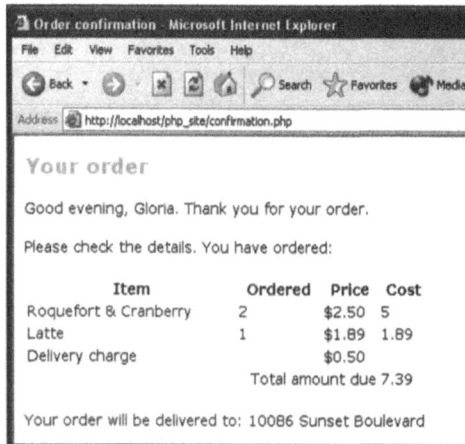

**Figure 11-17.** PHP has done all the sums for you.

If you look at Figure 11-17, you'll notice there's a problem. Instead of printing out 5.00 as you would need on

a real e-commerce site, PHP left out the decimal point and trailing zeros. You can fix that later, but the important thing to take away from this exercise is the way PHP can individualize pages. You have no way of knowing in advance the person's name, address, or how many items he or she will order, but gathering information in a form, storing it in variables, and using arithmetic operators to perform calculations opens up a whole range of new possibilities on your websites.

As far as a computer is concerned, any figures entered via a form are, in fact, strings, not numbers. PHP is savvy enough to realize that, although the number of items ordered is a string, it treats it as a number and performs the calculation you want. This would be impossible in a Java program. What happens if you enter "two" instead of "2"? Try it. PHP is not that clever, but it doesn't stop the script from working. That's useful in one respect, but it does mean you have to be careful about what type of information gets passed to your variables. Form validation is one answer, but there are also ways to check within PHP.

Before moving on, take another look at the calculation for the total amount.

```
$roqCran * 2.50 + $latte * 1.89 + 0.50;
```

For a more complicated e-commerce site in real life, the calculation of total price would probably be done in a more efficient way. The purpose of this exercise is to demonstrate how the order of precedence shown in Table 11-4 ensures the right amounts are multiplied before everything is added together. If you wanted to make doubly sure, you could play cautious and use brackets.

```
($roqCran * 2.50) + ($latte * 1.89) + 0.50;
```

**21.** Try it, but this time, instead of using Split or Code view, click the PHP icon in the cell next to Total amount due. This will reveal the contents of the PHP script in the Property Inspector (see Figure 11-18). It shows just the script itself, without the surrounding PHP tags. You can make any changes you like in the Server Markup box, and they will be applied when you save the page. This technique is best used for short scripts, and may not always be the most appropriate, but it is useful to know, particularly if you want to check on the contents of a

PHP script in a large page with lots of static XHTML. Instead of being mesmerized by the mixture of XHTML and PHP, you can see the bare bones of the script in isolation.

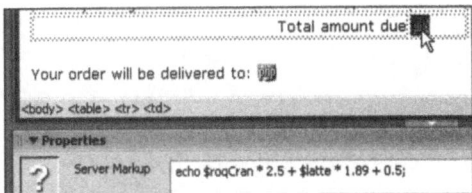

**Figure 11-18.** Viewing and editing PHP in the Property Inspector

## Summary

After all that, you deserve at least a croissant and latte! You're already on your way to a solid understanding not only of PHP, but of how Dreamweaver MX 2004 can make it easier to use PHP with your existing web design skills. You've covered a lot of ground, learning

- The basic grammar of PHP; how it's embedded into XHTML, the way it treats white space, and the importance of getting things right, particularly closing simple statements (instructions) with a semicolon

- How variables are used to store and manipulate information

- The use of echo and of the concatenation operator (.) in displaying text to the screen or browser

- That PHP treats text strings in single quotes as plain text, but processes any variables included as part of a string when enclosed in double quotes

- How PHP does both simple and complex mathematical calculations using either raw figures or numerical values held in variables

- And perhaps most important of all, how PHP can bring your web pages alive by individualizing them with input from online forms

In the next chapter, you'll build on these foundations by looking at how PHP makes decisions, and getting your online form to send information to your e-mail inbox.

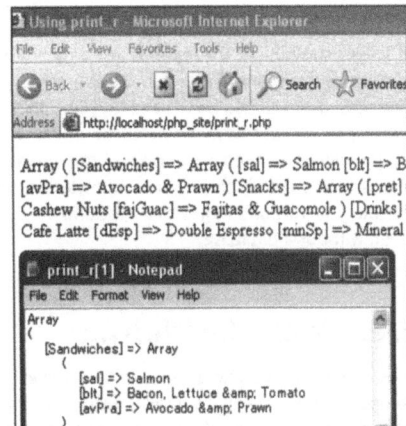

## Chapter 12

# PAGES THAT THINK
# FOR THEMSELVES

**What we'll cover in this chapter**

- Making decisions
- Formatting currencies with `printf()` and `sprintf()`
- Hiding unwanted output
- Controlling program flow
  - `if` statements
  - `switch` statements
  - loops
- Using loops to alternate table row colors
- Storing related information in arrays
- Using built-in PHP and user-defined functions
- Saving PHP code for reuse
- Sending form output by e-mail

If you're straining at the leash to get a database-driven site up and running, bear with us. We show you how Dreamweaver MX 2004, PHP, and MySQL all fit together in Chapter 13, but to make database-driven sites work really well, you need to know a little bit about the mechanics behind them. This knowledge will also enable you to build pages that respond to user input even without a database.

## Decisions, decisions...

The power of web pages made with a server-side language is their ability to make decisions. As you've already seen, you can change the content of the page based on input from a form, and PHP can perform calculations. But what if...?

Say you don't want to charge for delivery on orders that come to a minimum value? Three basic devices—**comparison operators**, **logical operators**, and **program flow control**—enable you to implement such decisions with PHP. Before studying the details, let's try it out.

> ### Waiving the delivery charge

1. Open confirmation.php, the file you created in the last chapter (it's also available on the friends of ED website). You're going to offer customers free delivery if their order comes to a minimum of $10. To make the calculations easier to handle, make some changes to the large block of PHP close to the beginning of the page. Find this line in the code.

   ```
   $latte = $_POST['latte'];
   ```

2. Add four new lines immediately below it.

   ```
   $priceRoqCran = 2.5;
   $priceLatte = 1.89;
   $totalRoqCran = $roqCran * $priceRoqCran;
   $totalLatte = $latte * $priceLatte;
   ```

3. These new variables hold the price of each item and calculate the cost of the number ordered. By putting all the prices together, you can update the code a lot more easily whenever the prices change. (You have only two now, but imagine searching

through a page with dozens scattered all over the place.) You've probably also noticed the trailing zero has been left off 2.50. PHP doesn't use it. Note also that your calculations are now composed solely of variables. Use variables to hold values that are likely to change or that you want to manipulate. Use actual numbers or strings of text only for things that will remain constant. The price may not change very often, but the number ordered will differ with every new customer. Storing the result of each calculation in $totalRoqCran and $totalLatte makes the next stage of the process a lot easier.

4. Go through the rest of the page, and update all the lines with calculations like this.

   This line

   ```
   <td><?php echo $roqCran * 2.5; ?></td>
   ```

   becomes

   ```
   <td><?php echo $totalRoqCran; ?></td>
   ```

   This line

   ```
   <td><?php echo $latte * 1.89; ?></td>
   ```

   becomes

   ```
   <td><?php echo $totalLatte; ?></td>
   ```

   This line

   ```
   <td><?php echo $roqCran * 2.5 + $latte *
   ➥1.89 + 0.5; ?></td>
   ```

   becomes

   ```
   <td><?php echo $totalRoqCran +
   ➥$totalLatte + 0.5; ?></td>
   ```

5. You may be wondering why the delivery charge in the last line has not been changed to a variable. It will be changed, but you should get into the good habit of checking at each stage that things are working as expected. When you first start working with variables, it's easy to make mistakes. Load order.html into a browser and make sure the calculation is correct. If everything is working properly, you should get something like Figure 12-1.

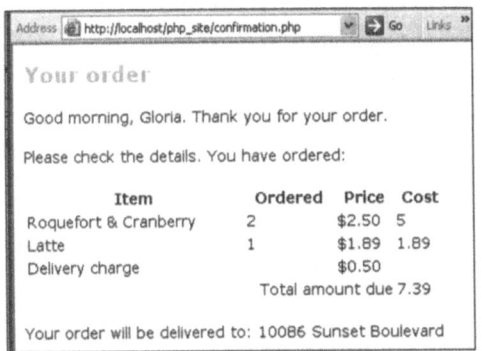

**Figure 12-1.** The code has changed, but the output is the same.

6. To work out whether to charge for delivery, all you need is to add together $totalRoqCran and $totalLatte. Then get PHP to make a decision like this.

```
if (the total is $10 or more) {
  delivery is free;
}
else {
  delivery is $0.50;
}
```

7. Add a new block of code following $totalLatte = $latte * $priceLatte;

```
// Calculate the delivery cost
if ($totalRoqCran + $totalLatte >= 10) {
  $delivery = 0;
  }
else {
  $delivery = .5;
    }
```

8. Pause a moment to see if you can follow the logic of that new block of code. The if and else structure are the same as in step 6. The only thing you may be unfamiliar with is >=, which means "is greater than or equal to" in PHP. We'll come back to this in more detail later.

9. Now you need to reflect this change in the rest of the page. Highlight the 0.50 delivery charge in the output table as shown in Figure 12-2.

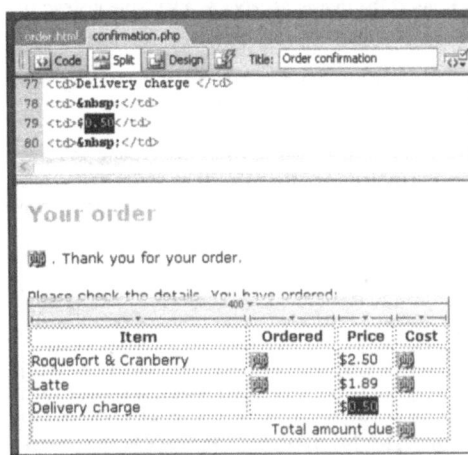

**Figure 12-2.** Highlight just the figures, not the dollar sign.

10. Delete the 0.50 and insert a block of PHP code so the line looks like the following (you can use the Echo button on the PHP Insert bar to save typing):

```
<td>$<?php echo $delivery; ?></td>
```

11. To reflect the actual delivery charge in the Cost column, change the <td> </td> (line 80 in Figure 12-2) to look like this.

```
<td><?php echo $delivery; ?></td>
```

The only difference is the dollar sign in the Price column. Note that the dollar sign is *outside* the PHP tags, so it's treated as ordinary XHTML. It's not part of a variable, but plain text. The dollar sign in $delivery, though, tells PHP to treat $delivery as a variable. If you are working with dollars as a currency, this can be very confusing at first, but it's important to understand the difference.

12. A few lines further down in Code view, locate the following line:

```
<td><?php echo $totalRoqCran +
➥$totalLatte + 0.5; ?></td>
```

**199**

**13.** Insert the delivery charge as a variable instead of a number, like this.

```
<td><?php echo $totalRoqCran +
➡$totalLatte + $delivery; ?></td>
```

**14.** Test your page again. Order something you know will come to less than $10. Then try it with an order over $10. Your page should have started to make decisions, as shown in Figures 12-3 and 12-4.

| Item | Ordered | Price | Cost |
|------|---------|-------|------|
| Roquefort & Cranberry | 3 | $2.50 | 7.5 |
| Latte | 2 | $1.89 | 3.78 |
| Delivery charge | | $0 | 0 |
| | | Total amount due | 11.28 |

**Figure 12-3.** The PHP script determines there is no delivery charge.

| Item | Ordered | Price | Cost |
|------|---------|-------|------|
| Roquefort & Cranberry | 3 | $2.50 | 7.5 |
| Latte | 1 | $1.89 | 1.89 |
| Delivery charge | | $0.5 | 0.5 |
| | | Total amount due | 9.89 |

**Figure 12-4.** The PHP script determines the delivery charge automatically.

**15.** The page is beginning to look quite good, but it's spoiled by PHP chopping off any trailing zeros from your currency amounts. It's easy to fix with one of PHP's built-in functions, `printf()`. Find the code in the Cost column that displays the total cost of croissants.

```
<?php echo $totalRoqCran; ?>
```

**16.** Change it to this.

```
<?php printf('%.2f', $totalRoqCran); ?>
```

**17.** Do the same with $totalLatte in the next row, and with both instances of $delivery in the following row.

```
<?php printf('%.2f', $totalLatte); ?>
<?php printf('%.2f', $delivery); ?>
```

**18.** Then change the code that calculates the total.

```
<?php printf('%.2f', $totalRoqCran +
➡ $totalLatte + $delivery); ?>
```

**19.** Save and test your page. Try it with an order you know will require trailing zeros, such as the one shown in Figure 12-5.

| Item | Ordered | Price | Cost |
|------|---------|-------|------|
| Roquefort & Cranberry | 3 | $2.50 | 7.50 |
| Latte | | $1.89 | 0.00 |
| Delivery charge | | $0.50 | 0.50 |
| | | Total amount due | 8.00 |

**Figure 12-5.** The `printf()` function adds in the required trailing zeros.

**20.** The `printf()` function modifies output to fit a pattern you can specify yourself, and then displays it. The patterns can be rather cryptic, so we don't intend to go into detail here other than to show you how to format currencies. The way you use it is as follows:

*printf('pattern', output to be formatted);*

**21.** The pattern being used here ('%.2f') tells PHP to format the output as a number with two decimal places. If you want to include the dollar or other currency symbol, add it before the percentage sign inside the quotes, like this.

```
$cost = 2;

printf('$%.2f', $cost);        // $2.00
printf('&pound;%.2f', $cost);  // £2.00
```

Note that since the pattern is enclosed in quotes, the semicolon at the end of &pound; is not treated as the end of the statement (see the discussion about semicolons in Chapter 11).

Typing these `printf()` patterns can be tedious and it's easy to make mistakes. Fortunately, Dreamweaver MX 2004 makes life easier by enabling you to store the necessary code as a snippet (more on that later). To learn more about `printf()` and its related function sprintf(), visit the PHP online manual at www.php.net/manual/en/function.sprintf.php. (You'll be using sprintf() later in the chapter.)

**22.** Now that you know how to format currencies, you can make the figures in the Price column dynamic too. Change the code in the Price column for "Roquefort & Cranberry" from <td>$2.50</td> to <td>$<?php printf('%.2f', $priceRoqCran); ?></td>. Repeat for Latte, with $priceLatte as the variable. Your prices are now fully dynamic, and need be changed in only one place, where the value of the variables is originally declared. Try it and see.

You have made quite a few improvements to confirmation.php, but before explaining in detail how you get PHP to make decisions, there is one more thing we'd like to show you.

**23.** In Design view, click anywhere inside the Delivery charge row, and then highlight the entire row by clicking the <tr> tag in the Dreamweaver status bar, as shown in Figure 12-6.

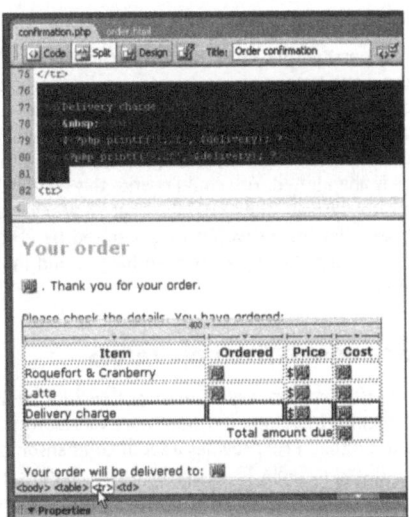

**Figure 12-6.** Highlight the entire Delivery charge row.

**24.** This shows you in Code or Split view the starting and finishing points of the row, where you need to insert some new PHP code, as follows:

```php
<?php
if ($delivery > 0) {
?>
<tr>
<td>Delivery charge </td>
<td> </td>
<td>$<?php printf('%.2f',$delivery);?></td>
<td><?php printf('%.2f',$delivery);?></td>
</tr>
<?php
}
?>
```

**25.** Save and test your page. First try an order that comes to less than $10. confirmation.php will work the same way as in Figure 12-5. Then try it with an order that comes to more than $10. The entire Delivery charge line will disappear, as shown in Figure 12-7.

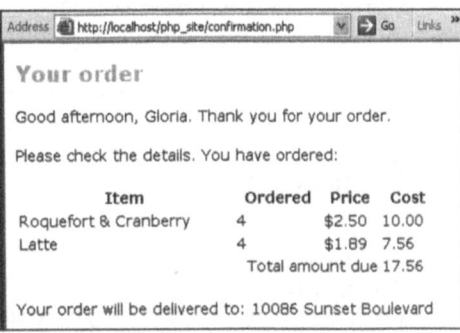

**Figure 12-7.** PHP decides not to display the delivery charge when the minimum value is reached.

Of course, you could tidy up the design even more by making sure the figures in the columns line up neatly (either using CSS or horizontal align for individual table cells), but the important thing here is that you got PHP to make intelligent decisions about what to display. Your code remains the same, but the output is no longer constrained in the same way as static pages.

**201**

# How PHP makes decisions

Let's take a closer look at the PHP decision-making process.

## Using if statements

Just as in everyday life, decisions are made by asking if something is true. In PHP, this is called an if statement, and it is the simplest form of conditional statement. if statements follow this pattern.

```
if (condition) {
    All code inside these braces is executed
}
```

The condition being tested for is enclosed in parentheses. If it turns out to be true, the entire block of code within curly braces is carried out. If it's false, the code is ignored. It's important not to mix up parentheses and braces. They are easy to confuse both in print and on the computer screen, but PHP will get very upset if you try to use the wrong ones.

- Conditions are enclosed in parentheses ().
- Code blocks are enclosed in curly braces {}.

Take another look at the code you created in step 24 of the last exercise.

```
<?php
if ($delivery > 0) {
?>
<tr>
<td>Delivery charge </td>
<td> </td>
<td>$<?php printf('%.2f',$delivery);?></td>
<td><?php printf('%.2f',$delivery);?></td>
</tr>
<?php
}
?>
```

The condition being tested for is ($delivery > 0). The mathematical symbol > means "greater than," so this code tests to see whether the value held in the variable $delivery is greater than zero. If it is, all code inside

the braces is executed. "Hold on a minute," you may be saying. "There is no code between the braces. The closing ?> tag comes immediately after the first brace."

In Chapter 11, we told you that PHP lets you embed code straight into your XHTML. The reverse is also true. The PHP engine sees the opening brace and looks for the closing one. If the condition is true, it executes everything between them. The fact that you may be switching between XHTML and PHP is not important. As long as the braces match up, the if statement will be executed.

```
if (true) {
?>
<p>This XHTML will be displayed.</p>
<?php
}
?>

if (false) {
?>
<p>This XHTML will never be seen.</p>
<?php
}
?>
```

This is possible because PHP parses (or processes) the entire page before attempting to send it back to the browser. That's why you get only an error message if something is wrong with your script. As soon as it encounters an error, PHP stops processing and the page is abandoned. You could rewrite this section using echo to display the XHTML. That way everything between the braces would be generated by PHP, but that adds unnecessary work both for you and the PHP processor.

## Using comparison operators

The most common way of making a decision in an if statement is to compare two or more values. To enable you to do that, PHP provides a set of comparison operators (listed in Table 12-1). As the name suggests, comparison operators compare values, which are always handled in pairs.

**Table 12-1.** Comparison Operators in PHP

| Operator name | Symbol | Description |
|---|---|---|
| Equality | == | Determines whether two quantities are equal. |
| Inequality | != | Determines whether the values are not equal. |
| Identical | === | Determines whether the two operands are identical. To be considered identical, they must contain not only the same value, but be of the same type, for example, both strings or both integers. |
| Not identical | !== | Determines that two operands are not identical (according to the same criteria as the previous operator). |
| Greater than | > | Determines whether the value on the left is higher than the one on the right. |
| Less than | < | Determines whether the value on the left is lower than the value on the right. |
| Greater than or equal to | >= | Determines whether the value on the left is of higher or equal value to the value on the right. |
| Less than or equal to | <= | Determines whether the value on the left is of lower or equal value to the value on the right. |

Comparison operators don't require much explanation. They are used to test whether something is true or not; thus, they **return** (or produce a result that is) either true or false.

```
$a = 5;
$b = 10;
if ($a > $b) // returns false
if ($a < $b) // returns true
```

Perhaps the only two comparison operators that are difficult to grasp are **identical** and **not identical**. As shown in Table 12-1, for two operands to be identical, they must contain not only the same value, but also be of the same type. An example should make this clearer.

```
$aNumber = 5;            // integer
$itemsOrdered = '5';     // string

$aNumber === $itemsOrdered // false
$aNumber !== $itemsOrdered // true

$aNumber = 6;  // now 6, still an integer

$aNumber !== $itemsOrdered // still true

$itemsOrdered = 6; // now an integer

$aNumber === $itemsOrdered // true
```

As noted in Chapter 11, a single equal sign (=) in programming languages does not mean "is equal to." It is the assignment operator, which sets the value of a variable. To compare two operands to see whether they are equal, you must use the **equality operator**, which consists of two equal signs (==) with no white space in between. This crucial difference occasionally trips up even experienced programmers, so it's something to bear in mind if your script returns unexpected results when trying to test two items for equality.

### Mixing up the assignment and equality operators

1. Create a new PHP page called equality.php. Enter the following code anywhere between the <body> tags:

```php
<?php
if (10 == 5) {
  echo "Oh no it's not!"; // won't execute
  }
?>
```

2. Save it and preview in your browser. You should see nothing. The comparison is deliberately nonsensical to ensure the if statement returns false.

3. Amend the code slightly by removing one of the equal signs from the first line.

```php
if (10 = 5) {
  echo "Oh no it's not!"; // won't execute
  }
```

4. View the page again. Instead of a blank page, you should get an error message like that in Figure 12-8.

An error was generated because you tried to assign a value to an integer, which can't be done. If you do this with a variable, though, you'll get no warning, and your scripts will almost certainly start producing totally unexpected results.

5. Delete the previous section of PHP code, and replace it with this.

```php
$itemsOrdered = 5; // set the variable

if ($itemsOrdered = 5) { // check number
  echo 'Yes, five items were ordered';
  }
```

6. Test it in a browser. It works! Who needs the equality operator? Hold on a minute...Reset the variable in the first line to any other number and test it again.

```php
$itemsOrdered = 20; // set the variable
```

7. The browser should still have displayed Yes, five items were ordered. To explain why, we need to do one more test. Change the code so it reads as follows, and then preview in a browser:

```php
$itemsOrdered = 20;
echo "Variable is set to $itemsOrdered";
echo '<br /><br />';
if ($itemsOrdered = 5) {
  echo 'Yes, five items were ordered';
  }
echo '<br /><br />';
echo "Variable is set to $itemsOrdered";
```

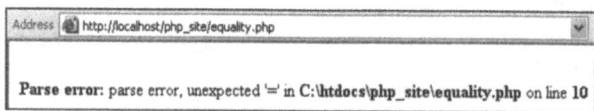

Address http://localhost/php_site/equality.php

**Parse error**: parse error, unexpected '=' in C:\htdocs\php_site\equality.php on line 10

**Figure 12-8.** Using the wrong operator generates an error.

**8.** The results are shown in Figure 12-9. Instead of testing whether $itemsOrdered equals 5, the assignment operator has *changed* the value of the variable. Remember, an if statement always tests for true or false. PHP looks at $itemsOrdered = 5, and determines that this is an instruction to set the value to 5, which has been done; therefore it's true. Not only have you got a wrong answer, the changed value of your variable will ruin any further calculations. PHP issues no warning because it's done exactly what you asked it to do. The importance of distinguishing between the assignment operator (=) and the equality operator (==) cannot be stressed enough.

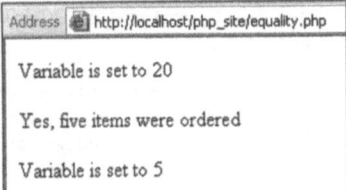

**Figure 12-9.** Using the wrong operator produces false results and *no* warning.

## Back to decision making

Comparing just two values is often not enough. To handle more complex decisions, PHP offers both logical operators and further decision-making structures.

**Logical operators** are described in Table 12-2. Their use will become clearer when they are shown in action.

In the following example, the || operator tests if one *or* the other expression is true.

```
if (10 > 5  || 10 == 5)  {
   echo "it's a half truth"; // will display
   }
```

To save time, PHP doesn't bother testing the second expression if the first one is true. So this construction still returns true even if both comparisons are successful.

What happens if you use the && operator instead?

```
if (10 > 5 && 10 == 5) {
   echo 'Pigs might fly'; // won't happen
   }
```

To display "Pigs might fly," *both* expressions must evaluate to true.

**Table 12-2.** Logical Operators Used in PHP

| Symbol | Example | Description |
|--------|---------|-------------|
| && | if ($a==0 && $b==1) | Checks both conditions. Similar to the **and** symbol, but has a higher precedence. |
| and | if ($a==2 and $b==3) | Checks both conditions, but has a lower precedence than &&. |
| \|\| | if ($a==4 \|\| $b==5) | Checks to see if one of the conditions is true. Same as **or**, but has higher precedence. |
| or | if ($a==5 or $b==7) | Checks to see if one of the conditions is true. It has a lower precedence than \|\|. |
| xor | if ($a==8 xor $b==9) | Determines if one of the two conditions is true, but not both. If both cases in the example are true, overall it will return false. |
| ! | if (!isset($a)) | Determines whether something is false; in the example shown, if the variable $a has not been set, it will return true. |

**205**

You can also create more complex if statements like this.

```
if ($a > 100 && $b == 130 && $c != 99) {
  // do something
  }
```

Although there is no real limit to the number of conditions you can use in an if statement, you should try to use no more than three. Any more and the syntax can become ugly.

Sometimes you may want to execute some code if the condition is false. Although it is possible to use two if statements, it's more efficient to use an if… else statement.

## Using if… else statements

The construction of an if… else statement is very simple, and it mirrors the type of decision you make in everyday life.

```
if (it's raining) {
  I need my umbrella
  }
else {
  I need my sunglasses
  }
```

In the next example, the equality operator in the if statement makes a deliberately nonsensical comparison. Because it's bound to return false, whatever is contained in the else statement will be executed.

```
if (10 == 5) {
  echo 'Yes, 10 equals 5'; // won't display
  }
else {
  echo 'No, not equal'; // will display
  }
```

But what happens if you need to check against more than one set of conditions? Think back to confirmation.php in which you assigned the hour of the day to the $date variable. That uses an if… elseif statement to display a suitable greeting.

## Using if… elseif statements

The structure of an if… elseif statement is straight-forward.

```
if (it is raining) {
  I need my umbrella
  }
elseif (it is sunny) {
  I need my sunglasses
  }
else {
  I don't need either
  }
```

Perhaps the only difficult thing about the if… elseif structure is the need to remember that elseif is written as one word in PHP.

So, let's now take a closer look at the if… elseif statement in confirmation.php. The variable $date contains the hour of the day (an integer between 0 and 23).

```
if($date <= 11) { // if between 0 and 11
  $greeting = 'Good morning, ';
  }
// or if after 11 and before 17 (5pm)
elseif ($date > 11 and $date < 17) {
  $greeting = 'Good afternoon, ';
  }
else { // otherwise
  $greeting = 'Good evening, ';
  }
```

Of course, life isn't always as simple as that. Your choices may depend on others, for example:

```
if (it is raining) {
  I need my umbrella
  }
  if (no umbrella and light rain) {     // 1
    I can run to the bus stop
    }
  else (no umbrella and heavy rain) {// 2
    I'll have to call a cab
    }
elseif (it is sunny) {
  I need my sunglasses
  }
```

```
if (I've got some money) {        // 3
  I'll go to the beach
  }
else {                            // 4
  I'll just go to the park
  }
 }
else {
  I'll sit in the garden
  }
```

Conditional statements 1 and 2 are nested inside the first one (it is raining), and are considered only if it is true. If it's not raining, they will never be put to the test. Similarly, statements 3 and 4 are considered only if the conditional statement "it is sunny" resolves to true. "I'll sit in the garden" will only be considered if it's neither raining nor sunny, but because there are no other options, it will be always be implemented if the decision process gets that far.

Although you can nest conditional statements to cover all eventualities, the more choices you have, the more complicated it becomes to keep track of them.

## Using switch statements

The switch statement is designed to make multiple choices simpler. It tests a single variable against any number of possible cases, and takes the following form:

```
switch(variable being tested) {

  case 'possibility 1' :
  // do this
  break;

  case 'possibility 2' :
  // do something else
  break;

  default :
  //do this if none of the cases match
 }
```

A good use for a switch statement would be to display information in different languages on a website.

```
switch($language) {

    case 'Spanish':
    //go to Spanish page
    break;

    case 'French':
    //go to French page
    break;

    case 'German':
    //go to German page
    break;

    case 'Russian':
    //go to Russian page
    break;

     default:
    //no language specified, go to English
  }
```

Points to note about switch statements.

- The opening switch($variable), the entire construct is enclosed in curly braces.
- Each possibility being tested is preceded by the keyword case.
- If testing for a matching string, use the string in quotes after case.
- The criterion being tested for is followed by a colon.
- Even if a match is made, PHP will continue testing all remaining criteria unless you use the keyword break (followed by a semicolon) to tell the switch statement to stop.
- A default value is not required, but is recommended to prevent your script from generating errors.

**207**

# Handling repetitive operations with loops

Loops allow you to execute the same bit of code over and over again until a certain condition is reached.

## The while loop

The while loop is very simple in form.

```
while (condition is true) {
//execute this code
}
```

The following example shows the while loop in action, displaying all the numbers from 0 to 5, as shown in Figure 12-10.

```
$a = 0;
while ($a <= 5) {
  echo "$a <br />"; //displays number
  $a++; // increases $a by 1
}
```

**Figure 12-10.** A simple while loop in action

A while loop tests the condition to see if it's true, and if so, performs the code inside the braces. In the example just shown, the final line of code within the braces increases $a by 1 each time it is executed. The loop then returns to the top and tests the condition again. Provided $a is 5 or less, the code will execute again. Once $a reaches 6, the condition is no longer true and the loop stops. The biggest problem with a while loop is that if you set a condition that is always true, you create an endless loop that either fills the browser with garbage or freezes output. You must always make sure the condition will eventually return false.

## The do... while loop

The do...while loop is similar to the while loop except the condition is evaluated at the end of each iteration, rather than at the beginning. This means that the loop will always execute at least once, even if the condition is never true.

```
do {
  //code to be executed here
  } while( condition );
```

You may find some use for this loop, but it isn't used often.

## The for loop

The for loop works in a very similar way to the while and do...while loops, but it includes a counting mechanism with the condition being tested.

The for loop takes the form

```
for (initialize counter; test; increment) {
  //execute this code
  }
```

To show how it works, the following for loop produces exactly the same output as the while loop in Figure 12-10.

```
for ($a = 0; $a <=5; $a++) {
  echo "$a <br />";
  }
```

Combining the counting mechanism and the condition makes for very neat coding that is easy to understand.

- The first expression within the parentheses shows the starting point.

- The second shows what is being aimed for.

- The third shows the change being made in each pass through the loop.

Most of the time, you will come across for loops that use the autoincrement operator ++ or its negative counterpart --, but the counter is not limited to single steps. The following code displays numbers starting at 100 and reducing by 20 at a time, as shown in Figure 12-11.

```
for ($a = 100; $a > 0; $a = $a - 20) {
  echo "$a <br />";
  }
```

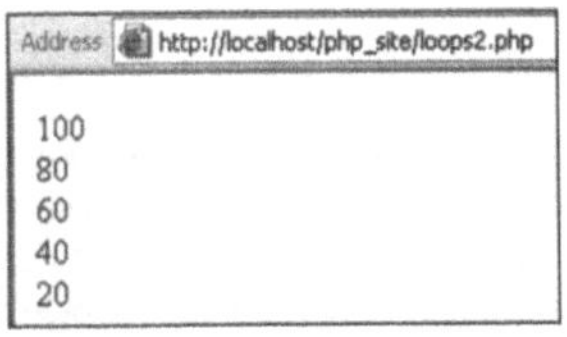

**Figure 12-11.** for loops are not limited to single steps.

A more efficient way of expressing the $a = $a - 20 in this expression uses what are known as **combined assignment operators**.

## Shorthand using combined assignment operators

You will often want to perform a calculation on a variable and assign the result back to the same variable. In the for loop just shown, 20 is subtracted from $a and the result reassigned to $a. Instead of typing it all out, you can use the following shorthand:

```
$a -= 20;
```

Table 12-3 lists the main combined assignment operators and shows how they are used.

**Table 12-3.** Combined Assignment Operators Used in PHP

| Operator | Example | Equivalent to |
|----------|---------|---------------|
| += | $a += $b | $a = $a + $b |
| -= | $a -= $b | $a = $a - $b |
| /= | $a /= $b | $a = $a / $b |
| *= | $a *= $b | $a = $a * $b |
| %= | $a %= $b | $a = $a % $b |
| .= | $a .= $b | $a = $a . $b |

The final combined assignment operator (.=) is extremely useful in building variables that contain long text messages like this.

```
$hamlet = 'To be or not to be, ';
$hamlet .= 'that is the question. ';
$hamlet .= 'Whether \'tis nobler ';
$hamlet .= 'in the mind to suffer…';
```

This shorthand certainly comes in handy when gathering all the text fields of a form that you want to send in an e-mail.

### Using a loop to alternate table row colors

1. You're now going to combine arithmetic operators, conditional statements, and loops to create a table with alternating row colors. This technique relies on the content of the table being generated dynamically, so it's easier to explain it in isolation rather than incorporate it into order.html and confirmation.php. Create a new PHP file in MX 2004, call it table_rows.php, and add the following code between the <body> tags.

```
<?php
echo '<table width="200" border="1">';
for ($i = 1;$i < 11;$i++) {
  if ($i % 2) {
    $class = 'odd';
    }
  else {
    $class = 'even';
    }
echo "<tr class='$class'>
  <td>Row number: $i</td></tr>\n";
  }
echo '</table>';
?>
```

2. For this code to work correctly, you also need to create two CSS classes. Because you are using them in this page only, create them in the XHTML <head>. You can use Manage Styles in the Property Inspector if you prefer, but it is much quicker and easier to code them by hand. Locate the closing

**209**

</head> tag and type the following code immediately above it:

```
<style type="text/css">
<!--
.odd {background-color: #FFFFFF;}
.even {background-color: #FFFFCC;}
-->
</style>
```

3. Save the file and preview in your browser. You should see a table with alternate white and pale yellow rows (see Figure 12-12).

4. You should be familiar with the for loop by now. $i = 1;$ initializes the counter to 1. $i < 11;$ sets the condition (count up to 10—or to put it another way, "less than 11"). $i++$ increments the count by 1 each time the loop is executed.

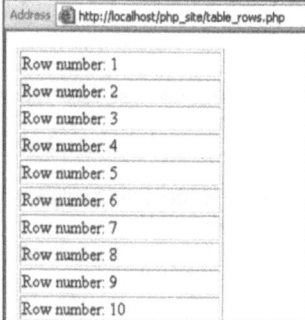

**Figure 12-12.** A dynamically generated table

5. The next step in the code—an if… else statement—should also be familiar, but the condition the statement tests does need explaining. $i \% 2$ uses the modulo operator to divide the current number by 2 and return the remainder. If the number is even, the remainder will be 0. If the number is odd, the remainder will be 1. Because conditional statements check whether a value is true or false, you probably expected the following:

```
if ($i % 2 == 1) {
  $class = 'odd';
  }
```

So how does it work without the comparison? Like most programming languages, PHP treats 0 as false. Any other number equates to true. In other words, using the modulo calculation on its own returns the same result as a fully expressed condition. You could now rewrite the condition in confirmation.php (see step 24 in the first exercise of this chapter) simply as if ($delivery) because it's testing for a value greater than 0.

*The only things PHP regards as false are*

- The integer 0 or double 0.0
- The keywords false and null
- An empty string ('') and the string '0'
- An array with no elements
- An object with no values or functions

> *Anything else is regarded as true. You can ignore objects at this stage because none of the code in this book uses them, but arrays are covered in the next section. What this means in practice is that if a variable contains any value other than those just listed, it will return true when tested as the condition of an if statement.*
>
> ```
> $reply = 'yes';
> if ($reply) // true
> $reply = 'no';
> if ($reply) // still true
> $reply = 0;
> if ($reply) // false
> ```

6. Most of the line that creates each table row is ordinary XHTML sent to the browser by echo, along with the value of $class and $i. You haven't seen the \n at the end of the line before—the backslash tells you that it's an escape character (like the backslash used to escape single and double quotation marks that you learned about in Chapter 11). It creates a new line in your XHTML output. This has no effect on the way the page is displayed in a browser, but can be very useful when you need to sort out a problem with your page. Open the source code for table_rows.php (View ➤ Source or Page Source, depending on your browser). It should look like Figure 12-13.

**Figure 12-13.** New lines make for neat source code.

7. Remove the \n and view the page source again. Imagine there's a mistake somewhere in your page. Which would you prefer to use for troubleshooting—the neat code in Figure 12-13 or the jumble in Figure 12-14? One important thing to note about \n is that it creates a new line only when used within double quotation marks. If you use single quotation marks, PHP will treat it as literal text.

# Arrays

An **array** is a special type of variable that holds a list of values. Because each element in an array shares the same name, you distinguish them by referencing each element's **index** (or **key**). The simplest arrays use integers as indices. What may surprise you is that PHP starts counting at 0, so the first item in an array is not 1, but 0. There are two ways of creating arrays: using the array() construct, or using [ ] after the variable name.

The following examples show both ways of building the same array:

```
$names = array('George', 'Craig', 'Beckie',
    'Kylie', 'Steve', 'Nancy', 'David');

$names[0] = 'George';
$names[1] = 'Craig';
$names[2] = 'Beckie';
$names[3] = 'Kylie';
$names[4] = 'Steve';
$names[5] = 'Nancy';
$names[6] = 'David';
```

**Figure 12-14.** Code generated without \n

**211**

The following code displays the value of the third element in this array:

```
echo $names[2];//displays Beckie, not Kylie
```

Although numerical keys are very useful, they're not easy to remember. To get around this, you can use a string instead of a number (although you can't mix both types in the same array). You have already worked with an important array of this type, $_POST['formName'] in which 'formName' represents the name of an input field in a form submitted using the POST method.

PHP creates the POST array automatically, but when you need a new array that uses strings as each element's key or index, there are again two ways to do it.

```
$lang = array('en' => 'English',
              'sp' => 'Spanish',
              'fr' => 'French',
              'de' => 'German',
              'ja' => 'Japanese');

$lang['en'] = 'English';
$lang['sp'] = 'Spanish';
$lang['fr'] = 'French';
$lang['de'] = 'German';
$lang['ja'] = 'Japanese';
```

The only difference is that the array() construct uses => to assign the value of the key, rather than the normal assignment operator (=).

> *This type of array has one little peculiarity. Array keys that use strings instead of numbers should normally be enclosed in quotation marks like all the examples shown. However, if you use an array item in a double-quoted string, you must leave out the quotes around the key. This is one occasion when including one type of quotation marks inside another does not work.*
>
> ```
> echo "$lang['fr'] spoken"; // doesn't
> ➥work
> echo "$lang[fr] spoken"; // works
> ```

Retrieving the value of this type of array element is much easier. With no number to remember (or search for), you simply use the string as the key.

```
echo $lang['fr']; // displays "French"
```

## Looping through arrays

There are several ways to loop through an array. With an array that uses a numerical index, a for loop is very useful. The $names array created earlier contains seven items, so you could display each of them by running the following code:

```
for ($i = 0; $i < 7; $i++) {
  echo $names[$i].'<br />';
  }
```

You may wonder why the condition being tested for is $i < 7. As the loop runs, it feeds the value of $i to the key of the array variable, beginning with 0, so 7 represents the eighth element of the array. You want to stop at 7, so "less than 7" (in PHP terms) actually means "less than 8" in everyday language. Unless you've worked with other programming languages, this takes a while to get used to.

The for loop is used frequently when displaying results from a database. The database server tells you how many results it has retrieved, so it's very easy to implement. Frequently, though, you have no idea how many elements there are in an array, but you want to display them all or perform an operation on each one. In such circumstances, the foreach loop is exactly what you need.

## The foreach loop

The foreach loop is used exclusively with arrays. It takes two expressions.

- The name of the array you want to loop through
- A temporary variable to handle each item in the array

The basic pattern is

```
foreach (array name as variable) {
  // do something with the variable
  }
```

It's easier to understand when you see it in action. To display the array called $names that was created earlier, you need to set a temporary variable for each one, such as $individual, like this:

```
foreach ($names as $individual) {
  echo $individual.'<br />';
}
```

That produces the output shown in Figure 12-15. Note that foreach is one word. Putting a space between "for" and "each" generates an error.

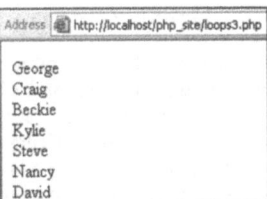

Address http://localhost/php_site/loops3.php

George
Craig
Beckie
Kylie
Steve
Nancy
David

**Figure 12-15.** The output of a foreach loop

The foreach loop also enables you to access both the key and the value by using the following pattern:

```
foreach (array name as key => value) {
  // do something with both key and value
}
```

Applied to the $languages array, the following code creates the output shown in Figure 12-16.

```
foreach ($languages as $key => $value) {
  echo "Key: $key Value: $value<br />";
}
```

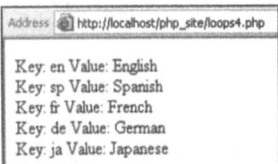

Address http://localhost/php_site/loops4.php

Key: en Value: English
Key: sp Value: Spanish
Key: fr Value: French
Key: de Value: German
Key: ja Value: Japanese

**Figure 12-16.** Accessing both key and value of an array

## Multidimensional arrays

An array is a list of variables. It is also a variable in its own right. Consequently, there is nothing to stop you from using an array as a variable within another array. In fact, you can nest arrays as deeply as you want (or at least, if you have the courage to do so).

```
$menu = array('Sandwiches' =>
  array('sal' => 'Salmon',
    'blt' => 'Bacon, Lettuce &amp; Tomato',
    'avPra' => 'Avocado &amp; Prawn'),
'Snacks' => array('pret' => 'Pretzels',
  'cashNut' => 'Cashew Nuts',
  'fajGuac' => 'Fajitas &amp; Guacomole'),
'Drinks' => array('latte' => 'Cafe Latte',
  'dEsp' => 'Double Espresso',
  'minSp' => 'Mineral Water (sparkling)'));
```

In this example, $menu is an array with three elements ("Sandwiches," "Snacks," and "Drinks"). In turn, each of these elements is an array containing an additional three elements.

To display the value of an item in a multidimensional array, you use both array keys in succession like this.

```
echo $menu['snacks']['pret']; // Pretzels
```

To display the entire contents of $menu (as shown in Figure 12-17) requires two foreach loops.

```
foreach ($menu as $category => $items) {
  echo "<h2>$category</h2>\n<ul>";
  foreach ($items as $item) {
    echo "<li>$item</li>\n";
  }
  echo "</ul>\n";
}
```

The first line of the code loops through the $menu array, finds the key of each element, and assigns it to the temporary variable $category. The value of each element is assigned to $items, but the value of each element is also an array in its own right. Therefore, line 3 performs another foreach loop extracting the value of each key in the subarray as $item.

**213**

Don't worry if you find this difficult to understand. Loops go around in circles, and it's easy to find yourself going around in circles trying to figure them out. Rather than attempt to cram everything into one structure, it's often better to break things down into smaller tasks. A simpler way of creating the $menu array is to create the inner arrays first (to save space, we'll show just one).

**Figure 12-17.** Displaying the contents of a multidimensional array

```
$sandwiches = array('sal' => 'Salmon',
    'blt' => 'Bacon, Lettuce &amp; Tomato',
    'avPra' => 'Avocado &amp; Prawn');
```

Then create the $menu array.

```
$menu = array('Sandwiches' => $sandwiches,
    'Snacks' => $snacks,
    'Drinks' => $drinks);
```

This multidimensional array can be displayed using the same code as that used to produce Figure 12-17, and the result is exactly the same. But this approach has two great advantages:

- You can now access items in the subarrays directly, that is, $snacks['pret'] rather than $menu['snacks']['pret'].

- It will be a lot easier to understand your code when you come back to it in six months.

**214**

You probably won't create multidimensional arrays yourself for a while. It's sufficient to know of their existence and that loops can be nested. The real importance of arrays will become apparent when you start working with databases in the next chapter because all database results are treated by PHP as an array. Loops are also essential for dealing with database results because, sadly, echo does not work with arrays, even if they contain only one item. You must always use the array key or a loop to display the contents of an array.

```
$vegetables = array('beans');
echo $vegetables; // displays "Array"
echo $vegetables[0]; // displays "beans"
```

A useful way of finding out what an array contains is to use print_r(). This displays the contents in something resembling human-readable form. print_r() also works on multidimensional arrays. Figure 12-18 shows the output of $menu, both as seen in a browser and as the underlying source code. Using the browser's View
➤ Source is usually much easier to understand.

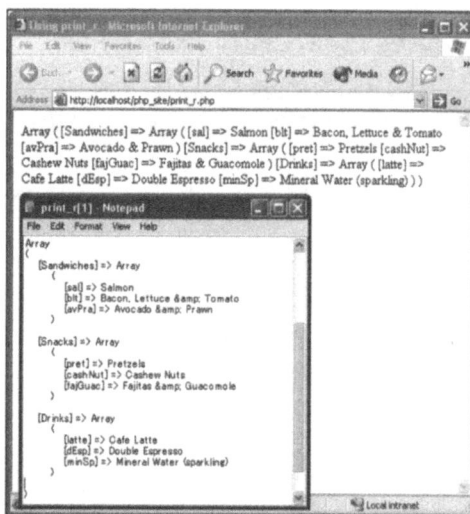

**Figure 12-18.** Viewing the contents of a multidimensional array with print_r()

print_r() is a built-in PHP function, bringing us neatly to the final section of PHP theory. (Was that a groan or a cheer?)

# Functions

The name says it all: **functions** do something useful. There are two basic types: those already built into PHP and those you build yourself. You've already met three built-in functions.

- date()
- printf()
- print_r()

The obvious thing common to them all is that they end with a pair of parentheses. Sometimes you can use a function just as it is.

```
$today = date(); // assigns current date
```

Other times, you set **parameters** between the parentheses. Parameters tell the function what you want it to do.

```
$hour = date('H'); // assigns current hour
```

PHP contains an astounding number of built-in functions (more than 2,700), many of them highly specialized. Most people are content with using just a few dozen of the most useful ones, and you'll learn about some of those in the rest of this book. Also, do take time to explore the online PHP manual at www.php.net/manual/en/.

Functions that you create yourself look and work in a similar way to built-in functions. The basic form is

```
Function functionName(parameters, if any) {
    Statements to be executed
    }
```

To show you how to build your own functions, we are going to bring together some of the techniques you have learned in this chapter to create a simple currency converter.

### A custom-built currency converter

1. Create a new PHP page and save it as format_ currency.php. Switch to Code view and position your mouse pointer before the XHTML doctype on

Line 1 and create several new lines to give you some space to work in (see Figure 12-19).

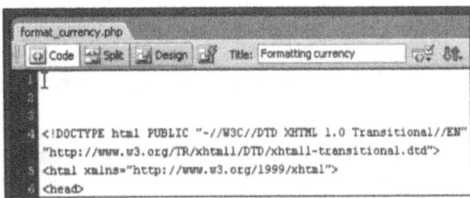

**Figure 12-19.** Create space above the doctype.

Don't worry about anything above the doctype putting browsers like Internet Explorer 6 into Quirks mode and affecting your CSS. You're going to put PHP code in this space that will not be sent back to the browser. In fact, this is where Dreamweaver MX 2004 stores a lot of the PHP it generates when working with databases.

2. Type the following code in the space you have just created:

```php
<?php
function currency($val,$curr) {
  // match $curr to appropriate symbol
  switch($curr) {
    case 'US':
    $symbol = '$';
    break;

    case 'UK':
    $symbol = '&pound;';
    break;

    case 'EU':
    $symbol = '&euro;';
    break;

    //if no match, use ?? as warning
    default:
    $symbol = '??';
    }

  // return $val formatted as currency
  return printf("$symbol%.2f",$val);
  }
?>
```

**215**

With the help of the comments in the code, you should be able to work out for yourself how the function operates. It uses a simple switch statement and then uses printf() to format the output. After processing everything, the function uses the **return** keyword to send the result back to the script. Forgetting to return the result is a common beginner's mistake in building functions.

3. To **call** (or use) the function, all you need are the two parameters: a value (either as a number or a variable that holds a number), and a string that tells the function which currency symbol to use. Type the following code between the <body> tags of your page, save it, and load it in a browser. You should see the output shown in Figure 12-20.

```php
<?php
currency(20, 'EU');
?>
```

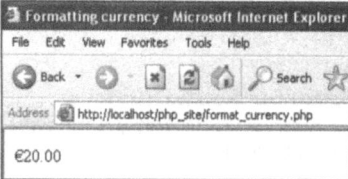

**Figure 12-20.** Output from the custom-built currency() function

Typing so many lines of code to get so little output may seem like a waste of time. It would be if you wanted to display just one currency amount on a page, but what if you needed dozens of currency conversions? The same code does it over and over again. You could also get the function to do some calculations for you. Before doing that, though, there are a couple of improvements you need to make.

4. You may have noticed that the code used to call this function doesn't use echo. That's because printf() not only formats strings; it also displays them. What if you want to format a string without displaying it? The answer is to use sprintf(), which works exactly the same way, except that it *returns* a formatted string instead of displaying it. Amend the final statement in your currency() function to read like this:

```php
return sprintf("$symbol%.2f",$val);
```

5. You can now use currency() to assign a formatted value to a variable like this:

```php
$euroPrice = currency(20, 'EU');
```

6. Still, you must always use an uppercase string to specify the currency. Another built-in PHP function can help here. Locate the following line:

```php
switch($curr) {
```

7. Change it to

```php
switch(strtoupper($curr)) {
```

At first sight, strtoupper() looks an impossible tongue-twister, but it's easy if you think of it as "string to upper" because that's what it does: convert strings to uppercase. You can now enter the $curr parameter in any combination of uppercase and lowercase because PHP will convert the input to uppercase before attempting to find a match in the switch statement.

The parameter it takes is the string you want to convert. You could do the conversion first and then use the switch statement like this.

```php
$curr = strtoupper($curr);
switch($curr) {
```

PHP is quite happy to use a call to a function as the parameter to another function. It's fast and efficient like that.

strtoupper() has a counterpart, strtolower(), that converts everything to lowercase. Two related functions, ucfirst() and ucwords(), convert the first letter of a string and the first letter of each word to uppercase.

```php
$play = 'AS YOU LIKE IT';
$play = strtolower($play);
echo $play; // as you like it
echo ucwords($play); // As You Like It
echo ucfirst($play); // As you like it
```

8. Another refinement you could add is to convert a dollar value into the other currencies. Amend the code as follows:

```
case 'UK':
$symbol = '&pound;';
$val *= 0.57;
break;

case 'EU':
$symbol = '&euro;';
$val *= 0.81;
break;
```

Note the use of the combined assignment operator (see Table 12-3) to recalculate the dollar value.

9. The following code produces the output seen in Figure 12-21:

```
<?php
$us = 50;
echo 'US: '.currency($us,'us').'<br />';
echo 'UK: '.currency($us,'uk').'<br />';
echo 'EU: '.currency($us,'eu').'<br />';
?>
```

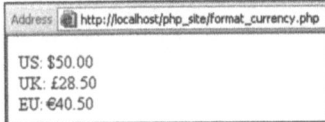

**Figure 12-21.** Converting a dollar amount with the custom-built function

Currency rates fluctuate daily, so this function as it stands would probably not be appropriate on a real e-commerce site. It's not intended as a solution, but as a way of stimulating your imagination to the virtually limitless possibilities offered by creating your own functions. As with the multidimensional array example, it's best to break down problems into easily manageable tasks. Don't try to build a single function that does everything because you will soon find you need another one to do something slightly different. Keep your functions concentrated on a single task or part of a task, so that it will be easier to recombine them to do something new.

# Reusing PHP code with the Snippets panel

To become a good PHP developer you need to start building a library of reusable functions. A good place to store such code is the Dreamweaver MX 2004 Snippets panel, which you learned about in Chapter 9.

### Making a snippet to format currencies

1. Open the Snippets panel in the Code panel group or via Window ➤ Snippets (*SHIFT+F9*). MX 2004 doesn't come with any pre-installed PHP snippets, so create a new folder. You can use the method shown in Chapter 9 or click the New Snippet Folder icon at the bottom of the Snippets panel (see Figure 12-22). Call the folder PHP. An annoying thing about MX 2004 (some call it an "undocumented feature"—others call it a bug) is that if anything has been highlighted in the Snippets panel beforehand, the new folder will become a sub-folder of that item. Clicking in any other part of the Dreamweaver interface doesn't clear the highlighting. Let MX 2004 create a new empty sub-folder, immediately right-click (*CMD*-click) it, and select Delete. When a dialog box asks for confirmation, click OK. Any new folder created now will be a top-level one.

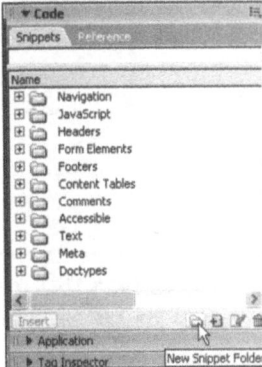

**Figure 12-22.** Make sure nothing is highlighted before creating a new folder.

**2.** Highlight the PHP folder you just created, and click the New Snippet icon immediately to the right of the New Snippet Folder icon. Fill in the dialog box as shown in Figure 12-23 and click OK.

**3.** Note that the Snippet type should be Wrap selection. The code in Insert before is **sprintf('$%.2f',** and in Insert after just a closing parenthesis. To create a UK sterling sign instead of dollar, enter **&pound;** instead of "$"; to create a euro symbol, enter **&euro;**. If you need to format currencies using a comma instead of a decimal point (as in some European countries), replace the period after the percent sign (%) with a comma.

**4.** To apply the format to a number or variable that contains a number, highlight the number or variable, and with your Dollar format snippet highlighted in the Snippets panel, click Insert or double-click the Snippet name (see Figure 12-24). That's it!

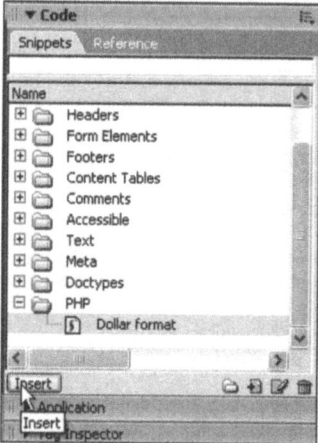

**Figure 12-24.** Inserting the Dollar format snippet

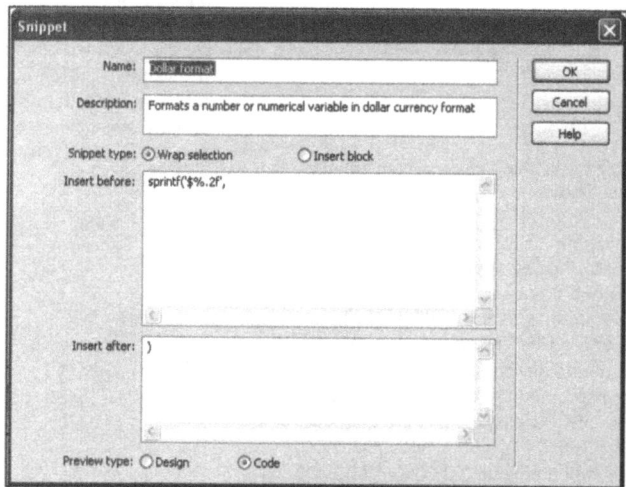

**Figure 12-23.** Creating a currency format snippet

## Mailing the output of a form

With everything you learned in this chapter, there are many enhancements you could make to order.html and confirmation.php, the files you have been working on since Chapter 11. For example, you could convert order.html into a dynamic page and use arrays and loops to generate a much more extensive menu. You could also use if statements to decide which menu items to display on confirmation.php. Such improvements, however, would probably warrant rethinking the project to work with a database.

You'll be looking at databases in detail in the next three chapters, but there are occasions when you either don't have a database available or the information doesn't warrant being stored that way. That's when PHP's mail() function comes in useful for getting information from a user to you.

1. Open confirmation.php and insert a form beneath the existing content. In the Property Inspector, set the Action to acknowledge.php and the Method to POST. Insert a Submit button in the form and set the button's Label to Confirm order.

2. Insert a hidden field into the form using the Forms Insert bar or via Insert ➤ Forms ➤ Hidden Field. Hidden fields, as you may remember from Chapter 8, are used to provide added functionality to a form without displaying anything in the browser. You are going to use a series of hidden fields to transfer information from confirmation.php to another page that will send the e-mail. There are other ways of doing this, as you will discover when you study sessions in Chapter 14. The reason for using hidden fields here is to store the information you want to e-mail as the contents of a form. This way you can adapt the script in step 5 to handle any online form.

3. Name the first hidden field name and fill in the Value in the Property Inspector as shown in Figure 12-25.

echo copies the value of $name into the name hidden field.

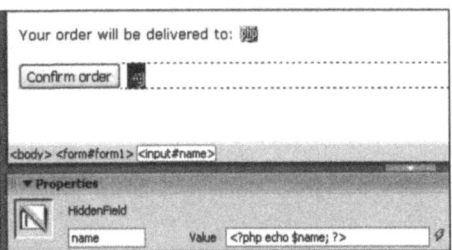

**Figure 12-25.** Creating the first hidden field

4. Insert six more hidden fields with the following names and values. This will transmit the information from confirmation.php in the same way as if a visitor had filled in a form with text fields of the same name.

```
address        <?php echo $address; ?>"
roqCran        <?php echo $roqCran; ?>
latte          <?php echo $latte; ?>
delivery       <?php echo $delivery; ?>
totalRoqCran   <?php echo $totalRoqCran; ?>
totalLatte     <?php echo $totalLatte; ?>
```

5. Create a new PHP page and call it acknowledge.php. Insert the following code between the <body> tags:

```php
<?php
$mailAddress = 'me@mydomain.com';
$subject = 'Order for ED\'s Online Deli';

// get and format the time now
$now = date('H:i D, F j');

// calculate cost of order
$total = $_POST['totalRoqCran'] +
  $_POST['totalLatte'] +
  $_POST['delivery'];

// build email text
$msg = "Order received at $now\n\n";
$msg .= "Name: $_POST[name]\n";
$msg .= "Deliver to: $_POST[address]\n\n";
$msg .= "Roquefort & Cranberry:
  $_POST[roqCran]\n";
```

**219**

```
$msg .= "Latte: $_POST[latte]\n\n";
$msg .= 'Total: '.sprintf('$%.2f', $total);

// send email
mail($mailAddress, $subject, $msg);

// acknowledge order
echo '<h1>Order sent</h1><p>Thank you</p>';
?>
```

The script in acknowledge.php uses the POST array to gather the information submitted by a form, and stores it in $msg. This is the text to be e-mailed. Although the e-mail text may consist of many sentences, mail() needs it stored as one long string in a single variable. Here it is built using a combined assignment operator (see Table 12-3) to make the code easier to read. And to make it equally easy for the recipient to read, new line escape characters (\n) are inserted to break the text up into paragraphs.

Note how the keys of the POST array have quotation marks when calculating the total, but not when incorporated into double-quoted strings (refer to the "Arrays" section, earlier in this chapter. for an explanation).

The core of this script is the following line:

```
mail($mailAddress, $subject, $msg);
```

It uses the built-in PHP mail() function to send the e-mail, using three parameters.

- The address the mail is being sent to
- The subject line
- The text of the message itself

Sending mail from an online form is really as simple as that with PHP. To find out about optional parameters you can use, see the online PHP manual at www.php.net/manual/en/function.mail.php. You can also find out how the date() function formats the date at www.php.net/manual/en/function.date.php. date() has about 30 options that enable you to represent the date in a wide range of formats. Using the code just shown results in a formatted e-mail like that shown in Figure 12-26.

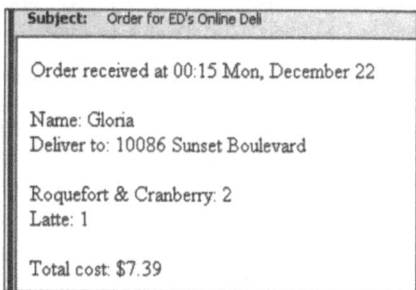

**Figure 12-26.** Confirmation of order received by e-mail

**6.** To get this to work, you need to assign your own e-mail address to $mailAddress and upload the files to your ISP's server. As long as the server is configured to handle PHP, it should work without problems. If you do encounter difficulties, ask your ISP if you need to use any special parameters with mail(). This script will not work on your local development machine unless you have configured php.ini to interact with a mail transport agent, the explanation of which is beyond the scope of this book.

## Summary

This chapter and the preceding one have been something of a crash course in PHP. We hope you're not feeling like crash victims, but more like survivors empowered and enthused to put this new knowledge to use. These two chapters cover all the core features of PHP, and even if you decide to switch to a different server-side language in the future, you will find this information gives you a flying start. Although the syntax may be different, all server-side languages have the features you just studied in common:

- Variables
- Data types
- Calculation
- Handling text as strings
- Decision making with comparison operators and conditional statements
- Handling repetitive tasks with loops
- Built-in and user-defined functions

The ability to manipulate files and individual pieces of information give server-side languages immense power. Both PHP and Dreamweaver MX 2004 use this power to great effect when it comes to handling the output from databases. You will be relieved to learn that MX 2004 does a lot of the database-related coding for you. First, though, you need to install the MySQL database management system on your computer. That's what you're going to do as soon as you muster the strength to turn to the next chapter.

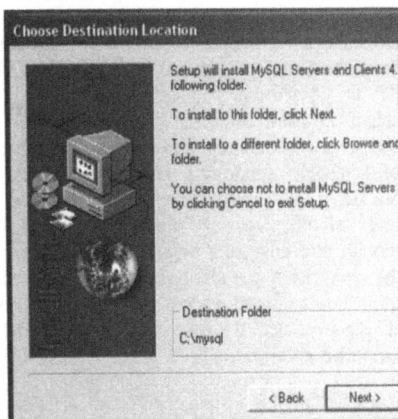

## Chapter 13

# PHP/MYSQL:
# THE REAL DYNAMIC DUO

**What we'll cover in this chapter**

- Installing MySQL and phpMyAdmin
- Preparing MySQL and Dreamweaver MX 2004 to work together
- Building a PHP application that stores information in a database
- Retrieving this information

Originally Dreamweaver created only static web pages. To create pages with server-side languages, such as ASP, JSP, or ColdFusion, you needed a separate product called UltraDev. When MX came out in 2002, the two products were merged, and PHP was added to the list of languages supported. Unfortunately, in the first release of MX PHP was unable to use many of the features offered for ASP and ColdFusion. Apparently, though, the engineers behind Dreamweaver felt that the rapid rise in popularity of PHP meant it was better to include a limited feature set rather than nothing at all. However, with the release of MX 2004, PHP/MySQL support is greatly improved.

You have already installed PHP and Apache. To start working with databases, you now need to install MySQL. You're also going to install a helper application to make working with MySQL a lot easier. The good news is that they're both free and installation is quite straightforward. So, without further ado...

## Installing MySQL

MySQL is the most popular open source database management system. It's fast, powerful, and ideally suited for the development of busy online databases. It's used by well-known organizations like Cox Communications, Associated Press, Texas Instruments, and NASA. Some database professionals criticize MySQL because it doesn't yet support all the advanced features available in commercial database systems such as Microsoft SQL Server. Most, if not all of those features are available in MySQL 5.0.0, which first appeared in an alpha version on Christmas Eve 2003. However, under no circumstances should you be tempted to learn MySQL and build database-driven sites on such an experimental version. Nor should you use MySQL 4.1.x, which is expected to be available in a beta version around the time this book is published, until it's declared stable. The MySQL development team is working at a fast and furious pace, and new versions are thoroughly tested by an army of experienced volunteers, so you can expect the advanced features to be available by the time you're ready for them. In the meantime, use the latest stable version.

The latest stable (or production) version of MySQL at the time of this writing is 4.0.17. You can download the necessary files direct from the MySQL website at www.mysql.com/downloads/mysql-4.0.html.

If you're put off by the size of the download (22.8MB), you might want to consider installing the latest version of the 3.23.xx series of MySQL, which is roughly half the size (12.8MB). Many ISPs have not yet upgraded to MySQL 4, and the MySQL team is still updating the 3.23.xx series to fix any major bugs discovered (although no new features will be added). All the files in this book will run on either version of MySQL, so the choice is yours. The download page for the older version is www.mysql.com/downloads/mysql-3.23.html.

> *Before proceeding with installation, it's worth pausing a moment to explain the difference between MySQL, mysql, and mysqld because they can easily be confused. MySQL refers to the entire database management system and is always written in uppercase (except for the "y"). The other two are always written in lowercase and refer to the two main programs essential to working with MySQL. mysqld is the **daemon** or server that runs in the background listening for any requests made to the database. Once it has been started, you can ignore it. mysql is the client program used to feed those requests to the database itself. All communication with MySQL is done through the client, which is normally referred to as the MySQL monitor.*

### Windows installation

1. Whichever series of MySQL you choose, make sure you get the version for Windows complete with installer. This comes packaged in a self-extracting zip file. Browse to the folder where you downloaded the MySQL zip file, and double-click it. It will extract the necessary files into a new folder as shown in Figure 13-1.

**Figure 13-1.** Contents of the unzipped MySQL file

2. Close any other programs you have running, and double-click the SETUP.EXE icon in the unzipped folder. The install wizard starts and displays the opening screen, shown in Figure 13-2. Click Next to start the installation process.

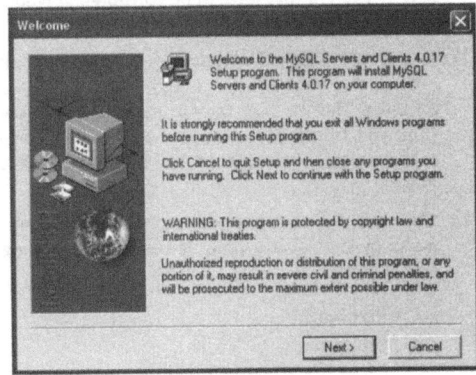

**Figure 13-2.** Starting the installation of MySQL

3. The next screen (see Figure 13-3) contains important information if you want to install MySQL in a folder other than the default setting (C:\mysql). Click Next.

4. You are then given the opportunity to change the default installation location (see Figure 13-4). It is recommended you accept the default. Click Next.

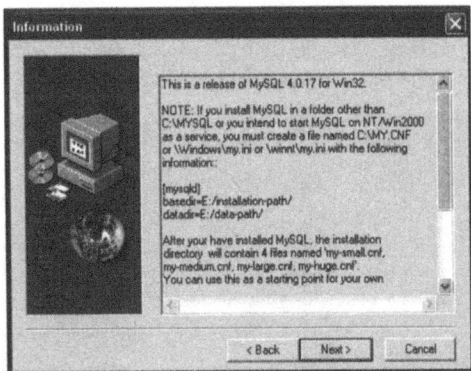

**Figure 13-3.** Read the instructions if you're planning to change the installation location.

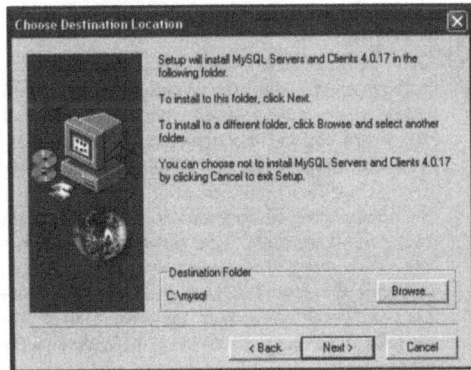

**Figure 13-4.** Accept the default installation location.

5. The final screen offers you the choice of a Typical, Compact, or Custom installation. Accept the default (Typical) and click Next. The installation process starts. Although that's all there is to installation, you now have to start the MySQL daemon.

6. The daemon needs to be running to enable you to connect to the database. Assuming that you accepted the default installation destination, open the C:\mysql folder. The contents should look similar to Figure 13-5.

**Figure 13-5.** The contents of C:\mysql after installation

7. Open the `bin` folder (it stands for "binary" and has nothing to do with the Windows Recycle Bin). Locate the `mysqld.exe` icon and double-click it. (Take care you get the right one; there are many files with similar names.) A Windows command prompt appears briefly on your screen and then disappears. Like all daemons, `mysqld` runs in the background, so there is no outwardly visible sign that it's running. The easiest way to check is to open the Windows Task Manager (press *CTRL+ALT+ DEL* on recent Windows systems), select the Processes tab, and look for `mysqld.exe` (see Figure 13-6).

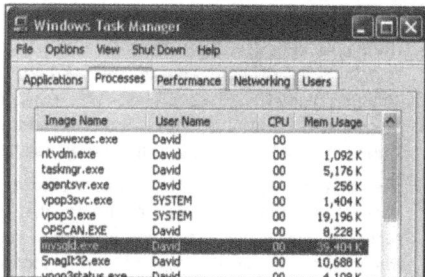

**Figure 13-6.** Checking in the Windows Task Manager that `mysqld` is running

8. Now that you know `mysqld` is working satisfactorily, you need to close it down gracefully. To do this, open a command prompt. If you're not familiar with this, you can do it via Start ➤ Programs ➤ Accessories ➤ Command Prompt. Alternatively, Start ➤ Run, type cmd, and click OK.

9. The command prompt provides a way of communicating directly with programs that don't have a Windows graphic interface. To access MySQL, type `cd \mysql\bin` and press the *ENTER* key.

10. Type `mysqladmin shutdown` and press the *ENTER* key. Use the Windows Task Manager again to confirm that `mysqld` has indeed shut down. You could have used the Windows Task Manager to kill the process, but this can have unpredictable results. At best, `mysqld` will shut down and you will keep all of your data intact. At worst, you could scramble your databases and your data would be toast! Even though you have not created any of your own databases yet, MySQL has an extremely important database that lists all users and their permitted access levels. If that were to be corrupted, it would create serious problems.

11. If you are running Windows NT, 2000, or XP Professional you can (and should) install MySQL as a service. This will start MySQL unobtrusively every time you boot your computer. Still at the command prompt, type `mysqld --install` and press *ENTER*.

12. You can now start and stop `mysqld` at the command prompt at any time by using the following commands:

```
net start mysql
net stop mysql
```

*If in the future you need to gain access to some of MySQL's more advanced options, you must remove it as a service, although for the majority of readers the current setup will be fine. The command to remove MySQL as a service is* `mysqld --remove`.

## MySQL monitor

The MySQL monitor is a simple command-line interface that allows you to connect and interact with the database. For anyone who has never worked with computer programs that use text commands rather than the Windows graphic user interface, it can seem a daunting prospect. However, it's not difficult, and direct interaction with the database can often tell you a lot more about what's happening with your database queries than when everything is hidden behind a seemingly reassuring point-and-click interface. For most of the work in this book, you'll interact with MySQL mainly through Dreamweaver MX 2004 and a very user-friendly system called phpMyAdmin. For the moment, though, open a Windows command prompt, and if you're not already in the mysql\bin directory, type cd \mysql\bin and press *ENTER*.

1. To start the MySQL monitor, type mysql and press *ENTER*. If the MySQL monitor can connect to the MySQL daemon, you should get a greeting message similar to that in Figure 13-7.

If you get a message like Figure 13-8, though, it means mysqld is not running on the local machine. If you get the error message, return to the previous section on installing and starting the MySQL daemon and try again.

2. To exit the MySQL monitor, simply type exit. You will be returned to the command prompt.

## Mac OS X installation

In Chapter 10, you used a package to install PHP, and that's the method you're going to use for MySQL. If you're really ambitious and know how to compile from source under Unix or Linux, feel free to do so. However, there is no real advantage to be gained from doing that.

1. Download the Standard package in the Mac OS X Package Installer downloads section from www.mysql.com/downloads/.

2. Double-click the .pkg file on your desktop. This will open the Mac OS X installer. Go through the installer as usual.

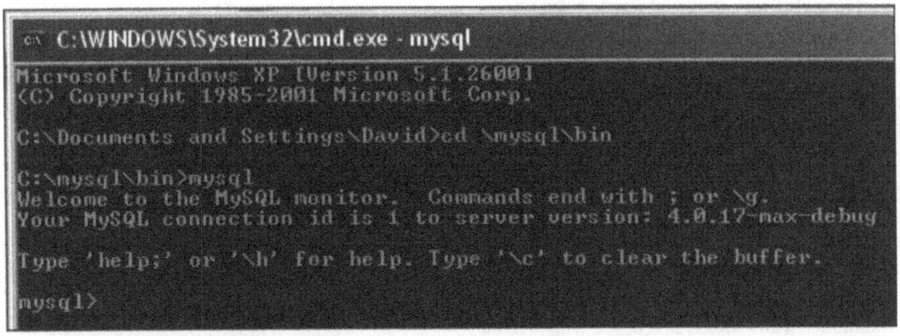

**Figure 13-7.** Opening the MySQL monitor

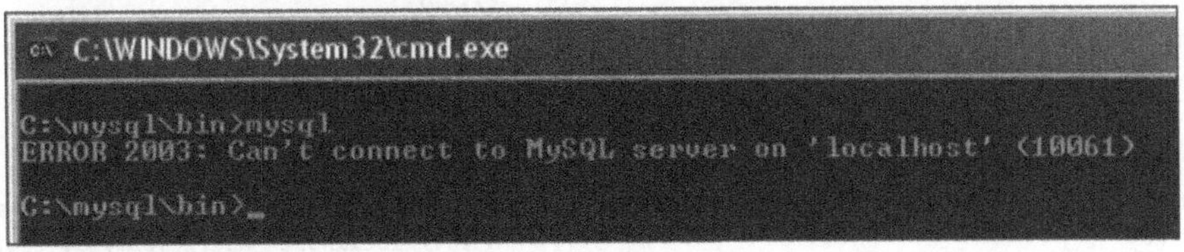

**Figure 13-8.** This tells you the MySQL daemon isn't running.

**227**

3. Once the installation has finished, open the Terminal application. To configure and start the MySQL database, from the command line, type cd /usr/local/mysql.

4. Change ownership of the data directory so that MySQL will have the correct permissions to run. Type sudo chown -R mysql data/. Enter your administrator password when prompted.

5. To start the server, type sudo echo, then type sudo ./bin/mysqld_safe -user=mysql &.

6. MySQL is now running and you can access the MySQL monitor from the command line. To avoid having to type out the full path to the mysql/bin directory every time, you can add it to the PATH in your environmental variables. The PATH is a string of text that lists the paths to certain folders. To view it, type echo $PATH in the Terminal. When you issue a command, the Terminal looks in these folders to see if there is a file there that matches. The PATH is easy to set from the command line by typing

```
echo 'setenv PATH
➥/usr/local/mysql/bin:$PATH' >> ~/.tcshrc
```

7. Close the Terminal window and then reopen it.

8. You can now access the MySQL monitor by typing mysql -uroot.

9. You can now run and create databases, tables, and so forth. You can also run PHP scripts with MySQL queries.

10. So you don't have to issue the start command every time you restart your Mac, you can install a handy little package from the creator of the PHP package. This will configure the Start up items in OS X to include the MySQL database. You can download it from www2.entropy.ch/download/mysql-startupitem.pkg.tar.gz.

## Testing, testing! (Windows and Mac OS X)

You should now be able to start the MySQL monitor, but there's one final test to check that MySQL is working correctly.

1. Open a text editor (like Notepad or SimpleText) and save the following as mysql_test.php in your web server's root directory. The following code connects to MySQL and uses the show status command to return information about the database:

```
<html>
<head>
<title>Test MySQL</title>
</head>
<body>
<?php
$host = 'localhost';
mysql_connect($host,'root','');
$sql='show status';
$result = mysql_query($sql);
if ($result == 0)
  echo '<b>Error '.mysql_errno().': ';
  echo mysql_error().'</b>';
elseif (mysql_num_rows($result) == 0)
    echo '<b>Query successful</b>';
else
{
?>
<!-- Table that displays the results -->
<table border="1">
  <tr><td><b>Variable_name</b></td>
  <td><b>Value</b></td></tr>
<?php
  for ($i = 0; $i <
➥ mysql_num_rows($result); $i++) {
    echo '<tr>';
    $row_array = mysql_fetch_row($result);
    for ($j = 0; $j <
➥ mysql_num_fields($result); $j++) {
    echo '<td>' . $row_array[$j] . '</td>';
    }
    echo '</tr>';
  }
?>
</table>
<?php } ?>
</body>
</html>
```

2. Save the file and point your browser at http://localhost/mysql_test.php, or for Mac users http://localhost/~username/mysql_test.php.

**3.** You should see a table with a long list of variables like the one in Figure 13-9. Don't worry about what they all mean—it's just telling you that PHP is "talking" to MySQL and your installation is fine and dandy.

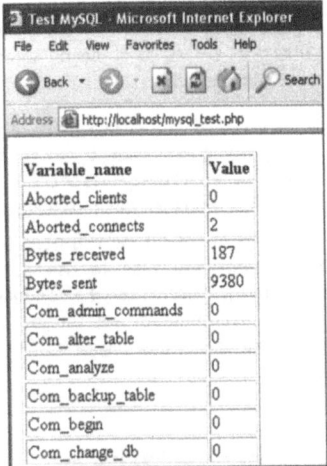

**Figure 13-9.** Confirming that PHP and MySQL are working together successfully

## Making MySQL secure

Windows users who don't have experience with Linux or Unix systems will probably be unfamiliar with the concept of a **root user**. *Root* is the name given to the main administrator on Unix-based systems, and MySQL follows the same tradition. In MySQL, *root* is a super-user account that has all privileges and can do anything, including deleting databases. (Mac OS X users should note that the MySQL root user is different from their system root.)

When you first set up MySQL, the MySQL root user requires no password to access the program. With such far-reaching privileges, this needs to be changed as soon as possible. Even if you are the only person using your computer, it's still a good idea to get into the habit of setting passwords. The next section is quite straightforward, so there's little reason to skip it. Moreover, the MySQL account on your ISP is certain to be password protected; it's also a lot easier to develop your sites locally that way too.

**1.** In Windows, open the command prompt and change directory to \mysql\bin. In Mac OS X, open Terminal. The instructions from this point on are the same for Mac and Windows.

**2.** Start the MySQL monitor by typing mysql -uroot. You should now be connected to the MySQL monitor and see the same welcome message as before (see Figure 13-7). The command-line prompt will have changed to mysql>.

**3.** MySQL user rights are stored in a database called mysql that is automatically created when the program is installed. This is the database that you need to change in order to secure future access to the program. At the mysql> prompt, type use mysql.

**4.** You will see a message Database changed. This doesn't mean changes have been made to the database, but that MySQL is now using the database called mysql and is ready to accept any instructions.

*The way you communicate with databases like MySQL is by using a set of instructions known as SQL (Structured Query Language) queries. SQL is not particularly difficult to learn, and although there are some differences in detail, the basic syntax is standardized across all leading relational database systems. By convention, anything that is part of the SQL syntax is written in uppercase. Everything else (such as the names of tables and data) is written in lowercase. This is, however, no more than a convention. You can write SQL queries entirely in lowercase, the only provision being that Unix or Linux-based systems (such as your ISP's is likely to be) treat database, table, and column names as case-sensitive. We observe the uppercase convention in the text of this book (although not always in figures) to make it easier for you to distinguish which part of a query belongs to the SQL syntax.*

*SQL, by the way, can be pronounced either "sequel" or "ess-queue-ell." The official pronunciation of MySQL is "my-ess-queue-ell."*

**229**

**5.** To give the root user a password, enter the following SQL query, substituting yourPwd with a suitable password of your own.

```
UPDATE user SET password =
➥PASSWORD('yourPwd') WHERE user = 'root';
```

**6.** Remove anonymous access to MySQL, using this SQL query:

```
DELETE FROM user WHERE user = '';
```

**7.** To tell MySQL to update the table and apply the new set of privileges, enter the following:

```
FLUSH PRIVILEGES;
```

The SQL queries and responses you should have are shown in Figure 13-10.

If the MySQL monitor didn't respond to your queries, check that you got the spelling right and used quotation marks where indicated. The most common mistake is to forget the semicolon at the end of the query. Figure 13-11 shows what happens when you do.

The MySQL monitor patiently waits for you to continue your query. Just type a semicolon and press ENTER/RETURN. The reason for this behavior is that the MySQL monitor allows you to spread queries over several lines (particularly useful when you have a long, complex query to enter), so it needs some way of knowing you have finished.

**8.** To see the effect of your changes, close the MySQL monitor by typing exit. Now try to get back into the monitor by typing mysql -uroot as before. The MySQL monitor won't let you in (see Figure 13-12).

**9.** To gain access in the future, you need to tell the MySQL monitor you plan to use a password. Instead of mysql -uroot, use the command mysql -uroot -p. It will then ask you for your password before letting you in (see Figure 13-13); so don't forget it!

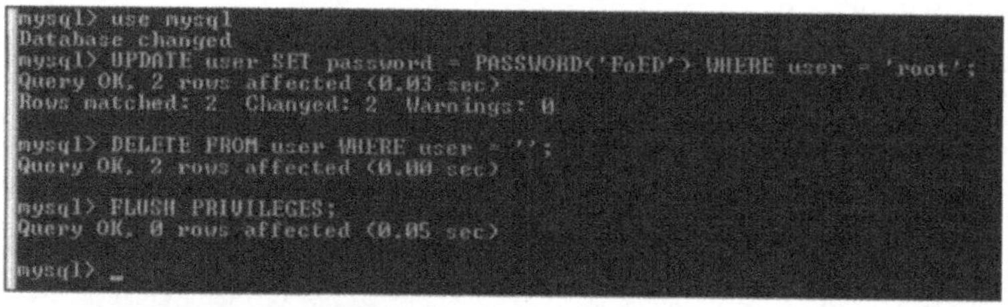

**Figure 13-10.** Securing MySQL before use

**Figure 13-11.** The MySQL monitor won't execute your query without a semicolon.

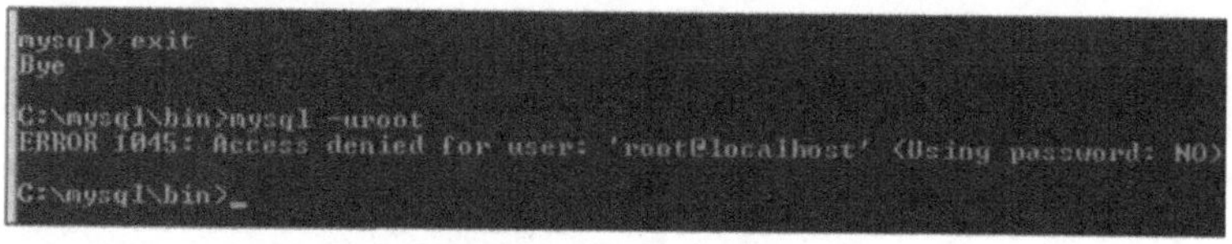

**Figure 13-12.** The MySQL denies access to root without a password.

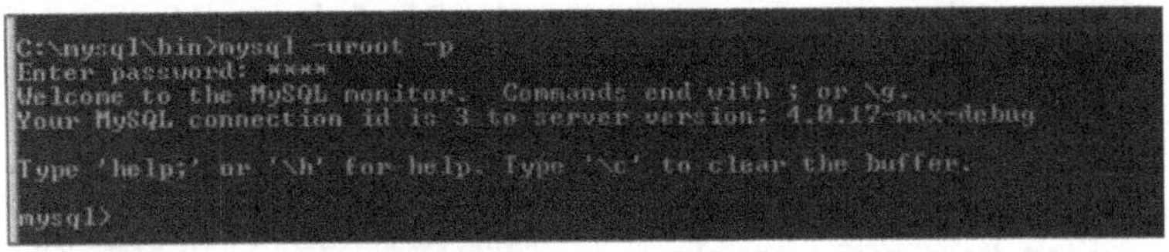

```
C:\mysql\bin>mysql -uroot -p
Enter password: ****
Welcome to the MySQL monitor.  Commands end with ; or \g.
Your MySQL connection id is 3 to server version: 4.0.17-max-debug

Type 'help;' or '\h' for help. Type '\c' to clear the buffer.

mysql>
```

**Figure 13-13.** The MySQL monitor is now secure.

*If you haven't already worked it out for yourself, -u and -p are start-up options for the MySQL monitor that specify username and password. The MySQL monitor doesn't mind whether you leave a space between -u and the username, but it does need to know which user is seeking access so that it can set the appropriate privileges. If you forget to specify the user, MySQL assumes you're trying to connect using the name you used to log on to your computer. If you forget to specify the -p option, MySQL assumes you're trying to connect without a password, and will refuse entry once you have removed anonymous access as described in the previous section.*

*So far, you have only logged on as the root user, but later you'll create a separate user with rights restricted to one database. When creating online databases, it's often a good idea to create a special user with privileges limited to a single database and read-only access (unless you're inviting others to submit information). That way, a malicious user would find it much more difficult to alter your database content. Fortunately, MX 2004 makes connection to MySQL with different usernames and passwords very simple.*

### Setting up your first MySQL database

In the next section of this chapter, you will install a very user-friendly GUI (graphical user interface) to MySQL called phpMyAdmin, but for the moment, continue using the MySQL monitor. The reason we want you to do this is that you may not always be able to rely on a GUI. The traditional way to manage MySQL databases on a remote server is to connect by Telnet or SSH (Secure Shell) and work directly at the command line in

the MySQL monitor. Telnet and SSH are quick and simple methods of communicating with a remote computer by opening up a Command Prompt or Terminal. Once the connection is made, you can work on the remote computer as though it were on your own desktop, even if it's on the opposite side of the world. To do this, you will need to be familiar with using the command line; so a little more practice should be useful.

1. If you are not still logged into the MySQL monitor, log in now. You're going to create a database called book_db. This is the database you'll be working with in Dreamweaver MX 2004. The SQL for this is CREATE DATABASE followed by the name of the database you want to create (quite logical, really). Type the following (as shown in Figure 13-14) and press *ENTER/RETURN* (all commands should be followed by *ENTER/RETURN*, so we won't keep repeating it).

   CREATE DATABASE book_db;

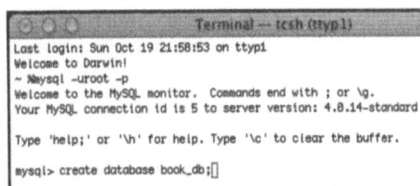

**Figure 13-14.** Commands in SQL queries are not case-sensitive.

2. The database will need some tables in which to store your data, but you'll create those later in phpMyAdmin. Right now, you need to add a user with universal rights over the database you have just created.

3. The `mysql` database is where user information is stored, so you need to tell the MySQL monitor you want to use the `mysql` database, just as you did in the previous section, "Making MySQL Secure." Type the command use `mysql`. (Note: use [database_name] is the only command in the MySQL monitor that doesn't need a semicolon at the end, although there's no harm in using one.)

4. The message database changed indicates you are connected to the database just specified (in this case, `mysql`).

5. To add a user with the correct permissions to read/write to the `book_db` database, use the following SQL query:

   GRANT ALL ON book_db.* TO name@localhost
   ➥IDENTIFIED BY 'mypassword';

6. Choose an appropriate name and password. In Figure 13-15, we used "spongebob" for the name, and "squarepants" as the password. Note that the name of the database is followed by a period and an asterisk. This means "all tables within the database."

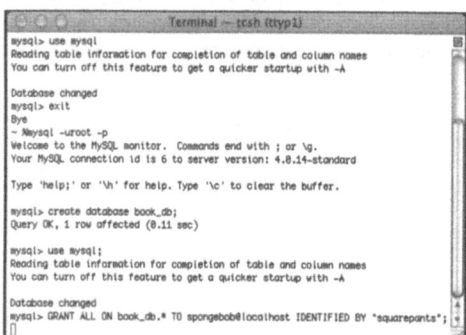

**Figure 13-15.** Creating a new user for the book_db database

7. Reload the table by typing FLUSH PRIVILEGES;.

8. The user spongebob is now fully authorized to work on the `book_db` database (but not any others). Close the MySQL monitor by typing exit.

# phpMyAdmin: A user-friendly front end for MySQL

phpMyAdmin is a collection of ready-made PHP scripts that you can use to create and edit MySQL databases from your browser window. Because it's written in PHP, the same version runs on both Windows and Mac OS X (as well as Linux). It's free to download and comes with plenty of online documentation and help forums. You can download it from www.phpmyadmin.net.

1. Download the file phpMyAdmin-2.x.x-php.zip where 2.x.x is the version number. In this example, we are using the latest stable release at time of this writing, v2.5.4.

2. Unzip this file to a folder on your hard drive, and open it. Depending on the method you used to unzip the file, this folder may contain another folder of the same name (phpMyAdmin-2.x.x). Select whichever folder contains the PHP files, and copy and paste the whole folder into your web server's root directory (C:\htdocs or /Users/~username/Sites).

3. Rename the new folder in your server root phpMyAdmin.

## Configuring phpMyAdmin

Before you can use phpMyAdmin, there are a few small changes you need to make to the configuration file.

1. Open the phpMyAdmin folder and find config.inc.php. Open it either in a text editor or in Dreamweaver MX 2004.

2. Locate the following code (it should be around line 39):

   $cfg['PmaAbsoluteUri'] = '';

This tells phpMyAdmin the address you will use in a browser to access it. Set this to the complete URL for your copy of phpMyAdmin. On Windows, this will be http://localhost/phpMyAdmin/. For Mac users, it will be http://localhost/~username/phpMyAdmin/.

   $cfg['PmaAbsoluteUri'] =
   ➥'http://localhost/phpMyAdmin/';

3. Next, you need to tell phpMyAdmin how to connect to MySQL. Look for the following block of code (around line 79):

```
$cfg['Servers'][$i]['auth_type']= 'config';
$cfg['Servers'][$i]['user']     = 'root';
$cfg['Servers'][$i]['password'] = '';
```

4. If you are setting this up on a computer that you're confident no one else will have access to, you can leave the first two unchanged, and enter your MySQL root password between the quotation marks of the password variable.

```
$cfg['Servers'][$i]['auth_type']= 'config';
$cfg['Servers'][$i]['user']     = 'root';
$cfg['Servers'][$i]['password'] = 'FoED';
```

Note that if you were to use the username and password that you created for books_db, phpMyAdmin would allow access to that person only, so it's best to log into phpMyAdmin as root.

A more secure method is to leave the user and password variables as they are, and change auth_type to http.

```
$cfg['Servers'][$i]['auth_type']= 'http';
$cfg['Servers'][$i]['user']     = 'root';
$cfg['Servers'][$i]['password'] = '';
```

This way you will be asked for your password before you can enter phpMyAdmin.

5. Save config.inc.php and point your browser at http://localhost/phpMyAdmin or http://localhost/~username/phpMyAdmin (depending on the system you are using). A welcome screen like that in Figure 13-16 should appear either immediately, or if you have chosen the http authentication method, after entering your username and password.

You will be delighted to know that you have now installed all the software that you need not only for the rest of the book, but that will enable you to design and build a wide range of database-driven sites in the future.

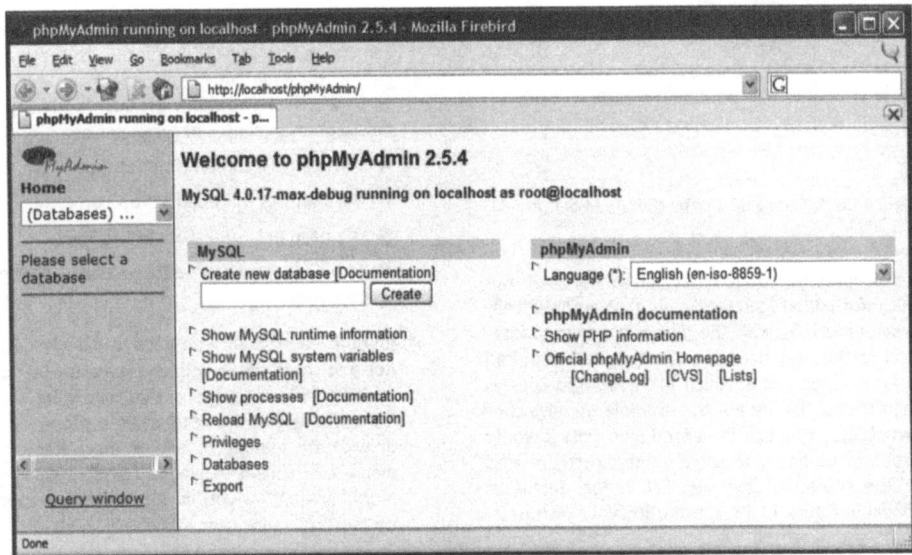

**Figure 13-16.** The phpMyAdmin welcome screen

**Connecting to MySQL from Dreamweaver MX 2004**

**1.** Open MX 2004 and select the php_site we defined earlier. Create a new PHP page called contact.php, open the Application panel on the right side of the Dreamweaver workspace, and select the Databases tab (*Ctrl/Cmd+Shift+F10*). Click the plus sign button and select MySQL Connection (see Figure 13-17). MX 2004 is a highly context-sensitive program, and it will let you create a connection to MySQL only if you have a PHP page open and a site and testing server already defined. You did that back in Chapter 10, so that part of the process is already complete. As you can see in Figure 13-17, the necessary steps are conveniently displayed in the Databases panel, and can be activated by clicking the links in the correct order. Once each step has been completed, MX 2004 puts a check mark against the item.

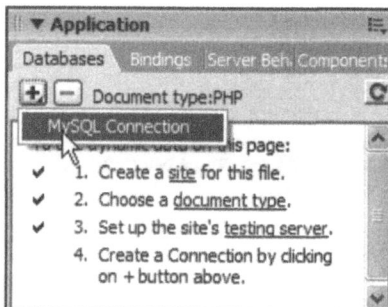

**Figure 13-17.** Setting up a connection to MySQL in MX 2004

**2.** A box opens for you to enter details. MX 2004 uses this information to create a file that automatically provides MySQL with the details it needs to connect to the right database. The first item required is Connection name, which MX 2004 also uses as the name of the file. For this example we have chosen myConn, although for a production site it would probably be better to use a name directly related to the subject of the site. Fill in the details as shown in Figure 13-18, substituting your own username and password.

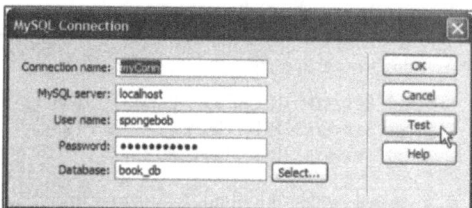

**Figure 13-18.** MX 2004 gathers information for the connection file.

*Something that confuses a lot of people is what to enter in the MySQL server field. While testing on a local machine, the use of "localhost" is fairly logical, but what happens when you're working with a remote server? In virtually all cases, the answer is still "localhost." This is because MySQL communicates with the web server that processes the PHP page. If the web server is on the same machine as MySQL, they are local to each other and use "localhost" even if the computer that requested the web page is on the other side of the world.*

**3.** When you've filled in the details, make sure you can connect to MySQL by clicking Test. You should get a message saying Connection was made successfully. If you don't get such a message, the most common causes of problems are

- The mysqld daemon isn't running.
- The user has not been set up correctly.
- You have not run FLUSH PRIVILEGES.
- You have mistyped either your username or password.

**4.** If you have problems, go back to the MySQL monitor and try to log in with the same username and password. If you can get in that way, there is something wrong with the setup of your site in MX 2004 or with the spelling of one or more items in the dialog box shown in Figure 13-18. If the MySQL monitor won't let you in, log back in as root and try creating a new user.

**5.** We hope everything will have worked without problem, so click OK. The connection you created will now be displayed in the Databases panel, but if you expand the Tables section, you'll see that none have been created yet (see Figure 13-19). To do that, you need to go back to phpMyAdmin or the MySQL monitor. In the exercise that follows, you'll use phpMyAdmin.

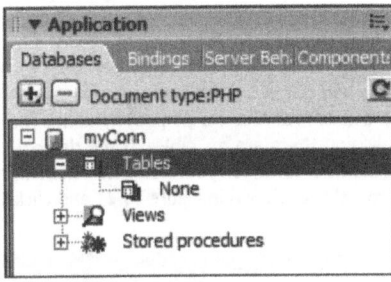

**Figure 13-19.** A connection has been created to the database, but there are no tables yet.

# Building your first PHP database application

Now it's time to build your first PHP database application—a contact form for a website. The form will contain just four fields:

- User's first name
- User's family name
- User's email address
- Space for comments

The structure and design have been kept deliberately simple, so you can concentrate on the principles of how it's put together without being overwhelmed by a mass of unnecessary detail. The steps you will follow throughout the rest of this chapter are exactly the same as you would take when designing and building a much more complex database application.

This is how we will proceed:

**1.** Plan the database structure.

**2.** Create the necessary database structure.

**3.** Plan and design the static part of the contact form.

**4.** Apply a validation behavior to the form.

**5.** Build the dynamic links between the database and form.

**6.** Test the system.

**7.** Build a dynamic page to retrieve and display the contents of the database.

As you can see, there is a lot more going on than in the construction of a static web page. Fortunately, MX 2004's integration with PHP and MySQL takes a lot of the hard work out of it through built-in **server behaviors** and **bindings**. Dreamweaver's server behaviors are basically custom-built functions, similar to those you learned about in Chapter 12. They enable you to perform common database-related actions, such as insertion and retrieval of data, updating data, and creating interactive navigation that lets users browse through several pages of results in exactly the same way as the major search engines like Google. Bindings (covered in Chapter 14) create a dynamic link between your web page and data retrieved from the database. Both are accessed from the Application panel you use to create the connection to MySQL (see Figure 13-17). If it sounds bewildering and mysterious, everything will become clear as you start to work with these new features. So, let's get to work ...

> A database-driven contacts page

## Step 1: Planning your database structure

For newcomers to database-driven sites, this is arguably the most difficult part of the whole process. Even experienced developers will tell you they often spend as much time planning the database structure as building the rest of the site. Getting the structure right is so important that it is time well spent. Whole books have been written on the subject, so we couldn't possibly go into all the details here. (For more information on the topic, we recommend *Database Design for Mere Mortals* by Michael Hernandez, published by Addison Wesley ISBN 0201752840). There are two important principles, though.

- Do not store more than one piece of information in each field.

- Do not store the same information in more than one place.

The contacts form you're building here is very simple, so there are not many decisions to be made—all you want to store is name, email address, and comments. That sounds like three pieces of information, but if you think about it, most people's names contain at least two pieces of information: first name and family name. Consequently, it's advisable to store them separately. When you first build a contacts list, you may think there's no need to separate them, but if you build a database with both names stored together, it becomes far more difficult to find everybody whose family name begins with P or M. With names, you could add fields for title (Mr., Mrs., Ms., Dr., and so on) and middle initial; and for addresses, the most sensible approach is to have separate fields for street, town or city, state or province, zip/postal code, and so on. That way, you can find all doctors in one particular area.

When you split everything up in this way, you need a method of identifying those items that belong together. You do this by creating a unique identifier called a **primary key**. Most of the time, this is simply a number that you get the database to create for you automatically. In MySQL it's called auto_increment. That means that in addition to the four fields already identified (first name, family name, email, comments), you need a fifth field for the primary key.

## Step 2: Creating the database table with phpMyAdmin

1. Open phpMyAdmin in your browser (refer back to the section of configuring phpMyAdmin if you've forgotten how). The drop-down menu on the left (Figure 13-20) shows you all the MySQL databases installed on your computer. Select book_db.

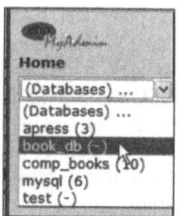

**Figure 13-20.** Selecting book_db from phpMyAdmin

2. This opens a page with information about the database and displays a series of tabs giving you access to the various features of phpMyAdmin. The page tells you there are no tables in the database, and presents a form for you to create one. Fill in the two fields as shown in Figure 13-21 and click Go.

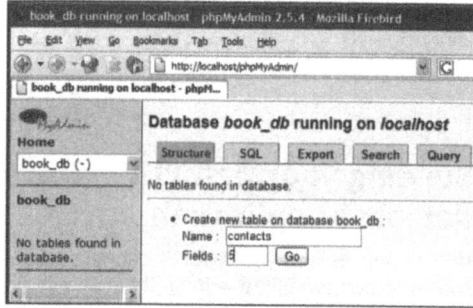

**Figure 13-21.** Creating a new table

3. phpMyAdmin now displays a page where you create the individual fields. Unless you have a very large monitor, you will probably have to scroll horizontally to see all the options. Fortunately, the ones that concern you most are toward the left. Enter the name in the Field column. phpMyAdmin's use of the word "field" is potentially confusing because what you're naming is not an individual field but instead the table column that will contain the individual fields. You can call table columns anything you like, as long as they contain no spaces, and are no longer than 64 characters. You can use numbers, letters, the dollar sign ($), and the underscore ( _ ), but you cannot use all numbers. There are a variety of naming

conventions, but the most important thing is to choose names that are meaningful. Call the fields contactID, first_name, family_name, email, and comments. Refer to Figure 13-22 to see how to fill out the entire form. We'll explain the other columns next.

**4.** The second column, Type, sets the table column type. The drop-down menu lists the 25 column types. Most of these you will never use, so we'll just explain the most important ones.

- VARCHAR is used for text or entries you want treated as a string. (For instance, MySQL strips leading zeros off numbers, so a product code or staff number that begins with 0 needs to be entered as a string.) VARCHAR holds a maximum of 255 characters.

- TEXT is used when you want to exceed the 255-character limit imposed by VARCHAR. It holds a maximum of 65,535 characters—longer than Chapter 12, which we think you'll agree is pretty long!

- INT is used for integers ranging from –2,147,483,648 to 2,147,483,647, or from 0 to 4,294,967,295 if UNSIGNED.

- DECIMAL is used mainly for money. The value is stored as a string, so if you want to perform calculations within MySQL, it may be preferable to store monetary values as cents or pence, using INT.

- DATE is used to store dates in the YYYY-MM-DD format.

- TIME is used to store time in the hh:mm:ss format.

- DATETIME, as you might expect, is used to combine the previous two types as YYYY-MM-DD hh:mm:ss.

> *Click the* Documentation *link under* Type *in phpMyAdmin to display the MySQL online documentation page, which explains all the column types in detail.*

You specify the maximum length of any field or any preset values in the Length/Values column. In the case of VARCHAR, any length between 0 and 255 characters is valid (although 0 would be rather pointless because you would not be able to enter anything in the field). DECIMAL is the only type here that needs a value: two numbers separated by a comma. The first number is the maximum width of the column (including any minus sign and the decimal point) and the second number is the number of digits after the decimal point. For example, a value of 6,2 permits numbers from –9999.99 to 99999.99.

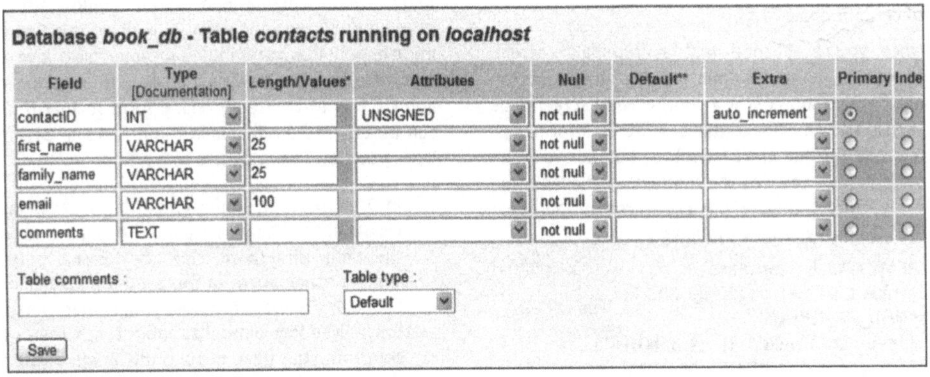

**Database *book_db* - Table *contacts* running on *localhost***

| Field | Type [Documentation] | Length/Values* | Attributes | Null | Default** | Extra | Primary | Inde |
|---|---|---|---|---|---|---|---|---|
| contactID | INT | | UNSIGNED | not null | | auto_increment | ⊙ | ○ |
| first_name | VARCHAR | 25 | | not null | | | ○ | ○ |
| family_name | VARCHAR | 25 | | not null | | | ○ | ○ |
| email | VARCHAR | 100 | | not null | | | ○ | ○ |
| comments | TEXT | | | not null | | | ○ | ○ |

Table comments :

Table type : Default

[ Save ]

**Figure 13-22.** The completed form for the contacts table

- The Attributes column offers three choices, the most important of which is UNSIGNED. This tells MySQL no negative numbers are permitted in the field.

- The Null column offers two choices. The default not null specifies that a field cannot be left blank. As you would expect, the alternative null permits blank fields.

- The Default column is where you specify what should be entered into the database when a not null field has no content.

- The Extra column is used to specify if MySQL's auto_increment feature is to be used.

- The Primary column is used to specify if you want the contents of that field to be the table's primary key. To select it, click the radio button. The remaining four columns are used for advanced indexing, and needn't concern you at this stage.

5. Check Figure 13-22 again to see the values selected for the contacts table. The most important one is contactID, which will act as the unique index to each entry in the database. Its column settings are INT, UNSIGNED, auto_increment, and primary key. The remaining four fields are used for text entries, so they have been set to VARCHAR, with the exception of comments, which has been set to TEXT because VARCHAR's 255-character limit is probably too small. The VARCHAR fields have been given appropriate lengths, and all fields have been left as the default not null because we want all of them to contain data.

6. Once you're satisfied that everything's correct, click Save. phpMyAdmin creates the table in MySQL and shows you a confirmation screen (see Figure 13-23). This contains a lot of information that will become more useful to you once you gain more experience. For the moment, just check that it says Table contacts has been created, and that the SQL query reads as follows:

```
CREATE TABLE 'contacts' (
'contactID' INT UNSIGNED NOT NULL
➥AUTO_INCREMENT ,
'first_name' VARCHAR( 25 ) NOT NULL ,
'family_name' VARCHAR( 25 ) NOT NULL ,
'email' VARCHAR( 100 ) NOT NULL ,
```

```
'comments' TEXT NOT NULL ,
PRIMARY KEY ( 'contactID' )
);
```

7. If there are any problems, click the Drop tab on the right side and start again.

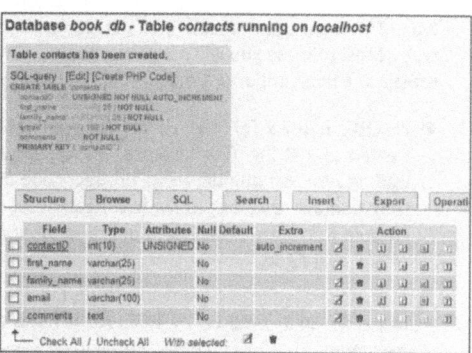

**Figure 13-23.** Confirmation that the contacts table has been created

## Step 3: Preparing the data entry form in Dreamweaver MX 2004

Now you've got a database table but no data. There are several ways of populating a database with information. You could do it all at the command line in MySQL monitor, but that's rather like eating peanuts with chopsticks—fun for masochists maybe, but not something we'd recommend. You could also put phpMyAdmin on your website, and get users to input information that way, but that would also give them control over your entire database. The most practical approach is to create an online form so that the data can be entered easily, but without handing over privileges you don't want others to have.

1. In Dreamweaver, confirm that the contacts table is visible in the Databases panel (see Figure 13-24). If the table isn't there, click the Refresh button, a small circular arrow in the top-right corner of the Databases panel. You will notice that contactID has a little key symbol to indicate it's the primary key. It also has filled in 10 as the length of the field. You could have done that yourself in phpMyAdmin, but it's not necessary because all

INT fields are a standard size. Notice also that each of the field (or column) names is marked Required. That's because you specified not null in phpMyAdmin. MX 2004 marks these as required to remind you that if a field is left blank, it will generate an error. The best way to avoid such errors is to implement some method of validation, which you'll learn how to do in the next section.

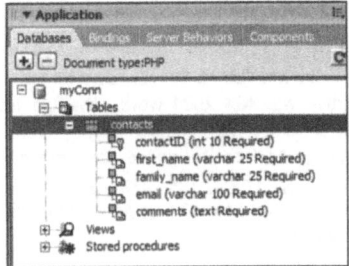

**Figure 13-24.** The contacts table is now visible in the Databases panel.

2. You're now ready to start building contact.php. Begin by inserting a form in Design view (you should have plenty of experience with forms by now, so we're going to keep instructions to a minimum). In the Property Inspector, name the form contact (see Figure 13-25).

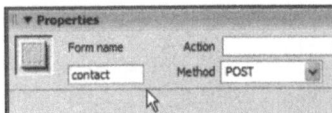

**Figure 13-25.** Naming the form in the Property Inspector

3. To keep the form tidy, place a table inside the form. Use the settings shown in Figure 13-26.

4. Complete the form so it looks like Figure 13-27. The left column simply contains labels for the three text fields and one text area on the right. You can use whatever labels you like for this column because they appear only on screen as a guide for the user. Feel free to include spaces and any formatting you like. In the Property Inspector,

however, make sure you rename each text field exactly the same as you named the fields in the contacts table in the "Step 2" section. They should be first_name, family_name, and email. These names will be used by PHP to make sure the data is inserted in the correct place, and must not contain any spaces (and will be case-sensitive on a Unix-based server).

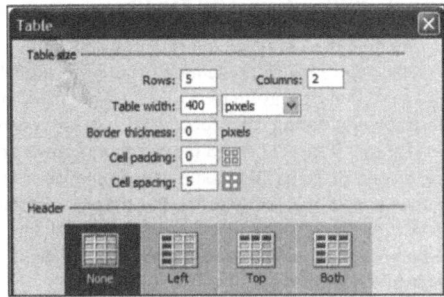

**Figure 13-26.** Settings for the table in the data entry form

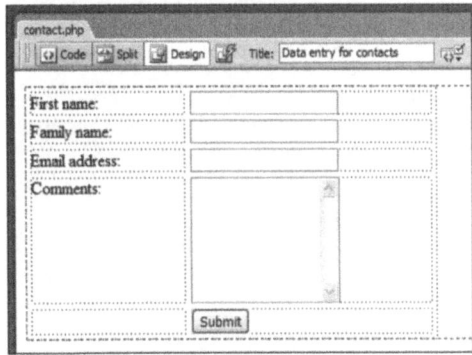

**Figure 13-27.** The completed data insertion form

5. The input field for comments needs to be bigger than a normal text box, so use a text area (Insert ➤ Forms ➤ Textarea or use the Forms Insert bar). The settings for the text area can be seen in Figure 13-28. By setting Wrap to Virtual, the text will wrap automatically on screen without inserting any new line characters when the content is inserted into the database.

**239**

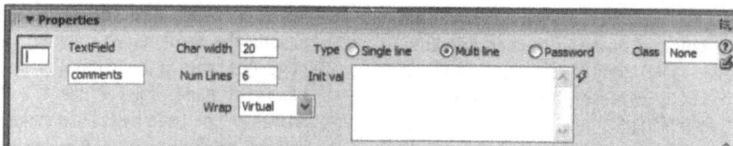

**Figure 13-28.** Settings for the Comments text area

## Step 4: Validating the form

You specified that all fields are required (not null), so you need some way of preventing users from submitting a form that has information missing. The way to do this is by **validating** the form data, which means checking that it meets certain requirements. There are several ways of doing this, some applying much more rigorous checks than others. For the purposes of this exercise, you're going to use a very simple validation method—one of Dreamweaver MX 2004's built-in JavaScript behaviors.

*Behaviors must always be applied to the correct element of a page for them to work properly. To apply a behavior, highlight the element to which it will be applied. Then in the* Behaviors *panel, click the plus sign button, and select the behavior from the context-sensitive menu that appears. If you can't find the behavior you're looking for, select* Show Events For *near the bottom of the menu and make sure there's a check mark next to 4.0 and Later Browsers. Dreamweaver MX 2004 comes with a good selection of built-in behaviors, and you can get many more that were created by independent developers (see the Appendix).*

*If you apply a behavior and later decide you don't want it, you should always highlight the element it was applied to, and open the* Behaviors *panel. There, you will find a list of behaviors that have been applied. Highlight the one you no longer want, and click the minus sign button.* **This is very important.** *If you try to remove behaviors any other way, you risk ending up with broken pages and large amounts of redundant code.*

1. Highlight the form (the simplest way is by clicking the <form#contact> tag on the Dreamweaver status bar). Open the Tag Inspector panel and select the Behaviors tab (*SHIFT+F3*). Due to the context-sensitive way MX 2004 works, the Tag Inspector label should have changed to Tag <form>. If it hasn't, go back to Design view and make sure the form is highlighted. The reason you need it highlighted is because you're going to apply a behavior to the form.

2. Click the plus sign button and select Validate Form from the drop-down menu (see Figure 13-29).

**Figure 13-29.** Applying the Validate Form behavior

**3.** The dialog box that opens will show all the named fields in your form. Select each one in turn (except email) and check Required and Anything from the options. For email, check Required and Email address. (See Figure 13-30.) Click OK when you are done.

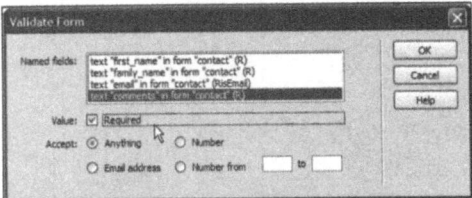

**Figure 13-30.** Filling in the Validate Form dialog box

**4.** The Validate Form behavior performs very simple checks, such as whether a particular field is required and if it should be an email address or a number in a particular range. It won't check, however, that the email address is a genuine one; only whether it *looks* like an email address. Save your page, press *F12* to preview it in a browser, and click the Submit button. You should get a message like that in Figure 13-31.

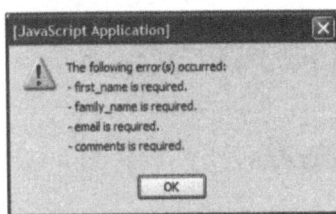

**Figure 13-31.** What happens when you try to submit an empty form

**5.** As you can see, the form validation is performed by JavaScript. If a user has JavaScript disabled, there's nothing to stop an invalid form from being submitted. In spite of its limitations, it's useful in stopping accidental submission of incomplete data. If you want to see how the behavior works, open Code view and look in the <head> part of the page, where you'll see MX 2004 has added two JavaScript functions.

## Step 5: Building dynamic links between the form and database

Now comes the really impressive part: getting MX 2004 to create all the PHP, and getting SQL to insert the information from the form into the database. In the previous section you used a behavior. This time, you'll use a **server behavior**. These are MX 2004's built-in functions that make creating server-side code a breeze.

**1.** Open the Server Behaviors tab (*CTRL/CMD*+F9) in the Application panel, click the plus sign button, and select Insert Record from the drop-down menu.

The dialog box that opens asks for the necessary information to create the PHP and SQL code, but MX 2004 does its best to help you by filling in as much as it can automatically.

Submit values from: requires the name of the form from which the data is to be drawn. There is only one form on your page, so contact is chosen automatically. If you had more than one form, you would select the appropriate one from the drop-down list.

**2.** Connection: this is automatically set to None. Open the drop-down list and select the connection you created earlier (myConn).

**3.** Once you've selected your connection, the Columns box will become populated. Because you used the same names for the text boxes and text area in your form as in the database table, MX 2004 automatically enters the correct value in each line. The only one that might seem rather odd is the first one, 'contactID' is an Unused Primary Key. Don't worry. This is correct. It simply means that no data will be entered from the form into the contactID field, which is exactly what you want because that field uses the MySQL auto_increment feature.

**4.** If any of the entries in the Columns box look like email in Figure 13-32, there's a mismatch between the name of one of your form fields and the names you used for creating the table in phpMyAdmin. In Figure 13-32, the error is caused by using e-mail in one case and email in the other. If this happens, click Cancel and check your field names again.

**241**

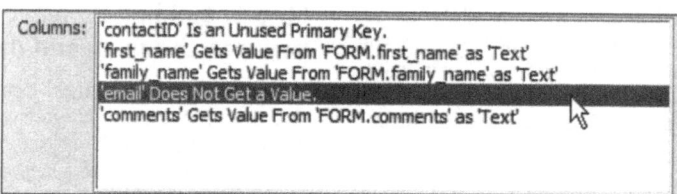

**Figure 13-32.** Mismatched field names cause an error.

5. In the Insert table drop-down menu, select the table into which the data is to be inserted. In your case, there is only one table available, so MX 2004 selects the correct one automatically, but you will need to set it yourself when your database has more than one.

6. Figure 13-33 shows what the correct values should look like. The final thing you need to do is enter the name of the page you want to send users to after the data has been inserted. Type thanks.php into the last field in the dialog box and click OK.

7. Create a new PHP page with a suitable "thank you" message, and save it as thanks.php.

That's all there is to it!

*After you have applied a server behavior or created dynamic text with the Bindings panel (see the next chapter), MX 2004 indicates its presence by turning the affected part of the page turquoise in Design view. Dynamic elements inserted this way are also listed in the Server Behaviors panel. If you ever make a mistake or change your mind about a dynamic element, the only safe way to remove it from your page is by highlighting the unwanted element in the Server Behaviors panel and clicking the minus sign button. Failure to do this will result in pages that produce unpredictable results.*

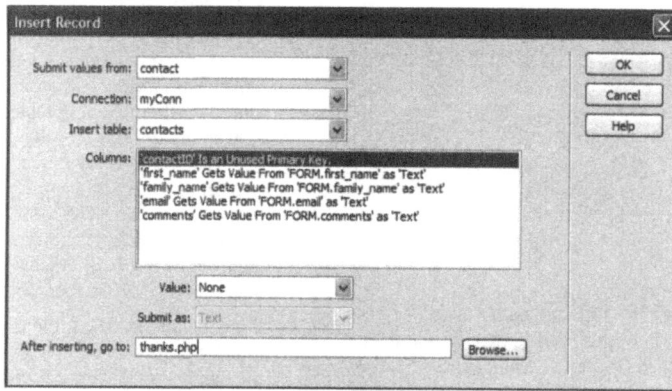

**Figure 13-33.** The completed Insert Record dialog box

## Step 6: Testing data input

**1.** You're now ready to test the form. Open your browser and point it toward http://localhost/php_site/contact.php. When you fill out the form and click Submit, you should be directed to the "thank you" message. But where has the data gone and how can you retrieve it?

**2.** To find out, open the MySQL monitor at the command prompt or Terminal, select the book_db database (use book_db;), and enter the following SQL query:

**SELECT * FROM contacts;**

That will show you everything in the table, although not in the most user-friendly of formats (see Figure 13-34).

```
C:\WINDOWS\System32\cmd.exe - mysql -uspongebob -p

C:\mysql\bin>mysql -uspongebob -p
Enter password: ***********
Welcome to the MySQL monitor.  Commands end with ; or \g.
Your MySQL connection id is 33 to server version: 4.0.17-max-debug

Type 'help;' or '\h' for help. Type '\c' to clear the buffer.

mysql> use book_db
Database changed
mysql> SELECT * FROM contacts;
+-----------+------------+-------------+-----------------------+----------
| contactID | first_name | family_name | email                 | comments
+-----------+------------+-------------+-----------------------+----------
|         1 | David      | Powers      | david@somewhere.nice.com | This is a te
st of the contact form. |
+-----------+------------+-------------+-----------------------+----------
1 row in set (0.00 sec)

mysql>
```

**Figure 13-34.** Viewing the results in the MySQL monitor

**3.** You could also use phpMyAdmin. Open phpMyAdmin again in your browser, and select book_db from the database list on the left side of the screen. Now that you have a table in the database, phpMyAdmin lists it immediately below the database name, again on the left side of the screen (see Figure 13-35). Click contacts to display the table details, and then click the Browse tab. You should see the same details, but in a much more readable format.

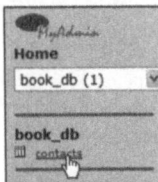

**Figure 13-35.** Accessing the contacts table in phpMyAdmin

Better still; move on to the next step to create your own page to display the database contents.

## Step 7: A dynamic page to retrieve and display the data

1. Create a new PHP page in Dreamweaver MX 2004 and save it as view_contacts.php.

2. Insert a table with the following values:

    - **Rows**: 2
    - **Columns**: 4
    - **Table width**: 600 pixels
    - **Border thickness**: 1 pixel
    - **Cell padding**: 0
    - **Cell spacing**: 0

3. In the four cells of top row of the table, enter First name, Family name, Email and Comments.

4. Select the Server Behaviors tab (*CTRL/CMD+F9*) from the Application panel. Click the plus sign button and select Recordset from the drop-down menu.

> *Recordset is the name Dreamweaver MX 2004 gives to a SQL query that retrieves a set of information from your database. You can have more than one on a page, and each one creates a PHP array (see Chapter 12) that allows you to retrieve the information you want and display it on the screen. The recordset is a multidimensional array in which each row represents a complete record identified by its primary key, and with each element labeled with the name of its corresponding column. Think of it is as a spreadsheet in which each field belongs to a row and a column that not only identify it as unique, but also provide a quick way of locating the field that you want and showing how different items relate to one another. For example, first_name in row 12 will always belong to family_name in row 12, even if you decide to display all the rows in a different order from how they were originally entered into the database.*

5. Enter my_contacts as the name for the recordset in the Recordset dialog box. If you plan to use several recordsets on a page or even on separate pages in the same site, it's a good idea to use a meaningful name that will still make sense to you in six months. For this exercise, you are using only one recordset, so my_contacts is fine.

6. Next, you need to specify which connection you are using. The dialog box offers you the option of defining one, but you don't need to. Select myConn from the drop-down menu. You will then see the rest of the fields in the dialog box become populated with details from your database, as shown in Figure 13-36. (If the dialog box looks different, it means you are in Advanced mode. Click the Simple button to switch modes. It's in the same position as the Advanced button in Figure 13-36.)

7. The Table field is where you specify the table from which you want to retrieve data. In this case, there is only one, so no change is needed.

8. The Columns field is where you specify the columns from which you want to retrieve data. (This is why we said phpMyAdmin's use of "fields" was potentially confusing. MX 2004 uses the correct database term by referring to the entire column, not just individual fields within a column.) A radio button toggles between All (the default) and Selected. You don't need to display the contactID for entries, so click Selected, and then highlight all the other column names by holding down *CTRL/CMD* as you click them.

9. The Filter field enables you to search for specific results, for example, if you want to find only records with first_name as "David." On this occasion, leave it at the default None.

10. The Sort field enables you to choose a column that will be used to sort the results. Choose contactID and Descending. This will display the results in reverse numerical order. Because contactID is increased by one with every new entry, the highest number (the most recent) will be displayed first.

11. Check that all the settings are as shown in Figure 13-37. If they are, click Test to make sure MX 2004 and MySQL are happy with the recordset you created. Click OK to close the test, then OK again to close the Recordset dialog box.

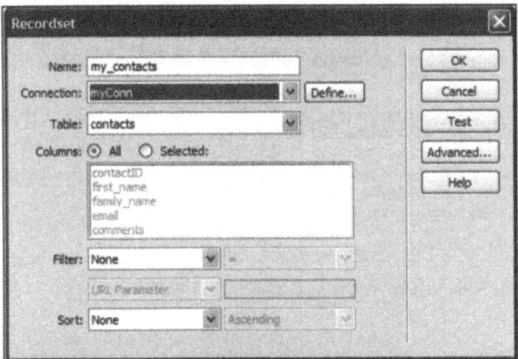

**Figure 13-36.** The Recordset dialog box

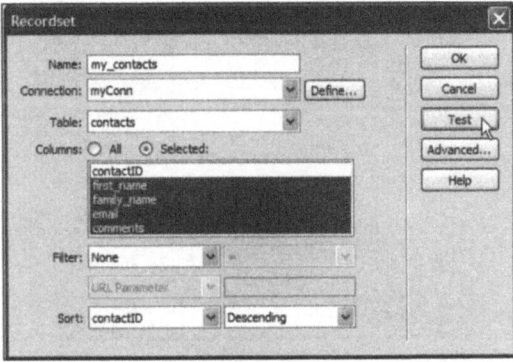

**Figure 13-37.** Preparing to test the recordset

**12.** Before performing the steps needed to display the results on your page, open Code view to see what steps 4 to 11 have achieved behind the scenes. Right at the top of the page, above the doctype, MX 2004 inserted eight lines of PHP (see Figure 13-38). The first one creates the connection between the web page and MySQL. The other seven are the recordset you just created. It contains all the necessary information PHP needs to display your data in whatever way you want.

**13.** Switch back to Design view and click inside the first cell of the second row of the table (directly beneath First name). Click the plus sign button in the Server Behaviors tab and select Dynamic text from the drop-down menu to open the Dynamic text box (see Figure 13-39).

**14.** Highlight First_name and then click OK.

**245**

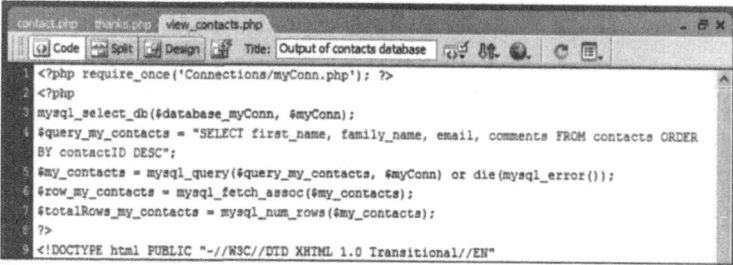

**Figure 13-38.** The code that drives the recordset

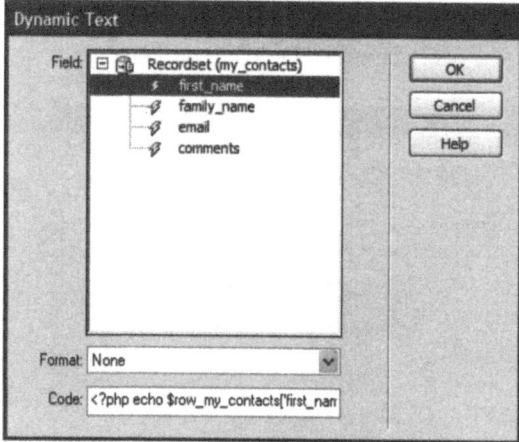

**Figure 13-39.** The Dynamic Text dialog box

**15.** MX 2004 will have placed the necessary code inside the cell to display whatever is retrieved from the first_name column in the database (see Figure 13-40). Because this is dynamic text retrieved from a database (unlike the dynamic text you created from an online form in Chapters 11 and 12), MX 2004 displays a more meaningful placeholder than the PHP icon.

**16.** Repeat points 13 and 14 with family_name and email.

**17.** Do the same with comments, but before clicking OK, you need to make a change to the code in the Dynamic Text dialog box. In the Code field at the bottom, locate the following line:

```
<?php echo $row_my_contacts['comments']; ?>
```

**18.** Change it to the following:

```
<?php echo
➥nl2br($row_my_contacts['comments']); ?>
```

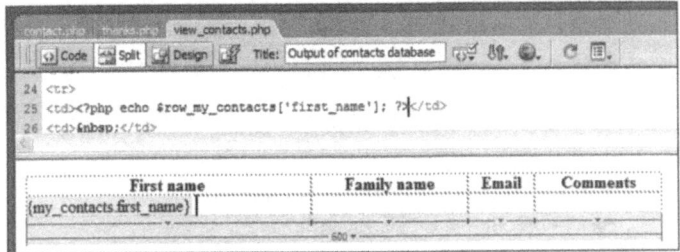

**Figure 13-40.** Dynamic text as seen in Split view

Your page should now look like Figure 13-41.

*Why do we do this? MySQL returns the data to the page as plain text, with normal line breaks. Unfortunately, web pages ignore line breaks, so you'll lose any new lines that people put in when they fill in the Comments box. To remedy this, you use another PHP built-in function nl2br() that replaces ordinary line breaks with the <br /> tag so that a web browser will format it correctly. The name of the function is easy to remember if you think of it as "new line 2 br." When making the change to the code, make sure you don't omit the closing parenthesis.*

19. If you test the page now using the Live Data button or by loading it into a browser, it will retrieve whatever you entered in the database. The problem is that it will display only the most recent record. Don't worry—MX 2004 has a Repeat Region server behavior that will fix that in a jiffy. Click anywhere in the second row of the table, and then select the entire row by highlighting the <tr> tag on the Dreamweaver status bar.

20. Click the plus sign button in the Server Behaviors tab, and select Repeat Region.

21. This opens the Repeat Region dialog box (see Figure 13-42), which enables you to choose how many records to show at a time. Leave the settings as they are and click OK.

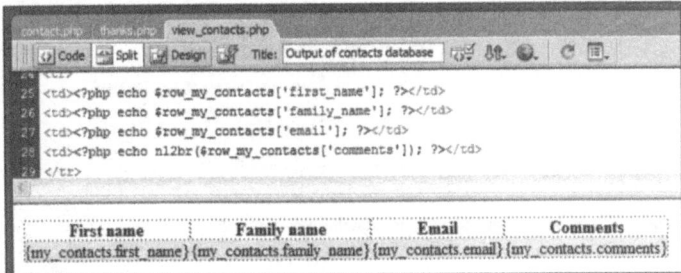

**Figure 13-41.** All the dynamic text code is in position.

**247**

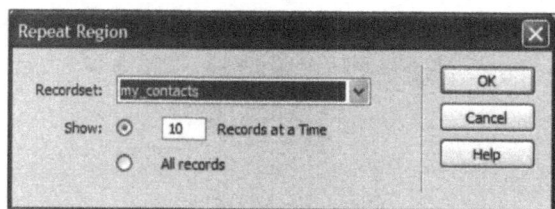

**Figure 13-42.** The Repeat Region dialog box.

**22.** Your row should now include the Repeat tag, as shown in Figure 13-43. This indicates the' server behavior has been correctly applied. If you look in the Server Behaviors window, you'll also see a line has been added that reads Repeat Region (my_contacts). If you ever want to change the number of records to be shown, highlight that line in the Server Behaviors window, and double-click.

It will reopen the dialog box for you to make changes. (You can do this with all server behaviors.)

**23.** Save the changes you made to view_contacts.php and view it in a browser, as shown in Figure 13-44. Congratulations, and welcome to the world of truly dynamic websites.

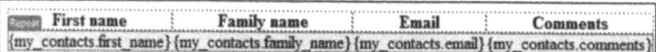

**Figure 13-43.** The row is now marked as a repeat region

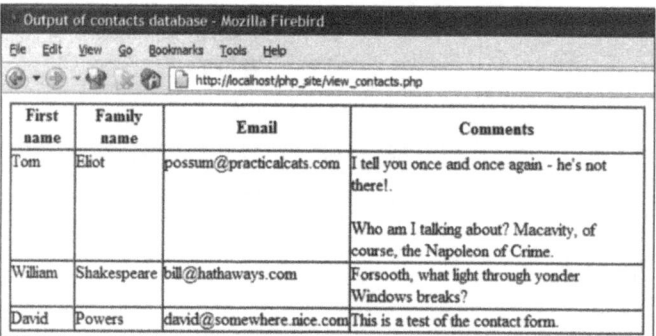

**Figure 13-44.** The output of your first database-driven application

## Summary

What you created may not be the most beautiful website, nor can we claim to have been particularly inspired with the sample content, but that wasn't the point. Such considerations would have gotten in the way of concentrating on the basic mechanics. It may not feel like it, but in the short space of a chapter, you've already learned the fundamental principles that are common to all database-driven sites, however large or small. The simple application you built could easily form the basis of a personal database for contacts, recipes, or for your own library.

In addition, you've installed the most popular open source database and communicated with it in four ways:

- At the command line with the MySQL monitor
- With phpMyAdmin
- Through the dynamic features of Dreamweaver MX 2004
- And most important of all, by building your own web-based interface

So far, you learned how to insert material into a database and retrieve it. MX 2004 has many other server behaviors that enable you to update your content, delete records, create dynamic page navigation, and make decisions about what to do when certain records aren't found. Over the next two chapters, we'll be looking at how to adapt what you have already learned and put it to genuinely practical use.

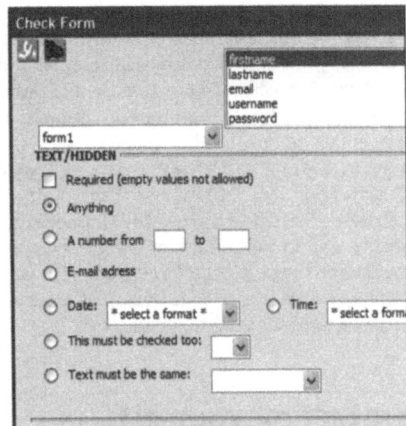

## Chapter 14

# SECURE LOGIN
# AND REGISTRATION

**What we'll cover in this chapter**

- Security issues in PHP
- Keeping track of information with sessions
- Using a registration and login application to password protect your site
- Using a third-party Dreamweaver extension for form validation
- Debugging techniques for when things go wrong

You don't have to be a secret agent to have information that you don't want available to every Tom, Dick, or Harry. But what if you want to put information online and share it with certain people, but not the entire world? In this chapter, we'll show you how to build a login/registration application using Dreamweaver MX 2004's new User Authentication behavior. The application relies on sessions, which enable you to keep track of information as a user moves from page to page throughout your website—a technique that has a wide range of uses wherever there's a need for persistent data.

## Protecting yourself from the bad guys

Sadly the Internet is no longer the innocent place it was when the World Wide Web was in its infancy in the early 1990s. Still, with a little care and planning, you can make sure you don't leave your websites wide open to attack.

You may recall back in Chapter 11 we advised you always to use the $_POST array to gather variables from forms. The reason for that is that the developers of PHP made a major decision with the release of PHP 4.2.0 in April 2002. They decided that certain variables, known as "globals" (mainly generated by forms and the web server), should no longer be automatically available simply by attaching a dollar sign ($) to their name. Before PHP 4.2.0, you could access the value of a form field called email by using a variable of the same name ($email). It was quick, simple, and automatic. Nowadays you have to use $_POST['email'] or $_GET['email'], depending on the method used to submit the form. The same applies to cookies and session values. Because most of this chapter is devoted to sessions, we thought it would be useful to revisit the subject in a little more detail.

Why change something that was so convenient? The developers of PHP concede that it is probably the most controversial decision they have made. The simple fact of the matter, though, is that it was just too convenient. Not only did it make life simple for PHP programmers, it made things just too easy for malicious scripters, as the following exercise should make clear. For a more detailed review of the problems inherent in having

globals switched on, see "A Study in Scarlet—Exploiting Common Vulnerabilities in PHP Applications" by Shaun Clowes at www.securereality.com.au/studyinscarlet .txt. The article was written before the release of PHP 4.2.0, but it gives a good insight into the reasons behind the decision to trade convenience for greater security.

In spite of the change, some ISPs decided to override it by altering the main PHP configuration file, php.ini, and switching the command register_globals back on. They apparently did so to avoid customers complaining that the upgrade had "broken" their scripts. If your ISP has adopted that policy, your websites could be at risk. Fortunately, it's easy to test whether register_globals has been set to on or off, and there are sensible precautions you can take to improve the security of your scripts regardless of the setting.

### Testing your site's security

1. Create a new PHP page and call it globals_test.php. Insert the following code between the <body> tags:

```php
<?php
if ($admin) {
  echo 'Welcome, come destroy my site!';
  }
else {
  echo 'Unauthorized, go away!';
  }
?>
```

2. Save the file, upload it to your website, and point your browser at the URL. You should see "Unauthorized, go away!"

3. In the Address bar of your browser add the following to the end of the URL: ?admin=1 and reload the page. If you're still told to go away, register_globals has been set to off, the more secure setting. If, on the other hand, you're invited to destroy the site...the message should be pretty clear. Your site is not as secure as it should be. (If you don't follow why admin=1 returns true, take another look at the discussion of true and false in the section on alternately colored table rows in Chapter 12.)

If the test shows that `register_globals` has been set to on, we recommend you contact your ISP and ask for security to be improved. If the ISP refuses, you may want to consider moving. If moving is not an option, you should definitely follow the security measures recommended in this chapter.

Even if your setting is the more secure register_ globals off, you cannot assume your scripts are 100 percent safe, and you should still build safeguards into your PHP scripts wherever user input is involved.

4. A very simple way of improving that script, even with `register_globals` on, is to change the conditional statement like this:

```
if ($_POST['admin']) {
  echo 'Welcome, come destroy my site!';
  }
elseif ($_GET['admin']) {
  echo 'Oh no you don\'t!';
  }
else {
  echo 'Unauthorized, go away!';
  }
```

It's still far from perfect, but if you try opening the page as suggested in step 3, it will no longer work because the conditional statement is checking for admin in the POST array, which contains only information submitted by the POST method and cannot be hijacked by information passed through a query string at the end of a URL. In fact, if a user attempts that, a different message is displayed.

## PHP superglobals

$_POST is an example of what are known as PHP **superglobal arrays**. There are nine of them, as listed in Table 14-1. Both the current and former names are still current, but you should use only the current shorter form because the longer versions are scheduled to be phased out.

The superglobals all take the same form: the name of the array followed by the name of the individual variable (the array key) in square brackets, for example, $_POST['admin']. The key should normally be enclosed in quotation marks, except when a superglobal is used as part of a double-quoted string. Your script will work without quotation marks, but it will generate warning notices if PHP notices are switched on (the setting recommended for a testing server in Chapter 10).

**Table 14-1.** PHP Superglobal Arrays

| Current | Former | Description |
| --- | --- | --- |
| $_GET | $HTTP_GET_VARS | Contains form variables sent through GET |
| $_POST | $HTTP_POST_VARS | Contains form variables sent through POST |
| $_COOKIE | $HTTP_COOKIE_VARS | Contains HTTP cookie variables |
| $_SERVER | $HTTP_SERVER_VARS | Contains server variables |
| $_ENV | $HTTP_ENV_VARS | Contains the environment variables |
| $_REQUEST | No equivalent | Contains the GET, POST, and COOKIE arrays together |
| $_SESSION | $HTTP_SESSION_VARS | Contains HTTP variables registered by the session module |
| $_FILES | $HTTP_POST_FILES | Contains variables related to files uploaded through POST |
| $GLOBALS | $GLOBALS | Contains all global variables |

The most important issue is that with register_globals off (as it should be by default), the only way to access information covered by the list in Table 14-1 is through one of the superglobal arrays. As the exercise demonstrated, you can prevent a malicious user from attempting to substitute the value of important variables by ensuring they are passed through the POST array. Even with register_globals on, you can increase security through inspecting the provenance of a value by checking for it in one of the superglobals, as was done in the final step of the last exercise.

To prevent having to type the name of the superglobal array all the time, a convenient method is to assign it to an ordinary variable the first time you use it: $admin = $_POST['admin'];. Thereafter, you need use only $admin.

It's also a good idea to test whether a variable has been set before attempting to use it. The built-in PHP function isset() returns true or false, but you need to realize it tests only whether a variable has been set, not whether it contains a value. Consequently, a form submitted by the POST method will set a variable for every form field, even if the user clicks the Submit button without entering anything. In this case, it's often better to test whether a variable is empty. Again, PHP has a built-in function for that. Here's how they work:

```
if (isset($_POST['admin'])) //true if set
if (empty($_POST['admin'])) //true if empty
```

## Other simple security measures

Another aspect of PHP that can leave your scripts vulnerable is the fact that you don't need to declare variables before using them. This is not really a problem if register_globals is set to off, but it's always a good idea to set the value of a variable before using it. For example, when using an if statement to test whether something is true, set the value to false first. Then you can be sure the result has come from your test and not from elsewhere.

```
$admin = false;
if (inAdmList()) { // user-defined function
  $admin = true;
  }
```

When accepting form input, you must always be on your guard. The contacts application you built in Chapter 13 has a serious weakness, which you should fix immediately if you have deployed it on your website. Apart from the obvious danger of someone filling the comments area with profanities, there's a less obvious and potentially worse problem. Figure 14-1 should prove the point.

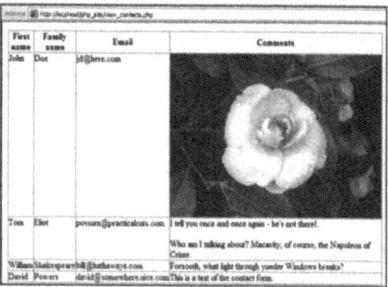

**Figure 14-1.** If you're not careful, user input can lead to unexpected results.

This was done by typing an <img> tag into the comments field. In this case, the result is quite pleasant, but consider if it had been pornographic or a multi-megabyte download. Even though the image was on a completely different site, the src attribute was a valid URL, so it would automatically be downloaded and displayed within your page. Moderating content before allowing it to be displayed on a website is one solution. Another, very simple security measure is to pass user input through the built-in PHP function strip_tags(). This will remove all (X)HTML tags from a string.

If you want to do this just for the comments field, you would add the following statement at the top of contacts.php within the first block of PHP code:

```
if (isset($_POST['comments'])) {
  $_POST['comments'] =
➡strip_tags($_POST['comments']);
  }
```

It would be safer to apply it to all elements in the POST array, but using a foreach loop will not work because of the way PHP handles array values. The most efficient solution is to modify the Insert Record server behavior created by MX 2004. Look for the following block of code in contacts.php (it should be close to the top, within the first dozen lines or so):

```
switch ($theType) {
  case "text":
    $theValue = ($theValue != "") ? "'"
➡ . $theValue . "'" : "NULL";
    break;
```

In the third line, surround the third instance of $theValue with strip_tags(), like this:

```
$theValue = ($theValue != "") ? "'"
➡ . strip_tags($theValue) . "'" : "NULL";
```

All (X)HTML tags will be removed from any user input, making your site much more secure.

*You may be wondering what on earth the PHP code generated by MX 2004 is doing with three instances of the same variable in one line. The PHP code uses the **conditional operator** (sometimes known as the **ternary operator**), a very useful piece of PHP shorthand that's a little difficult to get the hang of initially, but is actually quite simple. The operator itself consists of a question mark (?) and a colon (:). It evaluates the condition before the question mark. If the condition is true, it assigns the value between the question mark and colon to the operand on the far left. If false, the value to the right of the colon is used.*

*Confused? Perhaps it will become clearer if the statement is turned into human language. $theValue has already been set earlier in the script, but MX 2004 wants to format it, so the test being applied checks that it's not an empty string ($theValue !=""). If the test is true (it's not an empty string), $theValue is enclosed in single quotation marks. If the test is false (the string is empty), the value is set to NULL, which means the variable has no value. Don't worry if that's as clear as mud; just continue using if statements. The conditional operator is used a lot by advanced scripters, and even if you don't use it yourself, it's useful to know of its existence. Eventually you'll find yourself wondering how you ever managed without it.*

# Working with PHP sessions

The Internet is what's called a **stateless environment**. This means that each web page request is totally independent of any other such request. Although you may spend half an hour browsing several pages of the same site, many other people might be browsing the same page at the same time. Apache has no idea who is requesting each web page; it just serves up requests as they are received. To keep track of an individual user moving from page to page, PHP offers **sessions**, which can store information about a single user moving between pages. This enables you to create more complex applications such as shopping carts; after all, what good would a shopping cart be if it lost track of users (and their orders) as they moved from page to page? You wouldn't be impressed if Amazon's checkout consisted of a page that said, "Remind me again, who are you and what did you order?"

Sessions are variables that are preserved after your PHP script has finished executing. PHP stores them in a temporary directory either until they are destroyed by another script or the user closes the browser. Session variables can also be set to expire after a certain amount of time by defining a limit in php.ini. However, this is of less value to most web developers because they don't have direct control over the way PHP is configured. Sessions are deliberately destroyed to prevent anyone else from gaining access to information or privileges that may be stored in a session. As with many things, it's a lot easier to understand sessions once you see them in action.

### A simple session example

1. Create a new PHP page and call it session1.php. Insert a simple form with a text box called name and a Submit button. Set the form's Method and Action fields as shown in Figure 14-2. The Action field, as you will remember, is the file name of the page where information in the form is sent.

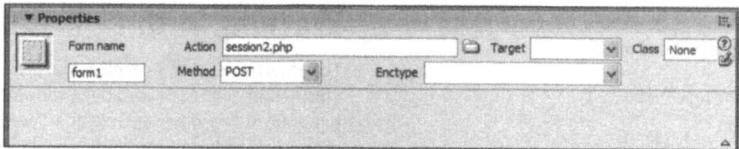

**Figure 14-2.** Settings for the form on session1.php

**2.** Create a new PHP page and call it session2.php. Go into Code view and insert the following code *above* the doctype, as shown in Figure 14-3.

```php
<?php
// initiate session
session_start();
// check POST array for valid data
if (isset($_POST['name']) &&
➥!empty($_POST['name'])) {
  // set session variable
  $_SESSION['name'] = $_POST['name'];
  }
?>
```

Let's break down the code within the PHP tags, line by line.

```php
session_start();
```

Whenever you use sessions in PHP, this line must be on every page that must access the SESSION variables. session_start() looks for an existing session, and if none exists, it will create a new one. Also, it must come before any part of the page is generated; that's why you needed to place it above the doctype. It's generally a good habit to make it the first line of script so you don't forget it.

```php
if (isset($_POST['name']) &&
➥!empty($_POST['name'])) {
```

This line of code performs the two tests mentioned earlier, checking to see if name has been set as part of the POST array *and* that it's not empty. The exclamation mark in front of empty is one of the logical operators listed in Table 12-2. When placed in front of a piece of code testing for a particular condition, it negates it. empty() tests to see if something is empty or has no value; !empty() checks to see if it does have a value. Note that 0 (zero) as a number or string (0 or '0') has no value, and is therefore regarded by PHP as empty.

```php
$_SESSION['name'] = $_POST['name'];
```

As long as the condition in the if statement returns true, a SESSION variable called name is created and assigned the value obtained from name in the POST array. If the condition returns false, the SESSION variable is not set.

```
session1.php  session2.php
Code  Split  Design   Title: Simple session 2
1  <?php
2  // initiate session
3  session_start();
4  // check POST array for valid data
5  if (isset($_POST['name']) && !empty($_POST['name'])) {
6    // set session variable
7    $_SESSION['name'] = $_POST['name'];
8    }
9  ?>
10  <!DOCTYPE HTML PUBLIC "-//W3C//DTD HTML 4.01 Transitional//EN"
```

**Figure 14-3.** Creating the SESSION variable

**3.** In `session2.php` insert the following code between the `<body>` tags:

```php
<?php
// check session var is set
if (isset($_SESSION['name'])) {
  // if set, greet by name
  echo 'Hello, '.$_SESSION['name'].'. ';
  echo '<a href="session3.php">Next</a>';
  }
else { // if not set, send back to login
  echo 'Who are you?
  ➥<a href="session1.php">Login</a>';
  }
?>
```

This if… else statement checks to see whether the SESSION variable has been set. If so, it displays a welcome message complete with the value of the variable, and creates a link to another page, `session3.php`. If the SESSION variable has not been set, the page tells the visitor that it doesn't recognize who's trying to gain access, and provides a link back to the first page.

**4.** Create `session3.php`. Start by inserting `<?php session_start(); ?>` above the doctype. Because you're using sessions, this line is obligatory. Without it, you cannot retrieve any existing session variables or perform any sessions-related functions.

**5.** Between the `<body>` tags of `session3.php`, insert this code:

```php
<?php
// check whether session var is set
if (isset($_SESSION['name'])) {
  // if set, greet by name
  echo 'Hi, '.$_SESSION['name'];
  echo '. See, I remembered your name! ';
  // unset session var
  session_unregister('name');
  // end session
  session_destroy();
  echo '<a href="session2.php">Page 2</a>';
  }
else { // display if not recognized
  echo 'Sorry, I don\'t know you.<br />';
  echo '<a href="session1.php">Login</a>';
  }
?>
```

The inline comments should be self-explanatory, but the two key items here are

```php
session_unregister('name');
```

`session_unregister()` is a built-in PHP function that removes a variable from the session array. Because it applies only to SESSION variables, it takes the variable's key as a parameter, in this case `'name'` instead of `$_SESSION['name']`.

```php
session_destroy();
```

This built-in PHP function removes the data stored for the current session. By placing it at the end of the code block, you have access to the SESSION variable up to that point, but from there on, the data is no longer available. The way it works will become obvious once you start using the three pages you just created.

**6.** Load `session1.php` into your browser and enter your name into the text box (see Figure 14-4).

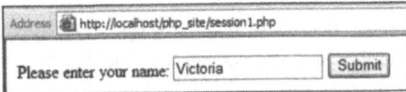

**Figure 14-4.** Step 1 of testing the session

**7.** Click Submit. You should see something like Figure 14-5. At this stage there is no apparent difference between what happens here and an ordinary form (as in the exercise at the beginning of Chapter 11).

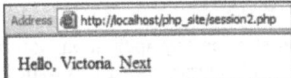

**Figure 14-5.** The session is registered.

**8.** When you click Next, the power of sessions begins to show. As you can see in Figure 14-6, the SESSION variable remembered your name even though the POST array is no longer available to it.

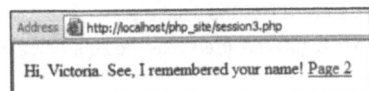

**Figure 14-6.** The session remembers your name.

**257**

**9.** Click the link to Page 2. The session has been destroyed, so this time session2.php has no idea who you are, as Figure 14-7 shows.

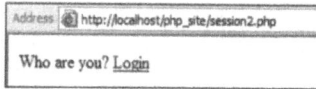

**Figure 14-7.** Same page as Figure 14-5, but it no longer remembers

**10.** Type the address of session3.php in the browser Address bar and load it. It, too, has no recollection of the session, and displays an appropriate message (see Figure 14-8).

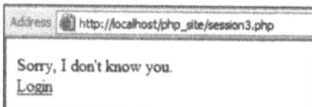

**Figure 14-8.** The session is completely gone.

We hope that brief tour of three pages will have demonstrated the power and the simplicity of working with sessions. You could adapt it to create a password-protected site. On the other hand, you could use MX 2004's built-in server behaviors, which is exactly what you're going to do next.

# Building a registration/login application

Before you start on any application, you must always take time to plan exactly what you want it to do. Say you have a website that you want to restrict to registered users. What would be useful?

- New users should be able to register themselves.
- The system must contain all the information needed to register and identify users.
- Information must be checked for validity before it's entered into the database.
- Once registered, users must be able to log in.

After a little thought, some answers present themselves:

- A web-based application form could be used to gather the information and register users at the same time.
- To identify users, first name, last name, e-mail address, username, and password will be needed.
- A combination of client-side (JavaScript) and server-side (PHP/MySQL) methods can be used to check the information.
- Once registered, access to the site will be controlled through an online form that checks the username and password.

### Building the database table and registration form

Now that you know what information you want to collect, you can plan your database table. You'll need six fields in the table, which will be called members, and you will create it in the same database as before (book_db). The fields will be memberID, firstname, lastname, email, username, and password. As in the last chapter, the memberID field (or column) is intended to provide a unique identifier for each entry, so it will be the table's primary key and use the MySQL auto_increment feature.

*Database experts would probably throw up their hands in horror (and rightly so) at the decision to create a second table in the same database to hold virtually identical information. It's something you should never do. The reason we're telling you to do it here is to prevent filling your MySQL data folder with a lot of small practice databases. In principle, though, you should create a separate database for each project to avoid mixing similar, but unrelated information. This becomes particularly important when you start creating projects that require more than one table (such as that in Chapter 15).*

1. Open phpMyAdmin in your browser, and from the drop-down menu on the left side, select the book_db database created in the last chapter.

2. In the Create new table section, enter the details for a six-field table called members, as shown in Figure 14-9, and click Go.

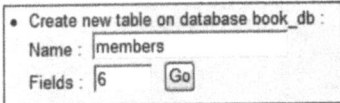

**Figure 14-9.** Creating the members table with six fields

3. Fill in the next screen with details of the fields as shown in Figure 14-10. We described all the options in detail in Chapter 13, so this should be quite straightforward. The only question you might have is why we suggested 50 as the length of the password. Surely nobody is ever going to use a password that long? The reason is that it's not a good idea to store passwords in plain text. You'll be using an encryption function, which results in a string much longer than the original password. If the length of the field is too short, users won't be able to gain access even if they type in the correct

password. That's because the database will have cut off the end of the encrypted version, making it impossible to match.

4. Click the Save button. Your database table is now ready. Next you will build the registration form.

5. Open Dreamweaver MX 2004 and create a new PHP page. Save it as register.php. Insert a form and a table inside the form. The table should have the following attributes:

- **Rows:** 8
- **Columns:** 2
- **Table width:** 400 pixels
- **Border thickness:** 0
- **Cell padding:** 5
- **Cell spacing:** None
- **Header:** Top

6. Select the top two table cells by holding down the *Ctrl/Cmd* key and clicking those cells. Right-click (*Cmd*-click) the selected cells and click Table, and then Merge Cells. Alternatively, use the Merge Cells button in the Property Inspector (see Figure 14-11).

**Database *book_db* - Table *members* running on *localhost***

| Field | Type [Documentation] | Length/Values* | Attributes | Null | Default** | Extra | Primary | Index |
|-------|------|------|------|------|------|------|------|------|
| memberID | INT | | UNSIGNED | not null | | auto_increment | ⦿ | ○ |
| firstname | VARCHAR | 25 | | not null | | | ○ | ○ |
| lastname | VARCHAR | 25 | | not null | | | ○ | ○ |
| email | VARCHAR | 100 | | not null | | | ○ | ○ |
| username | VARCHAR | 15 | | not null | | | ○ | ○ |
| password | VARCHAR | 50 | | not null | | | ○ | ○ |

Table comments :

Table type :
Default

Save

**Figure 14-10.** The settings needed for the members table

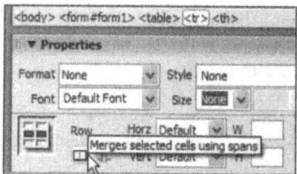

**Figure 14-11.** Using the Property Inspector to merge table cells

7. This will merge both cells into a single cell for the table heading. Type New User Registration inside the merged cells. Because you used Header: Top when creating the table in step 5, MX 2004 will have given the merged cells a `<th>` tag instead of the normal `<td>` tag. Most browsers render the content of `<th>` cells as bold, centered text, avoiding the need to use horizontal alignment or `<strong>` tags. This is just one of the many ways MX 2004 can help you create web pages that employ modern standards without the need for redundant tags. You can, of course, change the style of `<th>` tags with CSS to suit your own preferences.

8. Complete the table so that it looks like Figure 14-12. Opposite each text label in the left column, there should be a text field. Name the text fields in the Property Inspector as follows: firstname, lastname, email, username, password, and con_password respectively. As with Chapter 13, do not confuse the labels in the left column with the names you assign the text fields in the Property Inspector. The onscreen labels can be formatted any way you like for ease of reading. The names assigned in the Property Inspector are those used by the database: they should contain no spaces.

Also note that, this time, firstname and lastname have been written without underscores. Such differences are crucial to the way a computer will interpret them.

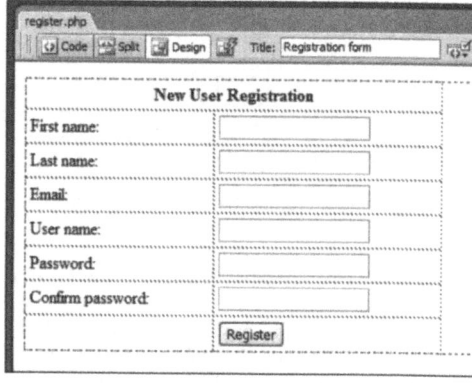

**Figure 14-12.** How the finished registration form should look

9. Two of the text fields need slightly different treatment: password and con_password. Make sure that the Password radio button in the Property Inspector is selected for these two (see Figure 14-13). This hides anything typed into a text box (usually by displaying stars or bullet points on screen) to prevent anyone looking over the user's shoulder from seeing what password is being used. You should be aware, though, that it does *not* encrypt the password. You have to do that separately (we come to that later).

10. The button in the final row of the table is a Submit button with the Label changed in the Property Inspector to Register.

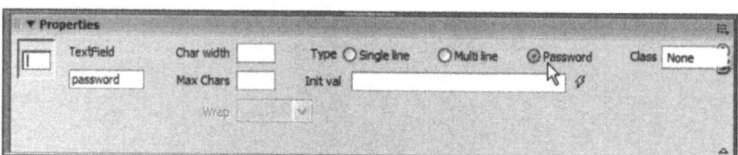

**Figure 14-13.** Selecting the Password option for a text box

## Validation

In the previous chapter, you used the Validate Form behavior built into MX 2004. Although perfectly adequate for simple checks, it doesn't offer enough options for a registration form. A far better solution is to use a third-party **Dreamweaver extension** called **Check Form MX**. It was created by Jaro von Flocken, a talented developer who has created a number of free extensions that add greater functionality to Dreamweaver. If you have never installed a Dreamweaver extension before, don't worry. It's very straightforward and you can find full instructions in the Appendix to this book.

Download Check Form MX from Jaro's site. His Dreamweaver extensions are listed and described at www.yaromat.com/dw/index.php (note that he's using PHP, so you're in good company). Oh yes, and the price is right: it's free.

### Applying Check Form MX and inserting data

1. If you have only just installed the extension, you will need to close Dreamweaver MX 2004 and then reopen it. This is because Dreamweaver initializes all extensions at start-up, so it cannot recognize new ones until it has gone through that process for the first time.

2. Open register.php again and highlight the form. Open the Behaviors panel in the Tag Inspector or via *SHIFT+F3* and click the plus sign button. In the menu that opens, choose Yaromat ➤ Check Form.

3. A dialog box like that in Figure 14-14 opens. As you can see, it's very similar to the one in the Validate Form behavior you used in the last chapter, but it has more options. It works the same way as the MX 2004 behavior: highlight each text box name in turn, and select the options required. One particularly nice feature is that Jaro's extension allows you to create more user-friendly error messages. We'll show you how to create them in a moment. First of all, though, select the options for each text box as shown in Table 14-2.

**Table 14-2.** Text Box Options

| Field Name | Required Check Box | Allowed Input |
|---|---|---|
| firstname | selected | Anything |
| lastname | selected | Anything |
| email | selected | E-mail address |
| username | selected | Anything |
| password | selected | Anything |
| con_password | selected | Text must be the same: password |

4. When setting the options for the final text box (con_password), after selecting Text must be the same, choose password from the drop-down menu.

5. Click OK and preview register.php in a browser. If you click the Register button without filling in any of the text fields, you will get an error message like that shown in Figure 14-15. It may be quite meaningful to you as a website developer, but put yourself in the position of a user. What does Field 'con_password' mean to them?

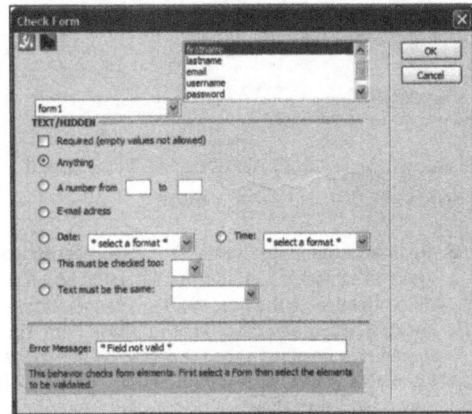

**Figure 14-14.** The Check Form dialog box

**261**

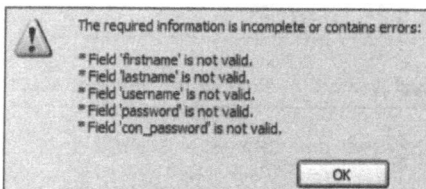

**Figure 14-15.** The standard error message from Check Form MX

**6.** Back in MX 2004, highlight the Check Form behavior in the Behaviors panel (see Figure 14-16) and double-click to reopen the dialog box. (Incidentally, this is the way you amend any Dreamweaver behavior or server behavior.)

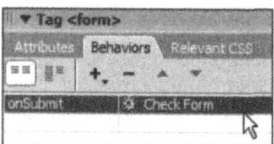

**Figure 14-16.** Double-click the behavior to amend any settings.

**7.** Once the dialog box opens, select each text field name in turn and enter something more meaningful in the Error Message box for each one. Some suggestions are shown in Figure 14-17.

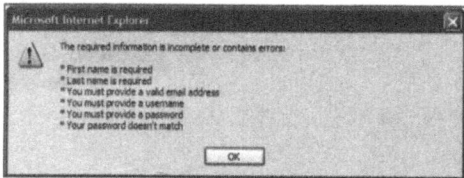

**Figure 14-17.** Customized error messages

**8.** The next step is to create the code needed to insert this information into the database. Much of this is identical to the procedure you learned in the last chapter, so details are kept to a minimum. You should now be able to see the members table in the Databases panel (see Figure 14-18). Go to the Server Behaviors panel, click the plus sign button, and select Insert Record.

**9.** When the dialog box opens, select myConn as the connection.

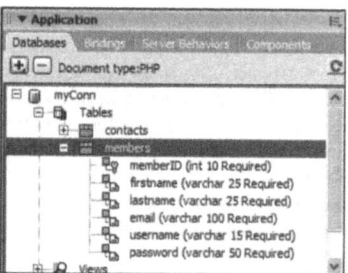

**Figure 14-18.** The members table displayed in the Databases panel

**10.** This next step is slightly different because you now have more than one table in the database. The Insert Table field in MX 2004 automatically displays whichever comes first in alphabetical order, so contacts is currently selected. You need to work on the members table, instead. Select members from the drop-down menu.

**11.** The Columns field should now be populated with a list of the correct fields. Check that all except memberID are marked as getting a value from the form. Figure 14-19 shows the correct values. If you have any problems, refer back to Chapter 13. Click OK and save register.php.

## Security issues

There are two problems:

- You don't want more than one user to have the same username.
- It's bad practice to store plain-text passwords in a database.

Here's the solution:

- Query the database to find out if the username already exists.
- Encrypt the passwords before storing them.

Time to roll up your sleeves again and do some more hand-coding.

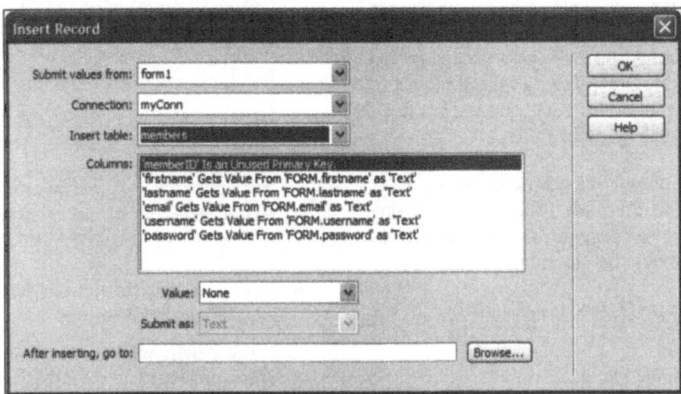

**Figure 14-19.** The Insert Record dialog box for members

**Avoiding multiple usernames and encrypting passwords**

**1.** In register.php switch to Code view and look for the following lines:

```
mysql_select_db($database_myConn, $myConn);
$Result1 = mysql_query($insertSQL,
➥$myConn) or die(mysql_error());
```

They should be on or around lines 41 and 42. Use Edit ➤ Find and Replace if you have difficulty finding them.

**2.** Amend the code by adding a new block in between the two lines as follows:

```
mysql_select_db($database_myConn, $myConn);
// SQL query to see if name already exists
$query = sprintf("SELECT username
  FROM members WHERE username = '%s'",
  $_POST['username']);

// submit query to database
$username_check = mysql_query($query);

// if entry found, issue error message
if (mysql_num_rows($username_check)>0) {
  print('Error: that username is taken');
}
```

```
else { // insert record and...
  $Result1 = mysql_query($insertSQL,
➥$myConn) or die(mysql_error());

  // redirect to thanks.php and exit script
  header('Location: thanks.php');
  exit;
}
```

This code does the following:

- A SQL query is created using sprintf(). In plain English, the query asks the database to select all entries in the username column that match the username submitted from the form.

- The query is executed by the PHP built-in function mysql_query() and the result stored in $username_check.

- mysql_num_rows() checks to see how many rows (or records) match.

- If more than 0 rows are found (in other words, there was at least one match), an error message is displayed—print() behaves in an almost identical way to echo.

- If no match is made, the data is inserted in the database and the user redirected to a "thank you" message (thanks.php was created in Chapter 13).

**263**

The reason for using sprintf(), which you learned about in Chapter 12, is to avoid problems with quotation marks. If you study the PHP code created by MX 2004, you will find sprintf()used all the time. It's by no means the only way to store SQL queries, but it is a very neat one once you get used to it.

3. That takes care of multiple username entries. Now, another tweak to the code (this time much simpler) will encrypt all passwords. Look for the following line (it should be around line 38):

```
GetSQLValueString($_POST['password'],
➥"text"));
```

4. Amend it so it looks like this:

```
GetSQLValueString(md5($_POST['password']),
➥"text"));
```

This uses the PHP function md5() to encrypt the password. This is a one-way encryption system (so it can't be unencrypted). So how do you match the password in the future? Simple. Encrypt it again, and compare the two encrypted versions against each other. There is no need to decrypt the password because all you are looking for is a matching pattern, not the actual meaning.

5. Now that you've finished making adjustments to the PHP code, test the form again. Press *F12* to preview the page in a browser. You may get a warning message like that in Figure 14-20. This is because you have altered MX 2004's server behavior by hand, and you can safely ignore it. The only drawback of altering MX server behaviors by hand is that once you do it, you cannot use the Server Behavior panel to make any further adjustments to that particular section of code. It's a choice most developers make, rather than be limited by what's available by default. It's also why we spent so much time earlier helping you understand the basics of PHP, so that making this sort of adjustment will eventually come quite naturally and not be a journey fraught with fear.

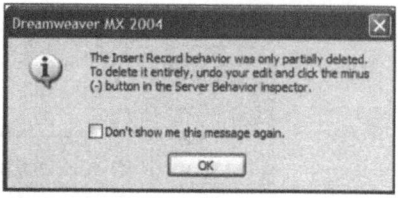

**Figure 14-20.** This warning message sometimes appears after customizing MX 2004 server behaviors by hand.

6. Enter your information (see Figure 14-21) into the form. Then click Register.

7. If everything worked properly, you should have been redirected to thanks.php. Now browse the members table in phpMyAdmin (instructions for how to do this were given in Chapter 13), and look at the password field. You'll see that the information has been encrypted, as shown in Figure 14-22. It also becomes clear why the password field was made so wide: a 9-character password has become 32 characters long in its encrypted form. If you want to allow your users to have longer passwords, you would need to make the field wider.

**Figure 14-21.** Testing the user registration form

| memberID | firstname | lastname | email | username | password |
|---|---|---|---|---|---|
| 1 | David | Powers | david@somewhere.nice.com | bottlewasher | cf0e909468da1a27628e83b5eb17ca1c |

**Figure 14-22.** The password has been encrypted.

**8.** Go back to `register.php` and try entering the same username again. This time, when you click Register you should get an error message at the top of the form, as shown in Figure 14-23. That means the SQL query you added in step 2 is doing its job. The problem is that all the text fields are now blank, so you have to go through the process of filling them in again; not very user-friendly.

Figure 14-23. What happens when the same username is chosen

**9.** Another little bit of hand-coding will easily fix that. In Design view, click the text box next to First name: to highlight it. If you now switch to Split view, you'll see the following code has been highlighted:

```
<input name="firstname" type="text"
➥id="firstname" />
```

**10.** Add some PHP code between id="firstname" and the closing tag, like this:

```
<input name="firstname" type="text"
➥id="firstname" <?php if
➥(isset($_POST['firstname'])) {echo
➥'value="'.$_POST['firstname'].'"';} ?> />
```

What's happening here is that isset() checks to see whether the POST array contains a value for firstname. As long as the form was correctly filled in, it should, so echo is used to insert a value attribute inside the text

field's <input> tag and set it to whatever the user originally entered in the field. It's at times like this that PHP can add that special touch to make your pages more user-friendly.

It's also at times like this that deep frustration can set in if all you get is an error message from PHP. Although this is a short piece of code, it's easy to mistype because it contains a sequence of single and double quotation marks and of square brackets mixed with parentheses that even experienced coders can sometimes find confusing. The block of code was copied directly from a working page, so unless a gremlin creeps in during the printing process, it can be taken as accurate. Let's just take a moment to explain how the code is put together.

The first part, if (isset($_POST['firstname'])), is an if statement, so it is enclosed in parentheses. Inside the outermost parentheses is isset(), which also uses parentheses to enclose the parameter it's testing for, $_POST['firstname']. That's why that section ends with ])). Match each one with its opening partner, and things become a lot clearer.

Perhaps the most potential for confusion lies in 'value="'.$_POST['firstname'].'"' because of the mixture of single and double quotation marks. If the name being stored in the variable is "George," what you want PHP to insert in the page is value="George". The need to display those quotation marks presents a problem because PHP also needs quotation marks to know how to parse the instructions you're giving it. There are several ways around this, but the one we chose is to use single quotes for the PHP and double quotes for the output to the browser, while the POST variable is sandwiched in between, using the concatenation operator (a period). Consequently, the first section 'value="' outputs value=" to the browser. The value of the POST variable (George) follows, and finally, '"' simply outputs the closing double quote after the name. If that explanation seemed a little too basic, just remember it's the small details that often trip up even seasoned hand-coders, so we felt it was worth spelling out in detail.

**11.** Make the same change to the lastname and email text field code, using $_POST['lastname'] and $_POST['email'] respectively.

**265**

**12.** Save `register.php` and test it again with an existing username. This time the first three fields should have retained their values, leaving the final three to be filled in again (see Figure 14-24).

**Figure 14-24.** The form now retains the user's name and email.

That completes the registration system, although there's a small touch you could add to `thanks.php`: create a link to `login.php` (the page you're going to create in the next section).

### Creating the login system

**1.** Open a new PHP page in Dreamweaver and save it as `login.php`.

**2.** Create a form with two text fields called `username` and `password`. The completed form should look like Figure 14-25. Apply the Check Form MX behavior as you did earlier in the chapter to ensure the user fills in both fields. Although the database will reject an incomplete form, the reason for applying the validation behavior is that it is carried out **client side**. In other words, it's carried out on the user's own computer, and not by the web server. When you're working on just your own computer for an exercise like this, the difference is immaterial, but client-side validation can save a lot of unnecessary delay in a real-world situation, particularly if the remote server receives heavy traffic or if the user is on a slow Internet connection. Any missing information is identified on the user's own computer before being submitted to the server.

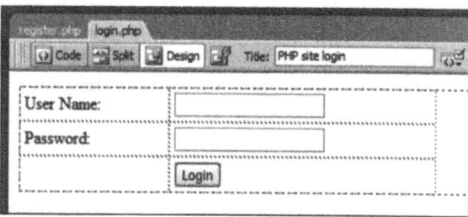

**Figure 14-25.** The login form

**3.** Open the Server Behaviors panel (*CTRL/CMD+F9*), click the plus sign button, and select User Authentication ➤ Log In User (see Figure 14-26).

**4.** In the dialog box that opens (see Figure 14-27), the first three fields are filled in automatically by Dreamweaver MX 2004, which makes an intelligent guess as to the values you want to use. In this case, they are correct. However, you have to tell MX 2004 which connection you are using. In Validate using connection, select myConn. The Table field drop-down menu is then populated with all tables available from that connection. Before making a selection, take a closer look at Figure 14-27. The Password column field at the bottom contains first_name (with an underscore). This is the first available field in the contacts table that you used in Chapter 13. Once you select the members table, the field will change to firstname (without an underscore). The point to note is that naming your tables and columns distinctively to prevent confusion is vital to maintaining your sanity when working with databases. With the small number of tables and columns currently in the database, they are relatively easy to distinguish. Not so when you have many more tables and columns. Select members.

**5.** You now need to tell MX 2004 which fields to use to log in the user. Select username for Username column and password for Password column. Pretty obvious really, but you need to make the selection yourself; MX 2004 won't do it for you.

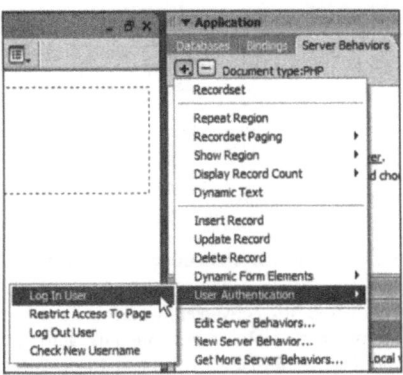

**Figure 14-26.** Applying the Log In User server behavior

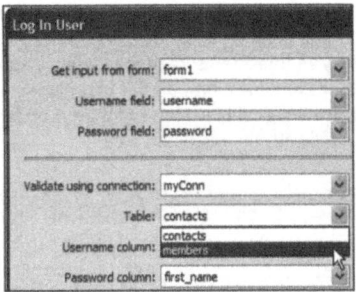

**Figure 14-27.** Select members as the table to be used.

**6.** Tell MX 2004 where you want to send the user if the login succeeds, and what to do if it fails. Fill in the appropriate fields as shown in Figure 14-28. At the foot of the dialog box is a section that allows you to specify whether to restrict access simply on username and password or on access level as well. You don't need to make any changes on this occasion because the members table doesn't have any way of distinguishing different levels of access. You could, however, at a future stage, create an access column in the table and assign different codes to individuals (for example, "guest," "administrator," and so on). For more information on how to do this, click the Help button in the Log In User dialog box and read the help files and related topics.

**7.** Click OK to close the Log In User dialog box, and then open Code view. If you remember, you encrypted the passwords stored in the database using md5(). Because this is a one-way encryption, the only way to compare a password entered in the login form with what's stored in the database is to encrypt the form's input the same way. Look for the following line (it should be close to the top of the page around line 14):

```
$password=$_POST['password'];
```

**8.** Apply the md5() function like this

```
$password=md5($_POST['password']);
```

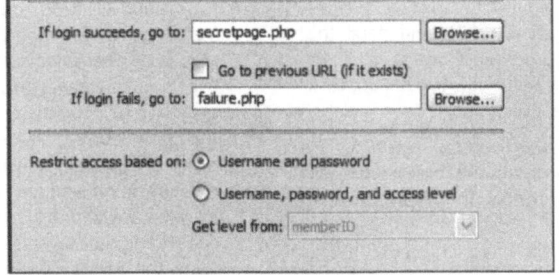

**Figure 14-28.** Set the destination pages for success and failure.

9. Don't forget the closing parenthesis after `['password']`. Save `login.php`.

10. You now need to create the two pages that users will see depending on whether the login attempt succeeds or fails. First, create a new PHP page in MX 2004 and save it as `secretpage.php`. Type an appropriate welcome message.

11. In the Server Behaviors panel, click the plus sign button and select User Authentication ➤ Restrict Access to Page (see Figure 14-29).

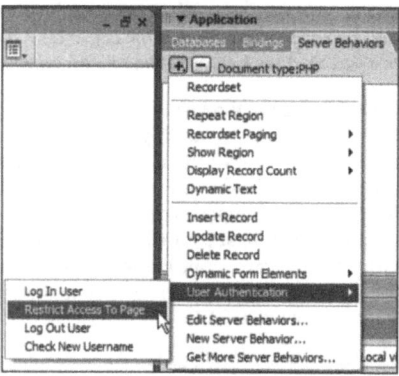

**Figure 14-29.** Selecting the Restrict Access To Page server behavior

12. The dialog box that opens (see Figure 14-30) is very straightforward. Make sure that the first radio option (Username and password) is selected for Restrict based on. If you were creating a more sophisticated login system, you would need the second option: Username, password, and access level. To find out more about how to set it up, click the Help button in the dialog box.

13. Enter `login.php` into the If access denied, go to field. This will direct a user to the login page if any attempt is made to bypass the login process. Click OK.

14. It may seem a bit abrupt to get rid of somebody immediately after logging in, but that's what you're going to learn to do next. While still in `secretpage.php` select User Authentication ➤ Log Out User from the Server Behaviors panel.

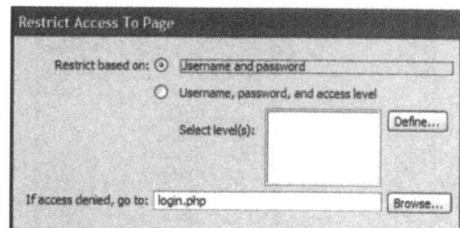

**Figure 14-30.** The Restrict Access To Page dialog box

15. The dialog box conveniently selects by default an option that creates a Log out link automatically (see Figure 14-31). All you need to do is tell the browser what to display after logging out. In the field marked When done, go to enter `login.php`. Although it may seem to be sending users round in circles, offering them the login option immediately after logging out means they can get back in again if they've forgotten something. Often, a login page will be combined with a site's main index page, so it's also a logical place to send visitors after they've finished with the restricted area.

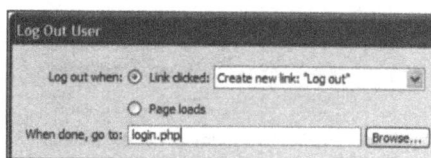

**Figure 14-31.** Using the Log Out User server behavior

16. Unfortunately, there's often a price to pay for having things done for you automatically. The Log Out User server behavior inserts the log out link wherever your cursor was positioned at the time, so you may have to move the resulting code. This is where the crash course in PHP earlier in the book should make things easier because you should have little difficulty in recognizing the code and what it does. However, if you don't want to do that, highlight the behavior in the Server Behavior panel and delete it, using the minus sign button (see Figure 14-32). Then click your mouse pointer in the right place and reapply the behavior.

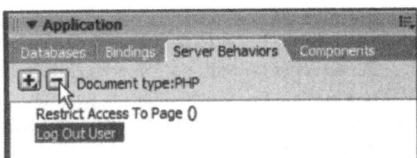

**Figure 14-32.** Use the minus sign button to remove behaviors before reapplying them.

17. Create a new page and name it `failure.php` (the page you specified if the login fails). Insert some suitable text and a link back to the login page.

### Testing the application

1. Assuming you created a username and password for yourself earlier in the chapter, open your browser and point it at `login.php`. Enter your details, and click Login. If you entered your username and password correctly, what you should see is `secretpage.php` similar to Figure 14-33. If you set up PHP the way we suggested in Chapter 10, though, you will probably see something more like Figure 14-34.

**Figure 14-33.** `secretpage.php` as it's meant to look

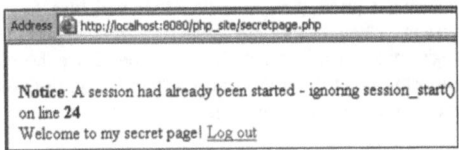

**Figure 14-34.** What you'll see if PHP notices are switched on

2. Why the difference? Figure 14-33 shows the application running on a production server on the Internet with PHP notices turned off. Figure 14-34 shows a testing server with notices switched on, and reveals a weakness in the way MX 2004 creates some PHP coding. MX 2004 does a brilliant job most of the time, but occasionally it inserts redundant code. What has happened here is that the Restrict Access to Page and Log Out User server behaviors both need a session to be running for them to work. Consequently, both use `session_start()` at the beginning of the code block they insert into the page, but only one session can exist on an individual page. PHP helpfully ignores the second call to `session_start()`, and it won't affect any pages on servers that have notices turned off. Still, it shouldn't be there. Open `secretpage.php` in Code view and locate the second instance of `session_start()` (it should be around line 24 as shown in Figure 14-35). Delete that entire line.

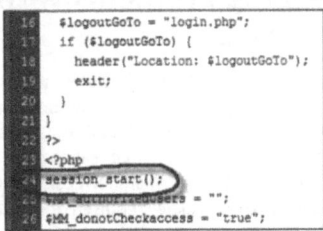

**Figure 14-35.** Remove the second instance of `session_start();`

3. After removing the second call to `session_start()`, your page should be displayed as shown in Figure 14-33. Click the log out link, and you should find yourself back at `login.php`.

4. One final test: try opening `secretpage.php` without first logging in. You won't be allowed in, and the browser will take you to `login.php` instead. If you were expecting it to take you to `failure.php`, the difference is that `failure.php` acknowledges a failed attempt at logging in (because of an incorrect username or password), while any attempt at bypassing the login process simply goes straight to the login page.

**269**

## Expanding the restricted area

This simple registration and login application contains only one restricted page. In most cases, you would want to have more pages in a subscribers-only area. Unlike protecting entire directories or folders with basic HTTP authentication, pages protected by PHP sessions have to be protected individually. This means you have to apply the Restrict Access to Page server behavior to every page you want to be part of a restricted area. Also, because you don't usually know when a user will want to log out, you need the log out server behavior on every page—assuming, of course, you think logging out is necessary. The session is destroyed automatically when the browser is closed, so that may be sufficient security for many sites. If it's an administrator's page with permission to alter the contents of a critical database, though, a log out procedure is likely to be a high priority.

# Debugging problems with PHP and MySQL

In the process of writing this book, we have gone through all the steps you're being asked to, in order to make sure they work as expected. It would be far from the truth, though, to claim that every step has gone without a hitch. Creating dynamic websites requires far greater care than is usually required for a static one. One little comma or semicolon out of place, and the code stops working. It's also easy to miss a step. The page itself may look fine, but underneath something's not quite working the way it should. All good programmers (for that's what you are, even if you use nothing more than MX 2004's built-in server behaviors) need to develop debugging techniques to help find out what's gone wrong.

MX 2004 already has some debugging built into its server behaviors. For instance, the Insert Record server behavior includes the following line of code:

```
$Result1 = mysql_query($insertSQL,
➥$myConn) or die(mysql_error());
```

The final section or die(mysql_error()) will display a brief error message if there's a problem with your SQL query. The message in itself may be enough to tell you what the problem is. For example, if you have misspelled the name of a column or field, you will get something like this:

```
Unknown column 'usename' in 'field list'
```

Sometimes, though, error messages are not so easy to work out. A common one is You have an error in your SQL syntax near.... Even more baffling is not a valid MySQL resource. In circumstances like this, the best way of tracking down the problem is to use echo to display on screen exactly what it is you're trying to ask the database.

MX 2004 submits queries to MySQL by storing the SQL as a variable (usually ending in __query), and passing it to the database using the mysql_query() function. Find the line where the query is stored before being passed to the database, enter a new line, and then echo the contents of the query variable to the browser. In the case of a Log In User server behavior, you would use

```
echo $LoginRS__query.'<br />';
```

Putting <br /> on the end makes it easier to distinguish the code being displayed from the rest of the browser output. Even if you don't understand what's wrong with the query yourself, you can copy the output and ask for help in one of the many online forums. Someone familiar with SQL will be able to help you much more easily if they can see the syntax of the query being used. Eventually, you will begin to spot many of the problems yourself, but if you don't know what's being sent to the database, you're only guessing what might be wrong.

It's also a good idea to echo other variables to the screen. When testing the code for this chapter, the login didn't work correctly first time. Since MySQL reported no errors, the suspicion then fell on the username and password variables:

```
$loginUsername=$_POST['username'];
$password=$_POST['password'];
```

Those lines were temporarily amended like this:

```
$loginUsername=$_POST['username'];
echo $loginUsername.'<br />';
$password=$_POST['password'];
echo $password.'<br />';
```

The answer became clear in an instant. The password was being sent to the database in plain text: we had forgotten to encrypt it with md5(). Trying to spot the problem by poring through the entire script line by line would have taken much longer.

Get into the habit of testing your variables with echo and you won't be admitting defeat; you'll be doing exactly what the experts all do. The earlier you adopt this good practice, the less likely you are to end up tearing your hair out over some seemingly insoluble problem. When dealing with arrays, don't forget print_r(), which you learned about in Chapter 12. It does for arrays what echo does for ordinary variables.

## Summary

We've covered so much. If it's still the same day as when you started the chapter, you've done extremely well. There have been a lot of hands-on exercises, and a little sprinkling of theory in there, too. We looked at

- Some common PHP security issues
- The superglobal arrays
- Session basics
- A simple example of how sessions work
- Building a registration/login application to put it all into practice
- How to begin problem solving for yourself

You are now well on the way to a solid grasp not only of PHP, but also of working with databases and MX 2004 server behaviors. It's time to combine these skills with those you learned in the first half of the book, and turn the Images from Iceland site into a practical online content management system.

**Chapter 15**

# CASE STUDY: A CONTENT MANAGEMENT SYSTEM

**What we'll cover in this chapter**

- Understanding content management systems
- Converting the Images from Iceland site to work with PHP
- Planning and building the database structure
- Converting static pages to dynamic
- Using the Recordset dialog box in Advanced mode
- Creating dynamic links
- Building and password-protecting the content management area
- Using an MX application object to build a dynamic navigation bar

In the last few chapters, we showed you how PHP, MySQL, and Dreamweaver MX 2004 work together to create dynamic pages. In Chapter 14, we also covered how to create password-protected pages. Now it's time to put everything you learned to practical use by creating a **content management system** for the Images from Iceland site that you built in the first half of this book.

# What a content management system does

The traditional way of building websites is to create each page separately and upload it to a server. When anything needs to be updated, even just a couple of words, the whole page has to be uploaded again. It's not a major problem for people competent at web design, particularly if they use a sophisticated XHTML editor like Dreamweaver MX 2004. For people with no knowledge of XHTML, though, it becomes a major undertaking. If they make a mistake, the design could collapse, and a designer has to be called in to pick up the pieces.

A content management system (CMS) avoids such problems by enabling users to modify content on a site through a web-based interface. The underlying code is untouched because all the content is entered into a database in plain text, and displayed on the screen using a server-side technology such as PHP. Content management systems assist not only inexperienced users, but are also useful on sites in which content is frequently updated, such as news sites, e-commerce applications, and personal web logs. The advantages are particularly strong for e-commerce: prices are entered only once into the database, but can be used on many pages and in calculations based on user input, such as in a shopping cart.

A CMS can be as simple or as sophisticated as you want. Entire books are dedicated to the subject, so we can give you only a brief glimpse of what's possible. By the end of the chapter, though, you will have converted the Images from Iceland website to a fully functional content management system.

**Preparing Images from Iceland to work with PHP**

First, you need to prepare the website created in the first half of this book to use the PHP server model. PHP site definition in Dreamweaver MX 2004 was covered thoroughly in Chapter 10, so we will only skim through the instructions this time. If you have any problems, refer back to Chapter 10.

1. If it's not already there, copy the site folder into the document root of your Apache installation. If you used the folder name originally suggested, Web - Images from Iceland, rename it simply **Iceland**. If you want to use a different name, replace any spaces with underscores. Although you can leave spaces in file names on your desktop computer, most web servers on the Internet do not recognize character spaces in file names. Get into the habit now of using file names with no spaces.

2. Create a subfolder called **admin**. You will need this later for your administration pages.

3. Locate index.html, contact.html, and about .html. These files will all use PHP code, so rename them **index.php**, **contact.php**, and **about.php**. If your operating system warns you that changing the extension of a file name may make it unusable, click OK to confirm you want to make the change.

4. Open MX 2004 and select Site ➤ Manage Sites. If you want to keep the original site you set up in Chapter 3, select New and then Site. Give your site a suitable name, such as Iceland_PHP (see Figure 15-1). Alternatively, highlight the name of the original site and click Edit. This will overwrite the previous settings, and convert the site to work with PHP. Once you're happy with the name, click Next. (These instructions assume you're using the Site Definition Wizard, which can be accessed from the Basic tag.)

5. In the next screen, select Yes, I want to use a server technology. From the drop-down menu that appears, select PHP MySQL and click Next.

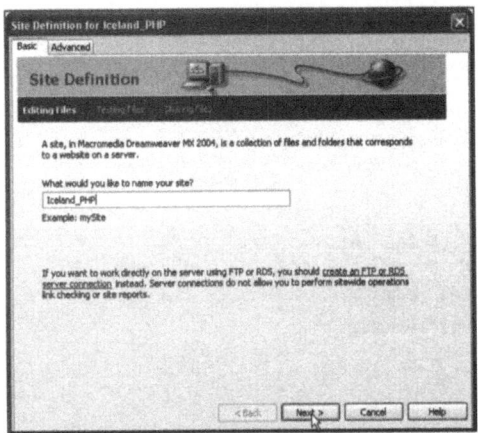

**Figure 15-1.** Enter a name for the PHP version of Images from Iceland.

6. In the next screen, select Edit and test locally (my testing server is on this computer). Make sure the text field contains the path to the new folder you copied into the Apache document root in step 1. Figure 15-2 shows the path on a Windows system. Mac users should use the path to their Sites folder. If you're creating a completely new site, Dreamweaver MX 2004 will have made an intelligent guess at which one it is, but if you're editing the previous site definition, it will still have the path to the old static site. Click Next.

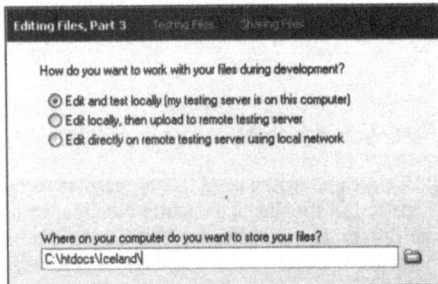

**Figure 15-2.** Setting up for testing locally

7. In the next screen, enter the full URL path to the files, making sure you include the trailing slash (see Figure 15-3). Mac users should include their username in the URL.

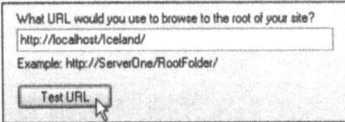

**Figure 15-3.** Enter the local URL and test it.

8. Click the Test URL button. If MX 2004 can't find the URL, recheck the previous steps.

9. When you get a success message, click OK. Then click Next.

10. In the next screen, you are asked if you want to use a remote server. Click No, and click Next.

11. The final screen displays the settings for your site. Check them, and if you are satisfied, click Done. Dreamweaver will create the site cache, if necessary. Once it has finished, click Done to close the Manage Sites dialog box.

12. The final stage of the conversion involves altering the links in the template file (Templates\main.dwt) to reflect the changes in file extensions you made to the three files in step 3.

13. Open main.dwt in MX 2004, and choose Edit ➤ Find and Replace (*CTRL/CMD+F*). This very powerful utility can be used to make changes on single pages, selected folders, or even entire sites. On this occasion, you need to make changes to the source code of the current document, so select those two options from the drop-down menus at the top of the dialog box (see Figure 15-4). In the Find field, enter **contact.html** (or .htm if that's the default extension you use for static pages); and in the Replace field, enter **contact.php**. In the Options area at the bottom of the dialog box, make sure Match case and Use regular expression are *not* checked. In this case, it doesn't matter whether Ignore whitespace is checked or not, but for most Find and Replace operations, you will need it checked, so it's best to set it that way and leave it. Once all the settings are complete, click Replace all.

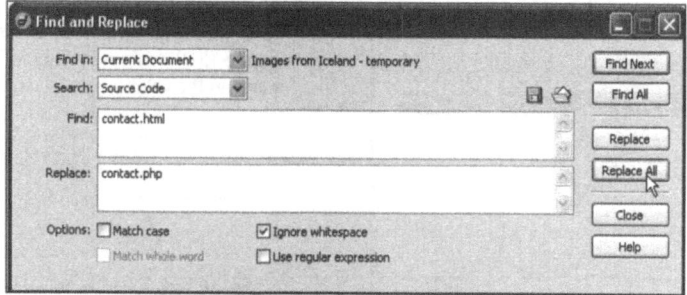

**Figure 15-4.** The settings for changing file names in the template

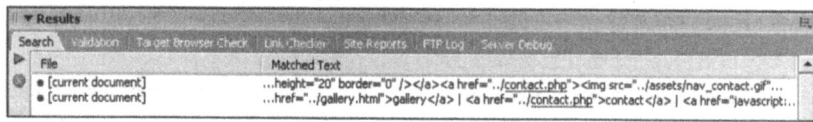

**Figure 15-5.** Results of the find and replace operation

**14.** MX 2004 searches through the source code of main.dwt and replaces all instances of contact.html with contact.php. The Results panel should open at the bottom of the Dreamweaver workspace, showing you what's been replaced and where. As you can see from Figure 15-5, it made two replacements in the page. If you double-click any of the items in the Results panel, MX 2004 highlights the changed item in whichever view you are using at the time. This is very useful for making sure you have not changed something by mistake.

**15.** Do the same for the two other files, index.html and about.html, replacing them with index.php and about.php. Two replacements should be made in both cases.

**16.** When you save main.dwt, you will get a warning about having placed an editable region inside a block tag. This same thing happened in Chapter 7, and you can safely ignore it by clicking OK.

**17.** The next dialog box that opens (see Figure 15-6) demonstrates one of the most timesaving features of MX 2004. It asks if you want to update all the other files created from the same template. You do, so click Update.

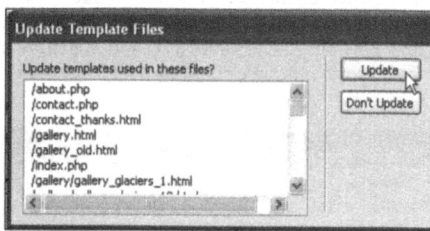

**Figure 15-6.** Updating files that use the same template

**18.** Like greased lightning, MX 2004 searches through the rest of the site, and updates the same six links on each page. Even though you left the old, pre-JavaScript version of the gallery pages in your folder, Dreamweaver updated the entire site in one tenth of a second! (See Figure 15-7.)

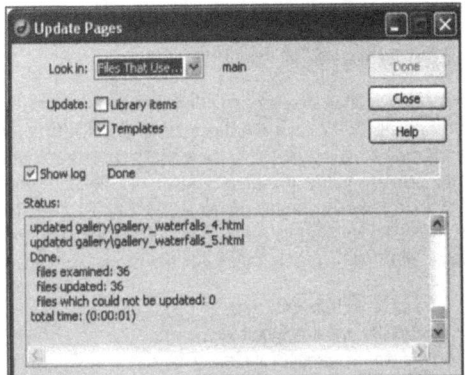

**Figure 15-7.** Results of updating all children files of the template

**19.** The Results panel is no longer needed, so get it out of the way by choosing Window ➤ Results (*F7*) or right-clicking (*CMD*-clicking) the top-right corner of the panel and choosing Close panel group from the pop-up menu.

Images from Iceland is now ready to be converted to a content management system.

## Defining and planning the CMS

To plan the structure of the CMS, you need to define exactly what you want to achieve. If you think about it, there are four main sections to the site:

- The index page carries news items that will need updating on a regular basis.
- The about page won't change so frequently, but must be updateable.
- The gallery page could be converted to work with a database, but is now pretty efficient thanks to the JavaScript display system you created in Chapter 9, so that's a project for another time.
- The contacts page contains specific information, such as e-mail and postal addresses that may need updating from time to time.

Although you're not going to convert the gallery to work with the database, it's very common to use images in connection with a content management system. For example, a staff records system will almost certainly store a picture of the staff member along with all other details. What puzzles most beginners is figuring out which column type they should use to store their images in the database. The answer is: you don't store images in a database. You store the image file name instead, and store the image itself where it usually would be—in a folder on the website.

Databases are good at storing text, which can be easily searched and indexed. Putting images in a database results in bloated files that will slow searching down to a crawl. When you want to display an image along with its associated material, retrieve the file name from the database and use it to build an <img> tag in the usual way.

One of the principal advantages of a CMS is that updating pages should be possible without using any XHTML code. In order to do this, each page needs to be adapted so that plain text drawn from a database will slot into the existing XHTML template. It also requires a web interface where a user can enter the necessary information into the database.

In ordinary circumstances, you would create a completely new database that serves only the CMS. This would ensure the integrity of information being stored. Because this is purely an exercise, we suggest you continue using book_db, the database created in Chapter 13. If you would prefer to create a new one, go back to Chapter 13 to review the necessary steps (creating the database in MySQL, creating a username and password, granting the necessary privileges, and flushing privileges before using the new username). Whether you create a new database or not, you will need to create the necessary tables to hold the new information.

To start with, the CMS requires three tables: one for each of the pages you are going to update dynamically. These will be called cms_news, cms_contact, and cms_about.

Decisions about what to put in the database need to be made with the final output in mind. By looking at each page in turn, you can determine which parts are likely to remain constant, and which will need updating on a regular basis.

## The cms_news table

This table will populate index.php, the front page of the site, with news items. A quick look at the static page reveals three areas that should be incorporated into the database (see Figure 15-8):

- Story date
- Story headline
- Story text

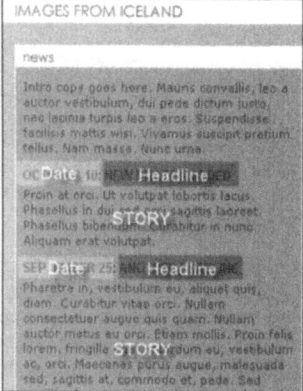

**Figure 15-8.** Identifying the areas in the news page to be fed from the database

The image area on the right will remain constant, as will the introduction (although this could also be updated from the database if required). Each news item will also need a unique identifier, so you require four fields (or columns) in the news table:

- **newsID**: the unique identifier
- **storyDate**: the date to which the story refers or when it was written

- **headline**: a brief description of the story
- **story**: the text of the story

In previous chapters, we provided detailed instructions on how to build each database table, so this time we are going to give just the bare essentials for each one. You can use either phpMyAdmin or the MySQL monitor to create the tables. If using the MySQL monitor, remember to change to the correct database (**use book_db**) first. The SQL query for the news table is

```
create table cms_news (
newsID int unsigned not null
➥auto_increment primary key,
storyDate date not null,
headline varchar(100) not null,
story text not null);
```

If you are using phpMyAdmin, select book_db from the database list, create a new table called cms_news with four fields, and use the SQL just shown to fill in the requisite fields. The 100 in parentheses after varchar is the length of that field.

## The cms_contact table

The cms_contact table will keep material in contact.php up to date. There are three areas likely to change (see Figure 15-9):

- E-mail address
- Postal address
- Telephone number

Again, you need a unique identifier, contactID, to act as primary key. If you like, you could also add fields to update other text areas of the table, but the SQL required for the basic cms_contact table is as follows:

```
create table cms_contact (
contactID int unsigned not null
➥auto_increment primary key,
email varchar(100),
post varchar(250),
telephone varchar(25) );
```

**Figure 15-9.** Three areas in the contact page that will be updated from the database

Generally, you would not create a single field for a postal address, but instead create separate ones for street address, town, state/county, zip/postal code, and so on. The reason they are all in one field here is because there is no need to sort or search through different entries. Only one address (the most recent) will ever be displayed, so it is simpler to create just one field for a content management system like this. When designing databases, there are few fixed rules. The main criterion is finding the right solution for each particular job. You should also think ahead: are circumstances likely to change, and if so, how? Flexibility in both thinking and design are likely to lead to better solutions.

You should also note that none of the fields (except the primary key) has been marked as "not null." You may decide at some stage that putting your postal address on the website in not such a good idea, or perhaps you want to remove the phone number while you're sick or on vacation. If the recordset shows the field to be empty, you can use a conditional statement to stop that part of the page from being displayed.

## The cms_about table

This table is very straightforward. It includes a unique identifier and a text field to hold the content. The SQL required is

```
create table cms_about (
aboutID int unsigned not null
➥auto_increment primary key,
details text not null);
```

**Initializing the cms_contact and cms_about tables**

Although the cms_news table will constantly evolve with new information, the two other tables will hold just one record that will be updated as required. You could create web interfaces to insert the original material and separate pages to update them. Because the main focus will be on updating, it's simpler to initialize these two tables with dummy material, and just build the update pages. If you're comfortable with the MySQL monitor, that's the quickest way to do it, but we'll also give instructions for phpMyAdmin. First, though, MySQL monitor:

1. Assuming you have already changed databases and are using book_db, enter these SQL queries at the command line:

   ```
   INSERT INTO cms_contact (email, post,
   ➥telephone) VALUES ('a','b','c');
   INSERT INTO cms_about SET details='a';
   ```

2. In phpMyAdmin, select the book_db database from the menu on the left, and then select the cms_contact table. In the window that opens, click the Insert tab. That will open a screen like that in Figure 15-10.

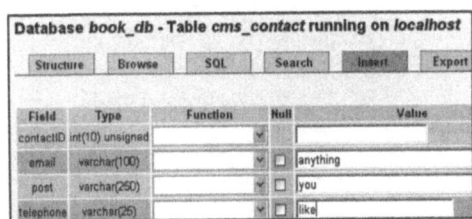

**Figure 15-10.** Initializing the cms_contact table in phpMyAdmin

**279**

3. Leave the Value field for contactID empty, and insert a small amount of dummy material in the remaining three Value fields. Click Go.

4. Do the same with cms_about. The only Value field that requires dummy material is details.

## Converting the static pages to dynamic ones

1. Once you set up the site definition and server model, the first task with building any database-driven site with MX 2004's server behaviors is to create a connection from Dreamweaver to MySQL. If you still have the template main.dwt open, close it because attempting to create a connection with a template still open is likely to result in undesirable changes to the template.

2. Open one of the PHP pages. index.php is a good choice because you'll be working on that first. Then select the Databases tab (CTRL/CMD+SHIFT+F10) from the Application panel, and click the plus sign button. Select MySQL Connection.

3. Fill in the dialog box, using cmsCon as the Connection name and substituting your own user-name and password. Test the connection by clicking the Test button, and then click OK.

4. You should now be able to view the connection in the Databases panel. If you expand the Tables listing (see Figure 15-11), you will notice that the connection shows all tables in the database, not just the ones you want to use.

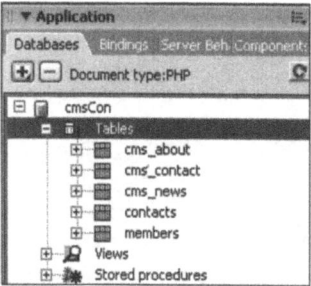

**Figure 15-11.** The CMS tables listed in the Databases panel

That's one reason for giving them all a cms_ prefix. That way they are all grouped together, and their meaning is immediately clear. Otherwise, you may confuse the cms_contact table with the contacts table created in Chapter 13. It may seem a small point, but choosing clear names for your tables is essential to good database management.

## Converting index.php

1. Open index.php. Highlight the text within the pageCopy region, and delete it. When you do this in Design view, MX 2004 assumes you want to retain the same formatting inside the editable area, so it won't select the opening and closing <p> tags (see Figure 15-12). After deleting the text, you need to go into Code or Split view to remove the remaining pair of <p> tags.

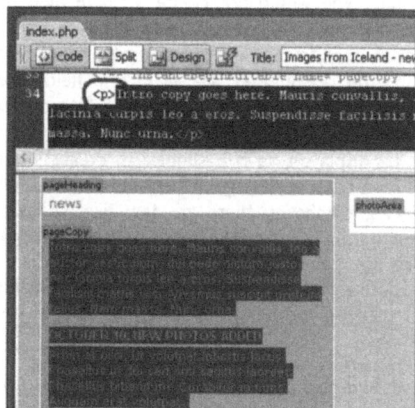

**Figure 15-12.** Highlighting text in Design view does not capture the opening tag

2. Create a recordset to retrieve data from the cms_news table by opening the Server Behaviors panel (CTRL/CMD+F9). Click the plus sign button and select Recordset.

3. Up to now, you have always used the Recordset dialog box in Simple mode. This time, switch to Advanced mode by clicking the Advanced button

on the right of the Recordset dialog box. Figure 15-13 shows Advanced mode, perhaps intimidating at first, but nothing to worry about.

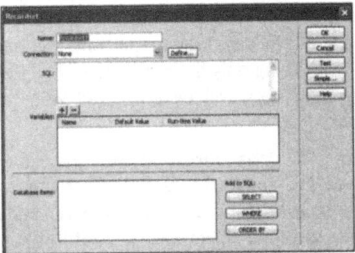

**Figure 15-13.** The Advanced mode of the Recordset dialog box

**4.** Advanced mode enables you to build your own SQL query, either by typing it directly into the SQL field, or by using the Database items and Add to SQL buttons in the lower half of the dialog box. To populate the lower half of the dialog box, you need to enter a name for the recordset and select

a connection the same way as in Simple mode. Enter **news** in the Name field, and select cmsCon as the Connection.

**5.** Once the Database items field is populated, expand Tables, and then cms_news, as shown in Figure 15-14.

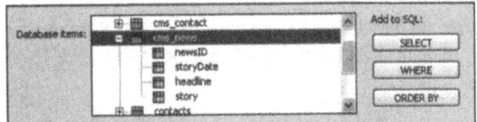

**Figure 15-14.** The cms_news table expanded to display its columns

**6.** The fields you want to retrieve from the cms_news table are storyDate, headline, and story. Highlight storyDate, and then click the SELECT button.

**7.** If you look in the SQL field in the upper half of the dialog box, you will see MX 2004 has begun to build your SQL query (see Figure 15-15).

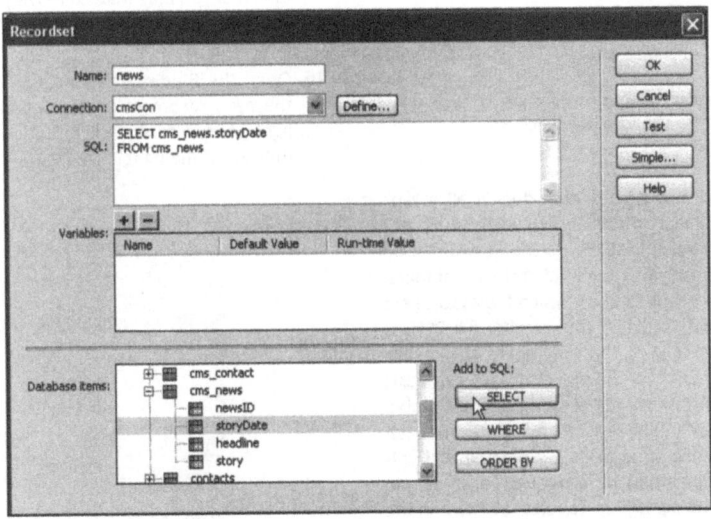

**Figure 15-15.** The SQL statement being built by MX 2004

**281**

**8.** Highlight in turn the two other fields you want to retrieve (headline and story) and click the SELECT button. You have to do it separately for each field. MX 2004 will not allow you to highlight more than one field at a time.

**9.** Highlight storyDate again and click the ORDER BY button.

**10.** Highlight newsID and click the ORDER BY button. Your SQL query should now look like Figure 15-16.

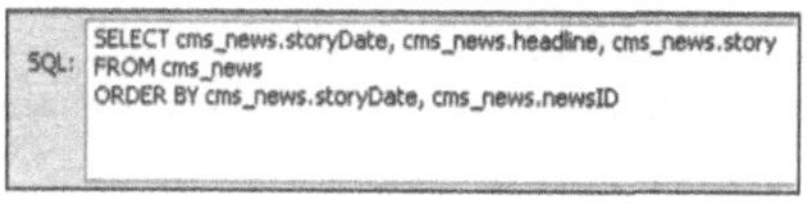

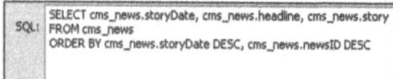

SQL: SELECT cms_news.storyDate, cms_news.headline, cms_news.story
FROM cms_news
ORDER BY cms_news.storyDate, cms_news.newsID

**Figure 15-16.** The SQL statement as built by MX 2004

**11.** That's almost perfect, but there are a couple of finishing touches you need to do by hand. Click inside the SQL field and position your cursor just before the comma in the third line. Insert a space and type DESC. Go to the end of the line; insert a space, and type DESC again. The amended SQL query should look like Figure 15-17.

SQL: SELECT cms_news.storyDate, cms_news.headline, cms_news.story
FROM cms_news
ORDER BY cms_news.storyDate DESC, cms_news.newsID DESC

**Figure 15-17.** The amended SQL statement for cms_news

**12.** Not too hard, was it? But what does it all mean? SQL is very similar to human language, so it's not difficult to work out. SELECT is the keyword used to select (or retrieve) material from a database. The database needs to know which tables to select FROM and what to ORDER (the results) BY. DESC is short for "descending," which means the results will be presented with the highest number or most recent first. Although you're using only one table in this query, MX 2004 uses the full syntax for each field by referring to both its table name and column name, separated by a period. So, in simple terms, this is telling MySQL to select all items in the storyDate, headline, and story columns from the

cms_news table, and to sort them in descending order, first by storyDate and then by the table's primary key. By specifying two criteria for the sort, you have greater control over how they are presented. If you miss an important item and want to add it several days later, it will come out of order if you sort using only the primary key. Any items with the same date will be presented with the most recent first.

**13.** Click OK. The recordset will be inserted in index.php above the XHTML. It's a good idea to save your pages after adding a server behavior to make sure that all your work is not lost if anything goes wrong.

**14.** Now that you have created the recordset to retrieve the content for the page, you need to insert the dynamic text. Steps 15 to 19 may sound complicated, but if you read them first, and study Figure 15-19 before working through them, you'll find they're quite straightforward.

**15.** Click inside the pageCopy editable area of index.php. During this stage, it's best to work in Split view so you can see where your code is being inserted. You may want to move your cursor onto a separate line in the source code to keep it neater and easier to read.

**16.** Open the Bindings panel (*CTRL*/*CMD*+*F10*). Expand the news recordset if it's not already open, highlight storyDate and click the Insert button at the bottom of the panel (see Figure 15-18).

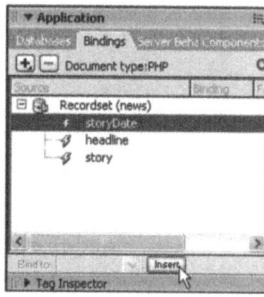

**Figure 15-18.** Inserting dynamic text from the Bindings panel

**17.** Click inside the Code section of Split view, and position your cursor immediately to the right of the PHP code that's just been inserted. Type a colon and a single space. Then highlight headline in the Bindings panel and click Insert.

**18.** Click inside the pageCopy area of Design view, and in the Property Inspector, change the format to Heading 2.

**19.** You should now have placeholders for the story date and headline on a single line, formatted as Heading 2. Check Figure 15-19 to see how everything should look in Split view.

**20.** Make sure your cursor is positioned after the PHP code for headline (as it is in Figure 15-19), and press ENTER/RETURN. MX 2004 will insert a pair of <p> tags separated by   (a non-breaking space) in the code after the closing </h2> tag.

**21.** Highlight the   to delete it, and with your cursor still between the <p> tags, insert the dynamic text for story by highlighting it in the Bindings panel and clicking Insert.

**22.** In the code part of Split view, highlight all the dynamic text and formatting you inserted since step 16, including the opening <h2> and closing </p> tags (see Figure 15-20).

**23.** With the code still highlighted, open the Server Behaviors panel, click the plus sign button, and select Repeat Region. In the dialog box that opens, Recordset should display news. Change the number of records to show at a time to 4. By doing this, you will show just the four most recent stories. Click OK.

**24.** MX 2004 will have placed a Repeat Region marker around your dynamic content, and the page should now look like Figure 15-21.

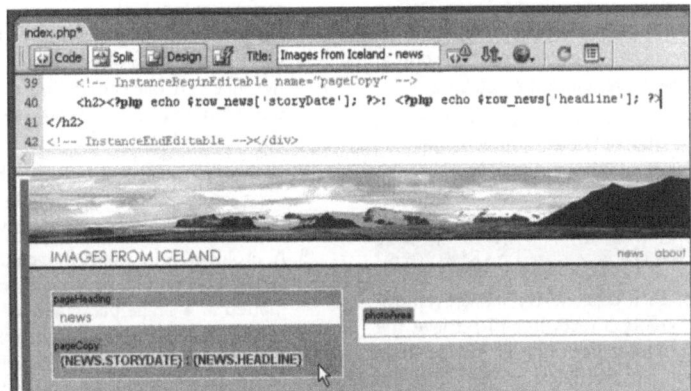

**Figure 15-19.** Dynamic text inserted for the story date and headline

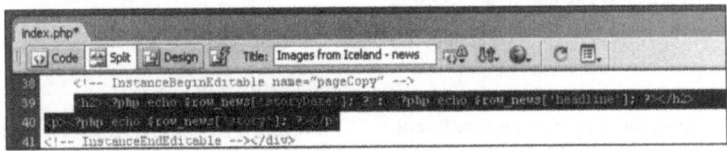

**Figure 15-20.** Select all the dynamic text and formatting.

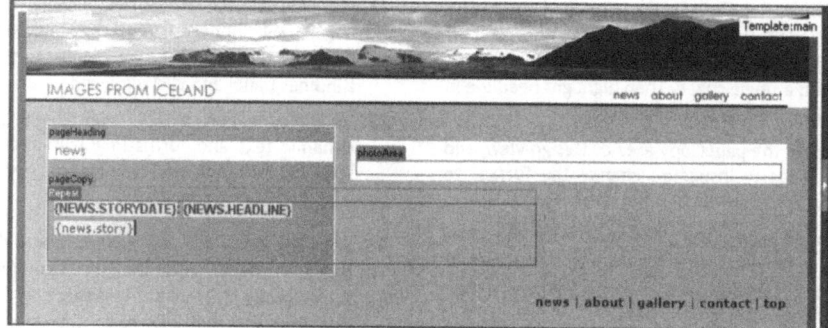

**Figure 15-21.** The index.php page ready to be populated with live data

25. Although that may have seemed like a lot of steps, they follow a logical sequence that you will find easy to implement after a little practice. Here's a recap: you created a recordset to retrieve the data, inserted dynamic text placeholders and ordinary XHTML into the page, and applied a Repeat Region server behavior. Although the page looks unattractive at the moment, it will come to life as soon as you start entering content into the database.

26. Save and close index.php. You'll need to do a little more work on it later, but now it's time to move on to about.php.

## Converting about.php

1. The process for each page is very similar: remove the static text, create a recordset to retrieve the dynamic text, and insert the code for the dynamic text. Open about.php and delete all the text in the pageCopy region.

As with index.php, when you delete the text in Design view, MX 2004 leaves a pair of <p> tags in the underlying code. You want to keep the paragraph tags this time.

2. From the Server Behaviors panel, create a new recordset. This time, the Simple mode is sufficient. Call the recordset about, use the cms_about table, and select just the details column (see Figure 15-22).

3. Click inside the pageCopy area again and remove the non-breaking space ( ) that MX 2004 placed inside the paragraph tags. If you do this before creating the recordset, Dreamweaver usually just puts in another one. It's also important to make sure you have your cursor in the right place before inserting the dynamic text. If you try inserting it immediately after creating the recordset, the dynamic text placeholder will end up right at the bottom of your XHTML code, just before the closing </html> tag.

4. With your cursor still between the <p> tags in the pageCopy area, open the Bindings panel, highlight details, and click the Insert button.

5. A problem with using the content management system on about.php is that all the text will be formatted as a single paragraph. A simple solution is to use the PHP nl2br() function, and make sure that *ENTER/RETURN* is pressed twice between each paragraph when text is entered via the web interface that you'll be creating later. In Code view, apply the function to the dynamic text code. Locate the following:

```php
<?php echo $row_about['details']; ?>
```

6. Change it to this:

```php
<?php echo nl2br($row_about['details']); ?>
```

7. Save about.php and close it.

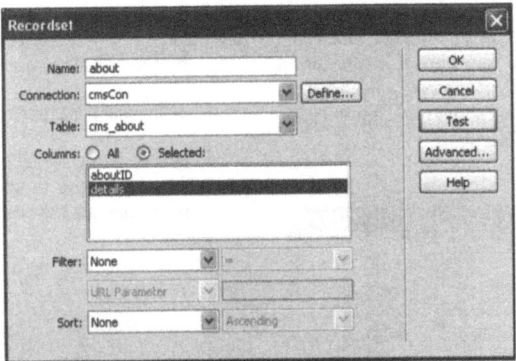

**Figure 15-22.** Settings for the about.php recordset

### Converting contact.php

1. Open contact.php. Create another recordset; this time call it contact. Choose cmsCon as the connection and cms_contact as the table. Select the email, post, and telephone columns (see Figure 15-23). Then click OK.

2. Highlight the existing e-mail address directly under the EMAIL label in the pageCopy region and delete it. Make sure just the <p> tags are left in the underlying code.

3. Select email from the Bindings panel and click Insert.

4. You now need to create a dynamic link for the e-mail text, so that the link will change automatically whenever the content is updated in the database. With <?php echo $row_contact['email']; ?> still highlighted, click the folder icon to the right of the Link field in the Property Inspector (see Figure 15-24).

**Figure 15-24.** The folder icon in the Property Inspector

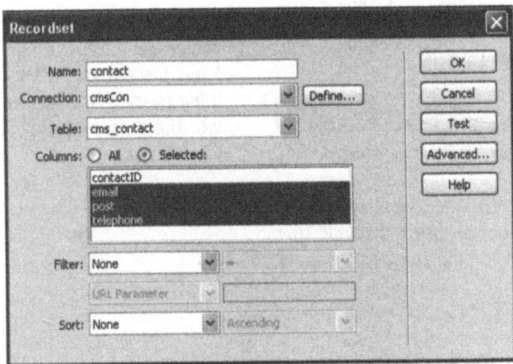

**Figure 15-23.** Settings for the contact.php recordset

**285**

**5.** The Select File dialog box that opens shows just the usual selection of files in the site, but if you click the Data Sources radio button at the top, it changes to display the dynamic text available from the current recordset, as shown in Figure 15-25. Select email and click OK.

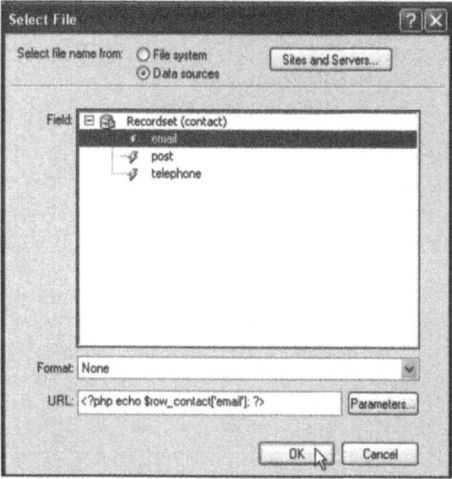

**Figure 15-25.** Selecting a link from data sources

**6.** MX 2004 inserted a dynamically generated hyperlink around the e-mail dynamic placeholder. To make it work as a mail link, position your cursor immediately after the href=" in Code view and type mailto: so that your code looks like Figure 15-26. Make sure you don't forget the double quotation mark after the equal sign.

```
<p><a href="mailto:<?php echo $row_contact['email']; ?>">
```

**Figure 15-26.** Converting the dynamic link to a mail link

**7.** Highlight the text under the POST label and delete it. Use the Bindings panel to insert dynamic text from the post field between the <p> tags.

**8.** To preserve any new lines in the text from the post field, apply the nl2br() function to the code, so that it looks like this:

```
<?php echo nl2br($row_contact['post']); ?>
```

**9.** Do the same for TELEPHONE. This time, though, you don't need to add the nl2br() function. Your pageCopy area should look like Figure 15-27.

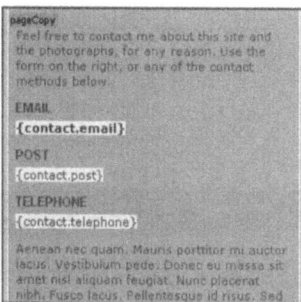

**Figure 15-27.** Dynamic text placeholders in contact.php

Another change you could make to contact.php is to convert the contact form to work with the PHP mail() function. We won't give go into that here, though. By now, you should have enough skill and confidence to refer back to Chapter 12 and adapt the instructions from there.

**10.** Save contact.php and close the file.

This is probably a good point at which to take a break. You've done a lot of hard work converting the Images From Iceland site to work with PHP. There's just one thing missing: the web interface to insert the content into the database. A dynamic site without content just doesn't fizz.

# Administering the CMS

Now it is time to turn your attention to the administration section of the CMS. When building such a system for a client, you will want to make the back end of the site just as attractive as the public parts, but right now we're going to concentrate on just the bare bones. Once you've mastered the technology of creating a CMS, you can devote your energies to making this section look however you want.

## Building the administration system

1. The administration section will contain six pages: a login page (login.php), an administrative menu (menu.php), and web interfaces for registering users and updating content (user.php, news_admin .php, about_admin.php, and contact_admin.php).

2. Create a new PHP page and save it in the admin folder as menu.php.

3. In menu.php, insert four text links to the following new pages in the admin folder: user.php, news_admin.php, about_admin.php, and contact_admin.php, as shown in Figure 15-28.

4. Because access to the administration system controls most of the content on the site, the first priority is to ensure that only authorized people can gain access. That means building a login and user authentication system just as you did in Chapter 14. The table and registration form will be almost identical, too, so you can use those if you prefer. The SQL for the cms_admin table is as follows:

```
create table cms_admin (
adminID int unsigned not null
➥auto_increment primary key,
firstname varchar(25) not null,
lastname varchar(25) not null,
username varchar(15) not null,
password varchar(50) not null);
```

5. Create a new PHP page and save it in the admin folder as user.php.

6. In user.php, create a table exactly the same as for register.php in the last chapter, only this time without a field for e-mail.

7. Apply the Yaromat Check Form MX behavior, again as you did in Chapter 14.

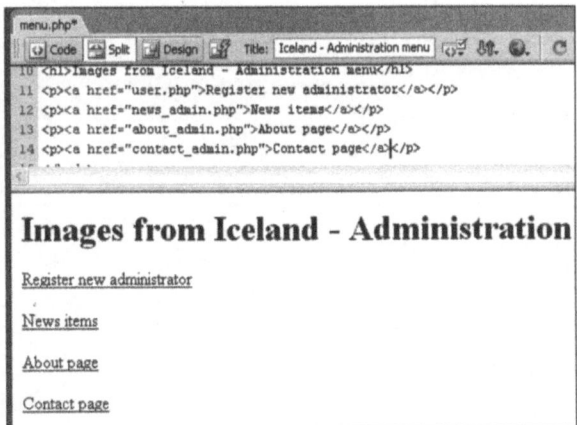

**Figure 15-28.** The administration menu for Images from Iceland

**8.** In the Server Behaviors panel, click the plus sign button and select Insert Record.

**9.** Set the connection as cmsCon, the table as cms_admin, and check that all columns will get the correct value. Click OK.

**10.** You need to make similar changes to the code as detailed in the "Avoiding multiple usernames and encrypting passwords" section of Chapter 14. Assuming you created the cms_admin table, this is what the code in step 2 of those instructions should look like this time (the differences are the table name and the page to which the user is redirected):

```
mysql_select_db($database_myConn, $myConn);
// SQL query to see if name already exists
$query = sprintf("SELECT username
  FROM cms_admin WHERE username = '%s'",
  $_POST['username']);
// submit query to database
$username_check = mysql_query($query);

// if entry found, issue error message
```

```
if (mysql_num_rows($username_check)>0) {
  print('Error: that username is taken');
}
else { // insert record and...
  $Result1 = mysql_query($insertSQL,
➡$myConn) or die(mysql_error());
  // redirect to menu.php and exit script
  header('Location: menu.php');
  exit;
}
```

**11.** Save user.php, load it in your browser, and register an administrator. If your page has been built correctly, you should be returned to the menu page after registering.

**12.** Create a new PHP page and save it in the admin folder as login.php. Insert a form with two text fields named username and password and a Submit button.

**13.** In the Server Behaviors panel, click the plus sign button and select User Authentication ➤ Log In User. Fill in the dialog box as shown in Figure 15-29.

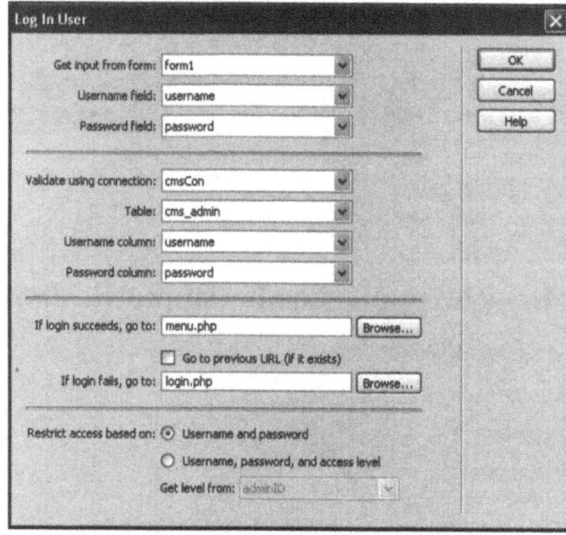

**Figure 15-29.** Settings for the CMS login page

**14.** As in the last chapter, after applying the server behavior, you need to open the page in Code view to encrypt the password. Find the following section of code (around line 12):

```
if (isset($_POST['username'])) {
  $loginUsername=$_POST['username'];
  $password=$_POST['password'];
```

**15.** Change the line containing $password to this:

```
$password=md5($_POST['password']);
```

**16.** Save login.php, and test it to make sure it's working. If it is, you should be taken to the menu page. Now, to the content management pages.

## Building the news management page

**1.** Create a new PHP page, and save it in the admin folder as news_admin.php.

**2.** Insert a form with two text fields called storyDate and headline, a text area called story, and a Submit button. The names of these fields are the same as in the cms_news table, so the MX 2004 Insert Record server behavior will automatically match the form fields with the appropriate table columns.

**3.** Click the plus sign button on the Server Behaviors panel and select Insert Record.

**4.** In the dialog box, set cmsCon as the connection, and select cms_news as the table. Check that each of the columns is correctly matched with the form field name.

**5.** In the field marked After inserting, go to, enter menu.php.

**6.** Unfortunately, dates present a problem to computers, not because they're difficult to handle, but because humans have so many different ways of writing them. Even in the English-speaking world, the British put the day before the month, whereas the North Americans put the month before the day, so January 2, 2004 is written 2/1/2004 in Britain and 1/2/2004 in the United States. To overcome this confusion, MySQL uses the ISO (International Standards Organization) format, which puts the largest unit first (the year) and goes to the smallest (the second). As far as the date is concerned, MySQL needs dates presented as yyyy-mm-dd, so January 2, 2004 becomes 2004-01-02. Because it's difficult to get humans to change life-long habits, you need to use some code to make sure the date entered in the storyDate field does not cause problems for database storage.

**7.** Open news_admin.php in Code view and insert the following block of code above all other code already inserted by MX 2004:

```php
<?php
function getTheDate() {
  // make sure return value empty
  $retVal = '';

  // check if date entered
  if (!empty($_POST['storyDate'])) {
    // assign to shorter variable
    $d = $_POST['storyDate'];

    // check if slashes used
    if (strpos($d,'/') === false) {
      $retVal = 'Error: Use slashes
➥to separate the date';
    }
    else { // if slashes, split into array
      $d = explode('/',$d);
      // remove any leading zeros
      $month = substr($d[0],0,1) == '0' ?
➥substr($d[0],1) : $d[0];
      $date = substr($d[1],0,1) == '0' ?
➥substr($d[1],1) : $d[1];
      // if year 2 digits, adjust century
      // 60 or above = 1960
      if (strlen($d[2]) == 2 && $d[2]>59) {
        $year = '19'.$d[2];
      }
      // 59 or less = 2000+
      elseif (strlen($d[2]) == 2) {
        $year = '20'.$d[2];
      }
      else {
        $year = $d[2];
      }

      // check the date is valid
      if (!checkdate($month,$date,$year)) {
        $retVal = 'Error: Date not valid';
```

**289**

```
        }
    // format for MySQL
    else {
        $retVal = '"'.$year.'-';
        $retVal .= $month.'-'.$date.'"';
        }
    }
    // if no date set, use today's date
    else {
        $retVal = '"'.date('Y-m-d').'"';
        }
    return $retVal;
    }
?>
```

This custom-built function checks whether a date has been entered. If so, it subjects the date to a series of tests, including checking whether it is genuine (using PHP's built-in checkdate() function). If the date is fine, it formats it for MySQL. If there are problems, it generates an appropriate error message. If no date has been set, it uses today's date and formats it in MySQL style. The function uses several string manipulation functions that we have not covered, but the comments should help you work out what's happening, if you read them in conjunction with the online PHP documentation at www.php.net/manual/en/ref.strings.php. If you don't want to have to copy it all, you can download the completed page from the friends of ED website. (Note: although this function accepts a variety of date formats, it works only with dates inserted as numbers separated by forward slashes. You could devise a function that covers a wider range of formats, but it's simpler to set rules for use rather than try to cover every eventuality.)

8. The code in the previous step is designed to work with the North American date convention, mm/dd/(yy)yy. To adapt it to work with European-style dates, locate the following lines:

```
        $month = substr($d[0],0,1) == '0' ?
➟substr($d[0],1) : $d[0];
        $date = substr($d[1],0,1) == '0' ?
➟substr($d[1],1) : $d[1];
```

9. Change them as follows (by swapping month and date):

```
        $date = substr($d[0],0,1) == '0' ?
➟substr($d[0],1) : $d[0];
        $month = substr($d[1],0,1) == '0' ?
➟substr($d[1],1) : $d[1];
```

10. Locate the section of code shown in Figure 15-30 (the line numbers may be different on your page, depending on how you typed in the custom function).

11. On the line immediately above the code, enter the following:

```
$theDate = getTheDate();
if (strpos($theDate, 'ror')) {
    echo $theDate;
    }
else {
```

This calls the custom function inserted in step 7, and uses the PHP built-in function strpos() to check whether the date contains an error message. strpos() returns the position in a string of whatever's held in the second parameter. The reason you don't use "Error" is because it returns the position of the first character. In PHP terms, that would be 0, which equates to "false." Consequently, you need to look for another part of the string. If there is an error message, the script displays it. If not, the else statement allows the MX 2004 script to continue.

```
86  if ((isset($_POST["MM_insert"])) && ($_POST["MM_insert"] == "form1")) {
87      $insertSQL = sprintf("INSERT INTO cms_news (storyDate, headline, story) VALUES (%s, %s, %s)",
88                      GetSQLValueString($_POST['storyDate'], "date"),
```

**Figure 15-30.** This section of code needs to be amended by hand.

**12.** You now need to substitute the new date variable for the one created by MX 2004. In the block of code shown in Figure 15-30, delete this line:

```
GetSQLValueString($_POST['storyDate'],
➥"date"),
```

**13.** Replace it with

**$theDate,**

**14.** To complete the changes, you need to balance the opening brace of the else statement in step 11. Locate this line (just before the closing PHP tag above the XHTML doctype):

```
header(sprintf("Location: %s",
➥$insertGoTo));
```

**15.** Insert a new line after the semicolon, and insert a closing curly brace (}).

**16.** To avoid invalid content being entered into the database, it's a good idea to apply some form of validation to the content administration pages. If you use the Yaromat Check Form MX behavior that you installed in Chapter 14, it will check for a variety of date formats, but it won't accept years as two digits, nor will it accept European-style dates without leading zeros. Because the custom PHP function created in step 7 does all the work, it's best not to attempt to validate the date with JavaScript. You should, however, make sure that the headline and story fields are required.

Phew! That was quite a tough one. As we explained at the outset, MX 2004 cannot handle everything you might want to do with a dynamic website (at least, not yet). So unless you want to be stuck with standard solutions, it's necessary to do some hand-coding yourself. The more you do it, the more flexible your own solutions will become. You need to do a little more date manipulation when it comes to displaying the output, but first let's make the web interfaces for about.php and contact.php. You'll be relieved to know they're a lot simpler.

**Building the management page for about.php**

**1.** The management page for about.php needs only one text area. Create a new PHP page, and save it in the admin folder as about_admin.php.

**2.** Insert a form, and insert a text area named details and a submit button inside the form. Label the button Update.

**3.** Add a hidden field to the form. In the Property Inspector, name it aboutID and enter 1 into the Value field, as shown in Figure 15-31. This will be used by MX 2004 to identify the record to be updated in the cms_about table. Because the same record will always be used, the value will never change.

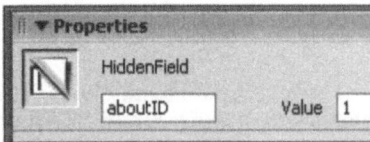

**Figure 15-31.** Using a hidden field to identify the sole record in the table

**4.** You don't want to have to change every single word whenever you update the content of about.php, so it will be useful to display the current content in the text area of about_admin.php. To retrieve the current content, you need a recordset. Create one from the Server Behaviors panel, call it about_adm, use cmsCon as the connection, and select the cms_about table.

**5.** Highlight the text area. Then, with the text area still selected, highlight details in the Bindings panel. Ensure that Bind to (at the bottom of the panel) is set to initial value and click Bind (see Figure 15-32). This will insert the content retrieved from the details field in the database, and display it in the text area, thus giving you a text you can edit rather than having to rewrite from scratch.

**Figure 15-32.** Binding the content of the details field to the text area

6. In the Server Behaviors panel, click the plus sign button and select Update Record. Fill in the dialog box as shown in Figure 15-33. This is almost identical to the Insert Record dialog box you have used on so many occasions. The important difference is that the reference to aboutID in the Columns field reads 'aboutID' Selects Record Using 'FORM.aboutID' as 'Integer'. You should highlight this item and make sure the Primary key box is checked as shown in Figure 15-33. The primary key passed to the Update Record dialog box determines which record is updated. Although you have only one record in this table, the same principle applies for tables with tens or even millions of records.

The only validation required on this page is to ensure that the details field is required.

7. Save about_admin.php and test it by loading it into your browser. It should display the dummy text you entered earlier in this chapter. Type some new text into text area, and click Update. You should be taken to the menu page. Click the link back to about_admin.php, and your new text should be visible in the text area ready for editing again.

### Building the management page for contact.php

1. The final administration file, contact_admin.php, is very similar to about_admin.php. Insert a form in the page with two text fields called email and telephone. Also create a text area called post and a submit button labeled Update.

2. You will use the same update record technique, so add a hidden field called contactID with a Value of 1.

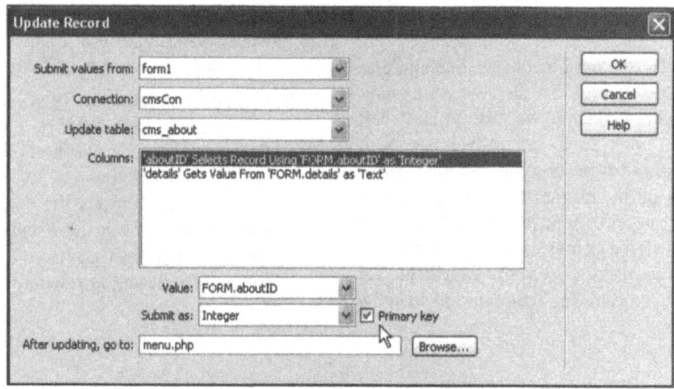

**Figure 15-33.** The Update Record dialog box

3. Create a recordset called contact_adm using cmsCon as the connection and cms_contact as the table.

4. Highlight each of the text fields and the text area in turn and bind the appropriate dynamic text to them from the Bindings panel, as described in step 5 of the last exercise. This will populate the email, telephone, and postal address fields with the current content ready for editing.

5. Insert an Update Record server behavior. It's the same procedure as in step 6 of the last exercise except you need to select the cms_contact table and make sure that contactID is used as the primary key.

6. None of the fields are required, but it may be worth applying one of the form validation behaviors to check that the email field is in an appropriate e-mail format. You can use either Dreamweaver's built-in Validate Form or Yaromat's Check Form MX.

7. Test the page in the same way as you did in the previous exercise.

### Securing the administration area

1. Once you know that everything is working, secure the administration area by applying the Restrict Access to Page server behavior to all files in the admin folder, except login.php. In other words, apply the behavior to about_admin.php, contact_admin.php, menu.php, news_admin.php, and user.php. You did this in Chapter 14, but if you've forgotten how, open the Server Behaviors panel

and choose User Authentication ➤ Restrict Access to Page. Set each page to go to login.php if access is denied.

2. It's also a good idea to give administrators the opportunity to log out. Because each content management operation always brings you back to menu.php, this is the only page where you need it.

3. In menu.php, position your cursor immediately to the right of the final link in the page. Press ENTER/RETURN to move the cursor onto a new line. MX 2004 will create an empty paragraph. This is where the Log out link will go.

4. In the Server Behaviors panel, click the plus sign button and choose User Authentication ➤ Log Out User.

5. In the dialog box, choose Log out when link clicked and accept the option to create a new link. In the When done, go to field, you could choose either login.php, or you could do as we did in Figure 15-34: take the administrator to the site's main page. That way, you can see the results of your handiwork as soon as you log out.

6. As we pointed out in Chapter 14, MX 2004 inserts session_start(); for each server behavior that uses a session, so you need to remove the redundant one from menu.php. Open Code view and locate the second instance of session_start(); (it should be around line 24) and delete it.

7. That's it! You should now have a fully functional content management system for Images From Iceland, complete with a secure administration area.

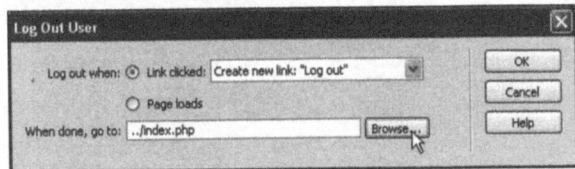

**Figure 15-34.** Set the Log Out User server behavior to take you back to the main page.

# Testing and refining the system

Before any website can go live, it's always wise to test it thoroughly. This is particularly important for sites that use server-side technology like this one. Check that you can log in and out successfully, that the update and content management pages work, and that everything is displayed as expected. If you enter a few stories in news_admin.php, the front page of the Images from Iceland site should look similar to Figure 15-35.

It's quite impressive, but look at the dates: they're still in MySQL format. Most people would understand them, but it would be better to format them in a more familiar way. You can do this a number of ways, but one of the most effective is to get MySQL to do the formatting for you.

**Formatting the news item dates**

1. Open index.php in Code view, and locate the following code (around line 11):

```
$query_news = "SELECT cms_news.storyDate,
➥cms_news.headline, cms_news.story FROM
➥cms_news ORDER BY cms_news.storyDate
➥DESC, cms_news.newsID DESC";
```

2. You're going to use the MySQL DATE_FORMAT() function to convert the date as it is retrieved from the database. The part of the SQL query you need to change is cms_news.storyDate. Amend it so it looks like this:

```
DATE_FORMAT(cms_news.storyDate,
➥'%M %D, %Y') AS 'storyDate'
```

**Figure 15-35.** Create a few news items to see how the site looks.

```
11  $query_news = "SELECT DATE_FORMAT(cms_news.storyDate, '%M %D, %Y') as 'storyDate', cms_news.headline,
    cms_news.story FROM cms_news ORDER BY cms_news.storyDate DESC, cms_news.newsID DESC";
```

**Figure 15-36.** The SQL query amended to format the date

3. The entire line should look like Figure 15-36, and the effect of the change can be seen in Figure 15-37. The function takes two parameters: a MySQL date or date source, and a string indicating the format required. The format codes can be combined with ordinary text or punctuation. In this example, we included a comma before the year. Some of the more commonly used format codes are listed in Table 15-1. You can find the full list in the MySQL online documentation at www.mysql.com/doc/en/Date_and_time_functions.html#IDX1373.

DATE_FORMAT() converts the data retrieved from the database, which is then given an **alias**, using the AS keyword. An alias is a way of identifying part of a database query result by a specified name. In this example, we used the column's original name as the alias. This may seem redundant, and is not required by MySQL, but PHP fails to recognize the correct part of the results array unless an alias is used. Using the original column name as the alias saves having to change the code used to display the date in the body of the web page.

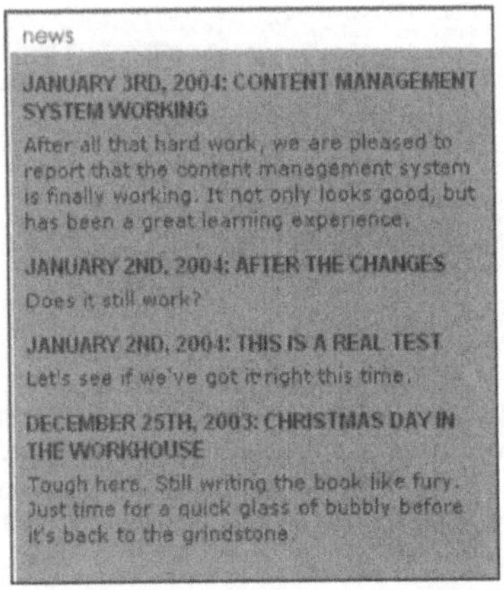

**Table 15-1.** Commonly Used MySQL Date Format Codes

| Code | Description |
| --- | --- |
| %M | Month, full text |
| %b | Month, 3 characters |
| %W | Weekday name, full text |
| %a | Weekday name, 3 characters |
| %D | Day of month with text suffix (for example, 1st) |
| %d | Day of month with leading zeros |
| %e | Day of month, no leading zeros |
| %Y | Year, 4 digits |
| %y | Year, 2 digits |

### Adding a navigation bar for news items

There are other refinements you could make to the content management system through the use of MX 2004's **application objects**, for example. Application objects are even more powerful than server behaviors because they enable you to create complex dynamic structures with the aid of one or two dialog boxes. As an example of the types of things they can do, you're going to add a navigation bar for the news page.

1. Open index.php and position your cursor right at the end of the coding for the pageCopy section (you need to be in Split view to do this accurately—see Figure 15-38).

```
59  <p><?php echo $row_news['story']; ?></p>
60  <?php } while ($row_news = mysql_fetch_assoc($news)); ?>
61  <!-- InstanceEndEditable --></div>
```

**Figure 15-38.** Positioning the cursor to insert the navigation bar

**Figure 15-37.** The news section after formatting the dates

**2.** Application objects are accessed from the Insert menu. Choose Insert ➤ Application Objects ➤ Recordset Paging ➤ Recordset Navigation Bar. In the simple dialog box that opens, the news recordset is already chosen because it's the only one on the page. All you have to do is decide whether you want the navigation menu to use text or images. Choose whichever you prefer and click OK. That's all there is to it!

**3.** MX 2004 adds a rather strange looking jumble at the bottom of the pageCopy area (see Figure 15-39), but its purpose becomes clear if you open index.php in a browser. If you have more than four items in the cms_news table, you will see a navigation bar like that in Figure 15-40 that enables you to move back and forward among your news items.

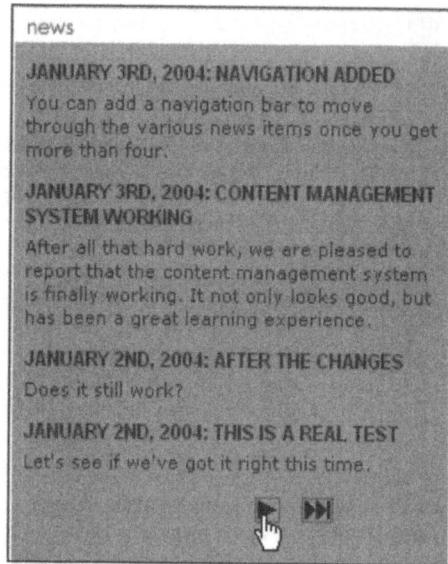

Figure 15-40. The navigation bar in action in a browser

**Figure 15-39.** The navigation bar as it appears in Design view

## Showing contact details selectively

Remember back to Chapter 12 when we showed you how to hide the delivery charge when the total price came to $10 or more. MX 2004 has a Show Region server behavior that works in a similar way with recordsets. Unfortunately, the standard choice is display all or nothing; you cannot choose to omit just one field. The good news is that it's very easy to adapt.

If you decide you don't want to show your e-mail details on the contact page for a while, you could simply use contact_admin.php to remove your e-mail address. The problem is that would still leave the email label on the contact page (see Figure 15-41). That's not very professional looking.

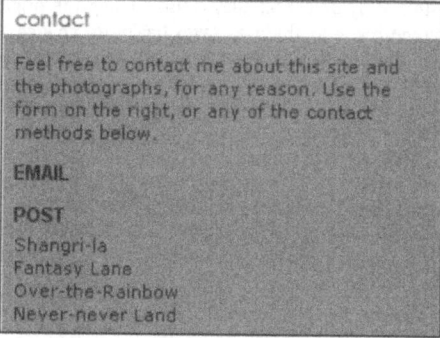

**Figure 15-41.** The email label still appears even if the field is empty.

**1.** Open contact.php in Split view, and highlight the EMAIL label and the dynamic text placeholder. You will need to go into the code to make sure you get the opening <h2> tag and the closing </p> tag (see Figure 15-42).

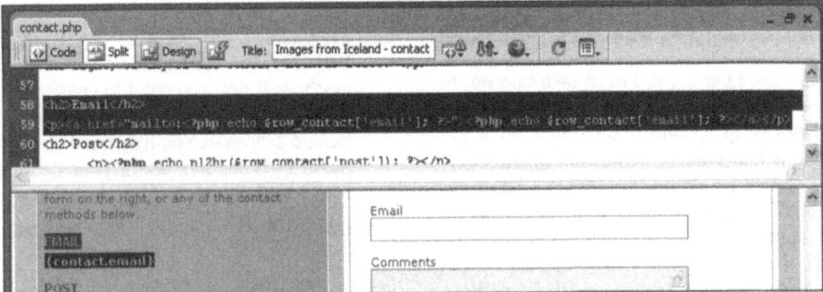

**Figure 15-42.** Highlighting the e-mail section

2. With the code still highlighted, click the plus sign button on the Server Behaviors panel and choose Show Region ➤ Show If Recordset Is Not Empty. The dialog box that opens simply asks you to confirm which recordset. Because there's only one on the page, just click OK.

You will see that MX 2004 has added two lines of PHP code, one before, and another after the highlighted section. It's the first line you're interested in. It should read

```
<?php if ($totalRows_contact > 0) {
➡// Show if recordset not empty ?>
```

This is a conditional statement that checks to see if the results from the database contain at least one row. If they do, it executes any code up to the closing curly brace in the other line that MX 2004 has just inserted. All you need to do is change the condition being checked.

The code that displays the e-mail address is located in the next line:

```
<?php echo $row_contact['email']; ?>
```

If $row_contact['email'] contains a value, you want to display it. Therefore, the test you need to conduct is to see whether $row_contact['email'] is *not* empty. The PHP way of doing that is to use the empty() function with the negative logical operator (see Table 12-2).

3. Locate this:

```
<?php if ($totalRows_contact > 0) {
```

4. Change it to this:

```
<?php if (!empty($row_contact['email'])) {
```

5. Save contact.php, and view it again in a browser. The email field is empty, so the EMAIL label is hidden, as shown in Figure 15-43.

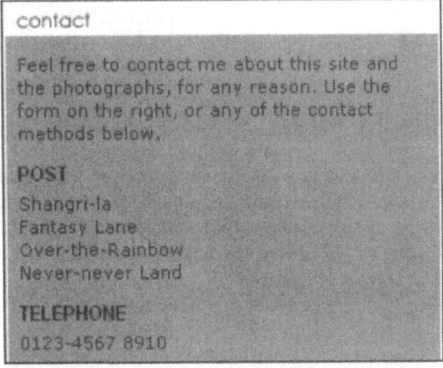

**Figure 15-43.** The empty field and its label are now hidden.

You can do the same with the post and telephone fields. Even though it requires a little hand-coding, using the MX 2004 Show Region server behavior is quite convenient because it puts the closing bracket in the right place, something that's easy to forget when working entirely by hand.

**297**

### Putting your site on the Internet

As we've mentioned before, you must take care not to infringe upon other people's copyright. You should not use the Images from Iceland photographs on a live website without first seeking permission of the copyright holder (details are on contact.html in the download files). You'll likely want to put your own images in a gallery or apply everything you learned in this book to a dynamic site of your own. There's virtually no difference between uploading a dynamic website and a static one. The normal way is to use an FTP client, such as the one built into Dreamweaver MX 2004.

1. To set up FTP access in MX 2004, choose Site ➤ Manage Sites, select your site, and click Edit. Open the Advanced tab of the Site Definition dialog box, and choose Remote Info. Select FTP from the Access drop-down menu (see Figure 15-44).

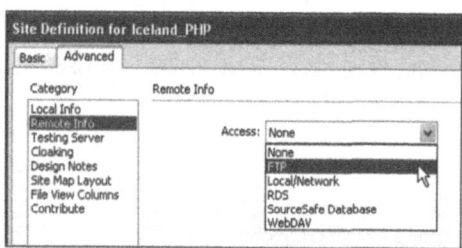

**Figure 15-44.** Choose FTP from the Access menu.

2. The dialog box changes to reveal a set of fields for you to fill in with the details for your remote server, using information that should be provided by your ISP. Figure 15-45 shows a typical setup.

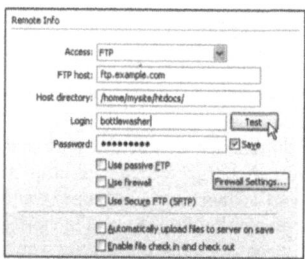

**Figure 15-45.** A typical FTP setup

3. Test the connection by clicking the Test button. If everything is OK, you'll get a message telling you that MX 2004 connected to your web server successfully. If not, you need to check the details and password (it may be case-sensitive). If you're behind a firewall, you may need to check the Use passive FTP option; and if your ISP offers Secure FTP, you should definitely check that option.

4. Once everything is set, click OK, and then click Done.

5. To upload files to your site, select them in the Files panel (*F8*), and click the Put icon (a blue up arrow, as shown in Figure 15-46).

Dreamweaver MX 2004 has a variety of commands that can make your remote server management more convenient. Consult the section on uploading files in the Dreamweaver Help files (*F1*).

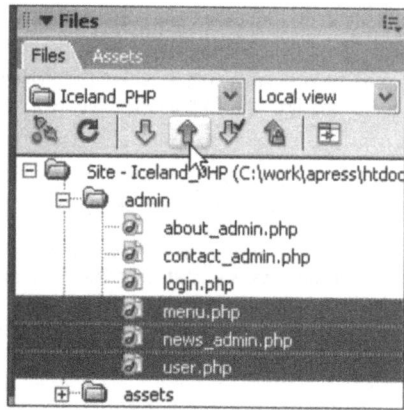

**Figure 15-46.** The Put icon

When working with a database-driven site, don't forget to upload the Connections folder and all its contents. Otherwise you won't be able to connect to your database. What about the database itself? How do you upload that? The answer is: you don't. To anyone who has worked with ASP or ColdFusion and an Access database, this may seem bizarre. Unlike Access, MySQL does not create a single file for each database; it creates a folder with separate files for the data, indexing, and tables. This file structure is one of the things that make MySQL both fast and lightweight. An Access

**298**

database with a few hundred records may be as large as 1MB. A MySQL database that size would hold several thousand records. To avoid damage to the data structure, you cannot just upload the files to a MySQL server while it's running. There are several ways of transferring existing databases, and you should check with your ISP to see which are available to you.

The best method, though, is to build and test your database structure locally. Insert only a minimum amount of test data. When you're satisfied everything is the way you want it, build it anew on your remote server and fill it with live data. One final thing: find out from your ISP about backup methods. There's nothing worse than building a superb database and discovering one day that a hard disk failure has wiped out all the data you so carefully built.

## Summary

We could go on and on, suggesting further improvements to your content management system, but there comes a point when you need to venture out and start making discoveries of your own. By this stage, you should be very familiar with Dreamweaver MX 2004. You should also have a solid understanding of the basics of PHP. Take time to explore the other server behaviors. What they do is usually obvious from the name. Try applying one to a page, just to see what it

does. Use the Help button in the dialog box for context-sensitive help. Explore the application objects in the Insert menu, too.

We also hope to have inspired you to learn more about PHP and MySQL. The MX 2004 Reference panel (Window ➤ Reference or *SHIFT+F1*) includes a copy of the O'Reilly *PHP Pocket Reference* with brief descriptions of hundreds of PHP functions. You'll also find the entire PHP and MySQL documentation online at www.php.net and www.mysql.com.

You should also take the trouble to consult the *Using Dreamweaver MX 2004* manual from time to time. Because it comes as a PDF file, many people never bother, but it's one of the best-written software manuals around, and at almost 800 pages, it contains a lot of information. It won't teach you how to build a website, but it will explain the correct procedure for doing something in Dreamweaver MX 2004. Two appendices cover the basics of database design and a SQL primer.

To help you move to the next stage, there are many excellent books, such as *Professional PHP4* by Luis Argerich and others (Apress, ISBN 1590592484), *MySQL* by Paul DuBois (Sams, ISBN 0735712123), and *The Definitive Guide to MySQL* by Michael Kofler (Apress, ISBN 1590591445).

Happy coding!

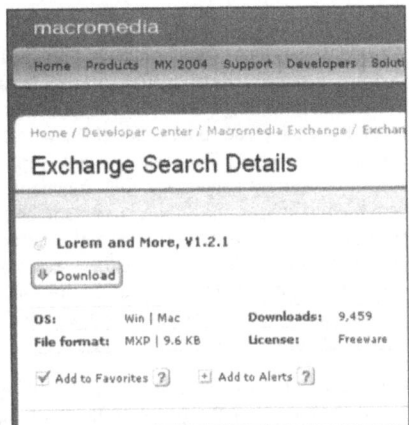

**Appendix**

# DREAMWEAVER EXTENSIONS

---

**What we'll cover in this chapter**

- Installing the Macromedia Extension Manager
- Installing extensions
- Removing extensions
- Finding extensions online

An extension is a package that allows users to add new features and extra functionality to Dreamweaver MX 2004. Extensions range from very simple additional features that enable you to add special characters such as fractions to your XHTML text, to very sophisticated tools that quickly generate a fully functioning menu with built-in images and CSS. A large number of extensions are free, such as the form validation extension we recommended in Chapter 14. Others are sold on a commercial basis. Whichever you use, they all depend on the Macromedia Extension Manager, which makes installation and management a breeze.

In this appendix, we'll look at how to install and manage extensions, and list some of the best places to download extensions.

## Obtaining the Extension Manager

The Extension Manager is common to all programs in the MX 2004 Studio, so you may already have the correct version of it installed for Flash MX 2004 or Fireworks MX 2004. It also comes bundled with Dreamweaver MX 2004, and it can be accessed from the Commands menu. However, it's a separate program in its own right, so you need to check that it has been installed and that you have the right version. The simplest way to do this is to choose Commands ➤ Manage Extensions within Dreamweaver MX 2004. If the Extension Manager has been installed, it will automatically open in a window like the one shown in Figure A-1.

Once it opens, check the version number by choosing Help ➤ About Macromedia Extension Manager. A copyright screen will appear with the version number in the bottom-right corner. It should be at least version 1.6. Click anywhere on the copyright screen to close it.

If the Extension Manager doesn't launch or the version number is lower than 1.6, you need to obtain and install the correct version before going any further. If your copy of Dreamweaver MX 2004 came on CD-ROM, the correct Extension Manager should be included. Locate Extension_Manager_Installer.exe, close all other programs, and double-click the installer icon. Alternatively, download the latest version of the Extension Manager from www.macromedia.com/exchange/em_download/. If you have an older version of the Extension Manager installed, Macromedia recommends that you uninstall your existing version before upgrading.

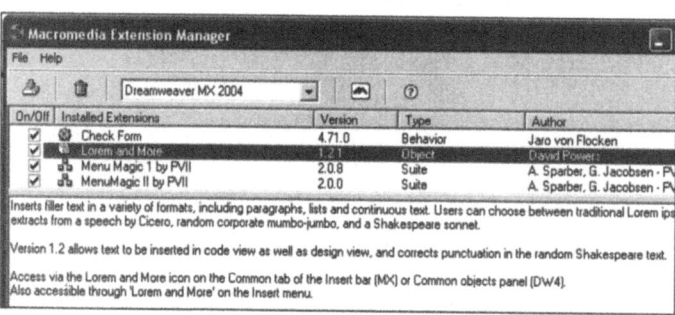

**Figure A-1.** The Macromedia Extension Manager

# How to use the Extension Manager

The Extension Manager performs a number of functions, some of which are needed only by the people who create extensions. These functions are never used by the vast majority of Dreamweaver users. Here, we're concerned only with the installation and management of Macromedia and third-party extensions.

Although you can open the Extension Manager by double-clicking its icon, the usual way to do so is either from inside Dreamweaver or by installing an extension. If you've never used the Extension Manager before, the top and bottom frames as seen in Figure A-1 will be empty. After you install extensions, they are listed in the top frame, and a brief description of what the extension does is displayed in the lower frame.

Once the Extension Manager is installed, you can open it by choosing Commands ➤ Manage Extensions within Dreamweaver MX 2004. Make sure you are connected to the Internet, and in the Extension Manager, choose File ➤ Go To Macromedia Exchange. This will take you directly to the Macromedia site. If you have never registered with Macromedia, you will need to create a user account. This is free of charge and unobtrusive. Once registered, you can browse the available extensions. There were some 900 available in early 2004, so you may find this overwhelming at first, but take a while to look at the wide range of categories. They include navigation, learning, accessibility, security, style, format, and many more.

One that you may find useful is Lorem and More, which was written by one of the authors of this book. It's a free extension that automatically creates filler material for web pages. You use it in the early stages of design to fill the page with dummy text so you can get a better idea of what the completed page might look like. As its name suggests, Lorem and More uses the traditional fake Latin text, Lorem Ipsum, and several other texts, including a Shakespeare sonnet, automatically formatting them as paragraphs, lists, and so on. You can find it on the Macromedia Exchange by searching for Lorem and More (see Figure A-2), or get it directly from the author's own site at http://computerbookshelf.com/tools/. It's only 10KB, so it's a quick and easy download.

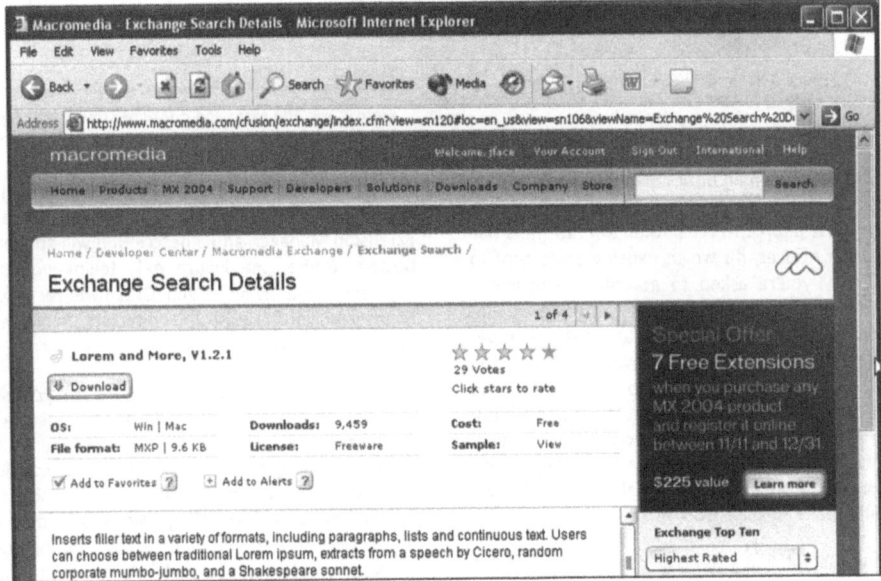

**Figure A-2.** Lorem and More on the Macromedia Exchange

### Installing an extension

Dreamweaver extensions are packaged in a single .mxp file (see Figure A-3). After downloading the file, there are two ways to install an extension:

1. Double-click the .mxp file icon. This should launch the Extension Manager and begin the installation process. Mac users may find this approach doesn't work if their operating system doesn't recognize the .mxp file type. In that case, use step 2.

2. Open the Extension Manager first, either from within Dreamweaver MX 2004 (Commands ➤ Manage Extensions) or directly, using whichever method is appropriate to your operating system. Then select File ➤ Install Extension.

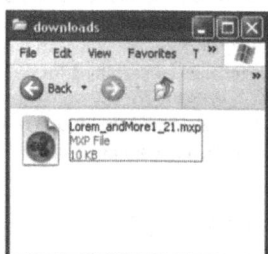

**Figure A-3.** Dreamweaver extensions come packaged as MXP files.

Either method will start the installation process, which begins with a disclaimer notice (see Figure A-4). You must click Accept for the installation to continue. Although most people never bother to read the small print of such notices, it's worth pausing a moment to consider why you're asked to accept. Dreamweaver Extensions are made by a wide range of people, including Macromedia employees. Most are highly competent, and any extension you download from the Macromedia Exchange will have been subjected to quality assurance tests to make sure they don't harm your computer or files. There is no obligation, though, to submit extensions to Macromedia for testing. If you get an .mxp file from a source other than the Exchange, you should make sure it's trustworthy.

By clicking Accept, you also agree not to distribute the extension without written permission. Some developers

sell extensions either as a business or as a way of supporting the cost of development, so unauthorized distribution would amount to piracy. Even in the case of free extensions, though, it's far better to get it direct from the developer or from the Exchange. Knowing how many times an extension has been downloaded gives a good idea of how successful it is, and will encourage the developer to keep it up to date and perhaps inspire new ideas. It also ensures you get the latest version available.

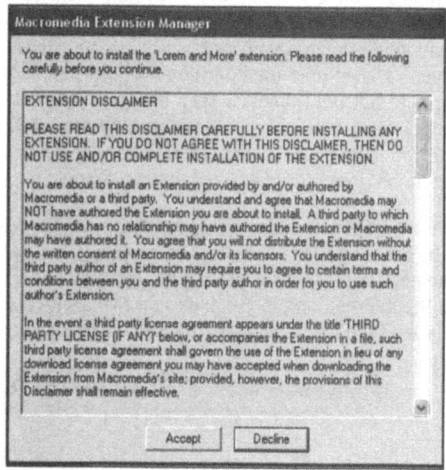

**Figure A-4.** The extension disclaimer must be accepted for installation to proceed.

After you click Accept, the installation process is automatic. Highlight the extension in the top frame of the Extension Manager, and a description will appear in the bottom frame (see Figure A-1) telling you how to access the extension within Dreamweaver MX 2004. Most extensions require you to restart Dreamweaver in order to initialize them.

3. If you downloaded Lorem and More, you will find that it has installed an icon on the main Insert bar (see Figure A-5). Click the icon and the dialog box shown in Figure A-6 opens. All the instructions for using the extension are in the dialog box. Choose the text type, formatting style, and amount of text to be inserted. The filler text will be inserted into your page when you click OK. As an alternative to clicking the icon on the Insert bar, select Insert ➤ Lorem and More.

**Figure A-5.** The extension installs a new icon on the Insert bar.

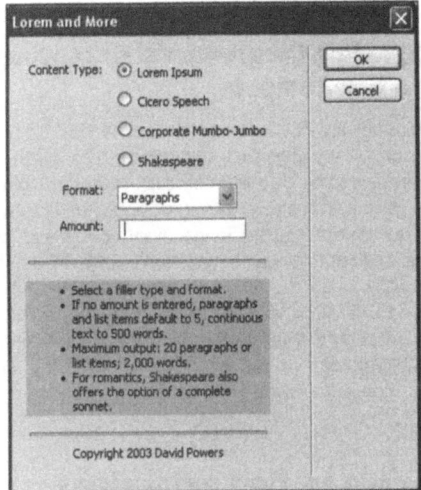

**Figure A-6.** The Lorem and More extension dialog box

## Extension compatibility

Considerable changes have been made to Dreamweaver since its first appearance, but the most important ones took place in 2002 with the introduction of Dreamweaver MX. The vast majority of extensions use JavaScript, not only to achieve dynamic effects on web pages, but also to manipulate code within Dreamweaver. Some older extensions are no longer compatible with the latest versions of Dreamweaver. You'll soon discover the problem because JavaScript error messages will start popping up as you're working on your page design.

Unfortunately, the error messages don't always indicate which extension is causing the problem. The only way around this is to start removing newly installed extensions until the problem resolves itself. An even wiser approach is to check compatibility before installing. The Macromedia Exchange gives compatibility details,

but only for when the extension was last tested. If it says MX or MX 2004, you're fine. But what do you do if it says DW3? Many old extensions still do the job perfectly (which is probably why they've never been updated), and will work on all versions of Dreamweaver. To find out if they're safe to install, visit the creator's website—the link should be on the extension's page on the Macromedia Exchange. Most developers are keen to test their wares on all versions of Dreamweaver, and will report known problems and compatibility issues on their own sites. If the developer's site is no longer there, proceed with caution.

Changes to the menu system in MX 2004 also mean some extensions will not work on earlier versions of Dreamweaver. If the developer created the .mxp package correctly, the Extension Manager will refuse to install extensions on versions earlier than those for which they were designed. The opposite doesn't apply, so some older extensions will appear in a different place in the menu that you might expect. This doesn't affect their functionality, but is obviously not ideal.

# Disabling and removing extensions

If you have problems with an extension or simply no longer want it, you can either disable it temporarily or remove it completely.

### Disabling an extension temporarily

1. In the Extension Manager, highlight the extension you want to disable.

2. Click the check mark in the On/Off column to the left of the extension name (see Figure A-1). The Extension Manager immediately starts the disabling process, and when it's finished, it displays a message like the one shown in Figure A-7.

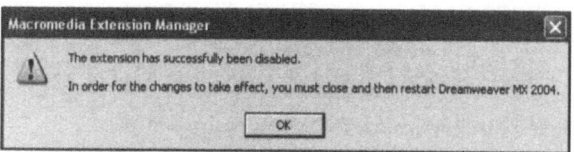

**Figure A-7.** Disabling an extension temporarily

3. Click OK, close, and restart Dreamweaver MX 2004 for the change to take effect.

4. To restore a disabled extension, simply click the empty On/Off box next to the extension name to toggle it on. Restored extensions are normally ready for immediate use without the need to restart Dreamweaver.

### Removing an extension permanently

1. In the Extension Manager, highlight the extension you want to remove.

2. Click the Remove Extension icon (see Figure A-8) or press *CTRL/CMD+R*, and click Yes when the Extension Manager asks you to confirm your decision.

When the process is complete, a dialog box will prompt you to close and restart Dreamweaver for the changes to take effect.

Once you've removed it in this manner, the only way to restore an extension is from an .mxp file.

## Upgrading Dreamweaver or moving to a new computer

Extensions are not automatically transferred from one version of Dreamweaver to another. The safest way when upgrading is to reinstall each extension anew as you need it. This also gives you an opportunity to weed out extensions you no longer want, but it can be a long, tedious process. If you don't want to do it all manually, open the Extension Manager, select File ➤ Import Extensions, and follow the instructions. The disadvantage of this approach is that, if you have compatibility problems, it can be difficult identifying which extension is the cause.

## Where to find extensions

Don't let the warnings about compatibility put you off. The vast majority of extensions are just fine. Some are little short of brilliant. Most will improve your productivity by leaps and bounds, so we strongly encourage you to explore the world of extensions and make them part of your everyday Dreamweaver experience. It's the fact that the program can be extended in so many ingenious ways that makes it such a superb tool for web development.

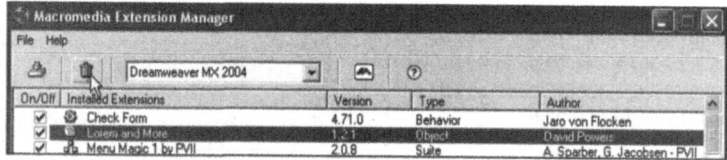

**Figure A-8.** Removing an extension permanently

In the previous section, we visited the Macromedia Exchange. Although it is probably the biggest source for downloading extensions, it's certainly not the only show in town. If you visit the sites of individual extension developers, you will get a better idea of how the extensions work and what they're for. The next sections list some of the better-known extension developers. Many of their offerings are free.

## Massimo Corner

www.massimocorner.com

Massimo Foti is one of the most popular extension developers around. His site is bursting with free extensions. It's worth a visit—you won't come away empty-handed. Don't be put off by the fact many were developed a few years ago. Massimo's skill with JavaScript is legendary. They haven't been updated because they don't need to be.

## Project Seven

www.projectseven.com

The team at Project Seven develops some of the most popular commercial extensions available, as well as many free ones, too. PVII extensions regularly feature in the Top Ten most highly rated extensions on the Macromedia Exchange. At one point in late 2003, they held the top eight positions. With products like Menu Magic I & II and Tree Menu Magic, which allow you to build JavaScript menus with a couple of clicks, it's not hard to see why. Al Sparber of Project Seven is as passionate about CSS as his partner, Gerry Jacobsen, is about JavaScript. They produce stunning designs, and share their knowledge through free online tutorials and a lively forum where you can ask for help should you encounter any problems.

## DreamweaverFAQ.com

www.dwfaq.com

Founded by Angela Buraglia, DreamweaverFAQ.com is home to many of the best-known writers about Dreamweaver. As the site's name suggests, it's crammed with sensible answers to frequently asked questions about Dreamweaver and web development. There are plenty of free tutorials, and it's where you can find the Snippets Exchange—more than 300 ready-made snippets for you to add to your collection. The DWfaq store offers a wide range of useful extensions, both free and for sale.

## DMXZone

www.dmxzone.com

Not only does this site have a large collection of extensions to download, it also contains many good tutorials and code snippets. Registration is required before you can download extensions, some free, others for sale. Some content is also available only on a pay-per-view basis.

## Community MX

www.communitymx.com

Community MX is mainly a subscription-only resource that provides tutorials and troubleshooting forums for its members. The contributors are some of the best-known names in the web design business, and quality is reputed to be high. The website offers a small amount of free material, including some free extensions. At the time of this writing, the free extensions were available to everyone without need to register.

## Yaromat

www.yaromat.com

We used Jaro von Flocken's form validation extension in Chapter 14. He has written a variety of other extensions as well. One of Jaro's best-known extensions is Layer 2 Style, which is indispensable if you use nested Dreamweaver layers (absolutely positioned divs) and need to support Netscape 4. Also available is a progress bar that indicates how much of a page has been downloaded, and a command that inserts automatic alt text for images. If you have difficulty finding the extension you're looking for, browse Jaro's site by category.

## Rawveg

www.rawveg.org

Home to Tim Green, one of the busiest and best PHP extension writers around. He is the creator of IntelliCART shopping cart extension.

## Dreamweaver MX Support

www.dreamweavermxsupport.com

Run by Gareth Downes-Powell, this site contains several PHP-based extensions and tutorials. Gareth's articles on troubleshooting Apache and MySQL are particularly useful.

## MM-Exporter

http://mm-exporter.joexx.de/index_en.php

Not really a Dreamweaver extension, but a very useful free utility created by Jörg Schmalenberger to back up and save all your important settings from Dreamweaver, including site definitions. It was originally known as DW-Exporter, but the name was changed to MM-Exporter in January 2004, when support was added for two other Macromedia products, Contribute and Flash. It is indispensable when you are faced with a computer crash or need to migrate to a new computer (Windows only).

## Computer Bookshelf

http://computerbookshelf.com/tools/

Last but not least we have the site of David Powers, one of the authors of this book. In addition to a small collection of Dreamweaver extensions, the site features personal reviews of web-related books.

# INDEX

*(continued)*

(continued)

*(continued)*

**329**

GPSR Compliance

*The European Union's (EU) General Product Safety Regulation (GPSR) is a set of rules that requires consumer products to be safe and our obligations to ensure this.*

*If you have any concerns about our products, you can contact us on ProductSafety@springernature.com*

In case Publisher is established outside the EU, the EU authorized representative is:

Springer Nature Customer Service Center GmbH
Europaplatz 3
69115 Heidelberg, Germany

**Batch number: 09474112**

Printed by Printforce, the Netherlands